A phenomenology of working class experience

This moving and challenging book by Simon Charlesworth deals with the personal consequences of poverty and class and the effects of growing up as part of a poor and stigmatized group. Charlesworth examines these themes by focusing on a particular town – Rotherham – in South Yorkshire, England, and using the personal testimony of people who live there, acquired through recorded interviews and notes from conversations. He applies to these life stories the interpretative tools of philosophy and social theory, drawing in particular on the work of Pierre Bourdieu and Merleau-Ponty, in order to explore the social relations and experiences of a distinct but largely ignored social group. The culture described in this book is not unique to Rotherham, and Charlesworth argues that the themes and problems identified will be familiar to economically powerless and politically dispossessed people everywhere.

SIMON J. CHARLESWORTH is a Research Fellow at Clare Hall, Cambridge.

Cambridge Cultural Social Studies

Series editors: JEFFREY C. ALEXANDER, *Department of Sociology, University of California, Los Angeles, and* STEVEN SEIDMAN, *Department of Sociology, University at Albany, State University of New York.*

Cambridge Cultural Social Studies is a forum for the most original and thoughtful work in cultural social studies. This includes theoretical works focusing on conceptual strategies, empirical studies covering specific topics such as gender, sexuality, politics, economics, social movements, and crime, and studies that address broad themes such as the culture of modernity. While the perspectives of the individual studies will vary, they will all share the same innovative reach and scholarly quality.

A phenomenology of working class experience

Simon J. Charlesworth
Clare Hall, Cambridge

CAMBRIDGE
UNIVERSITY PRESS

PUBLISHED BY THE PRESS SYNDICATE OF THE UNIVERSITY OF CAMBRIDGE
The Pitt Building, Trumpington Street, Cambridge, United Kingdom

CAMBRIDGE UNIVERSITY PRESS
The Edinburgh Building, Cambridge, CB2 2RU, UK   www.cup.cam.ac.uk
40 West 20th Street, New York, NY 10011–4211, USA   www.cup.org
10 Stamford Road, Oakleigh, Melbourne 3166, Australia
Ruiz de Alarcón 13, 28014, Madrid, Spain

First published 2000

Printed in the United Kingdom at the University Press, Cambridge

Typeset in Times NR 10/12½ [SE]

A catalogue record for this book is available from the British Library

Library of Congress Catologuing in Publication data

Charlesworth, Simon J.
A phenomenology of working class experience / Simon J.
Charlesworth.
p.   cm. – (Cambridge Cultural Social Studies)
Includes bibliographical references.
ISBN 0 521 65066 6 (hardback). – ISBN 0 521 65915 9 (paperback)
1. Working class – England – Rotherham.   I. Title.   II. Series.
HD8400.R68C48   2000
305.5'62'0942823–dc21   99–21510   CIP

ISBN 0 521 65066 6 hardback
ISBN 0 521 65915 9 paperback

Contents

Acknowledgements

This part of a book must have particular significance for someone who, ordinarily, should never have written one. There is something tragic in achieving literacy to encounter, time and again, the disinterest of publishers and journals alike and one's exclusion from the sites that give sense to the practices of culture; all of which ensure one's estrangement from the skills that makes a simple gratitude possible. After so much unemployment and the wastage of so much of my time, it is difficult to feel that what is written here has any value.

I was educated at Rotherham College of Arts and Technology; by all that is involved in that trajectory. I was taught to write by Jenny Greatrex and Martin Happs; introduced to sociology by Diane Bailey; and Eileen Walsh struggled in the face of my cultural deficits to teach me 'A' level English.

My writing style owes much to the influence of that milieu, to staff and students alike. If holding degrees were sufficient to protect people like us, then I, and many others, would owe these people a great deal. Martin Happs taught an assortment of ill-prepared comprehensive school failures, condemned to youth training and varieties of poor work, to compete with the best that get places at traditional English universities. I owe a debt to Dr Peter Ward who introduced me to philosophy and slaked a mind that had always hankered after concepts but never had the education to enjoy them. Like him, I still share a passionate interest in Wittgenstein that has often inspired me in the face of the corruption and bankruptcy of English higher education. It is a great pity that their efforts really count for so little in the face of the experience that many of us have had. Rotherham tech was the finest, and only real, intellectual experience that I have ever had. And it wasn't simply the teaching that helped us acquire the dispositions and cultural skills to get through 'A' level and enter university well educated and articulate, it was the atmosphere among the students which was egalitarian, non-hierarchical and based upon an unconscious sharing of resources and kindness that helped many of us recover the deficits that state schooling creates and entrenches. It is remarkable the kinds of sociality that emerge when people face odds that are against them, and put themselves at stake in such an inegalitarian and often cruel educational system. For many of us, doing 'A' levels was remarkably difficult and straining and our deficits demanded a huge amount of work and highly considerate teaching by people who had a deep sense of the nature of our experience and perceptions and a sense of how to 'translate' between our reference and that of the texts that we had to know. The atmosphere among the students is something that I have never forgotten. It was based on a consideration and solidarity that characterizes the best of working class culture. The maturity and decency of the students I knew at Rotherham tech could never have prepared me for the culture of the English university. The intense decency and qualities of friendship I knew at Rotherham tech had come to seem ever more miraculous as I had to deal with those who infest the English university system. I had come to be convinced, by the endless personal criticism, of me and the decencies that I expected from the world, that I had dreamt the forms of relation I had grown to maturity amidst, only to go back after my Ph.D. and to find the forms of relation unchanged. It is fitting that I acknowledge the deep influence upon my sense of life of students like Kevin Happs, Alex Matheo, Phil Hoares and Patrick Moran, who tragically lost his life, as well as Andy Sutcliffe, Jennifer Childs, Lindsay Robinson, Christina Whorley, Helen Old, Stacey and Angela. Above all else, they instantiated, practically, an ethical system and form of concern about human existence and the immediate value of human beings that I have found completely absent at university. They are people who stand, unknowingly, for the best I've ever known. When people have asked me, with all the self-evidence of the racism at the heart of English elite culture, why I am like I am; they are why. I have struggled to hold on to the decencies they embody, the schemata of perception, thought and action that structure their lives.

Whilst university was an experiential black hole for me, sucking all of human value from all I had known and everything that I was, and whilst I went to university without needing much by way of teaching, I nevertheless owe personal debts to: Professor Margaret Archer, Terry Lovell and Dr Tony Elger, who had the insight and compassion to treat me as the friend I never had there. I must thank Mr G. H. Tan for his friendship. At Cambridge, I must thank Professor Geoffrey Hawthorn for being prepared to supervise me when I encountered a cold indifference and critical atmosphere from staff and students alike who manifest a clear disdain for me and projects that seemed too parochial to an international community concerned with issues of a more global import. Geoffrey Hawthorn remains the only person in that department who engages me on anything more than a basis of minimal tolerance, but I must also thank John Thompson for being prepared to act as referee. I must also thank Michael Black for doing his best to convert a punctuation attuned to the rhythms of South Yorkshire dialect, into something approximating standard English grammar. At Clare Hall I'd like to thank Tony Edwards and the painters, especially Darren, for sharing a tea with me and, also, the secretaries Elizabeth Ramsden, Wenda Torrell and especially Paula Herbert, for being an island of humanity and for tolerating my need to have a good gab about the references of my life and to laugh occasionally. I'd also like to thank Professor Gillian Beer and Ed Jarrod for their support.

Mike Fox saved me from the madness of being the only one. We joked that if ever we got through and got published, we'd say that it was *in spite* of Cambridge University. It is difficult to express how hard it can be living amongst some of the most privileged people in the world when you come back to (or from) the context described in this work. Little wonder it was so difficult for people to know me. The homogeneity of elite educational institutions establishes conditions for the most ruthless forms of discrimination that I've ever seen. With so many elite bodies together, there is a savagery to the processes whereby personal relations are constituted that is paid for by the few exceptions who make it into such places.

However, for one three-month period there were some miraculous exeptions and I must acknowledge the friendships of Matt Long, Guillaume Mallet, Roel Stercx, Andrew Slayman (thanks for the computer and books), Peter Lyk-Jenson, Matt Kirov, Elizabeth St George, Anastasia Economu, Orietta Maizza, Fiona Somerset and Imogen Crowther.

In Rotherham, I must acknowledge the people that I have boxed and weight-trained with, some of whose surnames I still don't know: Mick Ford, Ian Wright, Danny Clerkson, Gary Turner, Tim McDool, Darren Skidmore, Trevor Sanderson, Paul Ashton, Craig Lambert, Tim McGuinness, Mat Evans, Wes Weaver, Dave Rudkin, Greg, Wes, Shane, Issy Birks, Cath and Simon Othen, Ron Rolli, Violet Lucy and Chris Sykes. And I'd also like to mention Steve Stokes who died whilst I was working on this, and thank him and his son Shaun, for all they did for me.

I must also acknowledge the assortment of people who have been my friends. Sylvia Hudson knew more than anyone what I went through. I must mention the mates who gave me back some self-respect and confidence after Warwick had destroyed it and who have tolerated me on Saturday nights ever since Cambridge did the same. I owe a special acknowledgement to Paul Bates and Jason Fitzgerald who articulate so much that is true of the world in which we live, but I must also mention Jimmy Beighton, Jason Barker, Martin Emery, Suzanne Pickering, Nicola Whitehouse and Avril. And, of course, Jason Mace and Kevin Timmins for similarly never judging harshly the difference in how we make ends meet. Sharing nothing in common but the spaces in which we live and a certain demeanour that ought, in a just society, to be inconsequential, these people share their time and space with me, something rare at university. I'd also like to thank Asif Zaman for his friendship and insight; Ian and Sue Beever; John and Sarah Becket for a consoling coffee; and the people at Sheffield Road and Rawmarsh swimming baths who have been friendly faces. I must thank Rosalind Johnson and Andy Bruce-Burgess and Stella Ciorra for staying in touch. Thanks are also due to Des Compston for his long-distance phone calls of friendship. And a big thanks is also due to Roger Cook and Neil Pridham for their friendship and kindness and also to Roy Enfield for being on my side throughout my years of exclusion. I must thank Patrick Pouw for liking my poetry and Kev and Michelle Gill for understanding so much at the heart of this work. And Mick Postans has been a similarly invaluable commentator on the nuances of our culture. I must also thank Marc and Corrin Bailly for their friendship and Dominic Olariu for explaining to me the subtleties of a different world. Thanks are also due to Professor David Cooper for a sympathetic reading of my interpretations of phenomenology. Dr Briget Fowler was kind enough to write to Cambridge University Press when the process seemed stuck.

I must thank Dusan and Helena Gutman, for treating me with kindness I'll never forget. Similarly, I must thank Sarah Barnes for crediting me with some sense of respect and trust and for allowing me the kind of friendship denied me by so many of her background.

I'd like to acknowledge the friendship and humanity of Lew Owen and similarly Dr Darryl Gunson for proving that friendships can survive university.

Thanks are also due to Clare Hall for electing me to a fellowship. I am grateful given the enormous pool of perfectly qualified, perfect specimens of university culture to whom their resources usually go.

Somehow it would be improper if I failed to acknowledge Pierre Bourdieu. It would have been impossible to write without his insight because I could never have given voice to the perceptions of the everyday existence in which I live.

I must thank Diane Wright Mick, Pat and Craig Wright for making me one of the family and for their endless generosity of spirit and deed.

Finaly, Joan, John and Martin Charlesworth and the memory of Walter Charlesworth.

1

Introduction: Dead Man's Town

Who taught you to hate the colour of your skin?
Who taught you to hate the texture of your hair?
Who taught you to hate the shape of your nose and the shape of your lips?
Who taught you to hate yourself from the top of your head to the soles of
    your feet?
Who taught you to hate your own kind?
Who taught you to hate the race that you belong to, so much so that you
    don't want to be around each other?
You know . . . you should ask yourself who taught you to hate being what
    God made you.   *Malcolm X*

Our relationship to the world, as it is untiringly enunciated within us, is
not a thing which can be any further clarified by analysis; philosophy can
only place it once more before our eyes and present it for our ratification.
                                            (Merleau-Ponty 1962: xviii)

This work is a description of lives in one of the old industrial areas of
Britain. It is focused upon the town of Rotherham, part of what was once
a whole network of interconnecting towns and villages that gave South
Yorkshire its distinct culture. An area that has suffered de-industrialization
and the attendant social consequences of poverty. It concerns deprivation
and its wider consequences, personal and social, and looks to locate the
problems socially and culturally. This book, and, more importantly, the
archive of transcription that it emerges from, is an attempt to set down a
living record, a testimony to the dying of a way of life; the extinction of a
kind of people.

   Yet describing the nature of working class people in an age of such fragmentation and atomization, especially where so many are so uncertain, is
not straightforward. There are, of course, the simple truths of what is

everywhere on the streets but, listening to politicians, these simple things are endlessly contested. The middle classes fear the crime that is related to the economic marginality and social exclusion of the poorest third of the society, yet they want their own wages free of the tax burden involved in funding a civil society. For the working class, themselves, for whom the economically marginal and socially excluded are family members and neighbours, they have had to deal in the most palpable way with the decline of their own economic role and social position. Since the early 1980s, the gradual decline of the culture of the working class has been one of the most powerful, telling developments in British society. The bleakness of English society, what lies around us in the faces of the urban poor everywhere, emerges from this context, and yet there have been few accounts of the transition and consequences from amongst those who are unable to buy their way out of the conditions and into the protected elite spaces of the English middle and upper classes.

The book works through looking at the personal testimony of people who expressed something revealing about the nature of their lives in this milieu. Testimony was taken through recorded interviews and notes were taken from conversations participated in and heard. The task of trying to capture the voices of working class people, emphasized the gradual effacement of a way of life based around a coherent sense of the dignity of others and of a place in the world. Those around forty have a coherent way of describing their lives and a sense of what has happened to the working class, but, as one comes down through the generations, one moves away from the efficacy of any narrative of the social, away from the co-ordinates of class, and encounters an arid individualism devoid of personal embedding in something beyond the ego. The coherence of a spoken common understanding based upon mutual respect and shared sources of value, becomes more and more infrequent until, among the very young, understanding and value seem impossible. An inescapable conclusion of the work seems to be that the most dispossessed individuals understand their lives the least and are certainly the least able to articulate their existence. At times it has seemed to me that the central issue of the work was muteness, silence, inarticulacy and the problem of accounting for the available sense that grounds these lives and which the silence rises amidst. One cannot adopt a formalized systematic procedure for recording this, one simply has to be amongst this life and do the best one can to see the traces in the details of these people's speech of the world as it is for them and to be sensitive to what it makes of them. And what is true of the recording of phenomena, is true of its writing. Many expecting sorrowful stories of poverty and moving testimony, the bleeding-heart prose that reassures readers of their own sensitivity, will find my prose frustrating. My first task is to elucidate the phenomena, not to write something that is easy to read.

Hence, documentary description is part of its method but not its sole aim. The work tries to bring to light the sources that contribute to making working class people recognizable as people of a certain type, subject to an objective meaning. My aim has been to try to illuminate the obscure processes that lead to the invisibility of the sources of everyday misery and stigmatization involved in the constitution of a group of people who know themselves in certain ways: ways that have consequence for their life-chances and forms of self-realization.

Although this purpose is sociological, the subtlety of the processes that concern me, have drawn me away from strictly sociological literatures towards anthropology and philosophy, particularly towards phenomenological ideas. Such writing is concerned to provide insight into how, through the human situation, phenomena come to have personal meaning, a lived-through significance that may not always be transparent to consciousness. The focus is upon involvement in a natural–cultural–historical milieu within which individuals discover themselves as subject to meaning. This tradition stresses that we can only understand human phenomena, such as language, in practice, or use. Moreover, this tradition shares Wittgenstein's effacement of the primacy of an inner realm of phenomena, private to each individual, by insisting that we appreciate the role of affective behaviour, and recognize the body as the realization, or objectification, of the soul. Of particular importance, this tradition embeds human communicative processes in what McGinn calls a 'pre-epistemic relation to other human subjects which is rooted in our immediate responsiveness to them' (McGinn 1997: 8). It is this tradition's sensitivity to the grounds of the human, to the conditions of humanity, that I have come, over and over, to experience as being important in understanding the lives of people whose social environment 'grounds' their humanity in ways that curtail their generative competences for language use and expressive behaviours; inhibits the mediums through which they might found a richer form of existence based upon a fuller realization of the potentialities embodied in the forms of association they currently realize.

These ideas, with their unusual sensitivity to the significance contained in the expressivity of the human body, are particularly suited to one of the key problems of this work. A disturbing feature of the world I am trying to capture is that it is being enveloped by silence. A silence that is not merely metaphorical, one that does not simply reflect these people's relationship to the political institutions of England,[1] but one which describes the form of their intimate lives. It is in the most personal dimensions of intimate life, that the cultural conditions of working class life are most pronounced and most disturbing.

Yet there is an important issue here. Writing involves one generating an order, and the documentary method relies upon ethnographic techniques, most importantly, upon the recording of testimony. A central aspect of this work has been the recording of voices that tell their own moving stories. These people chose themselves by showing that what for many has remained, in some uneasy sense, unspeakable, is not inexpressible if we are capable of recognizing and exploring the residual traces[2] of damaging, fracturing experiences that have been incorporated by individuals from the grounds through which they have become what they are. Yet what is impossible to represent here is the pervasive silence which surrounds the instances of testimony and which the resultant transcription only apparently contradicts. The sense of vulnerability-bound inarticulateness does pervade some of the transcription and is a reason why I tried so hard to preserve the verbal form of the speech, with all its inarticulate mumblings and broken lapses, but the form of the work cannot capture the bleak darkness of the invisibility of these people's lives to themselves. My task throughout has been to record the instances of expression that exhibit the conditions which render so many quiet. It is a paradox that rendering this intelligible depended upon getting these people to speak.

There is a central and pervasive hermeneutic aspect to the project, in that it is an attempt to understand phenomena, whose sense is 'incomplete, cloudy, seemingly contradictory – in one way or another, unclear' (Taylor 1985: 15); or whose sense coheres in a background of implicit meanings that exist before, and as a condition of, individuals' constitutive self-understandings. There is something paradoxical in this project of writing a culture whose being is not enshrined in self-conscious cultural representations and thus for which gesture and enunciation are the seat of identity. If one is to understand and represent this experience, we need a phenomenological hermeneutics capable of recognizing the importance of pre-discursive, pre-rational constituents of intersubjectivity. Without this, we will fail to recognize the forms of humanity that humanity takes for those whose being is shaped by the absence of freedom to become other than what they find themselves having to be. If we are capable of recognizing the human processes involved in the constitution of the inhuman and thus how what is spontaneously perceived as abject emerges from the conditions of human culture, then we can understand how critical, racializing, comments come to be made about people so highly visible because of their demeanour and yet who are also completely lacking in the resources to represent themselves.

I need here to point to the irony involved in producing too strong a sense of a group capable of articulating their own experience when the central experience the writing is trying to communicate is of a confusion based upon a radical dis-embedding of individuals from social conditions of sociality, and thus from forms of sense and, hence, of sensible coherence. It is as if slowly, carefully, descending everywhere upon the realm of these personal lives, a silence is falling like snow, erasing the pathways through which we might return, once again, to the village of our being. Yet, the truth is that, for many, those paths were being erased whilst we were struggling to find our way. One of Toni Morrison's characters insists: 'Listen here, girl, you can't quit the Word. It's given to you to speak. You can't quit the Word' (Morrison quoted in Nbalia 1991: 102). Yet, in Freire's sense of 'speaking one's own word' (Freire 1970: 121), from amidst one's experience and the judgements of the group who share that experience, many have, unknowingly, given up on the word. Its possibility belonged to spaces and habits whose conditions are gone. During a period of mass unemployment, in which work has become more atomized and more precarious, insecurity has become the condition of too many. Elementary solidarities of family, work and place, once consolidated by the culture of the trade union and tertiary education, have been washed away by the corrosive cleansing of *laissez-faire* economic practice; the logic of financial markets sacrificing for profit the cultural configurations that human decency requires. In place of the dignities embedded in these elementary solidarities we can see a fractured anomie, juvenile delinquency, crime, drug and substance abuse, alcoholism and a host of other problems. For too many the sands of their time and experience have been washed away from beneath them, taking with them the customary reference-points of their existence. For these people, the condition Camus described as 'the absurd' is a sociological, not a metaphysical, predicament:

A world that can be explained even with bad reasons is a familiar world. But, on the other hand, in a universe suddenly divested of illusions and light, man feels an alien, a stranger. His exile is without remedy since he is deprived of the memory of a lost home or the hope of a promised land. This divorce between man and his life, the actor and his setting, is properly the feeling of absurdity.   (Camus 1975: 13)

The reasons for our world have crumbled. Hard work and education seem to lead nowhere, and the endless round of consecutive governments' retraining policies are known for what they are. Many have learned the lie of the lies that sustained the old world and know no stories of a promised land. Yet, unlike the heroic figures of Camus' work, this experience of the absurd is different. These are not individuals divested of intuitive feeling for 'the chain of daily gestures'[3] (Camus 1975: 19), rather, it is as if the grounds of their practical belief, the networks of an older world, have been washed away, slowly erased so that they can never know the satisfaction of forms of coexistence that might bring the peace of value. Rather, the world they inhabit is fractured, no longer supported by a steady stream of habitual associations, and their personal, affective world is pre-constituted as chaotic: absurd. Yet this is the only sense we have ever known. So this is an absurdity that cannot know itself because it cannot experience the ontological security and social grounds upon which self-justification might be realized. There is only ambiguity and confusion. This is an experience of the absurd emanating from a realm that is fractured, perceptually aggressing and negating. It is a world whose solicitations lead to a relation to the world, a form of inhabitation, that holds itself at the primary level of habituation, as close as possible to a realized automacy that leaves individuals less affected by consciousness: knowing only through the comportment by which sense is realized; knowing the world through a medium and in a manner that emerges from conditions of deprivation and symbolic impoverishment; the price that body-subjects pay for the absence of humanity that we all require but which only the privileged are able to inscribe in their own protected social space. This experience of absurdity, then, emerges from an economic and cultural condition, and is manifest in the mental and physical ill-health that afflict people. This sense of the world haunts working class existence. And this is what one would expect if 'man is a being without a reason for being' (Bourdieu 1990c: 196); because, if it is fundamental to being that it is radically ungrounded, or groundless, standing in need of a sense of life produced by human association and the sources of value to which it gives rise, then the condition of being-in-the-world must be more problematic for those whose lives are most devoid of social consecration. That is, for those condemned to live their meaning through self-understandings based upon notions of utility and stigmatization.

The book begins with a brief survey of the history and demography of the area, and moves on to focus upon the experience of the people of the town by considering the sense that emerges from examples of everyday conversations. The work progresses through the form of a series of meditations about the relationship of persons to their social environment. Whilst this is a particular site, understanding the lives of these people gives us an insight into the nature of being working class in the traditional industrial areas of Britain. The task is to highlight key experiences and to focus on what is characteristic in them: that is, to focus upon what makes those experiences possible.

Throughout, I allow the transcribed material to represent itself, without directly interpreting at the surface level of the speech acts themselves, since these have illocutionary force (and of course, perlocutionary force). The material tries to capture the form and force of the speech that emerges from these people's practices and connect it with a modality of being and the series of social and economic conditions which that modality originates in, and which the speech exemplifies. I try to look beneath what is said, at what it offers: the possibility of recognizing the relation to human being that being working class instils. It is a humanist attempt to show the problems of a naive humanist universalism that fails the poor by failing to recognize the real personal consequences of being poor. The book tries to exemplify the extent to which humans become differentiated and come to live their marks; that is, come to live amidst a background of social meanings, positive and negative, through which they experience themselves as individuated, as a being of a certain *kind*. As Nagel puts it, '[for] an organism [to have] conscious experience *at all* means . . . that there is something it is like to *be* that organism' (Nagel 1979: 166). And this work is concerned to elicit the originary experience through which a person comes to experience the world, through life among others, as a distinct place through experiences which teach a certain relation to themselves, the world and experience. To be working class, then, is to be part of a socially realized category. The book deals with the category 'working class' as an ontological concept, one which traces the nature of its realization through social relations that define individuals' objective being, and thus create for agents the modes of subjectivization through which their world and their forms of comportment are realized as possible solutions to the problems of a world that opens up to them as, always, from birth onwards, the world of the subjects they objectively are, beings of a certain distinct kind. It is the world of the working class person that this book wants to communicate, and it is for these reasons that it homogenizes, because it is looking for what is shared across the differences of life style, gender or race that must necessarily striate a multi-ethnic community that is poor and deprived; at what allows us to know each other as people who share a commonality in the eyes of those who do not share what is obvious in us.[4]

This is not a Marxist interpretation of working class experience, yet one of the most important reasons for this approach is to try and show that the social and cultural resources for developing one's inalienable human capacities, what Marx called one's 'species being', of coming to fruition as a person of categoric value, are inequitably distributed, with the result that the possibility of the development of capacities important to personal fulfilment are frustrated. Moreover, I depict a relation to being, contained in working class people's economic and social conditions, that forecloses upon and makes almost impossible autonomous ways of becoming a self-developing subject, of value for oneself and to others; capable of founding through oneself and others an intersubjective realm of mutually constituted empathic self-involvement. If this study convinces, then the demonstration that this condition exists must be an indictment of the economy which produces this relation to self and personhood. In *Humanism and Terror*, Merleau-Ponty suggests that 'to understand and judge a society, one has to penetrate its basic structure to the human bond upon which it is built' (1969: xiv). This work tries to illuminate that structure, and to show how it creates forms of being through which its fundamental patterns of relations are realized by inscribing between bodies forces of attraction and repulsion that reproduce the structure: at a price inequitably distributed by those invisible scales of justice which settle destinies in a racist society.

This book, then, is not the sociological equivalent of behaviourist studies of the natural world. It hopes to describe not merely what people in Rotherham do, the tapestry of practices that are the backdrop to their life-projects, but how they feel, and why; and what those feelings reveal about their relationship to social reality; how their being is mediated such that they are the subjects of such feelings: how they are made subjects in this way.

The history of the area, and of the country, means that the main concern is with the lives of young people who left school to face mass youth unemployment and a life governed by poor working conditions, poor wages and the almost constant threat of trips to the Department of Social Security and Job Centre. I have interviewed a large number of people who I have met throughout my own life in the town. And, where it was not possible to record their voices, I have written down their comments at the first possible opportunity. Clearly, being male, I have more access to men's private, intimate conversations than to women's, but at least one third of my respondents were women, and women's voices are a significant contribution to the book. Similarly, a significant number of the quotations that I have used are from Asian men, with whom I have both worked and trained. There was a sense of common concern, among both the women I interviewed and the members of the Pakistani community, about how impoverished their lives in Rotherham are, and they felt it inappropriate to mark what is fashionably called their 'subject-position' in the text. Clearly, women and members of the Asian community experience a commonality of location, of a life-impoverishing entrapment that they feel as a collective fate that shapes their experience of time and space and which they feel is confirmed in their conversations with others. For these reasons, in my original text I have not recorded these differences, reciprocating the respect these people exhibited in their own intuitive sense of their own lives as situated by the common humiliations and degradations that structure life in the working class life-course. However, it is conceivable that some readers might share the feeling that a colonizing 'white male . . . doxic heterosexuality is absolutely taken for granted' and effaces differences of race and gender: a response which I have received from at least one reader of an earlier draft. I am happy to let these criticisms stand if only because the work of communication the writing emerges from is, in any case, one in which these issues do not seem to be prominent. What emerges spontaneously, I have recorded and used. That people have participated in the way that they have and contributed what they have felt important is significant in itself. Furthermore, there are literatures on recognized ethnic groups as there are on issues concerning sexuality, and it is obvious that women are a powerful group of spokespeople for the experience of women. There are many women enjoying careers speaking for the experience of women in a way that is simply not true for the experience of working people. It seems to me that the university has been too silent about an experience that too many share outside the domain of the academy and the politics of representation and legitimacy that absorb so many of the intelligentsia. In this context, it seems that this project has a certain logic to it.

The academy has not, however, been over-eager to embrace the view from South Yorkshire, which has recently been shown, yet again, to be among the very poorest regions in Europe. And certainly a sociological community committed to projects concerned with the latest forms of a developing modernity, and fashioning categories that help us understand its newest cultural configurations, was not going to share, nor particularly respect, an interest in the living archaeology of a decaying world that in their own genealogy is unimportant, unexotic and, as a phenomenon, simple. The problem, however, is that this pattern of social development is not particular to South Yorkshire: it is a global phenomenon leaving disempowered, dispossessed people the world over invisible within their own national cultures. Labour is unrooted, dis-embedded, being made migrant the world over, creating people so vulnerable and atomized that they carry the marks of their impoverishment in their bodies as oddity and illness. Cheap labour, scrounging a day here, a day there, a mass of bodies rendered worthless by ubiquity, fit to clean or lift, care or dig, mend or clear, yet invisible except as a threat, aliens among their own species. This condition is ontological, this is social difference, categorization, realized in the being of beings. How could bodies share this contemporaneity as a life-course and not share a large part of their being? This is the primordial ground from which individuation springs. This is the experience revealed in the talk of the people of the town, and it warrants the moral stand of commonality

that their communication exhibits and thus which I have felt a deep obligation to honour.

The original work was drawn from a base of forty-three interviews,
although the ethnographic element from which I have written down conversations from disparate spaces gives me a much wider base of material in
which to contextualize and extend the voices recorded. Moreover, these
sources together have provided me with a developing archive of the
thoughts of the people of the town. The original work was drawn from an
archive of 350,000 transcribed words. This has consistently been added to
and is part of an ongoing project. However, what emerged from men and
women of all ages was a remarkably coherent story of the loss of a way of
living that was based upon hard work and industry, within which there was
a sense of friendship and relation, of basic dignity and respect. Of something that one could live in. Of a once-present state, now lost, in which individuals could plan a future, buy a house, marry, have children, live a life
that, though constrained by the routines of work, offered some security and
some circumscribed pleasures. However, the decline of traditional industry
and its replacement with jobs governed by new working practices have
brought great vulnerability at work, through lack of companionship, as
well as at home through worry about the security of employment, its duration and the low pay most jobs offer. Such changes have meant that people
do not feel attached to a future, something about which they feel great
anxiety, a worry that touches virtually all aspects of their lives and which
makes their experience of the present one of a misery born of hopelessness.
It is a phenomenon Camus understood: 'A man devoid of hope and conscious of being so has ceased to belong to the future' (Camus 1975: 35) and,
one might add, 'to the present as well'. Writing about the nineteenth
century, Gash has written:

Some years before the general election of 1841 the realization was growing that
there was a social question to which middle-class sectarian and party conflicts had
little relevance. 'A feeling very generally exists', ran the opening sentence of Thomas
Carlyle's famous pamphlet on *Chartism* in 1839, 'that the condition and disposition
of the Working Classes is a rather ominous matter at present; that something ought
to be said, something ought to be done, in regard to it'. When intelligent and socially
conservative members of the educated classes considered the state of industrial
England and Scotland, two reflections usually occurred to them. One was the
instability of a society where thousands of men, cooped up in mean houses and
narrow streets, without savings, adequate poor relief or even gardens of their own
in which to grow food, could be thrown out of work or put on reduced wages at a
moment's notice because of trade depression. The other was what seemed to them
the artificiality of a system where the traditional framework of social life – commu-

nity sense, acceptance of rank and inequality, reciprocal feelings of duty and defer-
ence, the practice of religion, charity and neighbourliness – had been replaced by
the indiscriminate massing in particular areas for purely economic reasons of
people whose only link with their employer was the cash nexus. (Gash 1979: 187)

If the educated classes walked around the industrial areas of Britain today,
they might feel an affinity with their forebears. What is certain is that what
Carlyle called 'The Condition of England' question is again pressing in
Britain today and, now, as then, 'something ought to be said, something
ought to be done' (Carlyle quoted in Gash 1979: 187).

Clearly, this work concerns some of the deeper moral issues raised by
economic organization. Its particular concern is with the possible grounds
of inclusion of the people whose social existence it depicts. Social exclusion
and the possibility of creating the grounds of inclusion for such groups is
one of the main problems confronting Europe. The dislocation of the
industrial working class may be as significant at the end of the twentieth
century as the economic dislocation of Europe's peasants was at the end of
the nineteenth century. Yet, if we are to tackle this problem with anything
approaching good faith, we need an accurate understanding of the conditions of dispossession which their being-in-the-world was premised upon
before economic change rendered them a problem. We therefore need to
understand their recent experience and present social condition. This book
is thus not concerned to catalogue the changes that have occurred in social
and economic organization, but with the ontological and epistemological
questions raised in understanding the being-in-the-world of working
people in their present social conditions. It therefore develops an account
of working class culture as overdetermined by economic necessity and dispossession, something that has been true throughout the era of industrial
capitalism. However, as well as this general account, the book tries to recognize new strains within working class life that are a result of the rapid
decay, within one or two generations, of an older culture. But it does not
try to grasp this through the usual sociological and economic categories. It
is an attempt to use philosophical ideas ethnographically. To use ideas
drawn from philosophy to lay open to view a version of human life; to draw
connections and show why it is as it is. Frank has suggested that 'Only an
ethics or a social science which witnesses suffering is worthy of our energies
or our attention' (Frank, 1991: 64) and this work is an attempt to make this
more than the laudable self-justification of a profession desperately
needing to recover some credibility.

It is hoped that through considering this particular place and these particular lives, through engaging this particularity with a philosophical

anthropology, there will emerge insights of a more general nature into the processes whereby individuals become trapped and alienated from themselves, others and the possibilities of perception and the forms of experience contained in different forms of life. Yet, I hope that, out of the doom and pessimism of this topic, the dim light of these people's humanity might be seen to shine, however overpowering the surrounding darkness may be. It is thus a work that, through the construction of a particular example, hopes to transcend that particularity and engage its readers' compassion and thus extend their commitment. It is, therefore, a work of recovery, of a form of being that is dying because the economic way of life that sustained it is no longer viable. Yet it is a project of recovery, of not only a way of life that has become obsolete but, of a coherent form of life, a certain form of honour or dignity, one of the variants of human dignity, at a point when our need for that pre-capitalist sentiment, honor, is most pressing.

There will be little straightforward description in this book. The reasons for this will emerge as the writing unfolds and begins to constitute its object. Furthermore, this has been done because the culture that it describes is not unique to Rotherham and anyone can experience the equivalent in any British industrial town or city. The deeper moral of the story of Rotherham, the universal that lies in its particularity, must be the same for economically powerless and politically dispossessed people everywhere. Furthermore, it is a reconstruction of a *habitus*[5] (Bourdieu 1990a), of a distinct way of being, and the reconstruction is done through the words of people and reflection on the deeper issues raised by those words.

The study concerns an environment encountered as an unquestioned universe in which 'Shit happens', because 'It's the way the numbers come up'. It is a place in which one is subject to apparently random events to do with one's individual fate, yet which obey a logic embedded in the politics of region and place, of economic context and class. Furthermore, representing a group as the victims of injustice and suffering is unavoidably a moral act. It is a political representation to the extent that it is an attempt by a member of a group of people to bring into being a sense of the group's experience as having distinct grounds that stem from the political and economic relations in which their lives happen to have been lived.

My purpose is to produce an account in which the subjects of the research would feel recognized if it were relayed to them through the intermediaries that are likely to be readers of this study. The reason for this is that we live in a social world where the instruments, the concepts and forms of association that enable individuals and groups to produce political representations and political acts are very unequally distributed, leaving many dispossessed of the means to produce a discourse that might be the beginnings of a framing of an effective political representation in the political process. The problem is that spokespersons need to emerge from the group, and yet the conditions of the group and, importantly, its socially mediated relationship to the political process and the media of representation, have been such as to curtail the production of such persons. Furthermore those who do exist require instruments that enable them to defend their own people as the subjects of injustice, and this makes them partially dependent upon cultural intermediaries. The normal producer of cultural intermediaries is the university. However, there are reasons why this social field does not produce people capable of framing schemes of thought in which the social world is correctly recognized. The university transmits ways of seeing. And the transmission is made easier by universities selecting, from a pre-selected group, individuals whose education produces the transformation of the mind, body and self of students. Having selected a pre-disposed habitus, the university tends to produce the habitus of a distinct cohort who deploy schemata of perception that ensure the reproduction of the discourse and behaviours that our political culture demands. These individuals enjoy access to the means of production of the instruments of production of discourse (Bourdieu 1991) and they are unlikely, because of the combined effects of rupture and co-option involved in their education, to misalign themselves. Many move on to become professional producers of the schemes of thought and expression of the social world: politicians, journalists, high-ranking civil servants, who produce for the dispossessed a form of political culture that is fetishized. In relation to this political realm the dominated are condemned to occupy a position that renders them passive consumers of political ideas that are constituted for them elsewhere and in which they have no part.

Working class people require intermediaries in the realm of culture to relay their condition: that is, people committed to expressing their condition through the instruments offered by the field of cultural production. It is, in a sense, a matter of translation, but not from a foreign language: rather it is a translation from a different mode of being: a translation of indeterminate, embodied experiences of forms of domination and exclusion into a language that allows for respect of the experience, that captures it without doing violence to the nature of the experience. As things stand, four things determine class-cultural intermediation. Firstly, the Labour Party appears to have turned its back on working class people. The Labour Party is now dominated by individuals whose primary political experiences were university politics. It is no longer a party in which working class people can play any prominent role. Secondly, the Trade Union movement, the traditional field that produced working class spokespersons, is in serial decline and no longer plays that role in any extensive manner. Thirdly, the university system has both given up on working class politics and been swallowed up by a crisis of funding that has all but curtailed the production of working class intellectuals. Finally, with the massive changes to the field of the English university system, particularly the emergence of clearly defined routes through working class sectors of tertiary education on to vocational degrees at lower-end universities, there has emerged a hierarchy of courses and universities that militates against the kinds of nurturance that the production of genuine working class spokespersons requires. As the system has been massified, so too the grounds for the personal links that would allow for the recognizing of genuine cases, a kind of informal 'positive discrimination', have disappeared as working class students have found themselves negotiating a system that, whilst allowing for a greater rate of survival, has achieved this, at the cost of a devaluation of their qualifications. Importantly, while working class people are involved in higher education for the first time, most are being trained rather than educated in the traditional sense. There are too many factors to detail, that have contributed to the prevailing political culture and to the connected issue of the state of our academic institutions. The humanities and social sciences are key sites for the production of the *petit-bourgeois* professionals who have contributed to the current culture. And this is reflected in the culture of the university which treats issues of deprivation with a quiet disdain issuing from an arrogance born of security.

The result is that there is no interest in class within the university and among publishers. Apparently, 'people do not read books on class', so there is no market. It is a paradox of writing about a dominated group. Because of their condition of dispossession, they do not consume books about themselves. Hence, class as a topic has sunk to the bottom of the hierarchy of intellectual objects. Within the contemporary university, it is seen as a sign of backwardness to have any concern about class and one is met with a mixture of disbelief, ridicule and derision. There is no symbolic profit to be had from being a working class intellectual or scholar which means that one cannot simply be what one is, say what one has to say, without constant verbal and non-verbal violations. 'You aren't a black woman' and 'Rotherham ain't exactly East Harlem' capture the mood of contemporary radical culture.

The universities celebrate their ethnic diversity, whilst failing to recognize the forms of discrimination that have shaped the nature of their own space, to say nothing of the inequalities upon which British nation-hood stands. There is no acknowledgement of the conditions of exclusion and racial enmity that define the contours of English society and which the English university system is a product and microcosm of. English society is built upon a deep social apartheid; an economically based racism, which marks the flesh of individuals as profoundly as differences in skin pigment. This is why this work does not develop through the standard literatures on inequality and poverty. This is because one of the central questions for anyone who grows up in a deprived area, is to grasp the consequences of living in such environments. This issue is not simply one of inequality because deprivation concerns the relationship to other social groups within the social universe as a totality of relationships. It is perhaps this, more than anything, that creates for individuals (and groups) a trajectory, or destiny. For the consequences of their milieu can only be understood in the context of the history of relations that have contributed to the space being constructed as the space that it is. Moreover, the effects of this primary milieu upon individuals is part of the economic relationship that defines the space of their personal lives. Marked as they are by the primary conditions of family and school, they then face a labour market within which individuals are defined by their difference within a totality of objectively hierarchized patterns of difference. Carrying specific meanings, individuals must negotiate the world from their meaning, which has a social value, positive or negative. Although economically based, the phenomenon of inequality and deprivation becomes racial and social. One might, facetiously, suggest that being poor leads to being poor; that the exigencies of the social relations that deprivation is built upon mean that the marks of its conditions cannot be resisted and yet once incorporated are of consequence for life-chances and for the next generation. The philosophy of Simone de Beauvoir has always seemed strikingly relevant:

No factor becomes involved in the psychic life without having taken on human significance; it is not the body-object described by biologists that actually exists, but the body as lived in by the subject.   (de Beauvoir 1952)

The phenomenological ideas are an attempt to lay clear, to *show*, the sense that de Beauvoir's final clause, 'the body as lived in by the subject', might have, and to exhibit this temporal, existential structure for these people. This study concerns the institutional positions and the social grounds which lead to the imbuing, and taking-up, of a form of comportment that makes the world meaningful in a certain way; open to a certain form of corporealized subjectivity: a subjectivity that makes certain things show-up in the social universe, and which also leads these people to be possessed of an objective being, the result of which is that they suffer unemployment, low wages, job-insecurity and deprivation.

Understanding this means recognizing the processes whereby individuals come to be so clearly marked and condemned to the consequences of those marks. It means struggling to understand how an environment exists

for human persons; in what ways it is experienced through the long duration of maturation through specific mediating forms through which individuals become subjects and, simultaneously, objects. We need to be
sensitive to how the environment has an impact upon the corporealized
ways of being opened by being, and how for the poor this may lead to a
closure of potentiality in response to a world that is bereft of positive
human enforcement and fruition. Asserting this and understanding it are,
however, two different things. If the effects of this malaise are that a relative closure of being takes place, a refusal to be engaged by the world and
an inability to consider the grounds of experience, then we cannot directly
'read-off' this condition from practices. Orthodox observational methods
cannot help us here. And we need a way of recognizing the significance of
the way subjects are situated with regard the phenomena of their environment, how they are disposed to act in relation to their world. We need to
be sensitive to the sense manifest in what Wittgenstein called 'fine shades
of behaviour' (Wittgenstein 1958: 207). There is, then, something at stake
in understanding the relation of people to their environment. For those
living in deprived environments, it is the price they have paid with their
life-course and, often, their children's to boot, which we have a duty to
appreciate.

If we are to appreciate the impact of the barely perceived minutiae of an
environment that exists as an inexpressibly complex mixture of architecturally given space; of inherited historical sense; of social practices; of behav-
iors and institutions; of the space that particular persons live through as
body-subjects, then we need to understand the relation of persons to their
environment as something deeper than the relation of subject and object.
We need to have a developed sense of the ways in which human beings
inhabit the places in which they exist, and realize that the milieux through
which people come to understanding are cultural–historical contexts where
things count, or 'show-up', in distinct ways, the sense of which is carried by
the communal practices of one's immediate group *and* its relation to
national political and economic structures. Through life in a place we
become imbued with a sense of the world, of people and objects, through
the concerned involvement, unknowingly assimilated through a community's comportment, a comportment that reveals the world under distinct
aspects with a certain resonance or attitude. The spaces in which we live,
then, constitute a realm of shared intelligibility, disclosed in mood, through
which we come to dwell in a world defined primarily through its affective
dimensions and the possibilities of being which it circumscribes. We come
to know a world through an inextricable tangle of background skills and
discriminations that constitute the structure of intelligibility that we

unconsciously realize as the condition of personhood. Importantly, this assimilation is unselfconscious; embodied in the pervasive responses, motor skills and realized distinctions in the forms of comportment that are the inescapable conditions of being human. This way of approaching the relation of person and world thus places an important emphasis upon the corporeal, because the manner of being of subjects is that of embodied agents (Taylor 1989a: 3).

The body is the site of an incarnate intentionality within whose horizon self-realization and self-understanding take place. The 'lived body' is understanding, intention incarnate, and cannot be separated from the experienced world because it is through the particularity of the encountered world that individuals come to skilled, knowing comportment. It is the lived spatiality of the body which constitutes the basis of objective space:

Besides the physical and geometrical distance which stands between myself and all things, a 'lived' distance binds me to things which count and exist for me, and links them to each other. This distance measures the 'scope' of my life at every moment.
(Merleau-Ponty 1962: 286)

The lived-body is the *locus* of an intertwining of space and an unfolding meaning embedded, or opened-up, by the totality of the background practices and patterns of life which frame individuals' experiences of place. Place is the setting of the projects that come to make sense for us as we develop into the form of life in which we grow up. The world is therefore a *particular* world, come to be known in a particular way: a way that makes possible the realization of life-projects. The important point here, is that this is based upon the pre-personal project of the body as being-in-the-world. That is, that the initial 'world' through which we come to self-knowledge is one of taken-for-granted, non-cognitive attitudes to objects and other persons, manifest in forms of behaviour, or comportment, that 'teach', purely practically, the grounds of an affective-attitude; that operates like an attitude to existence and which is the body's 'style' of being. These styles of being constitute distinct social groups at the deepest level of being. Class is one of those critical mediations of being, and this book tries to show why, across the world, a Pakistani farmer of the Mirpur valley shares an attitude to perception, experience, persons, objects and belief with a working class person in Rotherham.

I perceive in relation to my body because I have an immediate awareness of my body as it exists *'towards'* the world. My sense of the world and my sense of my body cohere because it is as an inextricable mix, that I have learnt, through involved intimacy with others, the sense of both through each other. Our sense of space is thus mediated by life among the expressive bodies of others, an intercorporeality upon which our deepest beliefs stand as part of the stand on existence involved in membership of a group that has failed to universalize, or naturalize, its own comportment as justified-in-being, the happy flesh of the consecrated, honoured, dignified, valued, beautiful. The body thus involves a primordial, pre-reflective orientation that is passed on through a kind of 'postural impregnation' (Merleau-Ponty 1964: 118): a way of feeling the world which is an aspect of the body projecting itself into the world, apprehending significances.

Two things are important here. Firstly, this means that we inhabit the world not merely as perceptual subjects but also as affective beings. For our perceptions are always inhabited by an excess of meaning, originating in the primordial grounds of sense, which is more than sensation and which reveals the world of perception for what it is: the achievement of a body-subject which has a temporal structure enabling it to carry this primitive acquisition of horizons which allows a more determinate world of objects and projects to exist. This is the second thing of importance. This means that there is an 'ontological complicity' (Bourdieu and Wacquant 1992: 20) or mutual 'possession' (Bourdieu 1996b: 3) between a person and the world around them. There is a contact and communion between person and world within which the world becomes pervaded by a sense constituted from amid wider social relations. The source of the disclosure of sense is the everyday being-in-the-world of the people among whom we live. From amidst this, persons and things resonate with more sense than we normally cognize; they become possessed of an affective hue. We find persons or things becoming or unbecoming, beautiful or ugly, and this affects our responses and relations, creating fields of force, or a dimension to human existence that is felt through affinity, distance or repulsion, whose processes lie deep in the socialised body; a kind of bodily kinetic sensitivity, of unerring logic, that has grave consequences for individuals whose world and being fall towards the negative pole of social valuation.

This is what Merleau-Ponty calls the 'antepredicative unity of the world and our life' (Merleau-Ponty 1962: 61): the world of sense that language is used to articulate; a pre-objective contact between person and world sedimented in the body socialised into an intersubjectivity amidst the infinitely complex 'fine shades of behaviour' (Wittgenstein 1958: 207) through which we come to understand psychological concepts and their place in our form of life. This mutual 'possession', or 'ontological complicity', felt between persons and their world, arises from the point of space in which the individual is located and thus is defined both to themselves and for others, through the medium of the socialization that being a body-subject implies.

This is why Merleau-Ponty speaks of the body as 'the potentiality of a certain world' (Merleau-Ponty 1962: 106). It is a point expressed in more orthodox terms by Charles Taylor:

The fact of being inescapably in a world means that we cannot give a purely intrinsic description of the subject, one which makes no reference to what surrounds him in its meaning. This implication is strongly resisted by some of the most important streams of modern philosophical and scientific thought, for which the subject *ought* to be a potential object of intrinsic description, like everything else. The philosophical stance, that one can't start with a subject and relate him to a world, but can only describe the subject-in-world, has had to be constantly revived and defended against the mainstream of modern philosophy. A famous example in our century is Heidegger's passage in *Sein und Zeit*, where he talks about the way in which the subject is 'in' his world. The subject is not in the world in the way in which an intrinsically-describable object is contained in another, like water in a glass, for instance; rather the subject is in a world which is a field of meanings for him, and thus inseparably so, because these meanings are what make him the subject he is.

(Taylor 1989b: 2)

The relation of person/world is situated in the dynamic of body/space, and is thus socially located to the extent of becoming the site of a necessary particularity. These are the consequences of an appreciation of the lived body as the site of a generative capacity of practical understanding which enmires the person, knowingly and unknowingly, in an objective being. Place, then, as a social site related to other positions and social localities and known as a locality in which experience, memory and feeling are constituted, is critical to understanding being-in-the-world. And Merleau-Ponty's phenomenology of the lived-body allows us to understand how place is experienced through the founding of sense by human communities. Places exist to individuals as constellations of affective senses expressive of the life of those who inhabit them:

all these operations require the same ability to mark out boundaries and directions in the given world, to establish lines of force, to keep perspectives in view, in a word, to organise the given world in accordance with the projects of the present moment, to build into the geographical setting a behavioural one, a system of meanings outwardly expressive of the subject's internal activity . . . for the normal person his projects polarise the world, bringing magically to view a host of signs which guide action . . . I must reverse the natural relationship in which the body stands to its environment, and a human productive power must reveal itself through the density of being.   (Merleau-Ponty 1962: 112)

The conditions of such a 'density of being' are one of the targets of this book, and this means that 'particularity', or the location of human beings in *places* and the cultural relations that define regions as significant to the categorizing of beings, is fundamental to its more general relevance. The importance of place and of the phenomenal body are of critical importance because both mediate being so inescapably. Illuminating their relation will allow us to see the human condition as inescapably circumscribed by relations of domination which infuse space and subjects as part of the fabric of both. It is as though, finally, we are all parochial.[6]

Understanding a place, then, is a natural starting-point for understanding being. As Merleau-Ponty put it:

Traditional Psychology has no concept to cover these varieties of consciousness of place because consciousness of place is always, for such psychology, a positional consciousness, a representation, *Vor-stellung*, because as such it gives us the place as a determination of the objective world and because such a representation either is or is not, but, if it is, yields the object to us quite unambiguously and as an end identifiable through all its appearances. Now here, on the other hand, we have to create the concepts necessary to convey the fact that bodily space may be given to me in an intention to take hold without being given in an intention to know. The patient is conscious of his bodily space as the matrix of his habitual action, but not as an objective setting; his body is at his disposal as a means of ingress into a familiar surrounding, but not as the means of expression of a gratuitous and free spatial thought . . . I can therefore take my place through the medium of my body as the potential source of a certain number of familiar actions, in my environment conceived as a set of *manipulanda* and without, moreover, envisaging my body or my surrounding as objects in the Kantian sense . . . free from any attachment to a specific place or time, and ready to be named or at least pointed out. . . .there are my surroundings as a collection of possible points upon which this bodily action may operate, and there is, furthermore . . . the world as pure spectacle into which I am not absorbed, but which I contemplate and point out. As far as bodily space is concerned, it is clear that there is a knowledge of place which is reducible to a sort of co-existence with that place, and which is not simply nothing, even though it cannot be conveyed by a description or even by the mute reference of a gesture . . . The whole operation takes place in the domain of the phenomenal; it does not run through the objective world. (Merleau-Ponty 1962: 105)

This I take to mean that the deepest knowledge of a place is something that cannot be conveyed because it is carried in comportment (the mute structure in whose context gesture 'refers'), even 'transferred' in that medium of silent sense, through non-verbal cues that instil in space its contours of amiability or aggression. It is that realm which affects how things show up for us, but which we seldom think about because it concerns the world in which we are spontaneously absorbed in coping with the space we must negotiate in order to achieve our immediate projects. To put it simply, understanding the everyday world of places means understanding the spatiality of absorbed involvement, of being inhabited by its phenomenal sense. That is, to have been engaged, or produced by, its involvement-structure, such that one's body knows the sense that passes by 'postural impregnation' among those who share the space, and knowing that this sense haunts conscious attempts to constitute a world within that realm. That is, that this sense has the property of a background within which objects and one's life take place.

These phenomena are exemplified in the constant remarking, by working people, of the social decline and increased threat contained in urban space. It is common for working people, among one another, to speak of feeling 'dragged down' and invaded by what is around them.[7] For them, attempts to live decently with mutual respect in public, are thwarted by the manner they have to adopt in order to move through social space. The bodily knowledge amounting to a 'co-existence with that place' that Merleau-Ponty speaks of, is exemplified by the manner that one has to adopt in certain public spaces. For example, walking through town alone, it may be necessary to walk in a certain way, a way that exudes strength and a capacity for violence. Just as social psychologists have shown that there are signals that contribute to a woman's likelihood of being attacked – if she looks timid or not assertive, for example – so too one comes to know how to comport oneself in urban space so as to efface the threat of actual physical harm. Yet this method of comportment is also a way of entering into relationship with the world; in itself it is an experience of the place that emerges from the place's meanings. This is the place that spontaneously absorbs me because in the flourish of meaning I am carried into an affective reaction which carries me towards an immediacy of a certain kind of relaxed arousal that demands that I am sensitive to the possibilities contained in the situation around me. This is a form of unspoken knowledge of place that exists in manners of comportment that always mark those from 'the wrong side of the tracks', the 'rough part of town', and all the other euphemisms for people whose bodies betray their origins in poor communities low in status. And places exist as fields of such sense, which the body responds to against the wishes of one's conscious mind, because the primal sense of human space is given in the non-intentional, pre-verbal cues of comportment that reveal what really matters in that space. It is for these kinds of reasons that Heidegger in *Being and Time* talks of 'circumspection' rather than 'perception' (Hall 1993: 128), to refer to the way in which human perception is mediated by the practical background that always guides our interests and concerns.

The world of the street map and picture postcard that we call 'objective' is engaged with through the phenomenal body. It is the socialised, phenomenal body that inhabits, because it is inhabited by, a world full of resonances, of fear and anxiety and of pleasure. These people engage with the world at this affective level; seldom is that world contemplated as mere spectacle. This is what makes the traditional philosophy of action and ideas like Rational Actor Theory inappropriate to the description of their life-in-the-world, because theirs is a world that is lived in primarily as realized practices, behaviours latent with meaning, rather than self-transparent, conscious projects. For these reasons, this book is an attempt to illuminate how structural phenomena become manifest in the realm of sense and personal significance for people in Rotherham, part of the experience of existence contained in the language of human life, the language that they speak. The work is:

premised on the idea that *the most personal is the most impersonal*, that many of the most intimate dramas, the deepest malaises, the most singular suffering that women and men can experience find their roots in the objective contradictions, constraints and double binds inscribed in the structures of the labor and housing markets, in the merciless sanctions of the school system, or in mechanisms of economic and social inheritance.   (Bourdieu and Wacquant 1992: 201)

This work tries, throughout, to show the symptoms of this malaise. As a series of meditations on the nature of the personal suffering embedded in these social conditions, it might seem repetitive since it looks again and again at different manifestations of symptoms of the same malaise of being. Reader need to appreciate that the continual restatement of similar or related points in different ways and terms, to say nothing of the complexity and detail of the restatements, are necessary for me to identify the nature of the experience and phenomena because the multiplicity of form is essential in order to convey the distinctive characteristics of a 'field' of experience that is ambiguous and, too often, inarticulate. This book, after all, is concerned to elucidate the relation of working class people to their world and thus has a descriptive element, but what it depicts, the way that their experience emerges from their position, can only be described through the interpretative tools of philosophy and social theory. The interpretative frame illuminates by allowing us to depict the relationship between phenomena and realms that otherwise remain obscure. It is both an interpretation and a description.

It is a phenomenological method drawn from the philosophy of Merleau-Ponty and the sociology of Pierre Bourdieu, through which an attempt is made to reconstitute the powerful impact upon the subjectivity of these people, of the indeterminate, ambiguous, multi-faceted experience of the bleak darkness of a decaying urban, industrial working class environment. It is an attempt to restore what are too often separated: body and mind, understanding and sensibility – 'the social with which we are in contact by the mere fact of existing, and which we carry about inseparably with us before any objectification' (Merleau-Ponty 1962: 362). While this work tries to restore the context-conferring-sense to these people's utterances, it is not merely a social context of normative rules, a public realm of speech acts.

There is an irony in Merleau-Ponty's *Phenomenology of Perception*, in that his own considerations show that perception is inherently laden with culture (Langer 1989: 174). This suggests that bodily experience cannot be studied apart from the cultures in which we become knowing, feeling, body-subjects: agents endowed with a form of corporeal generative knowing beyond the merely cognitive and normative. And here is where the work of Pierre Bourdieu becomes of critical importance in situating the ontology. The notion of 'habitus', we will see later, crystallizes this condition of body-subjectivity precisely and gracefully. The context-conferring-sense, therefore, involves the history and culture that a person embodies: the habitus; that pre-objective contact between subject and world. This must be understood if we are to have a sense of the resonances and meaning of the environment as it is signified for the phenomenal body, through the experience of a life touched in all its moments by a place whose every phenomenal feature manifests the icy-presence of economic necessity. Hence, restoring the context-conferring-sense means being aware of what our experience owes to our being body-subjects in such a place, an incarnate subjectivity that is historically and culturally located. Thus, throughout, transcripted speech is dealt with as issuing from a context of incarnate subjectivity particular to the culture these individuals make incarnate. Hence the book tries to make visible the complexities of the primordial bond between person and world, as one in which the body as a socialized medium is the site of a generative capacity to structure our understanding of the world which makes this relation of subject and world one of ontological complicity. The context-conferring-sense, therefore, must involve a knowledge of what their experience owes to their embodiment, to the way that they *live* their bodies and *live* their marks as working class people. We must be aware of the duration of certain experiences like unemployment, and what the effects of that experience have been both upon the individual and upon the culture of the locality as a whole. This is:

to give oneself a *general and genetic comprehension* of who the person is, based on the (theoretical or practical) command of the social conditions of which she is the product: a command of the conditions of existence and the social mechanisms which exert their effects on the whole ensemble of the category to which such a person belongs (that of high school students, skilled workers, magistrates, etc.) and a command of the conditions, psychological and social, both associated with a particular position and a particular trajectory in social space. Against the old Diltheyan distinction, it must be accepted that *understanding and explaining are one.*   (Bourdieu 1996a: 23)

Merleau-Ponty's emphasis on the phenomenal body and the ontology that he formulates around notions like 'incarnate subjectivity' are important in understanding how working class people experience the social at a time of acute poverty and vulnerability. We need to understand the consequences of those conditions for people's subjectivities. This book concerns itself mainly with exploring the complexity of this, and in that sense it goes over the same insights a number of times, each time exploring a different aspect of the central relation between subject and world through a different lens, in the manner of Adorno (Adorno 1974). As each lens is used, we should become more and more aware of what it is that makes people become so naturalized to their world, what it is that makes them become so ingrained in the contours of their environment. It is in an effort to cast light on these issues that this work repeats its ontological presuppositions through different examples in order to cast light on working people's experience and what is at its heart.

My primary aim is not behavioural description of the practices characteristic of the place, because the space is not lived in as a spectacle, but through the involvement of the phenomenal body: as an "Orrable place: but what else is the'?', as 'an ugly shit hole of a place', 'dull and boorin", 'Fuckin' depressin". That is, through forms of involvement that originate in the body-subjects these people are; that is, in the forms of comportment characteristic of persons of the social category to which they objectively belong because they embody the particular culture that they do. So, to focus upon the practices in a descriptive, behaviouristic way, is of little help if we want to understand the experiences of their way of being-in-the-world. We need to be aware of their expression as issuing from their comportment, the form of involvement from which their speech issues, and treat what they say and do in the light of this.

For instance, the phrases of the people quoted, may appear to be responses of an aesthetic nature, but the experiences they emanate from are the least aestheticized. They emerge from brute being, from sensuousness, from pure embodied involvement, from the confrontation between a subjectivity and the horror of space that belittles, humbles and humiliates, of space that drives out the human, that doesn't allow the possibility of growth, of space that through its confinement, its constraint, its shoddiness, inscribes in the human soul those same conditions. These responses emerge from people on whom the green of Clifton Park and the flowers of the pedestrianized centre do not impact, because they feel it, through their embodied involvement, as a place full of aggression; where they feel 'There is so much hate in young people nahr' and, 'There's a lot of anger in people nahr. Round 'ere, people are just angry an' thi' just lookin' fo' a target fo' it.'

It is a place perceived in engagement as a series of direct primal significances in which one has to achieve certain goals that bring a life, but never with assurance, never without vulnerability. It is a place in which life is consumed by the ordinary everyday mundanity of a people who are excluded from anything approximating to a form of civil society. It is a life of banal tragedy in which human energy is sapped by the consummate wastefulness of a welfare system which aggressively disciplines working people so as to achieve the chimera of efficiency in the nation's human resources. So, perception of the environment rarely rises to that level of objectification that the conditions of contemplation might allow.

After the brief historical–topographical introduction, the spaces them-selves are described sparingly, only where it is absolutely necessary to com-municate the context of meaning. Here, I must make clear that the descriptive section in the next chapter is essential to locate these people in a way recognizable to the reader, but that is not the main concern of the book which addresses the problem of how human agents are trapped by the inertia-inducing social conditions of contemporary capitalism.

The book aims to characterize the relationship of working class people to the world, to express their social reality but without focusing upon their experience of place as a 'landscape'. The thought of Bourdieu is unique in the quality of its insights into the suffering of working class people in modern capitalism. His 'generative anthropology of power' (Bourdieu and Wacquant 1992) which aims to 'effect the dissemination of weapons of defence against symbolic domination' (Bourdieu and Wacquant 1992: xiv) is of great importance to that group of people who face the endless process of recategorization that being unemployed involves – being shifted between the Department of Social Security, endless new training schemes, the Job Centre and poorly paid work. It is difficult to find another contemporary thinker who has had the concern, will and energy to frame concepts capable of illuminating the forms of pain and degradation that working people confront in the progressive fragmentation of modern society. As he sug-gests:

I think that in terms of symbolic domination, resistance is more difficult, since it is something you absorb like air, something you don't feel pressured by; it is every-where and nowhere, and to escape from that is very difficult. Workers are under this kind of invisible pressure, and so they become much more adapted to their situation than we can believe. To change this is very difficult, especially today. With the mechanism of symbolic violence, domination tends to take the form of a more effective, and in this sense more brutal, means of oppression. Consider contemporary societies in which the violence has become soft, invisible.

(Bourdieu and Eagleton 1992)

The concepts that Bourdieu has framed into a distinct vision of the human condition provide the possibility of describing this condition, and the anxiety and suffering that these changes have now brought to the heart of working people's lives.

It is important to say that the use of this type of theoretical and philosophical writing at the heart of this study does not instate a distance between myself and the people concerned. The process of transcribing and writing was the exact opposite of this. I had to rerun and rerun tapes of interviews, reliving the feelings of the interviews, feeling along with the voices on them the significances that their conscious avowals emerged from; and I have had to immerse myself in this almost-silent pain in order to think through the problems of the people I have interviewed. It was a process of thinking through the feelings manifest in the grain of the voice, in the remembered moments of the interview and of living through the described dilemmas of the persons involved. It was a process of mobilizing the feelings in myself in order to re-constitute them linguistically. The reconstitution is this writing. I have tried to *show* through this description why these people suffer and how they suffer. The process of theorizing, the generalizations, the concepts, are not driven by the desire to create an objectifying distance, but to honour the suffering of these people in a way that is adequate to its significance: to do justice to them, to honour their lives. As Wittgenstein suggested (Wittgenstein 1980) the intellectual's task is comparable to that of a draughtsman whose job it is to arrange before our eyes the relations between phenomena, and this is exactly what my task has been: to take the everyday embodied understanding of the people and to set it within a pattern of thinking that draws out its latent significance, what I believe they are really saying to one another when they say what they say.

This process of reconstitution makes it clear that the embodied insights of these people are surprisingly close to some of the deepest formulations of thinkers like Bourdieu. When working class people speak about themselves and say things like, 'I don't enjoy workin' but yer've, I think yer just programmed into, yer, yer programmed to du [do] that work, *to work*, yer know what I mean?' or 'Well it's all we know in't it, is all wi'v [we've] ivver [ever] known, wi [we] wo [was] brought up fo' this', then they are using to express their culture concepts and notions of the relation between subject and world that are very close to the kind of notions developed by Merleau-Ponty as well as by Bourdieu.

One finds a very powerful sense in working people of the centrality of habit in their lives, a sense of habit that stresses determination by their environment. These are ideas that operate as an ontology, forms of explanation that help these people to understand one another. It is markedly different from the sense of freedom of the self that one finds so celebrated by people who are university-educated.

The marked similarity of thought concerning their social fate is an impressive confirmation of Bourdieu's writing, which does seem to have a deeply insightful and, above all, deeply human appreciation of the kind of lives led by these people. I resist the idea that the passages from Bourdieu's writings are a distancing of the people's lives and feelings because I have sometimes shown and discussed key passages with people in Rotherham in a genuine effort to work out some mutual understanding of life and what has happened here. I found that people were fascinated by the ideas and knew precisely what Bourdieu was expressing. These two responses are perhaps most interesting, in that they express precisely the relation Bourdieu himself sees between objectification and experience:

X: Is it 'ard this Bourdieu to read, like? 'Cos them bits ye'v read to mi, the'r [they're] fuckin' spot on. Ye' know it's stuff A've [I've] allous [always] felt but A've never bin able to explain. Ye know, like when Ah [I] wo at school an' college, an' it all meks perfect sense ahr [how] he explains it but Ah wun't never Ah [have] thought o'r it like that . . . is the'r 'owt [anything] by 'im that's simple, like?

And:

X: Ye know, Marx wo' fuckin' brilliant to read an' he explain ahr [how] the economic system works but wot wi'v nivver [never] 'ad is someb'dy who explained ahr [our] experience in detail, yer know, all the humiliation an' ah [how] thi get us to feel s' [so] inferior an' ah [how] thi exclude us an' all that shit . . . Ah [I] mean nahr [now] cos 'r all that's 'appened an' ahr thi'v changed everythin' arahnd ahr lives, an' wi' [with the] Labour party; workin' people need people to speak fo' em like that, wi [we] need someb'dy like 'im to se' [say] that all these in Labour Party and Tories, that wot the'r sayin's rubbish, that it's wrong an' to let it bi seen ah [how] people are sufferin' which is what that stuff you'd shown me ses.

These people passionately seize Bourdieu's interpretations of their way of living because much of Bourdieu's writing is an appeal to conscience on behalf of these people, for their plight to be recognized. The people I have talked to experience a deep satisfaction in being confirmed by a writer, and they often express a desire to read more of it, the problem of course being that Bourdieu's writing employs a highly technical vocabulary that demands a knowledge of certain problems in social theory to be intelligible. What they experience is characterized by Bourdieu himself in the following way:

In short, the laws of diffusion of scientific discourse mean that, despite the existence of relays and mediators, scientific truth is very unlikely to reach those who would have most interest in receiving it. Yet one may think that one would only have to provide the latter with a language in which they recognized themselves, or, rather, in which they felt *recognized*, that's to say accepted, justified in existing as they exist (which they are necessarily offered by all good sociology, a science that, as such, *explains* things). (Bourdieu 1993a: 23)

Therefore, the relationship between the analysis and the experiences of life contained in the transcribed material needs to be seen as continuous, each informing the other. The analyses have to be abstract because they are trying to speak about things that are primarily lived through as feelings and bodily dispositions. Capturing them requires them to be signified, to be brought into the light somehow; and doing justice to the depth of their importance depends upon developing an ontology, otherwise these phenomena remain phenomena of the 'surface' of social life, when they need to be situated as being at the core of social life. No matter how articulate the people interviewed are, no matter how powerful the transcribed material is, these people do not need merely our sympathy, or our pity, they need other people to understand the nature of their suffering as being lodged deep in the cultural relations of this nation and at the heart of its nationhood. Because of this, the passages from Bourdieu and Merleau-Ponty are equally important to understanding their lives. This book concerns experience: but to capture it, it must break with that experience, because the experience itself rests in something beyond the situated experiencing subject. The language used by the people I have quoted from in my transcribed material, manifests a world that their corporeality invests with often ambiguous, indeterminate significance. Their struggle to give voice to this experience is registered in the broken syntax, the sighs and truisms that are the impact marks of the world that they know, uncertainly, through the pointless pain of their boredom, the wastage their embodiment registers in its growing inertia to experience itself, the thrill of new experiences being replaced by fear born of rejection. The work, therefore, uses theoretical ideas to recognize and mark the traces, in the talked-about world of these people, of structures that are real and emergent because they are making themselves felt in human subjects and impacting upon the form of community their communities take.

I would also like to acknowledge that severe restrictions on any empirical research are set by being forced – as in my case – to work alone, and on a small income. It can be a costly exercise, and forms of analysis are restricted by one's income as well as one's expertise. Co-ordinated labour on research objects is desperately needed right now. But I can only acknowledge the consequences that accrue from my being a particular social subject and thus both able to produce accounts of a certain type of experience and forced to accept the limitations that spring from it.

Having established the nature of the work, it is necessary at this point to explain some of the key operating concepts of the study. All of them are central concepts developed and used by Pierre Bourdieu.

Introducing some concepts: practice, habitus, ethos, doxa, reflexivity

The meaning of many of the concepts will become clearer from the context in which they are used: but I will offer a preliminary sense of their meaning which will help the reader to enter the discussion.

(a) Practice

Bourdieu has argued for a 'unified political economy of practice' (Bourdieu and Wacquant 1992: 4) and symbolic power that integrates phenomenological and structural approaches into a coherent approach to social reality. This book is an exercise in that enterprise. However, throughout, the word 'practical' is used in the sense derived from Bourdieu's theory of practice, to denote what he calls a 'practical sense'. Now, what these ideas are trying to illuminate, that is of paramount importance to this book, is that people have a pre-reflective, infraconscious competence that is a result of their immersion within the realm of the social. It is this 'sense' that characterizes human practice. In Bourdieu's terms, the relation between subject and world is one of 'ontological complicity' (Bourdieu and Wacquant 1992: 20), between a habitus and the world which determines it. Our 'practical sense' thus guides us before we posit our goals as such; it provides a sense of horizons in which we construct conscious strategies, it renders our world meaningful by spontaneously foreseeing the immediate future immanent in our present.

(b) Habitus

The habitus is the socially constituted principle of perception and appreciation of the social world that we acquire in a particular social context which renders the world meaningful: it is the basis of our practical sense. At the heart of the habitus are our corporeal capacities, through which we learn habits or dispositions, through which in turn we are able to engage with the world of others. Much of what we are is habitual, but not simple repetition; rather it is recursive: we use the past to frame our future actions. Yet this is a matter of hexis, of embodiment, because it is the body that takes up the motor skills. The socially learnt postural and gestural sets are taken up to create distinct forms of motility, a corporeal style or distinct bodily hexis that marks us both positively and negatively as persons, so that our being is this blend of thought taking place within a flow that habit sustains. The past is sedimented in the body's present and is carried through to the future that it helps to make distinct.

(c) Ethos

We think of an ethic as a moral principle that is part of a coherent system of moral edicts, but Bourdieu uses the term 'ethos' to refer to the system of dispositions embodied in the habitus of a group, dispositions which operate practically as an ethical system. This might cover a range of everyday occurrences concerning what a group believes to be right – holding doors for people, being courteous – things that they would realize in practice without thought, part of the practical sense of a group. But they will consciously consider the ethics of their dispositions only when the principles one's actions embody cease to be part of the social world encountered. It is an important concept in this book, because the decline of industry has meant a decline in the old ethos. For instance, men who grew up to work embody a sense of respect for others that they feel strongly lacking in the younger generation, and the experience of this lack often forces them to articulate the ethical principles of their action because that ethos is on the point of dying. It is the habitus that transmits from one generation to the next the ethos of groups; clearly then, the ethos is also a class ethos, it is a specific embodied morality that operates in a practical mode and it governs the nuances of honour between people.

(d) Doxa

'Doxa' is used to refer to a complex set of ideas concerning the way in which we come to accept aspects of our environment and position as 'natural'. It deals with a way of thinking and feeling about our everyday world, the way in which we perceive it as given. It refers to that which we think *from* rather than what we think *about*. As such, it refers to those schemes of thought and perception which objective structures produce but which we experience as given and which we take for granted. Therefore, it is constituted by those systems of classification which establish limits to what we contemplate in discursive consciousness, thus producing an inability to see the arbitrariness on which the classification and the structures have been established.

(e) Reflexivity

The concepts that I have introduced so far provide an ontology that this thesis uses to develop an understanding of the problems it takes as its object. Accepting this ontology, we cannot then treat the position of the academic as somehow different and, thus, we need to see academic practice as embedded in the same manner. The differences that exist between this position and those of the people described, thus need to be brought into view and considered. Bourdieu's notion of a 'reflexive sociology' is based around such a premise. Bourdieu's notion of a 'reflexive' sociological method is implied in his ontology, and I use the term to depict my own work. The notion of 'reflexivity' has come to be somewhat modish in the arts and causes some disquiet. In this work, it means little more than a constant epistemic vigilance throughout the process of thinking, living and writing. 'Reflexive' denotes something different from 'Reflective'. Social commentary of all kinds involves reflection but, for Bourdieu, reflexivity involves a turning back upon the position of the knowing subject, a looking back at one's own knowing practices. Hence its target is not merely the individual analyst but the unconscious embedded in her social position, as well as the tools and operations of analysis. Wacquant describes the heart of the method as being 'the inclusion of a theory of intellectual practice as an integral component and necessary condition of a critical theory of society' (Bourdieu and Wacquant 1992: 36). What this means in this work is dealt with more fully in chapter 3.

These ideas will be developed throughout the work to develop an account of what it is like to live in Rotherham and to have this experience of class. First I would like to move on and introduce Rotherham, firstly through a brief history and account of its life and secondly through demographic data.

2

Rotherham: history, demography and place

This country had a grim will of its own, and the people had guts . . . There was no communication between Wragby Hall and Tevershall village – none. No caps were touched, no curtseys bobbed. The colliers merely stared: the tradesman lifted their caps to Connie as to an acquaintance, and nodded awkwardly to Clifford: that was all. Gulf impassable, and a quiet sort of resentment on either side. At first Connie suffered from the steady resentment that came from the village. Then she hardened herself to it, and it was a sort of tonic, something to live up against. It was not that she and Clifford were unpopular – they merely belonged to another species altogether from the colliers. Gulf impassable, breach indescribable, such as is perhaps non-existent south of the Trent. But in the Midlands and the industrial North, gulf impassable, across which no communion could take place. – You stick to your side, I'll stick to mine! – A strange denial of the common pulse of humanity.   (Lawrence 1994: 14)

Not a town in the land is unscarred by the dogmatic application of the market principle.   (Hutton 1996a)

Themes of power, coercion, and collective resistance shape landscape as a social microcosm.   (Zukin 1991: 19)

1. Rotherham: a brief history

Rotherham, the hamlet on the Rother, is one of those places characterized, in the heyday of industrial production, by smoke-excreting steelworks and the unearthly towers that supported colliery headgear. However the colliery headgear pokes its spoked rims over Victorian walls, its purpose is lost to generations now growing up for whom much of that industry has gone. Sheffield Road, the main road between Sheffield and Rotherham, was a stretch of land once full of steel-related industry. Amidst the dereliction

32

there, now stands Meadowhall, a shopping mall built to the dimensions of a cathedral which is visited by 20 million people a year. If one doubted that the lifestyle of working people based around the rhythms of employment has been replaced by nothing but their reconstitution as shoppers, who travel to spaces where they can experience the rush of bodies collecting for the only possible common purpose they know, then Rotherham is a town to consider. The urban decay of the centre, the dying heart of the place, is being replaced by a life of the periphery, for those mobile and affluent enough to chase life to the shopping sites. In America, the mall makes sense amidst the disparate open abundance of space, but in Britain, with its tightly compacted urban space, its flourishing has more radical significance. A redirection of income and social power that has its roots in the same processes that have destroyed the communities they now depend upon. So, for Rotherham, as well as the expansive, inhumanly scaled Meadowhall, there is Parkgate, a site where there were steelworks for hundreds of years but where there now stands 'Retail World'. These are both sites where once people mattered, economically, because they worked. And now the same people return to participate as consumers. Yet these areas were lucky: they were redeveloped for retail, for service and thus for consumption, however short-changed workers have been in the process of replacing well-paid manual work with low-paid service work. For the rest of the area, there is simply devastation, at one point, the largest areas of industrial dereliction in Europe.

Yet Rotherham's history was not always so bleak. It appeared in the Domesday Book (1086) as a town with its own mill, church and priest, and by the eleventh century Rotherham had its parish church and the houses that stood on the land which became the town centre.[1] By the beginning of the eighteenth century, Rotherham was a prosperous small market town with a population of two and half thousand people, a population which meant it was comparable in size to its neighbor on the River Don, Sheffield. Although the population rose to six thousand by the end of the eighteenth century, it was the coming of industry which shaped Rotherham into its recognizable form. The geology of the western side of the borough consists of coal measures sandstone whilst the east side consists of magnesium limestone. The Romans smelted iron at their Templeborough fort, and in the twelfth century monks at Kirkstead Abbey were exploiting local mineral resources (Munford 1995: 5). This coincidence of shallow seams of coal and iron ore alongside limestone shaped the destiny of the area. The sixteenth and seventeenth centuries saw the arrival of a furnace at Jordan, a slitting mill at Masbrough and a steel mill at Thrybergh. Coal mining and iron and steel production expanded in the mid-eighteenth century with

Abraham Darby's discovery that iron could be smelted using coke. But of more importance for Rotherham, the Don Navigation canal was completed in 1740, linking Rotherham to Doncaster and allowing for the cheap movement of heavy goods. It was this which led Samuel Walker and his brothers to bring their young iron business to Masbrough and start Rotherham's industrial revolution. The census of 1801 shows that Rotherham, consisting of Masbrough and Kimberworth, had a population that was almost 6,500. However, throughout the century, industrial growth meant a rise in population such that it stood at 10,500 in 1841, 19,000 in 1861 and 54,000 in 1901. This growth in the number of people meant the building of cheap terraced houses on the Masbrough side of the Don (Munford 1994). The extent of the industrial development was clear in the transport of goods on the canal. In the middle of the nineteenth century, when the railways began to steal much of the trade the canal, was carrying, in 1857, over 400,000 tons of coal per year, but the railways were moving double that amount. Hence, with chief industries of steel and coal, the railways became a crucially important service for the area. The first railway was the Sheffield and Rotherham Railway which opened in 1838; however it ran only between the Wicker in Sheffield and Westgate. However, the North Midland line opened Masbrough station in 1840.

In the nineteenth century, Rotherham's economy was diverse. Buildings in the Victorian period were likely to have kitchen ranges, fireplaces, stoves and railings, and these were made in Rotherham foundries such as Yates, Haywood and Co., George Wright's or Micklethwaite's. Wrought iron was produced at the well-known Midland Iron Company, and water and gas supplies were delivered through taps, valves and meters made at Guest and Chrimes which stands on the river Don, whilst medicines were kept in bottles made at Beatson Clark's glassworks. The Holmes and Northfield potteries produced earthenware, and Owen and Dyson as well as John Baker produced wheels and axles for railways all over the world. And all of this was built on the back of the coal from local pits. Yet it was for steel that Rotherham has always been renowned. The Walker blast furnaces at the Holmes were taken over by the Park Gate Iron and Steel Company. However the main producer of steel was the works of Steel, Peech and Tozer Ltd. They had works at Ickles and Templeborough which were founded in 1875, and which grew to stretch for a mile along Sheffield Road. The demand for steel in the First World War led to the installation of fourteen open-hearth furnaces at the Templeborough works. In 1918, Steel, Peech and Tozer Ltd joined Samuel Fox and Company of Stocksbridge, Appleby Frodingham Steel Company of Scunthorpe and the Workington Iron and Steel Company to form the United Steel Companies Ltd. This ensured that the Templeborough works expanded steadily so that by the 1960s, Steel, Peech and Tozer Ltd was the largest employer in the town, with a workforce of 8,500.

These factories served the country well during two World Wars. The outbreak of the Great War of 1914–18 saw many local factories turned over to production for the war, and the pages of the local paper, *The Rotherham Advertiser,* carried the names of the men who died in the local regiment, the York and Lancaster. They suffered badly at the Somme, and the list of names on the memorial that still stands in Clifton Park ran to 1,304. It was a similar story in the Second World War, with women serving in the services and the W.V.S. The town raised £5,000 to buy a Spitfire and £700,000 to adopt a destroyer 'HMS Rotherham'; and the Bailey Bridge was designed by Rotherham born Donald Bailey and manufactured by several local firms.

The Depression of the 1920s and 1930s saw Rotherham suffer deeply. In 1930 it was designated a depressed area. The 1980s were a similar time for the English working class, ravaged by unemployment, they were content merely to hang on to what work there was, too weak to fight even against the poverty that was ravaging their communities. As in the Great Depression, personal life for working class families was scarred by the strains of economic marginality and vulnerability. I will turn now and look at the view that is presented in demographic data.

2. Rotherham: a demographic view

We have, now, a sense of the Rotherham that has passed. I would like to move on and look at contemporary Rotherham. I will begin by looking at the demographic picture provided by the Census. This provides us with what might be seen as an 'official' and formalized sense of the place. It also provides for us a contrast with what emerges from the interviews as the human meaning of the world of demographic and economic statistics. As the transcription suggests, there is a serious gap between these two versions of the town's condition, or, rather, the world as it is lived, does not emerge from the statistics. There is a marked difference between the object constituted through the demographic information and the sense of a distinct place that emerges from people who have grown up here and who have grown up with a set of conditions so naturalized in their consciousness that although they may deal with the place practically as a set of problems to be responded to, they seldom appreciate what their lives owe to the economic background that has shaped the culture and practices of the place they inhabit. This range of issues concerning the relationship between subject and world will be central in the following chapters, but here I will focus upon the state of the local economy and look at income levels, rates of unemployment across the different groups in the town and, alongside these, rates of ill-health and housing conditions.[2]

Rotherham's population is quite large at 251,637. However, this is spread across twenty-two wards, and the town itself is an aggregation of much smaller villages. It is this aggregation of the population within the different areas that gives Rotherham the sense of being a 'small town'. As the size of the population shows, it is not a small place, but the nature of its division, making it possible to move seamlessly from area to area where the flow of life exhibits the same contours, gives one always the sense of being in a place characterized by familiarity and visibility. Moving through the areas that make up Rotherham, one hears slight differences in accent – a slur here, an inflexion there – and alongside such small differences one gets the gentle mythology of places separated by the slight differences of shared conditions. People say 'watch yerseln up the'er kid', yet there is little, if any, genuine ill-feeling across areas which share a common culture and destiny. This is hardly surprising, given that the same industries and the same type of casual labour have fed the way of life, giving the areas a common cultural history. These people share the same judgements, the same sense of the world and of themselves and they share a sense of their place in it. Above all, they share the same world of practices that Rotherham is.

Rotherham is a place still trying to follow the rhythms of work, where the week still moves towards its climax at the weekend and begins with the nadir of Monday morning. The actual style of life – of struggling for work, or of poverty-ridden idleness through the week and waiting for the Friday and Saturday nights out of pubbing and clubbing, of hoping for the adventure of sexual conquest – is the same for many towns and villages in South Yorkshire. It is a history sedimented in a common way of being, of making life amidst a set of choices outside of which there is nothingness, of seeing the world, of valuing people: a common store of predispositions, of attitudes, of ideas and a practical day-to-day life. These are the habits of deed and thought that being from South Yorkshire consists in.

But what does the Census tell us about the life of these places? The last Census uses the term 'Economic Activity' to refer to those people who are over the age of sixteen years and who are employed, self-employed, unemployed or on a Government training scheme. Now of the 199,117 people who are over the age of sixteen years, 117,523, or 59% are economically active. Economic activity – rates are higher for men, at 68,305 (71.2%), than for women, at 49,218 (47.7%). However, the trend in Rotherham is that this gap is narrowing as more women are entering the labour force whilst an older generation of men are retiring early through closures and redundancies in the area's traditional industries such as coal, steel and manufacture. The vast majority of men are employees: 49,008 (71.8%) compared to 7,202 (10.5%) who are self-employed. Among women who are economically active, the majority, 42,397 (86.1%), are employees, but only 2,195 (4.5%) of women are self-employed or in business. If we look at the 41% of people who are classed as economically inactive, 3,223 (3.4%) of men are in full-time education, 6,943 (7.2%) are unable to work because of long-term sickness or disability; 16,743 (17.4%) are retired, and 776 (0.8%) are looking after the home or family. A larger proportion of women are inactive, the total being 27,207 (26.4%). Among these, 3,230 (3.1%) are in full-time education; 4,028 (3.9%) are permanently sick and 19,444 (18.9%) are retired.

Of those in employment, 76.7% are working full-time (31 hours or more a week), with 22.3% working part-time. Nearly all men (96.5%) are employed full-time but nearly one in two women (47.8%) are employed part-time. Production-related industries account for 43.5% of male employment in Rotherham, with construction accounting for a further 13.6% and service-based industries for 42.3%. More than one in four (27.3%) are employed in craft-based occupations, with a further 20.9% employed as plant or machine operatives. Another 27.5% are employed in managerial or professional/associate professional occupations, with only 5.2% in clerical/secretarial jobs. Female employment breaks down as four-fifths employed in service-based industries, while 38.8% of working women fall into the category 'Other Services'. This category includes employment in local government, the civil service and the health service. One in ten women are employed in a category 'Other Manufacturing' which includes the two large employers, KP Nuts and Morphy Richards, but generally, production industries account for only 20.1% of female employment. Clerical and secretarial jobs account for 25.2% of jobs for women, and there are fewer women than men, only 23.6%, in managerial or professional/ associate professional occupations. Sales accounts for 14.7% of female occupations which appears low when compared to the numbers employed in Distribution and Catering.

Reading these figures, one inescapable question forces itself upon the indifferent reader: 'So what?' The figures tell us very little, especially in a town that has been described in the following way:

Rotherham, meanwhile, is the worst of towns. John Richards was experiencing the feel-good factor on Thursday, but he was only five years old and was sucking an ice cream . . . The town has a tired, depressed feel . . . It is beginning to represent Britain in Decline . . . There are council estates in the area with 90 per cent unemployment, with some pockets of the borough having the worst unemployment rate in Britain.

(Hillmore 1996)

And this was written by an outsider who hardly knows the place. If it seems this bleak to someone who isn't intimate with the bleakness, then what must the experience of living here be for those of us who have built a personal existence here and for whom this has been our opening onto the human world? As a backdrop to the bleakness Hillmore perceived, perhaps we should return again to the world of objectivity that the Census has made accessible to us. What has it to say that might help us to fathom the sense that Hillmore felt around him?

Nationally, the 1980s were a period of economic recession and restructuring unprecedented in the post-war period, and areas characterized by traditional industries, like Rotherham, experienced these changes profoundly. In 1981 alone, from an employment base of 82,000, Rotherham lost over 8,000 jobs in metal manufacturing and engineering and a further 8,000 jobs in coal mining, whilst the town's economic performance was amongst the worst in the country. A series of comparative studies[3] of 280 local labour market areas consistently placed Rotherham in the bottom 20%. The changes are obvious in alterations to the amount and type of employment available. The overall decrease of 8.7% in the number of jobs over the period from 1981 to 1987, a loss of 7,200 jobs, obscures important alterations in levels of employment in both coal mining and metal manufacturing, which fell by more than 50%. In 1978 there were 12,500 employees in metal manufacturing, and by 1989 this had fallen to 4,950. The industry around Sheffield has always sprawled into Rotherham, and the working class of both places have always shared very much culturally, there being a good deal of inter-dependence socially among the people who live in both places: but this has also meant, obviously, that the collapse of the steel industry in Sheffield has also deeply affected Rotherham people because so many travelled to work around the Sheffield road and its environs. And this scenario is clear for so many of the pits that surrounded the area. Many older men tell tales of how many pits they once passed while cycling around the area. The mining industry nationally, we would do well to remember, has lost in excess of 130,000 jobs:[4] this has hit Yorkshire hard, but limiting ourselves to the period from 1981, when there were still fifteen pits operating, there now remains only one, with even Maltby likely to close. As Hillmore put it:

Rotherham's civic motto, 'Thus Industry Flourishes', has an ironic tone now that the great twin industries of steel and coal are no more. The coal strike of 1984 began here at Cortonwood colliery. Cortonwood, Orgreave, Manvers, Thurcroft and Treeton – the names of dead collieries around Rotherham sound like the sad litany of English dead in Shakespeare's *Henry V* . . . For every new service industry that the council persuades to start up operations, that it lures to the area with incentives, another, long-established company closes down.   (Hillmore 1996)

Clearly, then, over the last fifteen years Rotherham's economy has been chronically vulnerable to national economic conditions. The problem has been that its main industries are those in most serious decline at a national level, whilst the fastest-growing sector of the national economy in the mid-eighties, Banking, Insurance and Finance, is severely underrepresented in the area. The loss of its traditional industrial base has severely affected the prosperity of the area. Gross Domestic Product per head in South Yorkshire has reduced dramatically from over 92% of the UK. average in 1981 to only 79% in 1989, and average earnings have declined by nearly 15% relative to the UK average between 1980 and 1992. Rotherham and its fellow towns have undergone the classic symptoms of deindustrialization, and they have not been able to recover from the loss of jobs in the coal and steel industries.

Male employment has therefore become more evenly distributed, but there do remain significant concentrations in the area's traditional industries. These are: Energy and Water with 11.7%; Metal Manufacture with 16.2%; Mechanical Engineering with 14.8%; Retail Distribution with 14.2% and Other Services with 13.1%. However, Female employment has been even more concentrated in the sectors of Retail Distribution with 24.8%, Other Public/Private Services with 44.3% and Other Manufacturing Industries with 11%.

When this book was originally written mining still accounted for the largest share of employment, even though the early 1990s saw the number of jobs in mining in Rotherham halved. But, since this work was originally written, Kiveton and Silverwood have both closed. In the mid-seventies, in Rotherham, approximately 10,000 people were employed in the mining industry. If the closure of Maltby, goes ahead, that will mean the loss of another 1, 235 jobs and will mean there will be no deep-mined coal being extracted from the Rotherham area. The old socialist's dream of no one going down a hole in the ground, will at last be true, but one has to wonder, in the spirit of those old soldiers who fought for what was right, and who still speak of the 'Socialist Republic', would D. H. Lawrence himself, were he alive, be happier with this state of the industrial masses, whose plight so absorbed him?

The slump in the national economy has had other effects on the area: particularly, it has affected the confidence of those local businesses that the Tory Government once trusted so much regeneration to, especially it has affected the confidence of small and medium-sized enterprises (SMEs). The level of vacancy rates for industrial and commercial properties is an indication of this, and it has risen from 12.8% to 13.1%. It is very difficult for local people, whatever their economic status, to maintain any optimism about the immediate economic future. And this is particularly the case in the wake of the latest bout of pit closures which are likely to cost a further 200 jobs directly and another 4,000 indirectly. This will push unemployment in the area to over 20% and reduce local GDP per person by another 3%. The fall in local demand has resulted in increased bankruptcies, with many other local companies reducing investment and shedding labour.

Indeed, Rotherham's industrial structure is now so weak that certain industries are no longer represented. Even local companies like Novenco Aerex and Salem Automation that have had some success in winning contracts abroad in the areas of engineering and manufacturing accept that any such success is overshadowed by what has seemed to local people as the never-ending closure of pits, a decision by British Coal that affects not only those who worked in the pits but many other sectors of the local economy. The estimates that I could get my hands on seem equally bleak. Forecasts from Rotherham Borough Council seem to offer little hope of a recovery people might notice. It is anticipated that Rotherham's traditional industries will continue to decline, particularly in the areas of energy supply, metal production and engineering. The future seems to be one in which unemployment will almost certainly remain higher than the national average. Estimates suggest that there would need to be at least 5,000 jobs created to bring present rates of unemployment to the national average. Over the last twelve-month period that I could find records for, the year ending April 1996, these show that the demand for labour in the Rotherham area has fallen, for the number of annual notified vacancies to local job centres was lower at 8,184 compared to 8,383 in the previous year. Rotherham's industrial structure continues to have an overrepresentation of those traditional industrial sectors which are in long-term decline. Local organizations have tried to introduce some diversification into the local industrial base, but service sector industries remain under-developed in comparison with the national average, and sectors like banking, finance, insurance and business show no sign of being anything other than poorly represented in a local economy that remains poor.

The traditional industries of metal and mineral production and chemicals now employ about 10% of the local workforce, with 75% of these engaged in metal manufacture. They have continued to streamline their workforces with 5,230 job losses between 1981 and 1991, and there are further redundancies forecast. During 1992 there were an additional 431 job losses and, nationally, this sector is forecast to decline by 15% by 2001. The same is true of those jobs that remain in the energy sector: the former public utilities of Water, Gas and Electricity which, following privatization in the 1980s, have continued to shed jobs in a continual drive to increase profitability and competitiveness, which has left them accounting for less than 1% of Rotherham's workforce. The metal manufacturing industry, quite apart from the redundancies of the 1980s, has faced serious problems throughout the nineties. It has faced problems because of over-capacity within the European Community's Steel Community and on top of that, there has been the problem of cheap imports coming into the country from East Asia. Much of the steel produced in the area has been shipped to America for use in the car industry and the industry has always been sensitive to fluctuations in demand for American cars. Indeed, The American government's introduction of protectionist import tariffs on steel in the mid-1990s had a damaging effect on the steel industry and the closure of the pits in the area further hit the local steel industry because a sizeable amount of local steel companies' production was used in the coal industry.

These problems also affect the related industry of engineering which currently accounts for 10.5% of the Rotherham workforce. This sector itself has seen a steady reduction in employment in those trades allied to heavy engineering and in the next few years the demand for semi-skilled machine operatives will continue to decline. Overall there was a loss of 560 jobs between 1981 and 1991, with an additional 168 reported during 1992. National forecasts are that employment in all sectors related to engineering will decline still further. The local transport industries are also in decline, despite growth in services like small taxi firms and driving schools. The transport industry accounts for 3.5% of Rotherham's workforce, with road haulage companies accounting for 50% of these jobs. Again in this sector, pit closures have hit local firms hard; rail freight has been particularly hard hit with Tinsley Rail Freight having closed; but it has also hit local road haulage companies some of which were almost completely dependent on British Coal for contracts. Again, these are local factors adding to what is a national trend anyway since, overall, transport is expected to decline in importance nationally with employment on British Rail forecast to fall by 10% between 1994 and 2001 and with other transport jobs expected to follow with a drop of 4%. Even the areas of postal services and telecommunications, which, in Rotherham, showed a small increase in the 1980s, are expected to lose jobs. Employment in this sector is forecast to decline by 2% up to the end of the decade.

Although the large job-losses in mining and metal manufacturing have to some degree been offset in gross terms by new jobs created in the service industries, the jobs that have been created have not offered replacement work for those whose jobs have disappeared, because although the majority of new jobs are in sectors previously underrepresented in Rotherham, they offer different types of employment opportunities to different types of workers. For instance, in 1981, 61.7% of jobs were occupied by men, and 19.4% of jobs were part-time. By 1987 male employment accounted for 54% of jobs and part-time employment had grown to 27.7% of the total. This change in employment is a result of employers in the service sector utilizing female employees in jobs that are generally low paid and insecure but which offer great flexibility. Consequently, these jobs are not seen as an alternative to the skilled work available in the 1970s.

Obviously, the decline in the numbers of available jobs has meant a big increase in the numbers of unemployed, despite the massaging of the unemployment figures over the period since 1980 by the government. In October 1980, the unemployment rate was estimated to be 8% in Rotherham, compared with the national rate of 5.5%. The highest levels of unemployment were recorded in January 1986, when 24,580 people were registered as unemployed, an unemployment rate of 23.5%. At that point the national unemployment rate was 13.9%. The late 1980s saw a reduction in the numbers of unemployed nationally, and by July 1990 the national figure stood at 6.4% whilst Rotherham's unemployed numbered 12,017, or 12.8%. Throughout the 1980s, therefore, unemployment rates have been consistently higher than in the country as a whole, and, though the national improvements have been reflected in Rotherham, the relative local position has actually got worse. In 1980, Rotherham's unemployment rate was just under one-and-a-half-times that of the nation as a whole, but by September 1990 it had increased to twice the national rate. In January of 1992 unemployment in the area had risen to 14.7% and rose again to 15.6% in January of 1993, when 14,980 people were officially registered as unemployed. Furthermore, Rotherham has one of the highest rates of long-term unemployment in the country.

Unemployment among the young is particularly important and its effects will emerge later in the interview material. Unemployment among the young is something that has been a problem for a long time; and is of great importance to the lives of people in Rotherham, something that has touched almost everyone in one way or another. There were 4,637 people under the age of twenty-five officially claiming benefit in Rotherham in April 1993, which is a proportion of 35% of the total unemployed. Yet unemployment rates remain much higher for young people, compared to the overall rate for Rotherham. Based on the 1991 Census of population, and taking into account unemployment growth since then, the unemployment rate for under-25-year-olds, in April 1993 was 33%. Careers information figures for school leavers show that there are fewer young people leaving school in Rotherham and that more are now going into further education, mainly as a result of their knowing they will be forced to college through Youth Training, and partly in the hope that obtaining qualifications will be a way of increasing their chances of entering the workforce at a later date. And of those who do leave school, the vast majority go straight into Youth Training. However, according to Rotherham Borough Council's Unemployment Unit, in January 1995, the number of young unemployed is now above 5,500. In this same period, a third of unemployed young people had been without a job for a year or more, and this includes many who have never worked. The proportion of young men unemployed or on Government Training Schemes in Rotherham was more than twice that of men aged 24–64. If Government Training Schemes are included, the unemployment rate of young women was four times higher than the figure for women of 25 and over.

In spite of the reductions in unemployment over the last few years, there remain many things to be concerned about. For example, 35% of all claimants are under the age of 25, and many have had little experience of work outside the government-sponsored schemes that they are forced to enter. Indeed, 35% of these young people have been unemployed for more than a year. In addition, at least 2,700 school leavers are engaged on the Youth Training Schemes that the government sponsors. In acknowledgement of the severity of these problems, Rotherham is a Designated Area for various forms of assistance to aid economic recovery and alleviate hardship. A defined Inner Area receives aid and City Grant from the Urban Programme; the whole borough is an Assisted Area, all except two wards being a Development Area (as part of the Dearne Valley, which is designated by the European Union as the largest area of industrial dereliction in Europe), and for aid from the European Regional Development fund and the European Social fund. An area of 260 acres in the central area of Rotherham is designated an Enterprise Zone, and seven rural parishes in the south of the borough have been designated a Development Area by the Rural Development Commission. But for all of those hoping for a future for their children that is better than their own present, it seems there will only be more of the same present. Predictions of future employment patterns estimate growth on a national scale of 2.5% between now and the end of the century but it is expected that for Rotherham and the Dearne Valley as a whole there will be no overall growth.

However, reading these figures, particularly as someone who has been a part of what it describes, who left school for nothing but Youth Training, who has looked as a young person for work one has to say that they tell no story. On top of that, one is left thinking that it has all been much worse for all of us, much worse, because we all know too many people among our families and friends who have lost, or who are worried about losing, their jobs. The real nature of the situation is captured more accurately by a Skill Audit of Rotherham carried out by the Business School of Sheffield Hallam University in 1990, which estimated that if account were taken of those, particularly women, who are not eligible to register as unemployed, and yet who would be willing to work if jobs were available, then the numbers out of work would actually be at least double the official figures.

Now that seems a much more plausible number but, still, none of this speaks of a human world, of a place where things matter, of a place that means something to those who are the numbers involved. Week-in, week-out the local newspaper, delivered free, warns of 'Perils of poverty':

Families in Rotherham are struggling to give their children three meals a day . . . With unemployment well over the national average at 16 per cent, and local employers offering some of the lowest rates of pay in the country, Rotherham Council's anti-poverty unit's survey paints a grim picture of debt and poor health.[5]

(*Rotherham Record* March, 1996.)

The same report informs us that 4, 000 jobs have been lost in the last five years; that this has left 20,000 people without work, and more than 55,000 people are now on income support, that is more than one in five of the borough's population, with 62% of all council tenants receiving housing benefit. The figures for rented accommodation are 42%, and in Housing Association accommodation this rises to 61%. In other forms of private rented accommodation the figure is 55%. The council is struggling with an ever-expanding waiting list for housing, there are almost 24,000 people now on its list. This is a result of the great sell-off of council housing in the early and mid 1980s. Between 1981 and 1991, in Rotherham, the number of council houses fell from 44.7% to under a third of total housing, and house-ownership rose from below a half to almost two-thirds. This reduction in the council's housing stock weakened the local Authority's capacity to provide housing. Of the 23,869 people who in 1994 were seeking accommodation, 6,074 were assessed as being 'eligible' for rehousing, but only 1,996 were rehoused. Obviously, waiting times are very long, with families waiting 1 to 2 years, single people up to 6 years, and those wanting older people's accommodation over 10 years. The length of time of waiting varies, but the worst is in Boston Ward, where the waiting-time for a family is 3 years, and for older people it is 14 years. In the period April to December 1994, 918 people applied to be accepted as homeless by the council, but only 218 were accepted as being in priority need. In order to get any kind of housing, therefore, from a Housing Association, a prospective tenant is likely to be in acute housing need. A quarter of those who are given such accommodation are statutorily homeless. Over a two-year period, 414 homeless 16–20-year-olds had to be accommodated in the Night Shelter operated by Rush House for an average of twelve nights each.

In a survey of one housing estate it was revealed that 15% of tenants said that they could not afford heating in the living room and bedroom, 13% were unable to afford a warm, waterproof coat and 21% couldn't afford new clothes. More distressing still, 9% couldn't afford 3 meals a day for their children. It cannot be surprising, then, that 80% of residents reported being afraid of not being able to continue securing the money to live and pay their bills, and two-thirds reported being unable, at one time or another, to pay their gas, electric or water bills. Furthermore, between April and November 1994, 67 % of people were refused lump-sum payments for basic needs from applications for community care grants through the Government's Social Fund. This number itself is an underestimate, because many people know that they will not get such a grant and, instead, apply for recoverable budgeting loans. With so little money in the pockets of local people, one would expect children to suffer, and apparently 12,100 children live in households that do not have a wage-earner, a figure that amounts to more than a fifth of the total number of children. There were 5,395 children living in over-crowded conditions, that is, with more than one person to a room. In the school year 1993/94, 9,756 applications for free school meals were approved: that is 23% of the total number of children in Rotherham's schools. A quarter of children, therefore, come from families on Income Support. Furthermore, people in Rotherham also suffer worse health than in other parts of the Trent region, with mortality rates being higher in every category with the exception of breast cancer. For example, the number of households in England and Wales that contain a person with a limiting long-term illness is 24.6%, and yet in Rotherham households this is 31.2%. Nationally, the number of households consisting only of people who class themselves as 'permanently sick' and not looking for work is 8.8%; in Rotherham the number is 10.7%, and 6 out of 10 people in Rotherham who suffer from a limiting long-term illness live in households without a person who is employed. Between April 1992 and March 1995, the number in the area receiving Sickness Benefit rose by 23% to 4, 693 whilst the number receiving Invalidity Benefit rose by 17% to 17, 657. The numbers of people who are now getting the disability premium through

Income Support rose by a quarter in this period because of the large numbers of redundant workers from the mines and other heavy industry.

And as one might expect in a town like this, the burden of debt is huge, at over £4 million, which is £23 for every adult. The replacement of the poll tax with the Council Tax has only had a minimal effect, with over 16,000 people owing Council Tax debts; which is 1 in every 6, with an average debt of £160.71. In 1994/95, 1 account in 4 was subject to a summons, and 1 in 8 resulted in a liability order being issued. There were 2,390 people having debts recovered from their earnings, and 499 more from their benefit. In March of 1995, 112 cases were with the bailiffs. In the same period, it was reported that there were 17,469 token or rechargeable key meters in use to supply electricity and recover debts, with the average debt to be recovered by Powerkey meters being £177. These are pressures on the individual that are worsening. For example, Severn Trent Water increased its charges by 35% between 1990 and 1995 and its sewerage charges by 29.1%. Similarly Yorkshire Water Services increased charges by 18.5% and sewerage by 23.4% and Rotherham Environmental Health and Consumer Advice Centre has reported that one in five of its clients need advice about debt to water companies. According to this organization, its average client had five debts totalling £3,514, and the average debt per creditor was £916.

And the low wages are as important a phenomenon as the unemployment. The Yorkshire and Humberside Low Pay Unit in its work found Rotherham to be one of the lowest paid regions in the country with employers offering the lowest hourly rates for full-time work in the country, notably through the job centres. £3.70 per hour is seen by many as a 'good' wage and contrasts with the Low Pay Unit's minimum wage-target of £4.15, and the Council of Europe's low pay threshold, fixed at 68% of adult full-time mean earnings, of £5.87 per hour. The Low Pay Unit estimate that according to the New Earnings Survey, in 1994, there were over 3,100 people earning less than £3 an hour and over 16,300 earning less than £4 an hour.

According to the local MP, Dennis McShane, about £2.9 billion, that is around £120 for every tax payer in the UK, is being paid out in the form of welfare benefits to people with jobs, a figure that has now almost trebled in the last four years. It amounts to a modern day Speenhamland system, with the state prepared to subsidize low-paying employers. And this is a growing trend as employers obviously have an interest in reducing their wages budget. If it continues to grow at the present rate, then by the end of the century, such employers will be subsidized at a cost to the state that exceeds the education budget. In Rotherham, for example, jobs are advertised at a rate of £1.44 per hour. Furthermore, there are 70,000 professional, management and education jobs with pay so low that the employees qualify to receive family credit.

These are the conditions for a thriving black market, with wages so low that employers in the area call in unemployed men to do a day's work for an extra few pounds on top of their unemployment benefit. And the social life of these people begins to operate like a primitive economy where people exchange whatever they can get their hands on and sell. The National Federation of Housing Associations, looking at the incomes of new Housing Association tenants, found that 61% of tenants had a net income of less than £100 per week and 93% had an income of less than £200, while the average income of lone parents was £38.28 below an amount believed to be necessary for a lone parent with one or two children on a low-cost budget. A further statistic that reveals the lack of money in the area is that 38% of Rotherham residents do not have a car, and among lone parents the figure is 72%. Clearly, the money that there is, is spent on essentials and there is little room for embellishment here.

3. Rotherham: a sense of the place

Having looked at the background to Rotherham, I am now going to try and give my reader a sense of Rotherham as a place. In chapter 4 I will argue that this type of description is problematic in that it is always, to some degree, the result of a social distance manifest in the description and the judgements that it makes. Bourdieu has remarked that all the words we use to talk about the social world are located somewhere on a continuum between euphemism and insult. And with characteristic wisdom, he makes the point:

how is one to refer to the hairstyle of a low-ranking clerk without exciting class prejudice and how is one to communicate, without seeming to approve it, the impression she inevitably produces on the eye attuned to the canons of the dominant aesthetic – an impression which forms part of her most inevitably objective truth?

(Bourdieu 1996: 32)

This is a deep and central problem for anyone talking about class, for there is no outside to this universe, and what often looks like an outside, the synoptic position, is one whose social conditions render it inappropriate for an understanding of the phenomenon.

But how is one to describe the sights of poverty and dispossession without stooping to the vernacular which carries the most immediate sense of the phenomenon of inequality and stigma: the wear in clothes, already out of date, the dirt in skin and cloth, faces prematurely aged, the look of ill-health and the dispositions of abused bodies between hyper-sensitivity and an absolute hardness? How is one to describe, in a way that does not reproduce prejudice, what one unemployed woman described, when she suggested that 'poor people smell like sweet biscuits'? It is for these reasons that I have effaced description in this work. There is nothing wise in describing vulnerable people through categories that are the product of their condition. There can be no neutral way to describe social practices because practices emerge from locations within a relational totality which means that one can't divest descriptions of their objective meaning. Furthermore, if class is to England what race is to other cultures, and working class to bourgeois what black is to white in the USA or South Africa, then there can be no neutral description of the lives of the working class. Our affective being is too tied up with class. As one, left-wing academic, said of friends of mine, 'I felt something very dark, menacing, like an evil, coming from them.' With so many unconscious strategies concerning comportment and being at stake, with so much unconscious investment involved and a realm of denial so deeply seated at the heart of English institutions, how can one write honestly about the lives of working people without inciting the mocking recognition of 'townies' that English undergraduates so love to mock. It is for these reasons that I embarked on this section of description with grave reservations.

More importantly, even though I have lived the life that I describe and so am part of those who live like this for want of any other way, there are times when I fear prose cannot avoid being received as parody.[6] Yet the source of this description is the deep sadness felt at all the hidden bleakness of this world. And yet it is a futile exercise because it is impossible to describe the life of this space without betraying one's own deepest prejudgements because it is through one's own dearest hopes and deepest fears that the phenomena of this world show up. This is why it is important to constitute these phenomena through a philosophical vocabulary of being-in-the-world, because in this way we can appreciate the human processes through which human subjects come to be *of* the world of their environment. However, there is an inescapable problem, in that few readers will want to read abstract analysis and many will want to know something of the life of the town. So, having registered my reservations about the enterprise, I will now provide a description of the life of Rotherham.

The industry whose roots were described in the first part of this chapter, would now make a better study for an industrial archaeologist rather than a sociologist. The industry that remains, is dotted about, its scars remain, but its impact as a place of work, of filth and grime and death, has steadily receded. It is difficult to mourn the passing of so much that brought so much misery, but it is impossible to find anything to appreciate in what has come to exist in its place. Freedom from the pit and steelworks, for the industrial working class, has been bought at the price of the loss of many other human forms through which dignity, self-respect, honour and human sociality were founded. Were England a more moral society, which valued the possibility of a civic culture, like Japan or Holland, for instance, then the economic changes might have been humanly managed. The aggressiveness and violence with which the de-industrialization was achieved in England tells us much about its social and political relations. However, the industrial past is still living in the dispositions of the old, who still speak to each other in public space and who embody a certain form of concern about matters of human consequence. But their culture is terminal. Not long for this world. The past is there, living alongside the present, but the future is an ally of the young who continue the tendencies of contemporary conditions. And so, the world is becoming a similar place, filled with different generations, sharing the same experience, but unknowingly, because the public forms of sociality and communication of an older order have been replaced with the atomization of 'life-long' education, unemployment and small-scale working environments.

In Rotherham, then, the presence of industry is felt more in its effect upon the space, in the density of the housing, in the type of housing and in its obviously being the housing of industrial workers. As one man put it:

M: Rother'am's a nothin' kind'a place, thi's nowt [nothing] 'ere [here], it' wo [was] just an industrial tahn an' all wot's [what is] 'ere, all wot you can see nahr [now], it wo just built fo industry rahnd [around] it. All these 'ouses wo just fo workers. It's like Sheffield shit, an' aht [out] cem [came] Rother'am.

At night one still hears the banging of the steelworks and the diesel engines of the railway shunting around what is not moved by road; and driving any way out of Rotherham one is confronted with the devastated remains of its decaying past. A past that has passed more rapidly than many would have thought: within fifteen years the destruction of major industries in the area has destroyed the culture of labour that had been at the heart of the ethics of the people here, of their way of life, of their forms of respect and of care. This destruction has meant the decay of care itself, both for the self and, with that, of care for others. One man in his late thirties observed:

Well . . .'alfe [half] a young 'uns nahr [now] 'ave got, it's nowt [nothing] to be excited abaht [about] is it? I mean 'alfe the fuckers an't [aren't] workin' ah [are] thi? Eh? That is their . . . that's the'r life, that's their life style gu'in' aht drinkin' actin' twat [daft], tekkin' a few drugs, chilled aht [out] in it? I mean, 'alfe'r these young 'uns don't giy [give] a fuck abaht 'owt [anything]. Even the'r selns [themselves]. I mean, if yer on' abaht thi' smell, the'r not bothered that thi smell, the'r not bothered abaht the'r dress, or 'owt, the'r just not bothered . . . [*Voice rises for comic stress*] it wun't bother them if they were du'in' [doing the] same in thirty years time.

Whilst this man's comments are by no means true of even the majority of young people, something important has changed in the dispositions and relation to self between those who left school to work in the pit as this man did and younger generations leaving school for life-long retraining under the guise of education. Clearly, things matter differently for those he describes, and it is a form of mattering based upon a different relation to self. One mediated by a different social location, one outside the regimes of manual work and formed amidst a realm of consumption and display. What this man sees as 'chilled out' is a relation to self less embedded in the strictures of respect for others, it is a relation to self that is based upon a public display of the body adorned with the commodified signs of fashion and sexuality. And what this man sees as their not caring is the atomization involved in their primary relation to self and others. For if I define my humanity through a consumption I wear on my body, then others' existence to me must be permeated by those same criteria. The spaces for a primordial experience of commonality, for building a world of common pulses and rhythms has evaporated, leaving only a fragmentation of selves within a common world which only a few recognize in the experience of one another. This, perhaps, illuminates one of Lawrence's central questions:

What would come after? She could only see the new brick streets spreading into the fields, the new erections rising at the collieries, the new girls in their silk stockings, the new collier lads lounging into the Pally or the Welfare . . . What would become of them all? Perhaps with the passing of the coal they would disappear again, off the face of the earth. They had appeared out of nowhere in their thousands, when the coal had called for them. Perhaps they were only weird fauna of the coal-seams.

(Lawrence 1994a: 159)

Lawrence could see the tendencies latent in that earlier stage of capitalism and could see that spontaneous human relations were being colonized by the forms of this developing productive system. Lawrence yearned for people to be free of the labour process which meant so much pain and misery for working class people. He yearned for an end to the kinds of personal tragedy that one local novelist captured, describing a scene he witnessed in the nineteen twenties:

I heard a woman weeping in the darkness of this place a week or two ago. She was standing well within the shelter of an alleyway so that her face was hid from sight, but not the outline of her form nor of her head which was shawl covered and very slight. I might have faltered, but I just dared not. It seemed to me that sorrow was very sacred in that moment, so I took my blundering feet away as lightly as I could. She was crying because her little son had been compelled to work on the night shift at the local ironworks. She had patted him away with fear and foreboding. For the first time in his life he would not sleep within his mother's house, within the territory of her tender fingers. And, she, good woman, fearful of the loco's [sic] and the molten metal, had crept into the alleyway . . . to weep.

I find it impossible not to think of her, but I know that save for these stray lines her sorrow goes with small remark.[7]

The Rotherham of this world and the world described by the ex-miner are clearly separated by the development of different economic conditions, conditions that have produced different forms of being, different 'objectivations of life' (Dilthey quoted in McCarthy 1993: 94), different possibilities for humans to realize themselves through. Yet clearly, the historical continuity is that these people are enmeshed within and defined objectively by their position in the total relations of British culture and the fields which define them, through different epochs, as working class people, fit for what is left them. Even in one of the very poorest regions of Europe, the possibilities for self-realization and recognized existence are the prevalent simulations offered as subject-positions by the multitude of media that surround. With these two poles of Rotherham's history in mind, it is worth pondering the relevance of a remark by Baudrillard:

We don't realize how much the current indoctrination into systematic and organized consumption is *the equivalent and the extension, in the twentieth century, of the great indoctrination of rural populations into industrial labor which occurred throughout the nineteenth century.* The same process of rationalization of productive force, which took place in the nineteenth century in the *production* sector, is accomplished in the twentieth century, in the *consumption* sector. Having socialised the masses into a labor force, the industrial system had to go further in order to fulfill itself and to socialise the masses (that is, to control them) into a force of consumption.

(Baudrillard quoted in Kellner 1989: 16)

The forms of domination have changed, multiplied and become 'softer'. The form that necessity takes is part of a different context, one of apparent abundance, in which a whole black economy supports the poor's need to exhibit their belonging to a world of consumer references that defines individuals as worthy, valuable or worthless. Suitable for relationships or not. Yet much remains: the great difficulty of acceding to possession, of getting the money to buy the things that are necessary and of the degradation and risk involved in getting the money. Life remains a strain and few know fulfilment. What hasn't changed is the conditions which determine these historically separate experiences: both are the result of economic and political decisions which ensure these people are dispossessed and lack the material and cultural resources to found a life of value, in which they have worth and thus can recognize worth in others.

For many of those who grew up with work and the values it imbued, the industrial decay and the decay of the forms of human value and respect that went with it, are obvious:

S: 'Ave you seen it change rahnd 'ere in last twenty year?

M: Fuckin' 'ell fire. [*Voice is slow with emphasis and M is choosing his words carefully and deliberately*] This, *without a doubt*, I don't se' [say] this lightly, I don't se' this . . . I don't . . . I bet, I'd get old films out, this'd got to be the best Fanny in England twenty year since. Best Fanny Brown [town] in England, best town in England. Full employment, people wi' money to spend, everybody wo' [was] sociable, everybody knew it, people wo lifted on and off 'r buses, people wo great. It's destroyed because this town, nahr [now] got the 'aves and the 'ave nots, and that's wot destroys society.

Another steelworker, in his late fifties, expressed the changes and the effects of the industrial decline:

X: It's 'ard to believe ahr [how] it's changed rahnd 'ere. You'll not believe this but A' [I] once 'ad five jobs in a week . . .

Y: What, an yer just weighed 'em up and took t' best?

X: Aye, I did 'em all and took one that I wanted. But, then the'r used to be fifteen thousand men at BOC [British Oxygen Company], where I am nahr [now], and thi's less than two thousand left, nahr.

S: Has that affected the town do yer think?

X: Oh, fucking ell, aye, it's 'ard to believe ahr it's changed.

Z: The playin' wi' people's lives aren't thi [they] and thi dun't [don't] care.

X: It's affected young nahr [now], 'cos [because] thi [they] dun't learn the same and the'r different. I remember abaht [about] twenty year since coming aht [out] o' a shop wi' a packet of biscuits that I'd bought and I 'ad one and didn't like 'em and so I gev' these biscuits to this kid who wo' [was] ahtside' [outside] shop but I'd never dare do that nahr. It's like wi' young 'uns tha' daren't se' owt to 'em any-mo'or else yer likely to get a load o'r abuse or a knife between ('t) ribs.

Y: Trouble is, I think tha's gotta stand up fo' thiseln [yourself]. Even if tha gunna lose tha's gotta tell truth as tha' sees it, even if tha gets nowt aht o'n it, tha's gotta stand up fo wot's right.

Z: Tha rait, thy 'as [You're right, you have].

X: Ow'd [old] X's allous [always] in 'ere 'avin' a good talk. He likes 'is conversation, ow'd X [*laughs*].

Z: Well, tha can't beat a good gab [talk]. It's wot we're 'ere fo'.[8]

For these people Rotherham was a place that was like some great carbuncle of the earth, like something the gods had placed here to produce the primordial forces nature required to keep the world turning. By day, its industry produced things that to a child looked like cloud, great streams of bulbous smoke that connected earth to sky, and yet by night the same industry glowed in its own flames. One man accustomed to travelling through the Don Valley at work and on his way there, gave a vivid description of the impression it all made:

Ah [I] used to travel to work through East End o'r Sheffield, afo'or [before] thi' [they] built Tinsley viaduct an' it wo [was] like Dante's Inferno. All that industry through the'er, it wo like lookin' at 'ell [hell]. 'Specially wi Steelo's [Steelworks] wi' [with] furnaces gushin' aht [out] flames o'r [of] molten steel. It' wo same wi' Manvers, we used to gu through the'er an' it wo like after bomb or sumat [something], it wo just barren, ugly, awful-nothing . . .

Yet, although the steelworks still stand, the density of the industry has gone and a generation and more has grown up with the factories empty, with the buildings derelict and the space vacated, except for the filth that a century's plundering of the earth has left. And they survey this as dead ground unaware of the significance of its destruction, a scar upon the land that marks the place where once a form of life was vital, urgent, busy, relevant and meaningful. On a shopping trip to Meadowhall or on a trip for a night out in Doncaster who would want to think about the past of some decaying structure or rotting wasteland?

Describing Rotherham as an architecturally structured landscape is a difficult and misleading task. The place, even according to many who live here, is ugly and depressing. Moreover, this manifests itself not just in the architectural structures that pattern the space, but in the manner and bearing, the comportment and style of behaviour of the people in the town, as one 25-year-old man makes clear:

People are depressed an' nut 'ouses [mental hospitals] are fillin' up, thi's [there is] mo'ore an mo'ore people wot just can't tek [take] it any mo'ore, thi's too much strain fo' 'em. Rother'am's like a gaol wiy'aht [without] any walls. The'r [they're] stuck 'ere but can't see the walls. Wot it's like is, people can't see wot it is that's causin' ahr thi feel, it's like the'r ill an' doctor can't tell em what's up and ca(n)'t du 'owt fo' 'em.

It is as though people are responding through a kind of somatic–affective sensitivity to the awful, grey, bleak misery of all that is around them. They are responding, being affected by, the latent human sensibility that is everywhere around them, disclosed through the details that are 'too many to mention': all those everyday nuances of social experience that humans must live ignoring, even though in experience it has touched them, left a trace of sense, like the stains of rain upon a window. There is a coherent sensibility involved in such spaces that, though it never quite rises to the level of an aesthetic, is aware of a density of meaning registered through their engagement with the place that affects deeply their sense of human life and spiritual well-being. The reasons for this are illuminated by Heidegger, who, discussing 'mood', contradicts our sense that such responses are 'interpretations'; rather:

A mood assails us. It comes neither from 'outside' nor from 'inside', but arises out of Being-in-the-world, as a way of such Being. But with the negative distinction between state-of-mind and the reflective apprehending of something 'within', we have thus reached a positive insight into their character as disclosure. *The mood has already disclosed, in every case, Being-in-the-world as a whole, and makes it possible first of all to direct oneself towards something.*   (Heidegger 1962: 176)

Mood emerges from existence amidst the goings-on of those with whom one lives, through which one acquires, posturally, gesturally, beneath the public language of a place, a *sense* of the world in its affective rendering for those, *here*, in this place. Here we have the sociosomatic roots of the ill-being that the previous speaker recognizes with the locution, 'nut 'ouses are fillin' up . . . people . . . just can't tek it anymo'ore'. We need to be sensitive that these reports are not merely 'recordings' of a reality, but that they disclose something of profound importance about their being-in-the-world, that their condition is not merely some psychological predicament caused by their predilection for certain interpretations of their world, but emerges from the way their public world is mediated by the social conditions that have grounded their form of life. That is, that through this shared intersubjective realm the world is encountered as modulating with anxiety, uncertainty and pointlessness. There is much, humanly, to be learnt living among what many see as the ugliness of such traditional industrial areas, and much to be learnt about humanity from the happy misery and dutiful hedonism of people whose lives are so constrained by the the poles of shit jobs and an increasingly regimented unemployment.

Living in an area like this means growing up experiencing things the media has made clichéd; but the world, for many, has moved on only in the desires it instils in our consciousness, and not in the living fabric of our practical lives. Rotherham is the mucky river running through the middle with the adjacent canal, it is industrial dereliction that is large in scale, like King's College and its Chapel, but uglier – monuments to the power-source of a different part of the English bourgeoisie. The pits, factories and steelworks stand like tombs from which the treasure has long ago been plundered but, nevertheless, in their scale and new-found vacuity they teach the same lesson of power and space that elite colleges do, only it is an uglier and more profound way to imbibe the truth of civilization. Rotherham, too, is going past the pockets of steelworks where that old history still runs on, oblivious to the presence of the newer history outside; or of those cut off from its danger-filled community and the *bonhomie* of nights out paid for by the earnings of its sweat-filled toil. Young children can just about still peer through the steelworks on Sheffield Road, at the minute figures fighting back the splashes of hell's flames that one can glimpse periodically spewing from that mysterious fiery place hidden somewhere behind the corrugated iron-cladding. Rotherham now is the mass of derelict office blocks of the staff that once fed the adjuncts of the steel industry.

Where there is greenery in Rotherham it is quickly covered in rubbish, in stolen traffic cones dragged home by stupefied youths. The spare land and car parks on which young people play football and cricket are covered with bags and cigarette packets. But, nevertheless, come the summer, one sees common ground used for the great kick-abouts one sees when kids are off school and working lads get a dinner break. And Rotherham too is a town where housing is occupied by families who once worked in the firms and industries that created the place and, of course, this concentration is what adds to the devastation once the employment is gone. The narrowness of the economic base means that they lose together, their economies become driven by an exchange of help in kind where money is no longer available. Their space becomes an ever more complex mixture of consumer fantasy, in the mode of a dispossessed class, and a primitive economy exchanging gifts and favours on the basis of honour. The space is often concentrated, the houses are close together, the majority seem to smoke, too many are overweight, ill, and often lame too young; and too many are clad in dirty, often cheap, clothes. Young children play, till late, on the streets, and many teenagers seem hell-bent on destroying or damaging anything that is public, a disposition that is rapidly transcending that boundary into the private. As one man asked:

Why du people destroy things that are of 'elp to 'em? . . . Thi's kids ovver the'er an' the'r kickin' them lights in an' the'r sisters or grandmuthers might need them lights at night to stop 'em gettin' attacked or raped. Ah just can't understand these kids nahr, thi' just destroy everythin'. It's like when thi want a piss, when Ah wo their age we'd a gone aht'a [out of] sight somewhe'er but nahr [now] thi just dun't gi a toss, thi' just gu anywhe'er, in front o'r [of] anybody. An' thi think it's cool to bi cheeky an all it du's is piss off any 'r adults that might 'elp 'em. Yer just think, 'why would Ah [I] bother to du [do] 'owt fo' 'em? Yer know? [*Sighs*]

The town centre always seems to be busy, and walking around Rotherham one sees the same people, especially young men, wandering aimlessly, with nothing to do and nowhere to go. The place seems always dirty, always noisy, with a preponderance on housing estates of dogs, kept for security, but often tied up, ill-kempt, who proclaim their discomfort morning, noon and night by barking inconsolably. The treatment of the dogs is symptomatic of the lack of care for other human beings that now characterizes these areas. It is as though sentience itself is of no meaning, as though the denial of their own capacity for complex self-knowledge has extinguished any possible appreciative relation to the living warmth of other beings endowed with life: an attitude one sees all-too-often extended to children. Young children seem to wander around a long distance from their parents, who seem caught up in looking in shop windows and then turning to shout, often abusively, at the child. And these are kids brought up on shopping-trips to McDonald's, a new generation of would-be consumers, whose desires, however impoverished they are and in whatever locality, will be those of multi-national companies who market products at them and entice them into consuming their dreams from an ever younger age, touching and shaping their most intimate tastes, shaping their feelings, ensuring that, whatever occurs politically, this generation of children screaming at their mothers for a Big Mac, will, more than likely, want more of the same. Furthermore, advertising is extending its implicate order of self-disciplinary concerns and images of self-fruition downwards, rendering younger and younger cohorts in its webs of signification, altering awareness and comportment, making sexual subjects of pubescent youths, extending the traditional problems of the urban poor downwards.

Rotherham is a town full of ever-closing shops, forever replaced by charity-shops selling second-hand goods; it is a town where prestigious shops never stay; as the long caravan that began with *Next*, was followed by the older names *C&A* and *British Home Stores* and which was recently followed by *Escom* and *Barratts* who decided to relocate in the 'Promised Land' of Meadowhall. Those condemned to the voyeuristic pursuit of the pleasure of shopping-through-windows are finding fewer and fewer commodity dreams to consummate their existence as consumers. After all, there can be few markers of poor areas less embarrassing than the worn-out old clothes that bestrew the charity shops that function as dustbins for people whose clothes were made to be cheap and dispensable in the first place. Rotherham is a town that every day is full of people with little to do but waste time that they are unable to structure with activity. Growing up here has made me aware of a distinct sense, in the faces, the bodies, the styles of dress, the scenes they involve themselves in, a sense that pervades the area, a sense that is a historical product, embodied and lived through, yet which could never be captured either in the official statistics nor through living here without growing up here.

Rotherham is a town which is growing ever more threatening. The pubs are half-busy all day, the off-licences do a brisk trade in cheap super-strong lagers and cheaper-than-cheap bottles of wine. Young girls sit outside the beer-offs and ask older people to buy them alcohol. At night it is a place full of gangs of youths of various ages who sit around the town, around its take-aways and around the ring road which after seven o'clock at night is full of young men in ten-year-old Fords and Vauxhalls, silencer-less, thrashing and bellowing their way past the strategically placed young girls, waving down lifts with anyone prepared to take them for a ride. Having a car, in whatever condition, is the mark of the accomplished adult. Without one, a man is a queer thing. And with a nice one, celebrity beckons. The grounds for the establishment of even acquaintanceship are semi-prostitutional; although there is nothing unusual in that, what is clear to anyone used to subtler, more effete and capital-laden forms of instrumental relation, is the paucity of the capital-forms involved and the ruthlessness of the manner with which relation is refused to those lacking capital. The capital that is exchanged for sex has a direct relation to the monetary: the car and how much money one has. There are no values celebrated beyond the monetary, and no interest in persons for anything approaching a human quality.

Unlike the world of work that was Rotherham for an older generation, for those who haven't worked in the mass industry, Rotherham is the town centre: that network of pubs, clubs and take-aways that form the reference points of the experience of the night out, that highlight of the week that takes place on Friday and Saturday. There is a main network of open-plan pubs, organized around the principle subject-position of voyeur; of observing others and of being seen. These are not places one goes to, to participate in human association, and it is an experience therefore not constituted through communal participation. Rather they are places that one goes to either to see or, if one is narcissistic enough, as many are, to be seen and to be admired. The *Tut and Shive, Feofees,* the *Cross Keys,* the *High Bar, Elliots, New York Rock Cafe, Jazz, The Emporium* and *Yates'* and, on a Sunday, *The Masons Arms*: these are the places that must be visited; and a night out means going to one or more of these, except for a weekend, which consists in going to *all* of them, and then going to a nightclub like *The Zone* and *Fifth Avenue* – or else to a pub that will carry on serving late and have music, such as *Feofees, New York Rock Cafe, Emporium, The Travellers* or *Shipmates.* These are all open-plan theme pubs and clubs, where the space is designed and used to be observed in. They are what people colloquially term 'meat' or 'cattle' markets. And, indeed, some of the men are steroid-ridden, swollen in a world where muscles matter. Men and women stand up all night and walk around in large circles, parading themselves, and surveying the value of what else is on this market, whilst also assessing what bodies compete with their own, and what their own capital will allow them to take from this arena and what use it will serve, how long its value will last before re-entering this market. These are not places where one experiences the slightest pretence of sociability. Their nature is almost counter-intuitive, and they are a lesson in how common sense emerges out of actuality counter-factually; because people, if questioned, say they go 'to meet people'; 'have a laugh'; 'talk'; yet it is striking how atomized the life of such spaces is. There seems little verbal communication going on, even amongst groups of friends. There is little interaction, and what interaction there is, is like physical comedy in its gestural exaggeration. Interaction between men and women could be scripted, there are standard openings and a small number of correct responses. What is said is unimportant, for this is an arena in which the truth of our society is clear: it is what you *are* that matters. Existence is bought with the value of the flesh. Concern for others, here, makes you vulnerable, it places you below everyone. What one sees is a circulation of bodies in terms of their value. People do not meet, except through the unconscious pulsions of an environment in which space is distorted by valencies of capital that bring some into the vicinity of speech; and there is a grudging respect of those who are winners, played out against a backdrop of silent invisibility. So, there is very little meeting of people who do not already know one another as competitors and the dominant activity is the showing of place to those who lack capital. Human recognition doesn't often occur. The activity here is the strange pleasure of consumptive looking, and the equally perverse enjoyment of being consumed as a sexualized object; and anything else is just weakness or a threatening madness. The music is loud, and at a weekend one will have to queue for entry; and, once inside, each bar is three and four deep, with queues for the toilets and insufficient room to stand comfortably with a drink. None of this can be unique, and nor can it be peculiar to small towns, so anyone from a working class area will recognize these scenes. But I do not want to dwell on the description of the place. It is the nature of the experience that I am concerned to elucidate.

Because this book is concerned with the lives of working class people now, in an area that is dissipating and fragmenting, in which work-places have grown smaller, with many working in very small numbers, with very high levels of unemployment and the criminality that goes with it, the experience of working people, although similar in its conditions, is now lived through serially. That is, for many, there is much isolation and little sense of anything approximating to a shared sociality that grounds experience in the common references of a common life. They may see the same old faces on the streets and out on the town but they do not know them, and, moreover, it is best kept that way, because in such space one never knows what kind of threat contact might be interpreted as. In a world of where people feel stigmatized, it is as though 'face' and 'respect' can only be maintained through non-contact and the maintenance of a heavily managed 'front'. Any approach risks provoking hostility. As one man put it:

X: Tha [you're] best-off [better of] sayin' nowt [nothing] nahr [now]. Yer just daren't. If you se' [say] 'owt [anything] to someb'dy, yer know ye'v got to be prepared to fait [fight] ovver it. Thi's just too much aggression nahr.

And this aimless aggression is experienced differently by older generations. As one woman in her late sixties put it:

X: It's awful rahnd 'ere nah [now].
S: Ahr du yer mean?
X: Well yer used t' be able to gu [go] aht [out] an' leave yer 'ouse unlocked, yer knew nob'dy'd [nobody would] bother yer but nah, yer dun't even feel safe gu'in' on bus int' tahn way some'r yung 'uns are. Wi mi just beein' aht'r [out of] 'ospital, Ah feel right worried when Ah'm abaht [aboout] but when Ah [I] get mi [my] money from post office, Ah'm [I'm] scared that someb'dy's gunna mug mi, yer don't know these days du yer?

And these changes are registered by a man in his mid forties:

X: When Ah [I] wo growin' up, mi fAther'd[9] [father would] du stuff fo' neighbour's an' they'd du same, watch each other's patch, like. Thi's none 'r that nah [now]. Ah mean, thy [your] age group an't no idea o'r that but Ah grew up wi' it, an' Ah've [I've] w'ked [worked] in steelw'ks like a lot'r [lot of] lads rahnd mi but even ma' [my] age group dun't really du any'r [any of] that. It's just like community's completely gone and all the'r is nah is like . . . you stay on your bit an keep t' yerself an' Ah'll stay on ma bit . . .

The world for this man is losing meaning and yet because of his memory of other forms of association, this stands out for him as significant. He can relate the loss of one with the emergence of what disturbs and clearly he is trying to point out the difference for those who never knew the grounds of anything different, for whom nothing else has existed. For some, life has never had co-ordinates embedded in a life amongst others, and hence their experience is remarkably difficult to articulate. Their actual experience is itself too empty, too problematic. As one man expressed the changes in his life:

Yer used to gu [go] t' [to] w'k [work] an' yer could see who thi' [the] exploiter wo' an' ah [how] much thi [they] wo [were] mekkin' [making] aht'a [out of] yer but nahr [now], well, Ah [I] just sit 'ere like a sack o'r spuds [potatoes] an' Ah dun't know wot's gone on in world. It's fuckin' difficult to talk abaht. Ah mean, Ah find Ah dun't 'ave owt to se' cos all A've done is waste mi day away, same as yesterd'y!

And this man points up a central difficulty. If he finds it difficult to communicate his own experience of confinement to a private realm of existence, if he finds it difficult to articulate an experience he clearly finds discomforting, then it has to be hard on the person who has interviewed them[10].

Therefore, whilst I have laboured very hard to produce a seamless piece of writing, tried hard to reclaim the sense of the lives of the people whose voices I have transcribed, it is important for the reader to be aware that this creates a sense of unity that is often absent from the lives of these people. There is an unavoidable sense in which my work must rub against the grain of its subject matter, producing an order that cannot be said to exist in the experience of the place with which it deals. And if this is too elliptical, evasive and uncertain for my readers' tastes then they should count themselves fortunate that they have not had to try to verbalize, articulate and authenticate a social experience that is, by its very nature, fragmented, dissolute, polysemic, ambiguous and yet nevertheless desolating. The problem of the nature of social experience never confronts us more than when we face lives that are bereft of the usual sociological co-ordinates or whose co-ordinates have been drastically shifted and re-oriented. Clearly, all cultural phenomena are oriented relationally and need, in order to be seen aright, to be placed in something approaching a complete picture. It is only this way that we will see that what has been a long-standing social trajectory, identity and life style, has actually changed deeply in its nature and as a lived experience.

Being working class and growing up in Rotherham, no matter what one has done occupationally, there is no way in which one can escape the experience of a social context that is like a stagnant pond in which we are the suffocating organisms. There is an absence of the social conditions that make optimism and hope a realiztic life-strategy. Furthermore, even those things that, because of the absence of work and an income, people participated in, in order to participate in experiences that might partially constitute 'a life', such as a place at a local Further Education college, have been radically altered as social experiences and identities. Local Further Education colleges have been used to hide levels of youth unemployment, and this has altered their fundamental nature as places that people could go to, to be free of the manifestations of discipline. Now, the young are coerced into training courses reproducing their experience of school and giving the colleges the same sense that pervades working class schools, where once they were full of working class people who had made a positive choice to return to education. The shifting sands of our cultural co-ordinates have acted to destroy the possibility not only of that inescapable facet of alienated life, the capitalist dream, but of the ability to dream authentically at all. For in areas that have endured such high unemployment, people are sensitive that education itself has become progressively devalued. As one young man reasoned:

Naow [no]. Well even people wi [with] good education's, wi A's and B's an that, they don't get good jobs, so if we get a G or an F, or whatever grade we get, we've got same chance o'r gettin' a job as wot they 'ave. They'll probably end up in dole queue anyway, or gunna [going to] college or whatever . . . or the'll just end up on streets . . .

And another, a little older:

Ah'm [I'm] at college, but Ah'd [I'd] rather bi' w'kin'. [S: Why's that?] College is shit. It's a lot'a w'k fo' nowt [nothing]. Ah've [I've] seen too many du it an' get nowt . . . [What abaht [about] w'k then?] well yer I know what jobs are like rahnd 'ere, the'r slave labour. Ah might as well stay we'er I am fo' nahr. W'k part time.

The existential frame of these lives has dissolved, leaving only the resources of the generative schemes of the habitus; schemes of embodied historical essence that contain the seeds of resistance. Yet this is a blind, dissipating, resistance that involves a great deal of internalized tension and frustration. What, allows us to see this as a resistance? And in what way can it be said to be blind? The answer is that these people's social identity is based upon a distancing of self from the affectations and formalities instantiated in the *petit-bourgeois* identities of those who are constituted through a different and differentiating relation to that culture which is constituted as always negative: the working class, in relation to which bourgeois and *petit-bourgeois* distinction-strategies make sense.

This is a resistance which refuses re-acculturation through the mechanisms that the state has organized to create good workers through the endless round of training schemes for the unemployed. It manifests itself in a general obstinacy towards the world, an identity that in other social universes would be seen as rude and impolite. On the streets in daily life it manifests itself in a general, practically operative, non-judgemental attitude to the world. Areas like South Yorkshire, in which unemployment and low wages have become a way of life that touches all of a person's family and friends, exhibit a sense of unconscious relation to domination that is almost palpable; it is as if the doxic effects of living conditions and the extent to which so many people are trapped produces a physical sense that, like a contagion, produces a general weariness in the bones of those who live here. But, if it is a resistance, it is a relation that is constituted as supportive of one another against the progressive encroachment of the decay of the way of life; and, to the extent that, as a practical relation, it does not constitute or name either its enemies nor its oppressive institutional sources, it is blind. But then, how does a group that has been systematically robbed of the instruments of its own resistance, without jobs, let alone unions, go about constituting itself as a political group?

Now that we have a sense of Rotherham's history, of its population and of it as a place, it is important that we move on to look at my relationship to the research 'object'. In order to understand the way in which the account is constructed, any researcher must be honest about this relation. The task of understanding the effect on the view-presented of the position in which the writer is producing the account, and able to see what they see, is logically prior to the account, even though the object of the account appears to have a universally accessible primacy that renders such considerations ephemeral. It seems important to recognize that academics have an interest in 'finding' objects about which they can write. It establishes for them many benefits that accrue from having a career, and it seems important to recognize that we have an interest in exoticizing the mundane, in describing things which gain more respect the further away they seem. A certain honesty, based on consideration of the writer's relationship to the object, and on the basis on which what is known *is* known may be the only way of offering readers the capacity to make up their own minds on these issues. To the extent that it gives critics the power to criticize the writer's work by being open about the motivations that fuel analysis and drive emphasis, it is worth making the work problematic, in certain parts, for certain categories of reader. It is perhaps what separates sociology of this kind from literature, in that style and texture of description must be sacrificed to accuracy, and description must be punctuated by theoretical considerations which whilst unnecessary to the sense of the description, illuminate a deeper point to be drawn from the detail. So I hope that my reader will understand my reasons for considering these problems. If at times it seems this text meanders and runs close to repetition, it is because the writing is trying to depict a very ordinary world, yet one which is full of misfortune and pain for the people who live like this. It is the mundaneness of this that makes it difficult to write about, but it is not like this to the people who live through it: for them it cuts to the quick and leaves them confused as to the deeper malaise in which they live.

3

Class and the objectifying subject: a reflexive sociology of class experience

> In other words, certain features intrinsic to theoretical cognition encourage us to misinterpret its true nature, to overlook the fact that it *is* a species of activity, a modified form of practical engagement with the world, and so only possible (as are other, more obviously practical activities) for environed beings, beings whose Being is Being-in-the-world.
>
> (Mulhall 1996: 42)

> People thinking in the forms of free, detached, disinterested appraisal were unable to accommodate within those forms the experience of violence which in reality annuls such thinking. The almost insoluble task is to let neither the power of others, nor our own powerlessness, stupefy us.
>
> (Adorno 1974: 57)

Chapter 2 considered the history of Rotherham, the nature of the population and the current state of the local economy. Yet the demographic and statistical account separates the phenomena recorded from people's experience of them. In itself it tells us nothing of the impact of these phenomena upon what people think or feel. The understanding of place presented in demographic statistics overlooks the everyday spatiality of places, an imbuing of lived meaning originating in the comportment of those who use the space. Objectivist description cannot account for the matrix of meaningful practices through which phenomena actually become meaningful. In order to begin this recovery of an amorphous, ambiguous sense that pervades life here, something that rests beneath other particular experiences, giving a hue to them, I want to consider what made me awake to this concrete experience of the real. One might begin with Oscar Wilde's remark about education, that it 'Is an admirable thing, but it is well to remember from time to time that nothing that is worth knowing can be taught'. And this is certainly true of what a people knows and why Bourdieu suggests,

'One cannot really *live* the belief associated with profoundly different conditions of existence . . . still less give others the means of reliving it by the sheer power of discourse' (Bourdieu 1990a: 68). What is most essential to a people's experience may be sedimented in the background practices they take for granted in referring and may be inscribed in their comportment and motility, the ways they have, unconsciously learned to *be* in a world. Moreover, human relations framed around an absorbed coping with a world that has become problematic, will not tend to produce the prolonged, developed, formalized narrations required to disclose the truths of experiences whose fundamental traces rest in comportment and in the depth of a duration that inscribes in demeanour marks that only habituation could answer for. Duration, habituation and locality are the natural, necessary conditions *through* which meaningful, socially recognizable differences are achieved and enshrined in the invisible sensibilities of discrimination.

The things I am interested in cannot be revealed by the statistics surveyed in the last chapter: my concern is with the perceptions of individuals enmeshed in the meaning located in the place of their existence. That is, I am concerned not with perceptions of occurrent[1] things but rather with perception as a kinaesthetic lived-bodily incorporation of the sense of the world. My concern is with this primordial experience in which meaning is 'in the process of being born', the primal sense forever taking shape, which social conditions have for body-subjects through the everyday anxiety that wells-up and recedes and through which the world's meaning takes shape. Statistics catalogue the conditions of a hidden suffering, immanent in the condition of the social, that is encountered personally and felt as discomfort, frustration, unease, guilt and fear. The significance of the phenomena of class, inequality, deprivation and powerlessness must be understood through their effect upon the manner with which people come to exist in the world; the ways in which their inhabiting or dwelling in a space of intelligibility, opens up for them affective states or sensibilities that are social in the sense that they are prior to a particular individual's feelings and govern the range of feelings available.

If it is fundamental to the existence and reproduction of class that it concerns powerful affinities and aversions to persons, things and spaces, then we will not understand such a phenomenon by gaining a detached clarity nor by exempting reflection from description of experience. For the people about whom this work is written, class is a circumscribed way of knowing the world that they did not choose; rather they grew to live within it, they absorbed it as the space absorbed them in demanding that they comport themselves in a certain manner in order to be successful within its parameters.

People who sit back from the world and write about class structure over-look the essential truth of class that experience of it is always from amidst a world-defining context experienced through the primordial realm in which selves take shape. That is, class is not a simple matter of understanding oneself through a role but a locating of the flesh through inhabiting a particular social realm, constituted by certain objects and certain relations on the basis of one's embodying incorporated forms that lead one to be treated factically, as an object possessed of an essence. These are objective processes that work upon the deepest realms of the intimate lives of persons. They are processes that condemn people to lifetimes of abuse and misery. How could the truth of such lives be captured except through an existential hermeneutic phenomenology that reclaims the objectivity of the subjective? As Heidegger puts it:

When one is oriented towards 'Nature' and 'Objectively' measured distances of Things, one is inclined to pass off such estimates and interpretations of deseverance as 'subjective'. Yet this 'subjectivity' perhaps uncovers the 'Reality' of the world at its most Real; it has nothing to do with 'subjective' arbitrariness or subjectivist 'ways of taking' an entity which 'in itself' is otherwise. *The circumspective de-severing of Dasein's everydayness reveals the Being-in-itself of the 'true world' – of that entity which Dasein, as something existing, is already alongside.*

(Heidegger 1962: 141)

Recognizing the objective basis of personal, often unspoken, feelings of the most profound degradation, humiliation, fear and alienation, is of the utmost importance if we are to recognize, in the generative structures of inter-corporeal synchronizations, predispositions to respond to others; a primordial sociality that constitutes an implicate order of the body indicating possible sources of human fulfilment if the social conditions necessary for such reciprocity could be universalized and the conditions for an ethics of communicative rationality, established.

The important point is that class is a phenomenon of the flesh, of coming to inhabit the world in a certain way through powerfully internalizing senses based in an objective hierarchy of relations within which individual sensibilities take shape. It concerns processes of desire and aversion, through which individuals come to be located within certain social fields. How can we understand these processes through second-order derivations based upon the resulting structures that emanate from these processes? To quote one class analyst, 'Once having taken a position in the occupational system, people assume social inequality. They are placed in society' (Koch 1996: 190). The question is, what does this mean? What is it to 'take a position', and what is it to 'assume social inequality'? What does it mean to be 'placed in society'? This concerns the deepest issues of being human and cannot be dealt with, as a phenomenon, through a detached stance whose aim is to classify the objective properties through which class is recognized. The view from nowhere is no more possible in the social universe than it is in the universe of cosmology. Any view on the social world orders and organizes itself from a specific position in that universe. Rather, all views must be based upon some primary sense of this phenomenon. Involvement is inescapable, it is something we cannot get clear of; the task is to analyse the conditions of one's own view, to recognize the angle of one's vision.

Moreover, everyday human existence involves an understanding of what it is to *be* that is manifest in everyday practices concerning others and objects. This understanding of being, is not exhaustively contained in the mental states of individuals. Rather, it involves a whole background structure of intelligibility that orients our concerned involvement, our circumspective coping with the world. What is of deepest importance in identity and being is thus manifest in our comportment, our bodily sense of our 'place' in the world emanating from the world contained in the place in which we live. In order to understand the phenomenon, one needs to know the comportment and what it discloses. Something of great importance follows. It is expressed precisely by Levin:

> Much of our comportment is choreographed by 'postural impregnation': a proximity and intimacy with others through which the gestures, postures, and bodily attitudes of others gradually inhabit my own body, simultaneously shaping me in their image and carrying forward my body's own implicately ordered needs.
>
> (Levin 1990: 38)

A condition of perception of the world is an experienced structure of being with others that is as fundamental as our relationship to the object-world. Through a variety of relationships, intimate and formal, there emerges a realm of self-understanding and absorbed feeling the condition of which is life with others, that grounds communal perceptions of things, 'the perceived world is a world experienced not simply for *me*, but for *us*' (Compton 1989: 137). Clearly, it is necessary to share the comportment of working people to know their experience and perception, which means being produced by the same cultural conditions and objective position.

Like the people whom I quote, I know of these phenomena because I am a person objectively categorized and treated in social life as a member of a specific category of persons: this is where the experience begins for each person. As a defence of my work, it is important that I consider my relationship to the people who undergo this experience and to the contours of the culture that they experience. Clearly, I am concerned with phenomenon that exist only for members of the category of people concerned, and the project of bearing witness to their suffering, the 'hidden injuries of class' (Sennett and Cobb 1973), means that the work is necessarily personal. The problem is that these phenomena of class's hidden injuries emerge only through persons' embodied subjectivity. To understand these effects requires a retracing of the processes creating the experience, from a position that enables one to grasp the dialectic of embodiment which comprehends their objective being-for-others amidst an overall structure of significances. It is only by being a subject within the totalizing structure whilst being also a *particular* embodied subject that has enabled me to do the research and to know this life. The dialectic of embodiment is thus at the heart of the method, and a reflexive sociology is a way of recognizing that the grounds of social understanding are contained in the positions in social space of individual researchers: a position mediated by their primary resources of different forms of capital. I recognize this, indeed it is because this work emerges from the context of domination and deprivation that Rotherham is, that it tends towards what Bourdieu renders as 'spurious primitivist participation'. Its insights and blindnesses are inextricable from the conditions of cultural dispossession and social exclusion that the work tries to capture[2].

It is an attempt to speak of the experience of these people, to enable their words to do justice to their condition and to set down a record of the humanity which the social and economic conditions of England rob them of, and which is particularly evident whenever they produce speech acts in the presence of those professionals who are normally[3] instituted to produce discourse on the social. When one understands this phenomenon as well as the cultural conditions that influence the production of authorized discourse on the social, one realizes why so little of quality ever gets written about one of the major injustices of English culture. Living every day witnessing the extent to which working people are trapped, whilst knowing also what barriers there are to the recognizing of the truth, it is easy to feel the urgency of the expressive interest Primo Levi captures in his writing:

From men who have known extreme destitution one cannot expect a deposition in the juridical sense of the term, but something that is at once a lament, a curse, an expiation, and an attempt to justify and rehabilitate themselves.   (Levi 1988: 37)

It is difficult not to feel that I am trying to justify these people's existence by showing that their experience *exists*. As Koch expresses the predicament:

a growing number of social scientists is proclaiming a society 'beyond status and class' . . . To their mind, neither the concept of stratification nor the concept of class is able to portray reality any longer.   (Koch 1996: 187)

And this position is simply a variation on the view fashionable among the English intelligentsia that class is no longer deeply entrenched. In such a context of silence on issues of class inequality, it is difficult to face with equanimity the powerful forces of exclusion that ensure the invisibility of class. The stylistic conventions of academic writing are the product of a specific trajectory, one that all too often empties the world of its biting, incessant, primordial wailing, giving reality a comfortable hue that moderate tones reflect. A 'thrown-ness' into life is the primary condition of person and world, and it is an artifice of constructions of knowing that knowledge is presented through the epistemic relation of distance, a relation itself socially artificial, standing as it does on the back of a relation to language and the world that has its root in an economic relation of distance, of privilege; the temporal and spatial organization that facilitates the studied leisure at the heart of the great universities of the world. This is the social context in which the elect adopt a neutralizing, distant disposition towards language and the social world (Bourdieu 1993a: 120).

Steiner warns that 'A neutral humanism is either a pedantic artifice or a prologue to the inhuman' (Steiner 1985: 87). This is a piece of writing that understands that its own grounds rest not in a mysterious election through which a consciousness contemplates but in the incarnate subjectivity of a historically and politically located body-subject whose flesh incarnates an irreversible destiny, an openness to being that is foreclosed upon because of the social and political conditions of the lives of the group to which he belongs. The task has been to understand how flesh becomes signified within culture, and how this is internalized by agents as active subjects engaged with a social and political context which creates a closure in their being to what, at birth, they might have become. And how can one be neutral to such a foreclosure, to the determination of human being when it rests in conditions that are inscribed in one's body and mind and which are lived through with others in a condition that is denied? To remain uncommitted is upheld by many in the academy as an achievement, as though adopting the 'scholastic point of view' (Bourdieu 1990d) equates with becoming part of a special species that comes to know in ways other than connectedness and belonging. To fail to be outraged is to fail in one's connection with the world and to fail to see the domination that the position of the scholar is predicated upon: the dispossession of those whom the political system requires to be what Galbraith calls a 'functional underclass' (Galbraith 1992), a group whose poverty is guaranteed in order to maintain the standard of living and relative prosperity of the very sections of the population that are politically important to election and re-election and whose own social reproduction is invested in the academic field. The cultural dispossession of the working class has become ever more critical now they are no longer tied into the capitalist economy by a culture of work, and the social problems of the ghetto are all too real problems of daily life for too many of the world's populations. The problems of drug, alcohol and solvent abuse, to say nothing of the demoralization caused by job insecurity and unemployment that are hidden in rates of ill-health and an increased suicide rate, as well as more crime against the person and property, are creating an urban environment that has become desperate for too many and which is becoming a more stringent separator of individuals as the inequalities of class embed themselves in the contours of culture itself, in the manners of the flesh, adding a sinister dimension to what was once soberly talked of as an economic phenomenon.

So are these conditions demanding a modest appraisal, modestly delivered? Or do they demand a little courage, in our recognizing, knowing and certainly in our facing these conditions in the incarnation of flesh and being that interviewing and transcribing requires? And then, if the world we find is ugly, remorseless, ravaging of spirit and youth, of mind and marrow, can we expect anything comfortable to emerge in its writing? Complacency is part of the hidden benefits of privilege, it is part of the mode of being-in-the-world that privilege fosters, and from this position the voices of those demanding redress always sound shrill, demanding, ugly. This is part of the opposition of distinction and stigma that characterizes the opposed class positions of comfort and struggle, and in regard to these matters it is difficult not to agree with Kafka:

If the book we are reading does not wake us, as with a fist hammering on our skull, why then do we read it? So that it shall make us happy? Good God, we would also be happy if we had no books, and such books as make us happy we could, if need be, write ourselves. But what we must have are those books which come upon us like ill-fortune, and distress us deeply, like the death of one we love better than ourselves, like suicide. A book must be an ice-axe to break the sea frozen inside us.[4]

To live in Rotherham is to be surrounded by people whose talk about their lives carries a sense of undeniability, that too often threatens to leave one speechless, that emerges from the bleak truth that these people embody and speak from: what has come upon them as ill-fortune, and if it does not communicate that distress, then it fails. My desire is to communicate something in these people that I have interviewed, 'some sense of common value that has nothing to do with intellect in the first place' (Bourdieu and Eagleton 1992b: 117) and yet to try and gather together a coherent sense from across the atomizing disparate distress of these people the sense of what life has become for many in England. The conditions of that decency are decaying very rapidly, and we have a duty to confront the awful, sometimes brutal nature of the decay of that way of life and to see, without euphemization that, as Adorno put it, 'there is no longer beauty or consolation except in the gaze falling on horror, withstanding it, and in unalleviated conscious-ness of negativity holding fast to the possibility of what is better' (Adorno 1974: 25). For the decencies of these people are very close to being lost, and the responsibility for the immense social misery that will replace it rests with those in power who have knowingly allowed it to happen and even has-tened the arrival of a newer order of even more exploitative work-schemes. Sociologists must confront the new sources of domination and suffering that are springing up around working class people and must explore the processes whereby that domination becomes embodied. These forms of domination are creating new conditions for working class souls that require new forms of bearing-witness that are possible only through new forms of sight: a sight dependent, ultimately, upon new forms of analysis.

New forms of analysis necessitate new styles of writing, and this is why my writing makes frequent use of direct quotations. There are several related issues here. The most important is my acute sense of the complex-ity of the experience I am trying to capture. I do not mean this in the nar-cissistic sense that it is *my* experience as solitary *cogito*, but that my life in Rotherham has drawn me, in ever more forceful ways, to confront in com-munication with others an experience of the decay of life and of shared class conditions, of a relation to an absent culture, felt through its effects on the social space we inhabit, just as power exercised elsewhere, gravity-like, distorts the space-time that constitutes the co-ordinates of life. The task of giving voice to this drives my style and explains my use of other people's writing to say better than I can what is true of these people's lives. The project is to make visible the nature of the suffering of ordinary people at key points in the changing landscape of capitalist society, where the restruc-turing of the economy and of the state's role in the labour market has seen the use of ever more subtle forms of symbolic violence alongside a progres-sive impoverishment of workers through increased unemployment, reduc-tions in social security payments and the connected problem of low wages.

The work of Bourdieu exhibits a profound grasp of the symbolic vio-lence involved in the creation of working class people; and his writing, I believe, captures better than my own the condition of these people's lives. It seems inappropriate to paraphrase when the insight's formulation owes so much to him. Furthermore, his writing often develops, within the same paragraph, six or seven themes which he interrelates like a closely woven tapestry to create a unique sense of the problems of domination and working class existence. I believe that his writing style is part of his message, that what he is saying can only be said indirectly. Paraphrasing Bourdieu's prose often betrays the message. I have also drawn deeply from the philosophies of Heidegger, Merleau-Ponty and Wittgenstein.

Wolfe has suggested that 'Social scientists are moral philosophers in disguise' (Wolfe 1989: 23) This is clearly true of a work concerned with the subtleties of the personal suffering created by complex, newly emerging forms of social organization and the continual restructuring of identities that they require to function smoothly. Deindustrialization has, clearly, had the effect of wrapping many in a powerful sense of entrapment, as low wages, the cheapening of the qualifications they might reasonably aspire to obtain, and the shortening length of time that they hold jobs, have given them a sense of inescapable destiny, of being individuals collectively overwhelmed by historical change. Absence of security and of respect create a crisis in the reproduction of the culture that many grew up with, such as the educational links with the trade unions, the presence of union people in the communities, and the decline of the old spaces that used to be those of working people, like the pub and club. Understanding the impact of these changes requires that we appreciate, in an extended and sensitive way, the nature of human being and in this, it is difficult to avoid the considerations of thinkers so concerned with the relationship of persons to communication, relation and being. Any account of human life has to operate with an ontology, with a sense of the nature of the lives that it is purporting to generate an account of. Therefore, it is better that these considerations be explicitly considered in one's investigative method.

This raises important issues of taste. It may be felt that this kind of prose relies upon mystification and over-elaboration in order to produce an impression of profundity and insight. Another view was offered by Gerth and Wright Mills, writing of Weber's writing:

It is obvious that this school of writing is not what it is because of the inability of its practitioners to write well. They simply follow an altogether different style. They use parentheses, qualifying clauses, inversions and complex rhythmic devices in their polyphonous sentences. Ideas are synchronized rather than serialised. At their best, they erect a grammatical artifice in which mental balconies and watch towers, as well as bridges and recesses, decorate the main structure. Their sentences are gothic castles.   (Gerth and Mills 1946)

This makes their writing often difficult to paraphrase because the meaning is so intimately linked with their style. My use of these ideas is also related to the type of experience I am trying to capture, which is manifest through the medium of the phenomenal body as a vague, amorphous kind of confused abjection; as boredom; a dull ache; apathy and inertia. These are the forms their human engagement has been reduced to. Recognizing the nature of this in transcribed material[5] requires the use of a developed philosophy of human existence which can inform us of an experience that underlies language itself and is experienced through the primordial subjectivity of their flesh and bone. The necessarily complex nature of this enterprise, the difficulty that exposition of these phenomena demands, is captured succinctly by Christopher Macann, who writes that Merleau-Ponty's philosophy:

sets about its task of reflexive interrogation directly, that is, as directly as is ever possible for a philosophy whose whole ambition it is to reflect upon the unreflected, to think the unthought, to name the unnameable, in a phrase, to adopt the laborious detour of language to express what, by its very nature, antecedes, and so provides a foundation for, language.   (Macann 1993: 160)

This task is very much at the heart of the primary aim of this labour of objectification. Like Merleau-Ponty, I want to try and show that in our thought about the social world, things that are closest in being are furthest away in analysis, that the structures of comportment and the strategies of distinction we invest ourselves in, get shifted from our analytic gaze and we fail to see the truth of the land that our comportment avows. Little wonder that what should be nearest in being – our relation to a land whose people are haunted by the most appalling divisions – is furthest away in our theorizing.

The photographer Robert Capa suggested, 'when the pictures are not good enough, get in closer'. The task of description is one of constituting 'objects' through using the whole tool box of categories that we have at hand through our education. Higher education makes available a world of constituted meaning by making the world available to us under various descriptions. However, this is a world that is foreign to the being-in-the-world of working people, and too many academics overlook that their epistemic vision has inscribed within its very conditions of existence the position of the scholar. Academic training makes available the sense, form and modality of an experience of the social that is the exact opposite of the relation to the social inscribed in the position of being unemployed, or of being a labourer, or taxi driver, or police constable. In learning to perceive the world as the subject of acts of knowledge it is too easy to 'swallow down' with the concepts a conceptual unconscious, imbibed through the position involved in being a participant in the arts faculties of universities, a sense of the world that I have been conscious, throughout, of being an alien to, and of being 'up against'. Therefore, my own learning, having taken place in a different place, through the experience inscribed in being positioned differently, within the university and the wider culture, has made me painfully aware of having to make concepts service a different experience, an unmediated relation to being involved in a world that in its aggression and potential for economic and symbolic violence ensures that individuals perceive the world through circumspective involvement, through dealing-with, a kind of practical engagement that forecloses upon the possibility of individuals experiencing the world through a deliberative thematic awareness that focuses upon isolated determinate phenomena. It is a kind of understanding that Heidegger best describes:

> The scientific projection of any entities which we have somehow encountered already lets their kind of Being be understood explicitly and in such a manner that it thus becomes manifest what ways are possible for the pure discovery of entities within-the-world. The articulation of the understanding of Being, the delimitation of an area of subject-matter (a delimitation guided by this understanding), and the sketching-out of the way of conceiving which is appropriate to such entities – all these belong to the totality of this projecting; and this totality is what we call '*thematizing*'. Its aim is to free the entities we encounter within-the-world, and to free them in such a way that they can 'throw themselves against' a pure discovering – that is, that they can become 'objects'. Thematizing Objectifies. It does not first 'posit' the entities, but frees them so that one can interrogate them and determine their character.   (Heidegger 1962: 414)

Reflexivity means being theoretically sensitive to the articulated structure of the referential whole, to the background of comportment that is the ground of intelligibility and which informs these people's lives and speech without being formalized or outlined or objectified by them. And this means not positing formulations of the phenomena of their lives, but rather being sensitive to the character of existence that social conditions circumscribe and which these people articulate in their being-in-the-world, even when they are consigned to silence. Clearly, this entails a hyper-vigilance to the work of construction, an awareness of the threat of distortion that certain concepts may involve. So, I have tried to frame a form of knowing, tried to fashion the main instruments for description in a way sensitive to the dynamics of these people's experience and thus to construct an account that makes manifest the engagement that is characteristic of human knowing and being.[6]

The task is to constitute for readers an intimate sense of a world that is seldom dealt with in these ways and which will thus be unrecognizable to most who read this book. This is partly because the sense that it tries to constitute is that of the corporeal sense that people come to share through sharing a place in the world and because the description tries to capture the nature of processes which language often depends upon rather than focuses upon. The difficulty of capturing the status of what remains as part of the necessary background to intelligibility and people's way of being is well expressed by Searle:

> There is a real difficulty in finding ordinary language terms to describe the Background: one speaks vaguely of 'practices', 'capacities', and 'stances' or one speaks suggestively but misleadingly of 'assumptions' and 'presuppositions'. These latter terms must be literally wrong, because they imply the apparatus of representation . . . The fact that we have no neutral vocabulary for discussing the phenomena in question and the fact that we tend to lapse into an Intentionalistic vocabulary ought to arouse our interest . . . There simply is no first-order vocabulary for the Background, because the Background is as invisible to Intentionality as the eye which sees is invisible to itself.   (Searle 1983: 156)

And there are similar problems in using language to capture the nature of processes. Particularly processes as convoluted and paradoxical as those facing the writer confronted with the silence and confusion involved in processes of displacement without movement; of the mutual enveloping of social and personal decay, of fear and insecurity; of the experiences that are part of the most profound aspects of the life of people in the communities in which they live. Yet, as more and more people are condemned by the labour and housing markets to positions of extreme vulnerability and insecurity, and a life-context of impoverished forms of self-realization, these conditions need to be recognized and understood so that we can confront the 'social costs of economic violence' (Bourdieu 1998: 129), and the possibility for an 'economics of well-being' (Bourdieu 1998: 129) might become part of our horizons. Yet this requires a break from the atrophied forms of common sense that life in the academy fosters; a social break premised upon an engagement with the grounds of forms of being other than that of the free-floating intellectual. We must remember that the world constituted from the 'scholastic point of view', from the position of the scholar free to consider the world's meaning, in-itself, occurrently, is a derivation that:

> I alone bring into being for myself (and therefore into being in the only sense that the word can have for me) the tradition which I elect to carry on . . . Scientific points of view, according to which my existence is a moment of the world's, are always both naïve and at the same time dishonest, because they take for granted, without explicitly mentioning it, the other point of view, namely that of consciousness, through which from the outset a world forms itself round me and begins to exist for me. To return to things themselves is to return to that world which precedes knowledge, of which knowledge always *speaks*, and in relation to which every scientific schematization is an abstract and derivative sign-language, as is geography in relation to the countryside in which we have learnt beforehand what a forest, a prairie or a river is.
> (Merleau-Ponty 1962: ix)

My task is the paradoxical one of trying to return to that world which precedes knowledge: that invisible realm of imperceptibles, the past living in the gestural, purely practical sense of this community as it is sedimented in the comportment of these people as they make a clearing for what matters in the way they make experience available for each other, unknowingly through their very existence. The human processes of this background may be too pervasive, too extensive and too subtly complex to be visible in any ordinary sense, yet they provide the grounds for our kinaesthetic lived-bodily presence to the world, the grounds of that which thought is the mere echo of: 'Thoughts are the shadows of our feelings – always darker, emptier and simpler' (Nietzsche 1974).

This is a book struggling to see afresh: struggling towards that rarest of moments in the academy when a problem that emerges from the world is constituted afresh. When it no longer wears the tired drapes of yesterday's metaphors and the ignominy of concepts that no longer fit, nor the powerlessness of words bereft of sensuous power which ensure that the phenomenon no longer 'lives' in our imagination because of the bankruptcy of a professionalized discourse whose language, arcane and sterile, lacks the power to effect the shift of perspective involved for insight to constitute itself from the blinding sheen of the self-evidence of a common sense that is so heavily constructed for us. These issues concern the nature of our forms of knowing; they oblige us to find a style of writing capable of framing a type of knowing that might affect our spontaneous forms of recognition, the aspects which comportment realizes in us, and bring some understanding of the grounds of being to our forms of association.

Philosophy offers a deepened understanding of what it is to be human and the possibility of recognizing sources of damage to human beings. It offers the possibility of an ethics, the capacity to evaluate injustice and to be aware of its grounds in our own immediate affective, practical sense. That sense whose origins emanate from the primordial connection to others that we share in comportment and which is logically prior to discursive consciousness, but which the scholarly mode of knowing appears to reverse for those who engage the world through the position of scholar, who enjoy a neutralizing distance and who are free to appropriate the world primarily through the apparatus of academic discourse. Our embodiment offers us a relation to alterity that is irreducible to discursive consciousness: in the generative schemata of corporeal subjectivity there is a prosocial order that is the condition of individuation but which is anonymous as the background assumed in self- and other-knowledge. In these times of marginalization and progressive impoverishment, where so many are consigned to quietude, we need to be awake to the possibility that there is a sense of 'Justice in the Flesh' (Levin 1990: 35), that justice:

is not just an abstract ideal, a principle conceived by the mind; it is also a critical measure rooted in the body. By virtue of the body, we carry within us a rudimentary, preconceptually formed, sense of justice. This experiential ground of justice cannot be recognized, however, unless we rescue the body from reification.

(Levin 1990: 38)

If this is the case, then we need the resources to recognize this and to allow us to recognize the flesh's sense of injustice. We must be able to recognize this in these people's speech and interaction.

At a time when societies are creating ever more impoverished, marginal groups, and new forms of political and cultural dispossession, new forms of alienation, to say nothing of the decay of the urban landscapes in which many of us grew up, we need an invigorated, humanized form of description that can witness the nature of these phenomena, not as pre-constituted objects but as phenomena that touch indelibly the most intimate forms of personal life.

Paul Gregg reports one aspect of the extent of this malaise:

Workers feel frightened. Opinion pollsters report massive levels of job insecurity among the workforce. Forty per cent of employees say they fear for their jobs and 60 per cent say insecurity has been rising.

Yet a succession of Ministers and commentators say that this insecurity is a myth . . . So is the public really subject to a kind of mass neurosis, or are the measures used to describe job insecurity missing the point?

People's expressions of insecurity are hard to quantify. For one thing, they are about people's expectations of the future, whereas any hard data on jobs are inevitably about the past.

Also, there is more than one element to security: feelings of security are a function of the level of protection one enjoys, the likelihood of losing one's job and the degree of hurt and loss that would result if one were made redundant.

(Gregg 1996)

Gregg's simile of neurosis is insightful, for it indicates a certain dread that has come to pervade life, something that has come to exist within the contextual frame of experience as a manner of being with a certain degree of generality. It is not a fear explicitly represented in consciousness, but something that interferes with the temporal structures of being-in-the-world, emptying practical existence of the meaning that is normally its bedrock, and that flows from sensuous involvement in daily life. This unconstituted dread comes to abstract me from my existence, it tears me away from that integration that emanates from my being a body-subject like others. I am torn from that meeting point of the world that I am:

my life is made up of meeting rhythms which have not their *reason* in what I have chosen to be, but their *condition* in the humdrum setting which is mine. Thus there appears round our personal existence a margin of *almost* impersonal existence which can be practically taken for granted, and which I rely on to keep me alive; round the human world which each of us has made for himself is a world in general terms to which one must first of all belong in order to be able to enclose oneself in the particular context of a love or an ambition.   (Merleau-Ponty 1962: 83)

It is this umbilical cord between body-subject and world that is disturbed by the destruction of the humdrum setting of our lives as personal time is arrested and one form of present comes to proclaim itself over and against the movement of time, displacing the subject's sense of the temporal location of practice, robbing new presents of their authenticity. It is as though life goes on, under this dread, as a grinning mockery of itself, and this alien subjectivity comes to inhabit the person, virus-like, destroying the programmes of the habit-body until enjoyment of the thickness of being is foreclosed upon, indefinitely – or until, perhaps, there comes a point when ontological security is founded, established, again. One man, talking about how he felt when he first knew he was going to lose his job, made clear this breakdown of the body's lived intentionality and the sense of embeddedness, or security, that is involved in our self-transparent absorption in the primordial realm of everyday being-in-the-world:

S: Can I ask yer abaht ahr [how] it meks [makes] yer feel?
K: Ye . . . [*sighs and pauses*] . . .'cos [because] yer just constantly on an edge, know what Ah [I] mean, yer constantly on an edge, unsettled, yer thinkin' all time: yer gu to bed at night an' yer laid the'er thinkin', I mean, 'What 'appens if Ah lose mi [my] job?' . . . it's allous [always] on yer mind . . . Yer can't 'ave a good time . . . yer can't relax . . . it's the'er all't time.

What is being described by this person is the breaking of the link between his lived intentionality and its pre-objective context: that is, the ungrounding of the intentionality his body incarnates in its movements, its practical projections in its pre-objective orientation towards its 'behavioural setting'. For this person's existence in this setting, the continuance of the habits that constitute the rhythms of the life of that context is being threatened by the potential sweeping away of the means to live that life: his income and all it guarantees in terms of the autonomy that a human life is premised upon. Clearly, the 'behavioural setting' is present in an unprominent way, this is clear in the feelings of conscious and somatic breakdown, as the problems of a new and threatening context obtrude.

The fear and anxiety of this man, the uncertain dread manifest in sighs and pauses, punctuated by the speed of his interjections, registering, in their rhythms, the raised heart-beat and the *sense* of veins coursing with adrenaline-rich blood, the somatic manifestations of fear; of loss and bewilderment, make explicit the unity of being-in-the-world. The psychic and the physiological are rooted in the intentionality of the body projected towards a world: but a world whose significance as a context of meaningful human action is heavily prescribed by the economics and politics of class, the things that constitute the 'beneath' of our coming into consciousness, the 'ungrounded way of acting' (Wittgenstein 1972: 110), the background through which we learn the practical belief of authentic being:

> Practical belief is not a 'state of mind', still less a kind of arbitrary adherence to a set of instituted dogmas and doctrines ('beliefs'), but rather a state of the body . . . Enacted belief, instilled by the childhood learning that treats the body as a living memory pad, an automaton that 'leads the mind unconsciously along with it', and as a repository for the most precious values . . . is the product of quasi-bodily dispositions, operational schemes.   (Bourdieu 1990a: 68)

Bourdieu calls them 'quasi-bodily dispositions' because, like Heidegger and Merleau-Ponty, he wants to frame a way of seeing that is a pre-objective view; and recognizes that 'being in the world' reintegrates Descartes' '"two *summa genera* of realities" – pure thought or extended being' (Langer 1989: 31), the physiological and the psychic – through a form of being that is peculiarly human, which straddles the distinction between behaviour and action by making our subjectivity incarnate, and which gives to our life the particular ambiguity that the spheres of sense and our involvement in its realms, its effects on our being, produce. We have to acknowledge, in Merleau-Ponty's famous phrase, that there are 'many ways for consciousness to be conscious', that:

> We cannot relate certain movements to bodily mechanism and others to consciousness. The body and consciousness are not mutually limiting, they can be only parallel . . . This distinction can survive only if there are *several ways for the body to be a body, several ways for consciousness to be consciousness*. As long as the body is defined in terms of existence in-itself, it functions uniformly like a mechanism, and as long as the mind is defined in terms of pure existence for-itself, it knows only objects arrayed before it . . . The intellectualist analysis, here as everywhere, is less false than abstract. It is true that the 'symbolic function' or the 'representative function' underlies our movements, but it is not a final term for analysis. It too rests on a certain groundwork. The mistake of intellectualism is to make it self-subsistent, to remove it from the stuff in which it is realized, and to recognize in us, as a nonderivative entity, an undistanced presence in the world. For, using this consciousness, an entirely transparent consciousness, this intentionality which admits of no degrees of more or less, as a starting point, everything that separates us from the real world – error, sickness, madness, in short incarnation – is reduced to the status of mere appearance.   (Merleau-Ponty 1962:124)

Once we recognize, with Merleau-Ponty and Bourdieu, that our embodiment in the world makes us perceptually and sensuously immersed in it in a way that challenges our usual academic thinking about these matters, then we can see that in contexts like the one I am describing, the decay of the world as it was can mean people being beset by the world as a place that comes to inhabit them negatively, as a world in which the meaning they are condemned to impregnating posturally, is abject, bleak, dark, ugly, unfulfilling and violating.

Given the link between our sense of the world and our comportment, that our consciousness is incarnate, then in such an economic context, understood in these ways, we would expect perception, *living*, to become the experience that Sartre called 'Nausea'. But this is not the same experience as it was for Roquentin in Sartre's *Nausea*. Perception does not float about for these people, rather the world as a referential-whole that they were embedded in and in which they experienced things as mattering, through which they experienced an investment in absorption; what gave quality to their lives, a certain mattering, has fallen away from them in that they have been withdrawn from their place in the practical, referential-whole of their world. Their world has lost significance, in that they can no longer experience the investment of being absorbed in what we call a 'meaningful context'; and in this situation of withdrawal, it is as if the world now stands out for them as a series of practices they are exempted from. The world has become occurrent to them, something they experience 'from the outside', that is, from a position of non-involvement. Possibilities no longer solicit them. They experience a radical discontinuity, an unsettledness emanating from the grounds of the body's projection into the future which creates a sense of the loss of meaning of their lives and yet which makes the meaninglessness of the world in which they live more explicit. It is a sense detectable in the words of one unemployed person:

X: A've [I've] bin rait [right] depressed miseln [myself] this week. An' fuckin' boored [bored] aht'a [out of] mi [my] mind. Ah just an't got a fuckin' thing to du [do]. It is strange, it just meks mi s' [so] upset. It's like beein' fuckin' ill, I feel sick an' I an't [haven't] bin [been] rait [right] fo' weeks. A'm just wastin' all mi life an' the'r in't a fuckin' thing Ah' can du. That's why Ah stay in bed su [so] late. Ah dun't wanna get up to feel su fed-up. [*Pause*] It meks mi feel strange inside . . . [*pause*]
S: What du yer mean?
X: Ah feel different, especially when Ah g' [go] aht [out]. Like Ah'll gu' [go] fo' a video or sumaht [something] an' when Ah'm [I'm] the'er Ah feel worried an' threatened a bit, like, an' Ah sort'a can't decide which t' 'ave, then Ah'll get 'ome an' Ah dun't [don't] wanna watch it but Ah'm boored an' Ah need sumaht t' du. So Ah watch it! But Ah dun't enjoy stuff at moment.
S: Du things not seem t' matter to yer?
X: No. Nowt [nothing] seems rait t' mi, not like it wo [was]. It's awful in it, gettin' older, fo this! That this is it. Signin' on', crap jobs . . . [*Pause*] . . . n' money . . . this place! [*Laughs*]

This man's nausea is embedded in his being enmired in a life-context that is not absorbing and where the meanings of the world that obtrude are too negative. Clearly, one could simply see this man as exhibiting the classical symptoms of depression. But there is more here. Heidegger said of anxiety:

Being-anxious discloses, primordially and directly, the world as world . . . This does not signify, however, that in anxiety the worldhood of the world gets conceptualised.   (Heidegger 1962: 232)

Heidegger's point is exemplified in the transcription. The condition of being out-of-work fractures the referential whole of practical engagement in which projects and concerns flow seamlessly together, locating the individual, through comportment, in a world. From this position in which everyday forms of motility and absorption are curtailed, everyday familiarity and the world as it was formerly lived fall into an unsettledness through which it becomes possible to experience oneself as worthless and meaningless, one is in the world but unable to secure meaning from the network of patterns of practices around one. It is like being in a familiar environment, in complete darkness, one knows the world is there but cannot know it in quite the transparency as when it is illuminated. As Heidegger put it, 'Publicness proximally controls every way in which the world and Dasein get interpreted, and it is always right' (Heidegger 1962: 165) or to have it put another way:

Being is being in, it is belonging to and being possessed, in short, participating, taking part, according importance, interest . . . And if the 'vanities of this world' have been perceived more often than the other social stakes in their true status as products of collective illusion, this is doubtless because the arbitrary nature of the game is more easily revealed, especially to the eyes of those who are excluded.

Bourdieu 1983: 1–2)

'Anxiety is not conceptual' (Dreyfus 1994: 179); it is an existential predicament, absorption ceases, and life seems like a game with no meaning. A life without public embedding in which these people must put forward an endless pretence, to the Department of Social Security and to potential employers, their lives are criss-crossed with regimes, regimes aimed at disavowing the truth their experience asserts in the face of a veil of public lies. Little wonder the matterings of life become problematic, and little wonder many feel sick and unsettled. The everyday practical lives of their communities have become fractured, and with them the sources of respect and value available have fallen away, leaving this amorphous sense of discomfort, unease and anxiety.

Yet this person's speech discloses something else. Unlike those experiences that are most readily described because they are discrete, temporally and spatially bounded, tied to the actual moment of a particular present which does not dwell in the order of objective time. Rather, it is a condition. That is, it is part of an on-going present that is part of a customary life, which does not exist *in its details* in consciousness. It persists as the context of the individual occurrences of their lives, almost as an 'unconscious'; it over-shadows, poisons the sensuous living of their present, both their choices and the 'happenings' they are subject to. And it is this which makes it very difficult for the unemployed to know, and hence to speak about, what is happening to them. They are powerless, humanly, to prevent the damage to their lives; and the alienation emanates from their isolation, the foreclosure of their lives from socially valued positions and responsibilities and, last but worst of all, their fortnightly ritualized humiliation at the hands of Her Majesty's Department of Social Security.[7] With all this affecting working class communities at many levels and in many different ways, there is little wonder that 'Workers feel frightened.' Their fears emerge from the grounds of humanity they share with the great thinkers of the world.

The lives of these people make clear that there is a link between the realm of economic organization and the most personal, intimate realms of human life. Economic policy has social effects and personal costs. And my task has been to frame a way of writing that, whilst being critical, thoughtful and illuminating, uses the instruments of objectification to show the affective significance of the primordial, that deep background that is the well-spring of our being, that network of relations which has been so fatally touched in recent social development. This destruction of the context of relations in which culture once existed, as a set of responses upon which a practically achieved ethos once existed, has left too many confused in a destiny which they experience through the fear and confused insecurity that local people have articulated. In the earlier transcription, what the individuals said emerged from a primordial understanding, from coping with changes affecting their affective responses, and the words described how these changes break through to, and disturb, consciousness:

Heidegger talks here of 'transparent coping' and of 'primordial understanding'. He is in complete agreement with Wittgenstein that our coping with the things we handle, our use of instruments does not require the presence of an 'intermediate consciousness' or 'cognitive state'. He talks of the things we encounter, chairs, books, hammers, as being 'ready to hand'. We are in contact with them not through our minds, by their presence in our thoughts as ideas, but through handling them, responding to their presence, given our intentions, purposes, desires, and affective susceptibilities. He agrees with Wittgenstein: our responses are not derived from our ideas, but rather our ideas are rooted in our responses.   (Dilman 1993: 10)

This is precisely what Bourdieu develops into the notion of an *ethos*, a range of implicit values that are practically achieved in a person's embodied responses to others, and which are the deepest form of moral existence (or, conversely, alienation), governing the recognition of others' value in existing (or, conversely, showing that they do not have value), granting their bodies space to feel comfortable and un-threatened in, and producing dispositions like generosity, 'a system of practical, axiological schemes . . . the strength of the ethos is that it is a morality made flesh' (Bourdieu 1993a: 86). And our ideas about the world are based upon the same schemes, the same practically engaged knowledge. But when those responses, as the medium of our relation to our environment, as the ways of life that mediate economic conditions, are brought into question by changes in the world, then our culture itself, as it is imprinted in our affective life, is called into question and we with it. There are two levels to the ontological insecurity: both the way of life and we ourselves fall into question.

For example, when the sense of honour that characterized a community has been destroyed; when the presence of large gangs of young people cut off from the relations in which an older generation learnt its values, and for whom those values of mutual respect can make no sense because they derive respect from their having no respect for others as an instantiation of their 'hardness'; and where joblessness and lack of housing force too many to a life that defies the rhythms of a working area and create endless petty irritations: that is, when a people have been produced with no presence in the world apart from their infractious presence on the streets, then the sources of value that characterized that older tradition become meaningless and anachronistic and those who embody that ethos will have to begin to distinguish when, with whom, that ethos operates. One man expressed clearly the change in the responses, in the 'ungrounded way of acting' (Wittgenstein 1972: 110):

It's just fuckin' rough rahnd 'ere nahr [now] an' it used to bi alrait [alright]. Tha [You're] just gettin' lads giyin' [giving] yer [you the] eye . . . when yer gu aht . . . some-b'dy's starin' at yer . . . an' f'st [first] to look away is the weaker one an' once thi' [they] see yer [you] as weak, then yer a target to 'em.

This person is in the world as a world with which he must first of all cope; but what this man is registering is that it has changed:

Ah [I] mean, Ah used to 'ang [hang] abaht [about] dahn [down] the'er [there] as a kid an' nahr it's full'r fuckin' tribes! Ah mean, them from E thiy all think the'r ten men. Thi' stare an' tha just 'as t' stare back an' laugh at 'em. Tha's gorra know who yer can treat wi' respect an' not bi [be] tekken [taken] fo' [for a] cunt . . .

This is a man of twenty-five years of age, so the youth he speaks of can be no more than eight to ten years earlier. Moreover, he is suggesting that it is the embodied responses of people in the area that are changing and display-ing an important shift in intent, purpose and affective engagement with the world of others. The ethos that he grew up with makes him sensitive to the change; it is an important shift, from respect to this aimless aggression, and this man sees no other way to accommodate to this change than by adapting his own embodied morality, by learning to distinguish between those deserving of respect and those he must show face to. So he must maintain his physical capital by keeping fit and strong, by honing his capacity to deal with physical aggression by finessing his fighting skills, and by ensuring the mutual protection of friends with those same capacities:

Tha's [you've] got to bi [be] able to scrap [fight] nahr [now], ye'v [you've] got bi known to bi 'ard. Ah mean it's all changed since we wo' kids. Ah mean, we'd scrap wi' kids 's [our] own age an that, but once thi' [they] went dahn [down] an' tha'd [you had] won, that wo it, it wo', 'rait, Ah can fight you: respect' and we'd *fuckin' nivver* [never] bother grown people. But nahr it's all changed, these gangs 'r young lads, the'r eyein' yer an' the'r threatenin'. An' not just that the'r carryin' nahr. *Ye'v got to* know aht to fight, an' it's best that thi' know that ye'v got 'eavy friends, friends wi guns, then the'll not mess wi' yer. Ah mean, Ah know decent lads an' A'd never have a disagreement wi' 'em but we've got no choice nahr. Like mi son, A'm teachin 'im to fight nahr [now]!

What these two passages demonstrate is that what Merleau-Ponty calls the 'habit-body' carries forward the sense of the world as it has been lived in, in the past; and this entails certain responses, ways of relating to that world; and this habitual setting is presumed around the subject in the encountered present. But, in this case, in these conditions, this presumed background of habits and responses and the practical sense of value they make manifest has changed. What was 'expected' to be there to reciprocate the practically projected schemes of gesture is no longer always there, and he is thrust into a future in which he must contemplate new schemes for existing, a different way of being because the old habit-world, the 'ethos' that he grew up with has decayed. So this man's speech is objectifying a change in human responses, and is registering his sense – in the feeling of his somatic responses, his practical, immediate, sensuous awareness, his embodied understanding, his comportment – of the falling away of the moral relations of people around him. It illuminates what Wittgenstein called 'fine shades of behaviour' (Wittgenstein 1958: 207) – those great subtleties of our doing and being our bodies through which we reveal our inherence in a realm of shared perceptions – our inherent perceptual ability to spontaneously discriminate such fine shades and make our responses to one another that of, as Wittgenstein put it, 'an attitude towards a soul'.

These feelings, even where they are those of aggression and dehumanization, rest in our affective reactions, which rest in our life in our communities, in the deeds through which we live, that create and justify our lives.

Hence it is this primordial orientation towards a setting wherein the habit-body of old ways and old expectations carries forward the 'present body', and in so doing brings forward a comprehensive past from which the present is dealt with, giving a form to a future that both anticipate. It is this carrying forward of a sense of practical honour in comportment that leads to the experience of its absence in the world of others. It is this sense of the decay of public life that creates, in many, such a sense of bleakness and leads them to conclude that the only way to live is to get out. The habit-body has come to expect the continuity of an environment created by the processes of capital and class. So much of our identity is based upon our embodied responses, through which we engage with our environment, and through which the significance that people and situations have for us crystalizes. The meaning of our world is always embroiled, fused-with, our affective modes of awareness, which reveal the primordial impact of economically based changes to the worlds in which people live.

If we are to recognize the economic origins of so much of the misery of individuals in these societies, we need to remember that 'Critical analysis should not be a conceptual neutron bomb, destroying living emotions and leaving structures intact' (McCann 1988: 27). The types of objective analysis through which these phenomena are usually constituted have given up on too much: they fail to capture the *human* grounds of people's being-in-the-world; the richness and fullness of an original experience, or the endless fusion of thought, action and emotion that human beings are, regardless of status or economic position. Of all disciplines, therefore, sociology has to operate somewhere between ontology and poetry. We need desperately to find a mode of writing that can articulate being-in-the-world and yet which has the sensitivity of a poet's sense of the deeper meanings locked away in the feeling-speech spoken by those we live among, and which ought to be the grounds of our thinking and writing. This work emerges from the experience it tries to convey through the insights of thinkers like Bourdieu, Heidegger, Merleau-Ponty and Wittgenstein, and it tries to develop a form of writing that escapes:

the deadly alternative between the dry objectivist detachment of scientific accounts and the more experientially sensitive involvement of literary forms.

(Bourdieu and Wacquant 1992: 66)

Such a style is necessary if we are to appreciate the significance of lives that social conditions are rendering meaningless. It is a task that makes unavoidable the 'laborious detour' that Macann (Macann 1993:160) described as at the heart of Merleau-Ponty's project.

We have seen in this chapter that the traditional notion of the epistemic situation as being that of a mind, through a withdrawal from the world, contemplating the meaning of objects, is a deficient mode of knowing the world. Rather, we must shift our attention to the world while remaining absorbed in the referential-whole of the background in which the place, and ourselves, exist. There is a striking difference between the transcribed words of local people and the commentary; but the difference is unavoidable if we are to understand the sense of these people's lives. And this is not a problem once we understand that sense is a phenomenon of the shared background which cannot be represented and thus cannot be communicated through formalizations: rather it makes itself manifest but cannot be abstracted from instances of the shared world of intelligibility. Hopefully, the commentary shows this sense in the transcription. It is only through an awareness of these issues and the distance inscribed in our analytical tools that we can maintain a 'Familiarity, which books cannot give, with the practical mode of existence of those who do not have the freedom to distance the world' (Bourdieu 1990a: 15). This is the only way for us to recognize the grounds of the common generative capacities upon which essentialized differences rest with all the foreignness of natural difference, and 'can thus be the basis both of a more acute awareness of distance and of a real proximity, a kind of solidarity beyond cultural differences' (Bourdieu 1990a: 15).

This, then, is a book that issues not from its author's gaze but from the more reliable tactile sense of embodiment, of being a subject of relations of domination. A sense of the world that emerges through the effects of a humiliation done to the flesh because the feelings these people are expressing are part of an unreflective-experience of brute being, of being-there. This is not an account that is built up through observation, through a withdrawal from the people and the phenomena that are described. It emerges through a reconstruction of the problems that are immanent in this life, written by someone who has faced the same cultural exigencies and done so through the same temporal and existential structures.

4

A landscape with figures?

Tevershall village – a village which began almost at the park gates, and trailed in utter hopeless ugliness for a long and gruesome mile: houses, rows of wretched, small begrimed brick houses with black slate roofs for lids, sharp angles and wilful blank dreariness.

Connie was accustomed to Kensington or the Scotch hills or the Sussex downs: that was her England. With the stoicism of the young she took in the utter soulless ugliness of the coal-and-iron Midlands at a glance, and left it at what it was: unbelievable, and not to be thought about.

(Lawrence 1994a: 13)

Space, of course, is alive
that's why it moves about;
and that's what makes it eternally spacious and unstuffy.

And somewhere it has a wild heart
that sends pulses even through me . . .   (Lawrence 1992: 192)

There is an internal landscape, a geography of the soul; we search for its outlines all our lives.   (Hart 1991: 1)

Lady Chatterley's Lover by D. H. Lawrence provides an insight into the ways in which comportment discloses perception, sense and experience. It illuminates the ways in which human beings' relation to the world is mediated by the way of life of their immediate class group. That is how the form of their relation to the world is inscribed in the immediate dispositions through which individuals come to be *in* the world as a place of the determinate sense inscribed in an individual's and group's position and location. Lawrence[1] shows clearly how place is mediated by class position. That is, how inscribed in the materiality of space, there are the invisible spectres of the referential-whole that, as background, always reveals the sense of place as somewhere in which we are either 'at home', indifferent or alien. Lives take place amidst this *sense* and our practical awareness, our accustomed-ness, to certain kinds of people, activities and distinct ways of life, and it is in our comportment that we are possessed of a primary, pre-cognitive, practical awareness of the ramifications of space. That it has a 'wild heart' as Lawrence put it, whose pulsions ensure we are always located amidst an internal landscape that possesses us, defines us to ourselves by framing the contours of the world in which we belong; a geography of the soul emerging from the very conditions of self-hood, identity and being-in-the-world as they all intertwine in the particular structures of being-in-the-world.

Perhaps the most famous attempt to capture the everyday lives of Yorkshire people is Richard Hoggart's *The Uses of Literacy*. Hoggart's work is interesting given the impact it had on the emerging field of cultural studies in England. Published in 1957, it was a book whose aim was to be 'a sort of guide or textbook to aspects of popular culture' and it became part of a reconfiguring of the Left intelligentsia in England. Hoggart's second chapter in *The Uses of Literacy*, has the title: 'Landscape with Figures – a setting'. Despite its concern with changes occurring in the working class culture of the time, what emerged was a view of the northern industrial working class as participating in a culture that was relatively static. It is an account guided 'by the degree to which working people still draw, in speech and in the assumptions to which speech is a guide, on oral and local tradition' (Hoggart 1957: 27). However, Hoggart was careful to point out the importance of 'changes . . . tending to cause the working classes to lose, culturally, much that was valuable and to gain less than their new situation should have allowed' (Hoggart 1957: 17).

Hoggart's early writing is mainly of historical interest now. The conditions he describes are long gone. The communities whose lives he described are now lost in the problems that face urban ghettos the world over. The forms of association Hoggart captured are lost to changes that have brought a radical anomie. The task of presenting an account of the experience of a group of people in a particular locality, might seem to presume the deployment of something like the notion of a 'landscape with figures'. However, whilst acknowledging Hoggart's text and its literary device, I really want to look, in this chapter, at why the idea of 'landscape' is inappropriate to the illumination of the nature of these particular people's world. Substantively I share little of Hoggart's world, but much of *The Uses of Literacy* was written about the South Yorkshire communities that concern this book and it is worth remembering that Hoggart's classic work has remained a standard reference for many educated middle class people who have no intuitive sense of the lives of working people and it thus seems appropriate to acknowledge Hoggart's contribution. Furthermore, for a generation of academics, the text enjoyed a kind of canonical status and the book remains in print at a time when publishers are not enthusiastic about works on class. The current status of the text indicates the power of the generation who currently control the institutions of academic culture. Yet, given how dated the text has become, one wonders, really, what it offers beyond nostalgia and the sense that things have improved. The text has become an irrelevance and the banality of its observations obscure truths one feels might always have been true for the class he described. There seems to me some justice in one critic's remarks that Hoggart's descriptions are reminiscent of 'a visiting anthropologist of a behaviourist persuasion'.[2] It is for these reasons that I chose to address myself to the notion of 'landscape' as a way of introducing insights that, whilst lacking the immediacy of Hoggart's descriptions, allow us, hopefully to see things of profound importance in working class existence that normally go unnoticed and unarticulated by working people because they constitute the unspoken, implicit sense that they come into being accepting as the necessary grounds of existence. We need to understand what it is that makes these people take up the relationship to the world that they do. If we can somehow grasp this, we might then articulate what is at the heart of their particular experience and find the larger truths of the forces that have marked these lives. The question is not, 'What do they do?' or 'How do they live?' but what is the sense of their experience beneath and around the particular experiences that they involve themselves in? The question is not simply that of 'lived experience', understood intentionalistically as the experiences of a subject dualistically involved in self-consciously monitoring and performing its activity whilst simultaneously enjoying an experience of that action; rather we need to understand the non-directed sense the world of action has that is deposited in the totality of practical and somatic forms given in the form of life and experienced within each personal life-trajectory as the long-duration of cumulative sense the world and each event in it has for subjects of this way of life and form of being.

Hoggart used the notion of a 'landscape' as a framing device, and, once we see why this device is flawed, my reasons for not pursuing what intui-tively must make most sense to readers, that is, to present a contemporary Hoggart-like 'landscape with figures', will be clear.

The notion of 'landscape' as a form of visual and textual representation is rooted, historically, in conventions of perspective originating in European art established early in the Renaissance (Berger 1972; Cosgrove 1984). These conventions of perspective make the surveyor's eye the centre of the visible world. Moreover, it is the vision of a spectator, divorced from a position within the world, free to survey the world *sub specie aeternitatis*, contemplating the scene surveyed as a 'landscape'. It is premised on 'the metaphysics of the present-at-hand and its bedfellow, the spectatorial premise' (Cooper 1990: 80). It involves a kind of absolute positionality. This stance is characteristic of anthropologists who, unable to orient themselves in a relation of immediate immanence to the world because of unfamiliarity, seek to relate to the particularities of place through the medium of representation. It is a representation that accounts for the detail of a world that unfamiliarity renders a 'scene' that demands an interpretation that solves, temporarily, the problem of the meaning of this space perceived from this standpoint of the spectator condemned to contemplation; rather than through involvement in the necessities and exigencies of the space as place. The relation of this mode of understanding to the lives of those to whom the place is familiar is like that of a map to those who know the place in another mode; except that this map is a visualization which deploys images whose meaning serves to produce a sense of familiarity born of preconstructed social knowledge, rather than a topographical schematic understanding of space divested of its lived sense.

Looking at the historical emergence of the idea of landscape, and focusing upon its visual or painterly dimensions, Cosgrove (1984) concludes that it is a restrictive way of seeing which privileges the position of outsider and their relation to the object. Moreover, this position implies the denial of any developed understanding of social and historical process: 'it is process [that] landscape as an ideological concept formally denies' (Cosgrove 1984: 32). The question confronting anyone concerned with a people's life in a place concerns the meaning of that place, and this is something that is foreclosed through the synopticism involved in the notion of Landscape. As Cosgrove suggests, 'there remains an aspect of meaning in landscape which lies 'beyond science', the understanding of which cannot be reduced to formal processes' (Cosgrove 1984: 17). We must retreat to the revelations of particularity, to living the life of the spaces, to the biorhythms of that geometry's population and the types of people the space and its use have created.

The idea of landscape substitutes the viewer's relation to the place for the people's own relation to it, because the conditions of that view have not been considered. Hoggart's 'Landscape with Figures', as a point of view, a way of seeing, implicates the point from which it is a viewing. It contains the clue to the conditions of possibility that give it its overwhelming plausibility as a subject-position for those likely to be consuming such an artefact of culture: it is an aestheticization. The work is a stylization of the world made to be consumed by subjects constituted in such a way that they constitute the object presented through the same schemata of perception, principles of vision, as that through which it was constructed, positing the world as spectacle and its people as 'figures' or 'characters'. This notional 'landscape with figures' is a horizon of consciousness in which phenomena are perceived in a quite different modality, one that is separate and antithetical. It tends towards a freezing of life, a suspension of time, and with it a resolution of all that temporality involves.

This is why we must avoid reproducing the errors involved in this presentation and find another medium through which to illuminate the processes that constitute a people and their place. This may help us avoid other presuppositions that are so prevalent in academic social commentary and appreciate that Rotherham does not exist for the people who live here as a landscape of symbols which mediate being towards different existential projects which involve coherent narratives of self and community. Rather, it is a series of spaces, in which some happened to be born at a particular historical moment and in which, often under pressure from state institutions, they manage to get through the points of the life-course relevant to them as best they can.

But what does *this* consist in? The notion of landscape, as far as I can see, is an attempt to portray the environmental character of the world, that space is a series of regions standing around the self; but it de-temporalizes the world and we do not get a sense of the primordial character of space as it is originally encountered as place. This encounter takes place through being born into a definite context of meaning carried in the ineffable details of the comportment we acquire from those around us, through which the world becomes meaningful as a subjective space, given in the objectivity we inherit through the mode of comportment through which we realize, unknowingly, a sense carried in all the elements of 'place' as a background structure of reference. Thus, we do not choose this 'there', or perspective or context, which we carry with us and which determines in advance our awareness, our apperceptions of the world. Individuals find themselves cast into a situation, which furnishes the context of plausibility, opportunity and decision. It is this context that operates as a clearing of sense opening a space of what is possible, what it *makes sense* to do. This practical sense of the realm of plausible possibilities embedded in the practices and discriminations realized in the comportment of the people in the place, gives sense to what an individual cannot choose to do or, even, what an individual may choose to do, only at the expense of doing something in pure privacy and meaninglessness. The space, or place, exists through realizable projects and availabilities, patterns of use and of users, all of which are practically negotiated daily. It is within this network, or field (Bourdieu 1990a), that things show up as possible and sensible, as though openings in the world solicit our realization of forms 'there to be done' as our realization of a commitment to life, our escape from inertia. An individual knows without much deliberation the range of the possible, and this is the realm of the unreflective sense common to the majority of the town's people. We might call this 'circumspection': a term Heidegger uses to describe the usual relationship between an individual and their environment: a kind of general everyday interaction with the world that exhibits a form of 'sight'. It is 'as if' self-conscious interpretation were manifest in co-ordinated, skilled interaction with the environment, yet this is achieved mostly without recourse to thematic awareness. This is possible because beneath the most basic directed intentionality of everyday coping, there is a background context which makes directedness possible. This unnoticed framework of practices and concerns is something in which we dwell: something that we take for granted and live *through*. It is the background within which things have significance, within which things show up as meaningful and actions have a point.

In this sense, we are not simply in the world, but rather we are amidst it, our world comes to inhabit us because we come to know it through our socialization into a way of being that discloses the world in a certain way, under certain aspects. Just as we inhabit language transparently, in that we are not aware of it establishing a space, or a clearing, of meaning through which we relate to others and the world, so, too, we inhabit the world through a network of non-referential coping practices and manners of comportment which imbue our experience of space with a non-referential sense that seems to inhere in space because it is our experience of spatiality. Thus, when we take in the world around us we do not synthesize a 'landscape' from multiple perspectives and sense-data, we do it through a background familiarity that can neither be reduced to specific self-referential actions, 'subjective intentionality nor objective muscle machinery' (Dreyfus 1994: 103), rather it is as habituated body-subjects, that we respond to solicitations contained in the environment. It is not a skill, but a readiness to cope with the situation enmired in the postural schemata and gestural *Gestalts* through which we deal with the world and involve ourselves in a human realm upon which the sense of the world arises as something 'given' or 'there', a pre-individual, pre-personal, anonymous order through which we find and fashion being-in-the-world. We can now recognize a non-cognitive intentionality through which we press into the possibilities available:

The phenomenal basis for seeing [existential possibilities] is provided by the understanding as a disclosive ability-to-be.   (Heidegger quoted in Dreyfus 1994: 191)

The realm of the possible is opened upon by one's ability to *be*. The existential possibility of unemployment, as well as its fear and anxiety, will show up as a possibility to someone who belongs to a social group likely to be consigned, by their comportment, to that social fate. Such an existential condition is unlikely to show up for someone whose ability to *be* discloses a world of opportunity. The existential possibility of being a successful university student and the sociality that it involves depends upon an ability to be, that is, upon a comportment based upon certain fundamental forms of corporeal hexis (those with positive status, high symbolic capital) that instantiate gestural and postural sets that manifest personality structures that relate internally to the social grounds which they manifest. The role of 'student' is given in one's ability to carry-off the absorbed, unselfconscious gestural repertoires through which an individual can open-up the possibilities of that international social universe.

If one is to encounter Rotherham as the place it is for those who have grown up here, then one must do so in the light of the understanding of being shared by those who inhabit it. But this cannot be done by simple observation. Because their perception of the town does not emerge from what is given occurrently[3] in the practices of the town. Perception need not be perception of objects. We have seen that the everyday way of acting in the world is one of absorbed coping or comportment, and need not involve an experience of a mental content, a 'decision' causing an appropriate bodily response; so too, perception need not be of visual experience, rather it may emerge from immersion in a realm that gives sense to sight[4] into which I am unselfconsciously absorbed. It is against this perceptual background that things are encountered when something 'out of the ordinary' occurs. This means that, on the whole, the place remains transparent to consciousness, and individuals do not consciously dwell on its characteristics, it is simply the 'there' of their lives which they press into, unknowingly, to realize their existence. Everyday being-in-the-world discloses the world, and 'looking' is a derivation that depends upon a more fundamental relation to the world that is mediated by life among others with whom we share our being-there as a way of being-in. Understanding Rotherham means understanding the habituated manner of comportment through which the place exists, *with* us.

This allows us to understand a fundamental anomaly that will emerge in this chapter, that the sense the town has to a spectator may be at odds with the life of the town. Rotherham town centre is kept clean and well decorated with flowers, and visitors often find it quite pleasant. Yet this is at odds with much of the description of the place by local people. There is thus nothing to be gained from describing the place as a spectacle: that is, by making the life of the town occurent, by removing chosen aspects of the hurly-burly of practices that go on at any one time, and de-contextualising them. Rather, we need a careful consideration of the sense that life has for Rotherham people. That is, a consideration that understands *their* being-in-the-world in the context of the kind of understanding of being-in-the-world contained in the works of Heidegger, Merleau-Ponty and Bourdieu. It is important to reconstruct the immediacy of the problems involved in living in and through certain spaces. The description that will emerge is that of engaged subjectivity, it is that of circumspection, of the place as it shows up within the horizons of the awareness involved in everyday comportment towards the situations and contexts of being in Rotherham. It is a presentation of place embedded in the problems involved in living in and through the relational-context of class that region mediates, a 'space' defined by the universe of forces that influence its contours and which also define our experience of place spatially and, for want of a better word, morally – that is, to ourselves and each other.

All of this makes experience of Rotherham what it is, while Rotherham itself, as the situation of existence, as a referential whole in which to seek satisfaction and life, may remain almost invisible, except for those points when it frustrates and thwarts human projects and it stands out as obstinate and conspicuous and we proclaim the abjectness of all that traps us. So, the town may have little objectified or representational meaning to those who live in it. Their feelings have nothing to do with the physical and material structures of the space in which they live and emerge from cultural relations that are not themselves *in* Rotherham. Readers who want exoticized descriptions of a strange way of life will be disappointed, because many of the peculiar stories oral historians used to record concerning the relation between working class life and the work process have gone. The people who tramp the streets because they have no jobs will not have the same stories to tell because all they have known is nothingness, the void of a life lacking meaningful spatial and temporal structure, and the invisibility of lacking an identity invested with a value recognized by others. It is a sense captured by one man:

Yer wun't [would not] believe it but Ah [I] w'ked fo eighteen y'r in pit an' then Ah've dun' nowt but bi unemployed. Life ended when Ah finished in pit an' it an't never started again. All thi's [there has] bin [been] is this nothingness. Mi life stopped. Ah'll niver [never] w'k age'an [again] an' so this is it fo' me, *forever*! Just bein' stuck wi' nowt!

This manifests the conditions that younger people have only known. A younger man expressed his sense of fate in the following way:

Let's face it, Ah [I] mean wi' wo' the forgotten generation 'cos thi' wo' no jobs fo' us an' thi' nowt fo' us to du. Wi' wo' just cheap labour t' keep wages dahn [down], an' no fucker wanted us. Wi' wo' the lost children 'r Thatcher's government, Ah mean, if thi' could'a done, thi'd a gassed us like thi' did in Germany cos wi wo' neither use n' fuckin' ornament. Wi' n' good fo' any fucker, n' good fo' us families, n' good t' us'selns an' n' use t' employers. Ah mean, thi' wo' nowt [nothing] fo' us, not a fuckin' thing. An' nahr [now] some'r us 'a [are] educated all that's appenin' is wi' bringin' dahn wages in what wi trained fo', yer ohnny 'ave t' look at FE [Further Education]. Ah've a job t' earn eight grahnd a year. Ahr lass earns mo'ore than me but wi' can't all train up an' w'k in'ealth services can wi?

Both these quotations in different ways make clear the personal effects of living a life devoid of the co-ordinates of social value. The reference to Germany and gassing is perhaps overstated for some people's taste but it is a reference that I have come across before and betrays a deep sense of these people's sense of themselves as devoid of value and utility. It shows a personal understanding of self-worth in terms of economic utility, a sense implicit in the culture of the labouring class. We can see, perhaps, some of the reasons why the youngest of the class, now, have given up on that traditional ethos of work and self-respect but why they have found little to construct a valued identity on beyond transgression. A person devoid of respect will tend towards transgression of the accepted forms of valuation, because – since they cannot be invested with the value of forms they cannot embody – their own strategy has to be that of subversion: of embracing and even celebrating their alienation as an emblem of what it is: their humanity, a human form that is degraded and stigmatized.

It is familiarity that is the modality of our knowing and perceiving Rotherham. Merleau-Ponty has taught us that our knowledge emerges from the stream of everyday life, from our practices: that it is a mode of doing, making knowledge and being specific to forms of practical engagement with the world. So, different ways of seeing or perceiving the world, depend upon our particular immersion in life as mediated by the culture and practices in which we are immersed: from which there emerges a way in which the world around us manifests itself to us. Our relation to place concerns more than an inert spatiality and includes our involvement with the world and other people. Our understanding must, therefore, contain a sense of destiny and fate, because being born into particular class locations at a particular historical moment involves individuals in being cast into a temporal frame and trajectory, that manifests the effects on individuals of overarching social and class processes that affect the life-course in all its details of living and being. The person attempts, through particular circumstances that call for particular resolutions involving the expenditure of life-time, to cope with a world in which they face a finite range of realizable possibilities. Knowing a place, therefore, exhibits a particular form of making manifest the problems of that world from the standpoint of practice.

Thus, characterizing an area through a description based upon observation the purpose of which is to create 'observations' which depict the place in relation to established academic literatures may be an enterprise that creates a sense of the place that is quite different from that of the experience of its inhabitants. People go about their daily lives and press into the available possibilities and at the level of the surface, of what we can see, there is little worthy of remark or note. But those who encounter Rotherham through a different route to knowledge, as the field of their existence and route to being; as a collection of resources in which to grow up and be in a life, would probably agree with an unemployed man who made the remark:

looking at Rother'am, yer know, if ye' [you] di'n't live 'ere [here] and know it, ye'd [you'd] think it wo' [was] a really nice place. Yer just can't see what it's like to live 'ere.

This person is suggesting that knowing the place involves something deeper than simply seeing it, that there is an experience of place that is intertwined with one's experience of life, or with how one's life is mediated by the institutional sites and public locations that individual experience takes place amidst. It is

the life of consciousness – cognitive life, the life of desire or perceptual life – is subtended by an 'intentional arc' which projects around about us our past, our future, our human setting, our physical, ideological and moral situation, or rather which results in our being situated in all these respects. It is this intentional arc which brings about the unity of the senses, of intelligence, of sensibility and motility.

(Merleau-Ponty 1962: 136)

This arc of intentionality is a projecting of a field of disclosedness, a space in which we encounter the world as a place in which we reach towards self-determination and realization by moving through this medium that is always more or less resistant and in which all distances are relative to position. This space of disclosure in which our intentional projection is embedded is the 'there' of absorbed coping and it exists as a space of determinate existential possibilities which in constituting the present, constrains the future. This public realm of implicit experiential meanings, the background in which individuals find themselves engaged in coping responses, through a network of sites, is how individuals come to be situated, socially, through comportment, both subjectively and objectively, in regard to an objective future inscribed in the position they occupy by being working class and living in Rotherham. The class habitus constituted through this experience provides a sense of the scope and practicality of their ambition, a sense of what they might aspire to possess and of what they might reasonably expect to achieve (and the obstacles that they might have to overcome). Our understanding must help us appreciate the extent to which the people of the town internalize a relation to culture that is a relation to the world, to themselves and to others that amounts to a heavily prescribed way of being; through a 'myriad of 'small perceptions' of everyday life' (Bourdieu 1990b: 5) that act as unnoticed, unrecognized sanctions which 'imperceptibly constitute, from childhood and throughout one's life, by means of constant reminders, this 'unconscious' which becomes paradoxically defined as a practical reference to objective conditions' (Bourdieu 1990b: 5). The town is not an 'objective' aesthetic space to the people, but a space in which they live and which inscribes in their lived-being dispositions that they enact as conditions of engagement with that reality, and which allows them to deal with the exigencies of their life; and this, in turn, marks them in objective social hierarchies as the objective beings they are. The 'sanctions' of experience are obvious in the speech of a young man of fifteen years of age who spoke to me about his experience of school:

S: What du [do] yer mek'r [make of] school?
It's not rait [right] good.
S: What meks yer se' [say] that?
Ah dun't see n' point in it. People wi' good grades end up du'in' fuck all, what's point?

Clearly, in areas like this, it is too clear to young people how constraining the labour market is and how worthless qualifications have become. This man, like many, could speak of older brothers and sisters who had trained for different jobs and yet never escaped the vulnerability of unemployment and Government Training Schemes. That the space of realizable possibilities, of what is available, of the realm of what it makes sense to do, is circumscribed by the horizons constituted by education, training and unemployment is indicated by one woman who remarked scornfully:

Ma' [my] son thi'v [they've] med [made] 'im gu [go] on these trainin' schemes an' its just cheap labour. Thi' [they] 'ad 'im trainin' t' be a welder, an then hi wo back on dole; then thi' 'ad 'im doin' joinery on ET [Employment Training] an' then hi' wo' back on dole age'an; *nah* [now] thi'v got 'im do'in' fork-lift truck drivin', so Ah guess next hi'll bi an unemployed fork-lift truck driver.

The practices, concerns and available paths of self-determination are circumscribed by a local economy that is intimately linked to regimes of education and training and to the mediations of the Department of Social Security. These networks are experienced as occasionally intrusive, and yet generally they are present amidst the background, or referential whole in which these lives take place. The space of realizable projects is mediated by this space. Even, those who are successful in escaping the direct solicitations of this space, must practically acknowledge and engage with how this exists, in the comportment and behaviours of others. This realm of 'familiarity in accordance with which Dasein . . ."knows its way about" in its public environment' (Heidegger 1962: 405), the set of comportment habits that are constantly active as our everyday orientation, our 'absorbed coping' is manifest in comments like the following:

It's like, in ahr [our] life, if wi wo' nice t' too many people, yer know, at dole [Social Security benefit] place an' that, ye'd just get tekken [taken] fo' a cunt. Yer would, thi'd [they would] fuckin' walk all ovva [over] yer.

Yet this kind of comportment is itself a response to a prevalent anxiety about one's social vulnerability that, while, it is a response to anxiety, also maintains that possibility within its horizons. Hence, the meaning of the place is infused with the experience of these sites. And these experiences operate as 'sanctions' that, through the threat of personal costs, 'encourage' individuals to pursue strategies, that whilst accommodated to the immediate demands of the social realm, curtail possible forms of self-realization. That the space of self-realization is dependent upon negotiating this space through what are effectively existential structures,[5] is clear in the following discussion among three female students discussing the immediate problem of getting some money whilst trying to escape their current predicament of low-waged work:

X: Ah'm tranna [trying to] sign-on. Are you signed on?
Y: Yeh, yer [you] 'ave t' [have to] get a learnin' contract from 'em [Department of Social Security] an' get W [teacher] to sign it fo' yer. Shi' did mine.
Z: An't [haven't] yer got n' money?
X: Naow [no]. Ah've [I've] gi'd [given] up mi job at kennels. Thi' [they] wo' [were] just treatin' mi [me] like shit. It wo' [was] 'ard w'k [work] an' shit money. Trouble is yer can't get nu [no] dole 'cos yer've [you have] got t' [to] bi [be] lookin' fo' w'k. An' yet all jobs are shit. So yer gu t' college t' giy yerself a chance 'a sumaht better but yer can't get n' money. Ye' ca't [can't] du both: yer can't get yerself off'a [off of] unemployed bi' betterin' yerself wi' education an' get a job.
Z: Thi' [they] ought t' leave yer alone if yer studyin'
X: Yeh but yer 'ave t' show em that yer lookin' fo' work t' get any money . . .
Y: Yeh, yer can't just se' yer at college.
Z: Du yer want t' gu t' university?
X: [*Negatively*] Ah dun't know. Ah' don't think so. Ah'm twenty nahr. Ah dun't know what Ah want t' du. Thi'r in't nowt really. Ah like science but Ah'm crap at it. [S: Du science X! Du science!] Ah said t' mi Mum other day. Ah said, 'Mum du yer think Ah'm clever?' An' shi said 'ye, course yer clever.' An' Ah said, ye' but du yer *really* think Ah'm clever?
S: Yer are clever X.

Z: yer should gu to university.
X: Ah just dun't know what Ah want t' du or whether Ah want t' gu.
Y: Yer get fed up wi'y it all dun't yer?
Z: What d' you want t' du Y?
Y: Ah've applied t' du primary school teachin' but Ah dun't know whether Ah want
    t' du it an' Ah dun't know if Ah'll get in. It's rait 'ard t' get in t' du, nah. [*nega-
    tively*] Ah really dun't know if it's worth gu'in'.

Clearly their present takes place in relation to a need to resolve the problem
of what they can do in life. Their opportunities are delineated by the work
opportunities that confront them, which they see as negative and something to be escaped but they realize that education is the only way for them
to escape low wages and poor conditions but this involves them in conflict
with the Department of Social Security because without work they need an
income which must come from benefit but they can't claim benefit unless
they are 'actively seeking work', so they are caught in a bind that demands
lies and the strain of deceit. Yet they are also troubled by questions concerning their own abilities and by whether they can firstly get into a university and then by doubts about the value of an education to them. But, in
the meantime, their experience of the present remains one of resolving the
problem of what to do with the now, to waste life in poorly remunerated
shit work or the gamble that education is for people of this category
without the confidence or symbolic and cultural capital to enjoy and make
successful an education-generated career. These incessant doubts that
silently nag at the conscience of working class people is acknowledged by
one man:

Ah [I] mean, when Ah left school, Ah trained up as a tool-mekker [tool-maker] an'
cun't [could not] see a future in it, although Ah'd nahr [now] bi better off if Ah'd [I
had] stayed in that, but Ah went to (t') Tech [technical college] t' du mi 'A' levels[6] an'
Ah just remember bein' scared all time 'cos Ah din't think Ah wo' clever enough t'
du it. Ah mean wi [we] wo' never brought up fo' any'r [any of] that an' all thi' did at
school wo' [*voice rises*] tell us ahr thick wi' wo' s' when Ah wo' doin' 'A' level Ah just
rememebr bein' racked wi' worry ovva whether Ah wo actually good enough or
whether Ah wo' just wastin' mi time. An' Ah rememebr talkin' to a lot'r people in
them classes who felt same. It weren't just me.

An important part of the conditions of their situation are thus these
realm of questions that emerge from social structures that delineate the
existential space of their existence. Moreover, this range of questions is
then mediated by the constantly intruding presence of the Department of
Social Security and its regimes of self-surveillance which force people to
apply for jobs as a precondition of having the money to try and 'better
themselves'. It is clear in the personal testimony that the world of these
people is disclosed through a socially mediated 'mood', or sense, that is

rooted in their objective situation, that is, in what the school and the context it led to, has led them to feel about themselves and their position. For the women, it is clear that they are both doubtful about their own abilities and pessimistic about the opportunities offered by a possible education the price of which is an extension of the current situation indefinitely, with the added problem of debt. It is a wise set of anxieties since so many of the previous generation have paid the price of a worthless education, as the man quoted earlier put it:

Education's a waste'r time fo' people like us. Ah mean, ahr [how] many'r lads wi' wo' at college wi' 'ave got anywhe'er? . . . Ah mean, Ah'd a bin [I would have been] better off as a tool-mekker. Ah mean, look at me, Ah've bin to university, Ah mean, Ah chose t' du sumaht vocational to avoid all shit that tha's [you've] bin through 'cos Ah allous had a sense that it weren't oppan t' [open to] us, but Ah've [I've] left university an' nahr Ah've 'ad t' gu [had to go] back t' agency w'k whe'er [work where] Ah' w'ked when Ah f'st [first] left school! Thi's [there is] lads the'er wo' [there who were] the'er when Ah wo', an' th'r miles better off than me, thi' din't get in debt gu'in' through university, thi' din't gu through the loneliness o' them colleges an' thi' an't wasted the'r lives endin' up stuck back wheer thi' wo' like us soft cunts'ave thi'? . . . Ah mean, Ah'm lucky, Ah've got a nice wife who stands by mi, shi' earns mo'ore than me, shi's main bread-winner in ahr family an' it dun't bother 'er, but it would a lot'r women. In that respect Ah'm lucky. But, well, [*voice drops*] it's all a load'r bollocks fo' us, education. Ah mean, Ah remember gu'in' t' [going to] college an' it wo' a fuckin' nightmare. Ah mean, Ah' wo', what, twen'y-five an' Ah wo' surrounded by these knob 'eads: way thi' laughed an' things thi' laughed at. Ah used t' look at 'em an' think 'What'r the fuckers laughin' at?' thi'd laugh abaht [about] stuff that wo' just *not* funny an' talk abaht [about] drag it aht [out]: thi'd still bi laughin' abaht same stupid fuckin' thing a week later! The'r sense'r 'umour an' everythin's just weird. It wo' a nightmare, worst days'r ma life, Ah wo' glad t' ged [get] aht. But it wo' just a waste, yer keep gu'in' fo' yer qualifications an''cos yer an't got nowt t' gu back t' but truth is that employers want twenty-one y'r old kids wi' degrees straight from college,'cos thi' don't know the'r arse from the'r elbows an' the'r miles better t' employ than cunts like us, so it's all a waste'r time fo' people like us.

With experiences like this now common in the area, there is little wonder that the young working class understand these problems, as the words of an eighteen-year-old man made explicit:

X: Ah'm [I'm] studyin' these 'A' levels an' Ahy [I] an't [haven't] a clue what Ah can du [do]. Ah wo' thinkin'a du'in' law but unless yer du it at a good university yer can't get a job.

S: Ah know it's 'ard in it?

X: Yeh. Ah dun't know, what t' du. Ah dun't wanna bi just stuck 'ere but thi's [there is] a lot'a people what've bin [been] t' uni an' come back an' are as stuck as ever. Yer might 'as well try an' work an' get a car an' 'ave them years in bag wiy'aht [without] giyin' [giving] up an' gettin' in debt fo what might bi nowt [nothing].

S: Well ahr but trouble is tha needs t' bi able to get a decent job an' the'r aren't s' many rahnd 'ere.

X: Studyin' shit, really though, in it? [S: Yeh, Ah'll giy yer that . . .] Ye' better off t' try an' 'ave a life nah [now], *Ah think*, get a car, some nice clothes, 'ave best life yer can.

This man has an obvious understanding of the risks involved in university education and knows that, for him, it may be a financial waste. This conversation makes clear the extent to which the background context that makes directedness possible is impacted upon by sites which impinge upon the sense of the public realm of these lives. Moreover, the public sites which meet in public space and define the biographical location of these individuals' existence, have consequences for the way the meaning of their lives, and the way aspects of the social realm, show-up for them and resonate with affective *sense*. This is manifest in the woman's questioning of her intelligence and in these people's reservations about university and any possible career. Living in this space must affect their future relation to public institutions. What emerges is an anxiety, pessimism and inertia based in the objective opportunities inscribed in the fields that mediate their social existence: a pessimistic inertia based in the sanctions of a social realm that has levelled so many and left them unable to escape. The struggle, anxiety and duress involved in this life emerged from a twenty-six-year-old man's comments:

X: A've [I have] 'ad [had] to come off dole [social security benefit] nahr [now], A' [I] just got sick o'r [of] it, thi' [they] wo' [were] hasslin' mi, an' hasslin' mi an' in end Ah [I] just cun't [could not] tek [take] it anymo'or. Every four weeks thi' wo' [was] sayin' to mi, 'What 'ave you applied fo'?' an' A'd [I would] se', 'oh A've 'ad no luck.' but then thi'd se', 'well tell us the companies ye've applied fo' and we'll ring 'em up and ask 'em' (S: Really!) Yeh! But A'm tellin' yer, Simon, the'r in't anythin' fo us in that job centre. Ah mean, why employ me when yer can employ an' eighteen year old fo' cheaper who yer can mould into the slave yer want? If yer an't got a career by ahr [our] age, yer fucked man because all the jobs are short term, money's fuckin' rubbish an' thi basically want young kids fo' 'em anyway. An' thi' se' to me up the'er, 'ye'v got to tek [take] sumat [something]. Ye' must be prepared to do anythin.' An' shi' tried to get mi to tek a bar job an' I ses to 'er, 'Look, it's against my religion to touch alcohol. Ah don't like bein' around the stuff, Ah don't like the smell of it, Ah don't like to bi near it. It's bad fo' people an' it's against ma religion to be involved wi' giyin' [giving] it t' people.' So she ses, ye'v got to come back in three days an' if ye'v not applied fo' nothin' then we're suspendin' yer benefit. So, A've come off'r dole nah, an' A've had to ask mi wife to sign on. That's why Ah want to do that at college 'cos at least it'll keep (t') Social off'r mi back fo' a year.

And, living in such a space, means that one must, to smooth one's passage, adopt the comportment that has evolved to smooth one's way in these locations.[7] So one adopts the forms of cynicism and realistic pessimism that allow one to confront a world in which nothing is ideal and in which sacrifices are demanded. Through the endlessly repeated, 'small perceptions' of constraint and worthlessness, one imbibes, without knowing, alongside the habits of surviving, an 'unconscious' that the world ensures our bodies never forget. Moreover, bearing this kind of personality, this 'prickliness' and subdued aggression, bearing the marks of the conditions of acquisition of the habits to survive this world, mean that our origins are imprinted within the very form of our being. Such an 'unconscious' and its conditions of acquisition, is perhaps best exemplified by an extended quotation from a young man, speaking about his experience of school:

S: If yer could mek [make] school better, ahr would yer like it to be?

X: Err. Well, if thi' [they] treated us wi' [with] mo'ore [more] respect.

S: Se', [say] if people who wo teachin' yer wo' [was] mo'ore like wot, se', Ah [I] am? And thi' [they] understood yer [you] more an' [and] that. Du yer think ye'd get on better?

X: Ye, 'cos [because] the'r big 'eads, thi' [they] think the'r better than we are. Ahrr, [yes] thi wun't be as much faitin' [fighting] either, cos faitin' it's tekkin all tension aht'a [out of] yer, an' [and] people who gu [go] rahnd [around] mouthin' off at yer an' pushin yer when yer not watchin' an' 'ittin' [hitting] yer in back 'er [of the] 'ead . . .

S: Does all that gu on then?

X: Oh arrgh [yes]. Bricks an' lot gu [go] in. My mate who gus boxing who used to gu theer [there (to a boxing club)] befo'ore [before] me, he 'ad a fait [fight] wi a kid from Treeton, this kid who I gu boxin' wi, this kid 'ad been arsing abaht [about] wi' [with] 'is [his] girlfriend, so this kid he ses 'just leave 'er alone, I dun't want to fait wi' yer, I know yer can fait mi' let's just leave it'. After lesson, dragged 'im in to arches, this kid from Treeton, dragged 'im into arches, yer know big Caterpillar boots? [S: Ye] Steel toe capped, kicked all his face in wi' them, jumped up on 'is head, [S: yer joking!] he 'ad cuts dahn 'ere, 'is face wo a rait mess, his eye wo' like that [*gestures with hand at swollen and bruised eye*], both eyes, all his nose.

S: Unbelievable, that's ahr yer kill people. I know lads who're like, 'ard [hard], who'r bouncers an' that who se' [say] thi'd never stamp on anyone's head cos that's 'ow yer kill sombody, it's fucking unreal that.

X: Thi' do though. It 'appens.

S: Du you fait a lot at school?

X: Ah fait when it comes to me, if I need to. I don't gu looking for it, thi's [there is] no point in looking for it. But if anybody ses 'owt . . . [*pause*] . . . It's not often anybody ses 'owt though anyway, if yer rait enough wi everybody and yer don't act as though yer better, it's alrait. No trouble. Ah've 'ad a few faits, abaht twenty odd faits, not that many, not a lot, not as many as some people.

S: Du yer get in trouble a lot?

X: [*spoken with a kind of unreconciled sadness*] Ahr, Ah'm in headmasters office tomorrer. [*sighs*]. Ahr, we just got back today. [*For a new school year after the summer holidays*] 'Cos last year wi' 'ad this time-sheet thing, in't [in the] staff room and every time yer mis-behaved in lessons teacher put dahn what lesson it were, wot yer did, wot yer name were, and I went, thi's loads a people 'ad 'em in ahr year, abaht fifty odd people that's 'ad these interview things wi 'ead master and't [the] year tutor and I went today and she ses 'right ye'v been on this list twenty-seven times', I cun't [could not] believe it me, all things she wo sayin' that 'ad been do'in', and then she said I wo' bullyin' people. I ses, 'I might'a dun all rest but I an't bullied people'.

S: Ye, I know, cos I can tell yer not a bully.

X: Mi brother wo bullied.

S: Wo'r'i [Was he]?

X: Ye, rait bad an' all. He used to get 'is face bashed in rait bad and get money tuk [taken] off 'im an' lot. I 'it one o'r 'em an' i' wo massive. I just din't like it. I din't like 'ow [how] i' [he] wo talkin' to mi [my] Mum an' that, yer know ovver it, gettin' it all out in' 'ouse instead 'er out on streets. So, he just 'it mi like that, I wo ohnny a first year, I wo ohnny abaht that 'igh an' he wo massive. He wo abaht same size as you, a rait big stocky kid, but thi' picked on littlest in class, thi din't pick on anyone the'r own size.

S: The'r always like that. [*Pause*] That must mek yer life a misery, then, livin' wi' that?

X: [*Voices lowers with sadness*] It's not very nice we'er we live. I mean, it's alrait like, thi's rait enough people, the's [there is] as many nice people as the'r [there] is rotten people, but rotten people aren't rait nice, I mean, 'im that got bullied, he wo set on fire, he wo' set on fire, X. Jesus, [*sighs*] God.

I have quoted this at length because it brings to light the nature of this environment as a place illuminated by a certain form of everyday living, of a certain interpretation of being. The testimony makes clear the extent to which the primary experiences of class rest in the inscription within an individual's comportment of a 'stock' of responses that exist in the shared environmental-whole through which people forge a life amidst a world that can be brutal and demeaning. Living in a world of continual possible threats like this, in which one must be prepared to 'fait . . . when it comes t' me, if I need to', involves one in absorbing somatically and habitually skills and forms of comportment that render one able to cope with the necessary exigencies of such an environment. And becoming habituated to such conditions involves the totality of one's comportment, it involves a whole system of aspects of awareness and embodied response that relate to a practical knowledge of the social realm in which one lives. If we accept Being-in-the-world as a unitary structure and understand a form of life 'in what it does, uses, expects, avoids – in the environmentally available with which it is primarily concerned' (Heidegger 1962: 155) – then what can we make of a world in which there is so little available, so much to avoid and in which expectations are so circumscribed? An answer to this is contained in the things that matter, in the ethos of the people concerned, in the aspects through which their world is disclosed and some of this is manifest in their talk. What they do, use, expect and have to avoid, is partially rendered in their conversation. What emerges is the extent to which the horizon of possibilities, what is there to be done, unfolds through a space whose contours are shaped by the local economy and its effects on the public culture and by the institutions of the Department of Social Security, Job Centre and educational institutions. Alongside this, they must cope with the environment as a space of people whose shared way of comporting themselves makes possible certain forms of respect whilst curtailing others. It is as though the way of being of those among whom one lives is infectious, as though one has to take it into oneself, regardless. To the young man quoted above, the place clearly shows up as negative, as one frustrating human self-realization. Even at fifteen, even in the face of his knowing no qualitatively better realm, he is aware that it isn't very nice where he lives. Moreover, his speech manifests the internal relation of this to his own way of being. There is an implicit acknowledgement that the conditions he describes involve him in forms of comportment acquired in order to maintain a level of dignity. This, however, then has consequences for him because it becomes part of a general 'attitude' to existence; part of the most intimate way the world is meaningful for him. Furthermore, the necessity of dealing with this as the condition for securing the possibilities that depend upon security and non-vulnerability – like the personal growth contained in the respect of others, feeling pleasure, the enjoyment of involving oneself in the world of others and finding justification in being what one is – disappears in the performative charade of dignity demanded by the maintainance of an integrity of self in the face of the moral, physical and psychic violations of this world.

The young man's speech brings the nature of this into view. There is here a distinct set of dispositions and a distinct way of feeling about the world which have an ethical dimension and which the environment 'demands' for passage through it to be 'smooth'. There is an emphasis upon a certain form of respect, that which people of little social status or objective value have traditionally created among themselves to permit them some circumscribed self-respect, however impoverished. This allows the 'decent' a circumscribed, limited, sense of human decency even though, as a form, in these areas, it is in decline. This man, working as he does every morning before school, already has a life which imitates shift work in its rhythms, and in that sense a pattern of his life is set, he has already learnt *this* life and the practical limitations of his sphere of existence. Embedded in the transparent coping demanded by such an environment, this man finds his being, there to be taken up in the patterns of habit and expression that are there, pre-existing, which have sprung from the ground of possibility contained in the environment into which he was born. That this is an environment of the levelled is manifest in the demand that one treat people equally, through a certain non-affected, bodily respect, 'if yer rait enough wi everybody and yer don't act as though yer better, it's alrait. No trouble.' What he is describing is the extent to which he must demonstrate in his corporeal style, his bodily hexis, a certain manner that must not be too obtrusive nor affected, that must not be able to be read as superiority. An ethos of the common, exhibited in common forms of address, an' 'alrait mate' or 'nah then yer fat bastard', a recognition and mark of respect that is part of a matrix of comportment-aspects that denote social position through which an equality is realized and experienced without this rising to the level of a formal ritual or an overt performance of honour. Being 'rait enough wi everybody' is a particular style that marks working class people to one another, and it emerges from the same practical sense of the world that creates tension for them when confronted with formal and semi-formal situations, or linguistic markets which demand the competence of legitimate speakers. In the transcribed speech we can see the habitus manifest as a system of durable dispositions to perceive and act; a set of embodied dispositions; postural and gestural sets, that are invested with values that characterize people's feelings about the world and which register the grounds of possibility of those feelings. It is comportment that gives the world to us and which make us what we are. When this man suggests: 'I din't like 'ow i' wo talkin' to mi Mum an' that, yer know ovver it, gettin' it all out in' 'ouse instead 'er out on streets . . .' there is displayed a basic need that the violations of the self not be brought into the private realm of intimate care-giving relationships which are personified by the mother. There is a strong concern that what has to be dealt with, be dealt with silently and with a stoical courage that, fearing the worst, confronts these conditions. This coping absorption anchors cognition, disclosing this world affectively in comportment, a way of knowing that is founded in the things that have to be done to get through the immediate moment and satisfy the demands of the future it contains. Environments 'trap' us because ways of feeling are connected to ways of being, a practical solidarity akin to commonality rather than conscious commitment that emerges from comportment; from the shared dispositions which make life in such places bearable. Thus a virtue comes to be made of necessity.[8]

We come to have a primary identification with the physiognomic perceptions of our comportment because our embodiment, our motility, is a real competence to us, something we deploy to bring people towards us, to enact a solidarity, to seek a solace amidst this turmoil. Yet in the conditions of our achievement of the comportment and forms of motility that are ours, amidst the degradation of the matrix of school, local economy, job centre and Social Security offices, we embroil ourselves more deeply in dispositions that entrap us as the objective beings we are. This man's commitment to who he and his family are, will never endear him to teachers, who can only accuse him of being a bully because they know of his commitment to that dignified and honoured practice of boxing. The ethical dimensions of the habitus are clear in this man's constant desire for peace and respect, and yet one sees his desire for respect being affirmed only through his capacities to resist: first to resist the teachers' insults and then to have to fight for himself and, if necessary, his brothers.

Yet it is in the description of an environment which puts these people under a barrage of differing negative influences that Bourdieu's insights really begin to emerge. In the transcription there is a sense of the negative solicitations contained in the fields which constitute the background of these lives. A further example of the 'small perceptions' of the background of individuals' lives emerges when the young man talks about his working life. Even though he is only fifteen, it emerges that he is already familiar with the feelings and dispositions of the shift-worker and is attuned to the commitments and way of being of the class to which, by experience, he belongs. The environment of his body has deeply shaped his perception of the world, but it is a world, as he describes it, that is not that of a 'Landscape with figures', but an account rich with the primal significances of the phenomenal body, of its sensuousness: here, of exhaustion:

S: Are you still working?
W: Ye, I'm du'in milk though nahr [now].
S: What did yer used to du?
W: Papers.
S: What, in't mornin'?
W: Err, mornin' and night, ye, I du some rait [right] hours.
S: Tell's abaht that then. Tell's, what times yer usually get up fo' that.
W: Abaht alfe five [about 5.30], quart' to six time, in mornin' and du [do] them straight from school, I used to, like, do at least thirteen paper rahnds a week and I used to get, what, fifteen quid back.
S: Did yer used to get up at alfe five and gu aht' [go out].
W: Ye, I'd du that for abaht [about] an 'our and then if I wanted to I could gu back to bed or else I could sit up watch telly or somat.
S: Then at night when yer got in from school, ye'd du it again?
W: Ye.
S: Wot's yer routine nahr [now]?
W: Well. I w'k [work] three days a week on' milk. This week's it's Mond'y, Tuesd'y, Wensd'y. Last week it wo' Wensd'y, Thursd'y, Frid'y, I w'k three days a week, but

them three days, s' next week it'll be Wensdy, Thu'sd'y, Frid'y, then back to Mond'y and I get up at abaht quart to four, an' I 'ave to gu dahn to, yer know bottom 'r Swallownest. [S: 'Naow.'] No, well it's just dahn end o'r't road an I 'ave to be theer for half past four an' . . .

S: Fuck'in 'ell.

W: I know.

S: At least that's three days a week. An ahr much du yer get fo that?

W: A fiva a day. It's not too bad. It's abaht three hours w'k but it's piss easy. Now't to it.

S: So it's three hours.

W: It's good fo' arms an all, yer know, liftin' milk an that.

S: It's still a lot three hours befo'or school.

W: Wi mi' boxin' like, I'm knackered. Like I'm tired nahr. [*8.15pm*]

S: Ye, I bet you are. 'Ave yer done one this mornin'?

W: Ye. It's alrait [alright] when yer up for an hour or so but then it starts tellin' on yer an yer eyes start shuttin' an that [*laughs*].

S: I bet it 'its yer abaht ten o'clock in't mornin' dun't it?

W: Ye, that's exactly when it 'its me that. When I've 'ad a cup'o tea an' that. I got 'ome from school tonight an' I walked upstairs [*voice intimates heaviness*], sat on mi bed, put music on, just put mi 'ead back an I wo asleep. That wo it, just gone.

The issues raised by this piece of transcription exemplify the relevance of understanding Heidegger's and Merleau-Ponty's insights if we are to understand what Bourdieu denotes as 'doxa'. The central question that emerges from a position outside of this context, the traditional question asked by radicals, is how can individuals live in such conditions and not become possessed of a consuming sense of the injustice contained in the details of their own experience? Yet this is the wrong question. Rather we need to understand why this does not rise to the forefront of consciousness, why individuals do not foreground the overall context of their practical lives. And it seems to me that Heidegger offers us a way to appreciate why this is so. If we accept the 'background as an originary kind of intentionality' (Dreyfus 1994: 238), as a kind of constant coping; of an absorbed responding to conditions disclosed by the habitus and ethos of the group to which one belongs, then we might appreciate how it is possible to live a life that is heavily circumscribed without necessarily understanding it in terms of linguistic procedures that constitute life 'transparently' in reflection as an object of conscious awareness. The political efficacy of this acceptance of the daily life-world is clear in this man's belief that the money earned is 'not too bad' and the work 'easy', even when he has to get up at hours his teachers are likely never to have worked. His acceptance of the injustice of working so early at such a young age is unquestioning. It demonstrates that this doxic relation to the world, for the dominated, is the most absolute form of conservatism. There is no more profound adherence to the established order than that pre-reflective conformism that emanates from one's sense of possibilities being the internalization of the opportunities inscribed in one's position.

It is as if the world speaks to us all from birth; as though we are constantly in communion with the mystery of an as yet unlived future that speaks to us, magically, of our place in the world of things and the universe of ways of life; such that we know, without mediation, who and what is ours, what we dare hope for and what we must fear. But this 'speaking' is that of the mime, for it articulates a sense that is indeterminate – and necessarily so, because these are original experiences that produce the means of thinking about the world, because the means to think discursively about the world emerge from what Merleau-Ponty calls the apprehension of 'an immanent sense in the sensible before judgement begins' (Merleau-Ponty 1962: 35). It is because meaning inheres in the social world that the dominated might be said to be 'condemned to meaning', in that the meaning of their social position flows through them as body-subjects and is too often something they are passively subject to. Looking at the young man above, confronted with such an environment, what chance does he have to turn away from it and take up his being-in-the-world, apart from labour and boxing? This man has qualities of engagement and decency, of a certain form of care, but his objective being is that of someone of his class, and he has little choice but to take up the corporeal style of a habitus based around a respect that is itself that of fractured, damaged people and which is based upon the sublimated threat of a potential capacity for physical aggression. Without this he risks, like his brother, moving from (minimally) self-respecting subject to object and target. Thus, it is a meaning that working people are condemned to live through, as the form of life that their environment offers. The environment itself, through its impact on the habitus of different age-cohorts, offers this sense that produces the sense of limits inscribed unknowingly in the ordering of the world. We must, therefore, follow Merleau-Ponty and reflect upon the unreflected, and hear beneath the voices a sense of this 'lost world'. A world lived through as the grounds of the body-subject, yet which, as the pre-personal grounds of identity, is seldom remarked upon or made the object of conscious reflection, and which manifests itself in occasional articulations, in snippets of conversation when thrown projection is frustrated and aspects of the background become foregrounded and articulated. Thus, what normally is not reflected upon, because it has been *lived* in its authentic originality, as the grounds of comportment, must still be recoverable. It is a question of acknowledging that what is unreflected upon is so because it is pre-reflective, antepredicative. It has the status of what

Wittgenstein called 'the inherited background' (Wittgenstein 1972: 15e), that functions like an orchestrating mythology.

Rotherham exists to the people who live here as an inherited background, and not as a landscape. Understanding the status of this background is at the heart of our understanding these people's relation to the world and their existence. If we understand this, then we comprehend their relationship to their being-in-the-world and cast light on their relation to the economic, cultural and political institutions of England. Much of what I have said concerning embodiment, comportment and motility, sometimes through the concepts of habitus and ethos, has been a way of thinking about our perception as inescapably a matter of engagement. As I have discussed the meaning of this cluster of ideas, it is clear that it necessarily involves a relation to a sense of 'background', a field of significance that grounds awareness in meanings disclosed through the forms of concern inscribed in the practices we inherit and the projects available to us. What these concepts do is to formulate the relation of person to sensible world as shaped by embodied culture, by comportment; by history incorporated in habitus; by form of life. What we have glimpsed, manifest, in the transcribed quotations is the nature of this engagement and the way it 'lights up' a world of distinct characteristics and hue; the way the world as it is experienced, or *lived*, is, inescapably, that of an agent with a particular manner of comportment, or corporeal style, a certain form of being human. Hence, in this model of being, comportment and a notion of the 'background' are mutually implicatory.

At this point, I'd like to make clearer the ramifications of this notion of the 'background'. Taylor expresses the nature of our relation to the context-conferring-sense, or 'background' as:

The context stands as the unexplicited horizon within which – or to vary the image, as the vantage point from out of which – this experience can be understood. To use Michael Polanyi's language, it is subsidiary to the focal object of awareness; it is what we are 'attending from' as we attend to the experience.

Now this is the sense in which I use the term 'background.' It is that of which I am not simply unaware . . . because it makes intelligible what I am uncontestably aware of; but at the same time I cannot be said to be explicitly or focally aware of it, because that status is already occupied by what it is making intelligible.

(Taylor 1993a: 325)

In other words, our perception of the sense of the world, our spontaneous experience of its being meaningful, takes place through our acceptance of a whole range of what we know to be there, in its 'place', as part of an immense network of interlaced practices; and it is from this that our perspective upon particular perceptions takes shape. Moreover, it is the network of significance deposited in the whole of inherited practices through which we come to understand the meaning of discriminable phenomena through the networking involved in being a practically engaged language-using being that renders particular perceptions sensible and our world spontaneously, intuitively significant such that, in most of our everyday way of being we do not have to ponder or contemplate whole areas upon which our existence depends. Hence, it is the vast totality of the practical dealings of the places in which we come to being that enables things to 'show up' at all.

This expresses what emerges from the transcription, that Rotherham as a series of spaces inhabited by people with distinct forms of comportment, to say nothing of the economic conditions acknowledged in the economic and demographic data, does not exist in the practical forms of engagement through which people go about their everyday lives, rather, these phenomena are felt through their effects on intimate, embodied life. The transcription has shown distinctions emerging that concern a practically engaged understanding that mediates the social that individuals encounter through a practical sense of what to avoid that results in a practically achieved negotiation of the 'decent' and 'rait enough' which leaves unarticulated the extent of the prevalence of the obverse and inarticulate the nature of 'decent folk' such that what exists is an individually achieved practical sense that hues humanity from the morass of a negative world on the basis of indescribable comportment-aspects that clue those to be avoided. It is this background of unspoken practical sense, the knowledge necessary to life in poor and deprived urban space, that we must be sensitive to. People's talk barely articulates these inscribed differences upon which much depends.[9] But it is a knowledge seldom articulated because it is part of an unarticulated background, a system of inscribed differences manifest in gesture and manner, the style that is taken to mark personal, natural difference, that marks working people to one another and yet which emerges often in the politically incorrect accounting-procedures that naturally arise from their environments. 'Ah wun't live the'er, it's full o'r druggies'; 'Asians from the'er all think the'r 'ard. Tha wants t' watch thiseln''; 'The rait slappers in the'er'; 'Thi' shag the'r cousins an' stuff dahn the'er'; 'Dun't leave car the'er, it'll 'ave n' wheels on when tha gets back t' it'; 'T' many student wankers up the'er.' Comprehension consists in awareness of the space of the town as a series of regions constituted through the comportment of those who frequent that space and lend to it its hue and perception of particularity is constituted in this light.

So that looking to construct Rotherham as a 'Landscape with figures', or as a set of figurative descriptions is wrong because the place exists through patterns of intelligibility that bring things into focus as actions to be taken and things to be accommodated to. Only a break with this primary milieu brings any recognition of it as a bounded, particular life. The referential whole begins to stand-out through conditions that render the normally there-at-hand, occurrent, when individuals cease simply pressing into the available possibilities disclosing the phenomenal realm through participatory engagement and become aware of the wordliness of their realm of being through experiences that throw into stark relief the nature of their lives as circumscribed by the culture of a class society. One sees such a realization when people work away, around more affluent people.

Clearly, there is a relation between experience and a certain kind of being-in-the-world: a relation that is world-shaping; and this exists through the implicit understanding that growing up into certain forms of comportment and patterns of relationships produces in one. It is knowing the aspects disclosed in that understanding of being, knowing the affective resonances of the world known through this way of being. Understanding consists in a way of inhabiting certain practices, because the background inhabits our actual dealings with people and things and is not separable from the disclosive activity of being, itself. Hence, if understanding is non-cognitive, pervasive and the product of circumspective awareness, we must be aware of this phenomenon whereby being establishes a space of affective sense that subtends practices and perception. Thus, the way of being cannot be read from practices without understanding what is 'there' as background. As Charles Taylor expresses it:

Our sense of things can be more or less articulate. But now we can see why the supposition that it could be totally articulate is misconceived in its very nature. I said that an engaged form of agency is one whose world is shaped by its mode of being. This mode of being provides that context in which the experience of this agent is intelligible, that is, has the sense it makes to the agent, as well as being understandable to an observer. World shaping is a matter of sense making. But the form can only determine the 'sense' things make for the agent, because the agent has some 'sense' of this form . . . Engaged agents are creatures with a background sense of things.

But why can't it all be articulated? Because it isn't a matter of representations, but of a real context conferring sense. As a real context conferring sense, our form of life is also the essential background to any articulation being meaningful. The short answer to why complete articulacy is a chimera is that any articulation itself needs the background to succeed. Each fresh articulation draws its intelligibility in turn from a background sense, abstracted from which it would fail of meaning. Each new articulation helps to redefine us, and hence can open up new avenues of potential further articulation. The process is by its very nature uncompletable, since there is no limit on the facts or aspects of our form of life that one can try to describe or of standpoints from which one might attempt to describe it.

The supposition of complete articulacy arises out of the Procrustean outlook of modern rationalism. Our understanding is supposedly made up of a finite number of not yet expressly foregrounded representations that are in some sense already there. Beyond this it is all hard wiring. What this completely misses is the irreducible content-context structure of engaged agency.   (Taylor 1993a: 328)

The form of involved coping, of engagement with the public world of our form of life that we have called circumspection, a way of non-thematized dealing with the world as it is revealed through comportment, does not represent a scene that is there to be recorded like a landscape painting. One needs to understand what constitutes the background at an affective level, and though talk reveals some of its elements, the background, as such, remains unsurveyable. I believe this is what people are trying to articulate when they say, as one woman said, 'Yet it looks alright lookin' aht the'er when sun's aht wi' flowers an' brick. It's underneath it all.'

Hence the paucity of overt description of scenes and practices in this work. The background articulations of this experience emerge in the talk, through the concerned involvement of the speaker in the totality of involvements that their lives consist in. What the woman above is struggling to do, is to register something that her everyday coping finds present in the world. Yet part of what she is trying to point out is that she finds herself engaged in strategies of coping through a continual negotiation with a realm in which she finds herself frustrated and continuously forced to deal with aspects that arise from the comportment of those around her that are not open to uncontestable or 'simple' description. Aspects that individuals register as a 'funny look', or a 'bad attitude', or through the concealed violence of the 'piss-take'. Thinking about this woman's assertion about the view from her shop window we might consider something Heidegger says:

In giving something a definite character, we must, in the first instance, take a step back when confronted with that which is already manifest – the hammer that is too heavy. In 'setting down the subject', we dim entities down to focus on 'that hammer there', so that by thus dimming them down, we may let that which is manifest be seen *in* its own definite character as a character that can be determined.
                    (Heidegger 1962: 197)

The problem for her is this process of focusing upon what is all 'in a certain manner', a certain 'feeling', such expressions acknowledge that there is a problem in the criteria whereby one might begin to focus on these aspects of the practical realm of her body's engagement. How is one to set down the subject and dim entities down so that the definite character of a phenomenon can be recognized when the criteria of identity are the subtle nuances of gesture, manner and comportment through which individuals unknowingly actualize and manifest their attitude to existence, an attitude that impacts upon those who cross their path? This woman, by her words, is trying to make an acknowledgement by attempting to restrict our openness to the scene, to the properties of light, colour and texture that might absorb an observer and hold her interlocutor to a 'view' disclosed in circumspective absorption. The interesting thing about this 'setting down of the subject' is that it depends for its sense upon the interlocutors being mutually embedded in a particular totality of involvements (our fore-having) which embeds this perception of this particular domain as it is encountered (our fore-sight) and which thus makes viable this interpretation (or fore-conception).[10] This fore-conception emerges from her own struggle to cope with her intimate environment, to make it open, recognized, apart from the pain of personal frustration. It is an attempt to establish a sense of the world so that certain kinds of predication can be made. It is an attempt to speak of what is true that depends upon the 'dimming down' of the scene as a landscape of occurrent properties, and upon the concerned absorption in our pre-interpretative understanding of the scene under the aspects revealed in the totality of involvements that grounds perception in that background.

There is a difference between speech-acts that describe specific occurrent properties of the town[11] and the kind of talk that I have tried to base my account of the town upon. Descriptions of features of the place can thus produce a sense of the place that defiles its nature.[12] Mulhall gives us some indication of the process of this covering-over:

In short, such assertions are, if not theoretical, at least proto-theoretical; they transform our relation to the object by severing it from its place in a work-world of practical concern and situating it solely as a particular thing about which a particular predication can be made . . . in a single movement, what is ready-to-hand is covered up and what is present-to-hand is discovered.   (Mulhall 1996: 91)

The point, as Mulhall explains it, is that assertions which focus upon occurrent properties restrict our pre-interpretative understanding of entities which are always part of a referential whole or network of involvements. They fix our awareness upon predicative meaning, upon the characterization asserted and this meaning becomes reified, fleetingly ungrounded from the seeing-as structure that underpins the sense of things. The meaning fixed by assertion, is different from that articulated in the network of connections of the field of significance upon which it depends for sense. Heidegger's point is that the interpretative-process, or forestructure, of assertion covers up the involvement-structures and referential-whole of articulations that ground our awareness of sense and understanding of the world. As Heidegger puts it:

The intelligibility of something has always been articulated, even before there is any appropriate interpretation of it.   (Heidegger 1962: 203)

In our comportment we instantiate an unexplicit, embodied, practical understanding of the sense of things – our shared pre-understanding; and from this, through interaction amidst the referential whole common to that form of life, talk, the existential–ontological foundation of language expresses the deeper articulations of the field of meaning. Talk amidst the dealings with the world recounts these unexplicit articulations, 'Discourse is the Articulation of intelligibility' (Heidegger 1962: 204) as Heidegger puts it. The field of significance that underlies human understanding is thus revealed in talk which is disclosive of entities in their being. The talk I have recorded and used, where it does describe entities as present-at-hand, discloses them through their readiness-to-hand. What talk lays bare is the interpretation, the fore-conception, which emerges from the form of life, from the involvement-whole. This allows me to restore the sense of the habitus of the person speaking, using their speech as an indicator of this phenomenal field, as a kind of sign-post of this sense-constituting capacity of the body-subject.

This makes clear the nature of 'the background' of sense and the relationship of the transcription to it. As Taylor summarizes:

The paradoxical status of the background can . . . be appreciated. It can be explicited, because we aren't completely unaware of it. But the expliciting itself supposes a background. The very fashion in which we operate as engaged agents within such a background makes the prospect of total explicitation incoherent. The background cannot in this sense be thought of quantitatively at all.   (Taylor 1993a: 329)

The intelligibility of experience always draws on this background understanding. The deeper sense of experience depends upon what underlies it, what it stands upon. Here is the crux of the problem of description: description requires a knowledge of the background to succeed in that the sense of articulations emerges from the sense of the unexplicit articulations of the field of meaning. The silences and ellipses in people's speech are their implicit, unknowing recognition of the background: those moments when the unsaid, shared, unspoken, passes between people, manifesting in knowing silences and appropriate gestures the shared sense of an unexplicit articulated awareness of a totality of involved reference that renders speech not merely comprehensible, but forceful, poetic, evocative, prosodic and moving. Talk, then, can articulate our pre-interpretative understanding of entities as being amidst a totality of involvements. Our background sense of place can be manifest in certain forms of assertion which articulate what concerns us in our interpretations, or the sense arising from our circumspective involvement, 'the background of . . . primary familiarity, which . . . is . . . present in [an] unprominent way' (Heidegger quoted in Dreyfus 1994: 103). This is clear in an example from the comments of one woman:

S: What du's tha [do you] think to Rother'am?
X: Crap!
S: Ye, but what else?
X: What du yer mean? Yer mean nightlife, like?
S: Well, just lookin' aht'a [out of] winder nahr?
X: It's shit. It's dead, it's boo'rin, thi's nowt 'ere, ohnny [only] charity shops. It's a
   bit like a ghost tahn [town] really. It's no place to live but wi''ere aren't wi?

This kind of talk calls each person's attention to the relevant aspects of the context and, when there is agreement upon the aspects or meaning portrayed in the detail, agreement about what the detail portrays, then the assertion functions transparently, it makes *sense*. When asked for an opinion of Rotherham this woman felt the one word, 'crap', uttered with a blank face, as though the question was one of an imbecile, in the tones of tolerant self-evidence and complete seriousness, was a satisfactory description of the place. She gave this answer knowing that the hearer would understand the sense the town has that she uses the invective of 'crap' to capture. She reaches spontaneously for 'crap', the immediacy of her response shows that the response is not one that issues from a careful weighing of possible responses; she is not contemplating different aspects of her perception or experience, but feels 'crap' captures the experience of stultifying banality the town engenders. It is like a short-hand that condenses the alienated frustration of working people's experience of place for those whose dispossession excludes them from the experiences and resources to articulate the direness of their position and experience. As expression, it crystallizes in a condensed meaning a whole relation to the world, attitude to existence and being, and instantiates this in a sense that relates to the referential-whole of their lives. Such talk emerges from and manifests the 'seeing-as' structure that underlies the meaning of phenomena. It is within this 'seeing-as' structure of meaning that entities are encountered and perceived (Mulhall 1993). The town is thus experienced 'under an aspect': Rotherham-crap is a direct expression of her experience; it has the linguistic form of exclamation rather than report, and it manifests an occupation with the experience that arises from the experience of being; one that impacts in a way that distracts the individual from a sense of fruition and comfortableness with life. It is similar in form to pain-behaviour and it shows that the experience is one of quiet duress. That this sense emerges from a general malaise is manifest in the words of one man:

Rother'am's like a prison wiy'aht [without] any walls, like people can feel these walls holdin' 'em in but thi' can't just walk aht on it, It's like a fuckin' big desert which nob'dy 'as energy t' walk aht on! [*Laughs*].

Moreover, this type of expression, like expressions we have seen earlier such as 'an ugly shit hole of a place' or 'Rother'am's a nothin' kind'a place . . . It's like Sheffield shit, an' aht [out] cem [came] Rother'am', and the 'Rotherham-crap' that we have just seen characterize the expressed experience, is the criterion for the experience it depicts, for the aspect of experience that it expresses. It shares the form that Mulhall describes:

'Now it's a rabbit!' is not being used as an ordinary perceptual report but rather as an exclamation . . . it gives expression to our visual experience in the sense in which an exclamation (such as 'It hurts!') manifests pain. The analogy Wittgenstein posits here is designed to highlight two features of aspect-dawning: first, that the form of words employed therein is a spontaneous reaction to what we see, a direct expression (*Ausserung*) of our visual experience rather than the end-product of an inference we make from the nature of our visual impression – no inner entity need be hypothesized to mediate between the perceived object and our verbal response to it. And secondly, it highlights the sense in which the verbal *Ausserung characterizes* the experience it expresses; like an exclamation of pain, the utterance of such a form of words is a criterion for the nature and existence of the visual experience of aspect-dawning – we have no independent means of specifying (or individuating) that visual experience in contrast to other such experiences except by means of the felt need to use that specific piece of verbal behaviour in this particular context.

(Mulhall 1990: 11–12)

These kinds of expression, exchanged in the course of everyday interaction are not just perceptual reports, but also constitute 'a cry of recognition' (Wittgenstein 1958: 198), and this is linked to the shared form of life, to responding and living in a certain way. It is no accident that these speech acts often form part of a lament, part of a regretting that the world is found to be this way and of the speaker's own life in it. This is clear in the following example:

X: Ahy an't seen yer fo' a bit. Ah thought tha' [you] might'a gone somewhe'er else: got aht'a [out of] this hole!
S: Bad in' it?
X: Worst mistake I ivver [ever] med comin' back 'ere. Ah've 'ad car brock [broken] int' four times an' two radios nicked an' wi' 'ad that back bedroom winder put through. Ah'r Y [*daughter*] wo' screamin' 'er 'ead off an' screamin' fo' mi not t' gu' 'aht to 'em. Ah went aht [out] but thi'd scarperred.
S: Ah know, it's awful.
X: It's fuckin' sunk rahnd 'ere. We are, wi' sunk.

These locutions manifest perceptual techniques that emerge from being situated in certain ways that 'attune' one to a certain kind of 'vision' of the world: it is a knowing one's way around, and these articulations are characteristic of continuous aspect perception. Perceptions made available by life in the contexts through which this sense becomes spontaneously available, significant, sensible and transparently manifest in the world around one.

In the example from the woman describing the town as 'Crap!', it is revealing that, when she was asked to elaborate, she assumed the question must be a request for an opinion of the nightlife of the town. The aspects of the environment that have led her to her spontaneous response, 'Rotherham-crap', the background of involvement-relations, the network of contrasts and interlaced patterns from which she makes judgements, are not something she is accustomed to describing. The town as a space is not constituted in discursive consciousness, it is the background that life issues from, a set of implicit, practical references, it is 'ready to hand' for her, to use Heidegger's idiom. What is striking about this is the readiness-to-hand of 'crap' as a form of description of her feelings about the town. The spontaneous exclamation 'Crap!' shows that the grounds for thinking through an intermediary process of interpretation are lacking and its purpose unnecessary. The readiness-to-hand of this exclamation as a meaningful description illustrates the extent to which this woman takes for granted this place and the experience that 'crap' is. This makes clear that being-in-the-world renders the world ready-to-hand as a condition of being what it is. Thus, this woman's relationship to the town takes place through her concernful dealings with the spaces. She talks of the town in terms of going out and in terms of shopping, the two activities she engages in through objectifying, self-consciousness. These activities, unlike her work in a chip shop, offer her the opportunity to be something a little bit more than an automaton. The town is encountered primordially as a medium through which people try to achieve a life. It is the domain of practical activity in which existence is manifest. Knowing the town is a matter of knowing the aspects under which it is experienced, and seeing the grounds that support the continuity of the aspect through which the background is felt in the attitude to life. This is a different way of recognizing what we saw earlier under the guise of 'habitus', which we might see as an embodied dispositional system of intentional projection; of continuous aspect-perception. It is the medium for the acquisition of something akin to what Wittgenstein called a 'world-picture' acquired tacitly through informal processes from childhood. Knowing this sense of Rotherham as a bounded whole, knowing the aspect-perception involved in the habitus, is the subject of what follows.

People who share this distinct experience of Rotherham will manifest this in the contrasts and comparisons they draw, in what they show is of importance in their lives. Their talk is a way of dealing with, a way of calling forth, social experience, but the deeper overall aspect through which they perceive remains unspoken though it has a generative efficacy in their linguistic products. One unemployed man in his mid-twenties tried to explain how what he felt of the place, his 'gut' response, was dependent upon familiarity with the unsurveyable detail of class experience that embeds comportment and reveals the place.[13] His comments highlight the nature of aspect-perception, of how we experience things as having 'fused' with the meaning we feel in our perception of them:

S: Look at this, 'ahd [how do] yer describe this?

X: It's depressin', [*Sighs*] it's very depressin. What can yer se'? Terraced 'ouses, rubbish everywhe'er, dogs barkin', but it's 'ard to put yer finger on why yer feel like that abaht [about] it . . . It dun't [doesn't] look nice . . .'ouses a' small. But what yer feel, it's not in ahr [how] it looks, it's, like, in the way that people are . . . [*Pauses*] . . . Anyway, it's not to du wi us [with our] environment. What thi'v done to us, is done, thi's no way back. These kids nahr that are just full o'r hate, yer can't ask 'em owt [anything] wiy'aht yer beein' prepared to scrap ovva it, thi's no way back from that nah [now]. Ye can't bi' good neighbours anymo'or. An we'er-ever [wherever] ye put 'em thi'd trash it like thi 'ave done rahnd 'ere. Class in't in the environment, it's in the' attitudes to everythin'.[14]

Like the woman quoted earlier he is trying to say that there is a deep sense of the place that is not available to those who do not share the position that means one must be involved in this experience. Yet he is also trying to say something else, that the background from which this perception emerges is one of class position. Where he suggests 'it's 'ard to put yer finger on why yer feel like that abaht it', he alludes to the nature of this experience as being one involving continuous aspect-perception: that in a sense, to 'see' or 'feel' about Rotherham in this way one needs to be held by this aspect, to have been 'taught' it through a familiarity with the social conditions, the unem-ployment, the Department of Social Security and the rest. The discomfort comes not from the aesthetics of terraced houses and rubbished greenery, but from a knowledge of what it all means in terms of human experience. From a knowledge of what patterns of comportment mean by knowing the conditions that have inflected them. Yet, our feeling under this aspect, seeing in this way, this man's use of his concepts, does not emerge from the learning of formulae. It is a matter of his life-long involvement with the life of the place, a life he recognizes as heavily prescribed by a lack of economic power and by a severe social vulnerability. It is a place he knows through relations of difference and similarity in experiential co-ordinates that only make sense against a background that remains tacit among those who live here. This knowing the place as an 'ugly', 'boorin'', 'shit-'ole' characterizes continuous aspect-perception; it is to have become skilled at seeing certain aspects in the environment, it is a learning of experience, a technique of cognition that has the status of 'being-to-hand' and which defies the normal notions of volition that we associate with the idea of 'technique'. It is to know the place as the world of a person who is objectively marked and for whom those marks ensure this experience of the world. The context confers the sense he registers as a body-subject in 'it's depressin'', but he is unable to go on and foreground his reasons for these feelings in representations of the environment that he can verbalize. Hence we get the self-deprecation obvious in the sighs and the pauses and the sense of futility of the effort of making it objective in 'What can yer se'?' This is a feeling that has always overwhelmed me in the face of this project and it is why so many feel so uncomfortable in the subject-position of interviewee asked to describe the town. It makes it clear that ordinary, everyday experience is always already founded in meaning and in an understanding of the world that I have tried to characterize through notions like comportment or habitus. We must therefore read the transcribed material bearing in mind the distinctive way in which human embeddedness in the world must be conceptualized; and then bear in mind what is particular to these people's relation to the world because of their class position.

This background manifests itself in our perceptions, and it fuses our perceptions with our way of feeling about our world in all possible aspects of our lives. This is the merit of Merleau-Ponty's notion of body-subject to depict the nature of our ability to perceive as being like an already acquired habit or skill. Even those sensory faculties that are most amenable to traditional philosophical descriptions are grounded in the thick of human life and deeply affected by those grounds. The importance of the notion is that it leads us to understand our sensory capacities as emerging from the particularity of our practice; and practice is the way the body comes to accomplish knowing, becomes capable of knowing the world. As Marx put it:

the senses of the *social* man differ from those of the non-social man. Only through the objectively unfolded richness of man's essential being is the richness of subjective *human* sensibility (a musical ear, and eye for beauty of form – in short *senses* capable of human gratification, senses affirming themselves as essential powers of *man*) either cultivated or brought into being . . . The *forming* of the five senses is a labour of the entire history of the world down to the present.   (Marx 1975: 301)

The practical beliefs of our form of life operate normatively; they provide criteria for how the world ought to look to the 'normal' eye, but they appear to us as the simple, neutral descriptions of an omniscient eye[15] because we experience meaning as assimilated to the world. It is as though our habitual life fuses our feeling-body within its environment. Our way of being provides subtle 'directions' to perception that we are unaware of, and so description takes the form of direct expression of experience that is primordially encountered. Instead of reports of a reflective, deliberative, aesthetic kind, one finds expressions that are closer to pain behaviour in form – exclamations that express a preoccupation with conditions that obtrude and affect us. This continuous aspect-perception, the practical belief through which we come to inhabit our world, is something we learn, not by satisfying ourselves of its validity through ratiocination but through our involvement in the world of others. It is part of an acquired sense of the world learnt as a practical system through comportment.

Wittgenstein insisted that 'Certain propositions must be excluded from doubt' (Wittgenstein 1972: 628) and this suggests that certain perceptions, disclosed in comportment through our practical understanding, are aspects of the background and articulate the form of life and cannot be grounded 'in' the scene experienced. And this is precisely what the man quoted above is trying to express when he says 'it's not in ahr it looks'. The same point is made by the woman who says that Rotherham is 'crap'. It is meant to signify a view that is shared but not articulated, but which is present in talk and in bearing, in all that is covered by 'being in Rotherham' or in being a 'Rother'am person' and part of those that are, as she put it, "ere aren't wi?' These types of exchange, like the young man who says, 'It's not very nice we'er we live' are invoking a way of seeing. But they are invoking a way of perceiving that is a way of feeling, based on a common way of being-in-the-world that has been learnt, purely practically, through comportment and concerned involvement, and which is thus 'not based on grounds. It is not reasonable (or unreasonable). It is there – like our life' (Wittgenstein 1972: 73). These statements are grounded in the multiple occurrences and repeated instances through which individuals come to acquire a coherent 'feeling' for the world; a process of acculturation that works through the gestural and habitual sets through which sense is imbued by a process of osmosis, body-to-body, through a kind of postural impregnation. We 'learn' through informal and tacit processes, and through this endless process of existence experience comes to 'educate' us into our fundamental, orienting sense of the world, a 'practical sense' that seldom rises to self-avowed belief.

We exist, therefore, against a background of practical existence in which our sense of the world inheres. In this context our discursive instruments, our linguistic habitus, are learnt as part of a totality of dispositions, of habits; both gestural and cognitive; as an inextricable dimension of being-in-the-world. We have seen how interpretation and mood are fundamental aspects of the world's being disclosed through our form of life as we acquire it as we learn to engage with the world. This means that experience is pervaded by values and resonances that shape our relation to the social world we encounter and which are expressed in comportment. Yet the conditions for acculturation into these forms of comportment are particular sites, particularly the family milieu and how this both marks and mediates being in regard to wider social institutions, particularly the education system and the social position it opens onto. Being-there is thus the opening onto a world revealed through a system of dispositions, of habitual comportment acquired through primary relationships that invest being-in-the-world, in all of its aspects, with a surplus of meaning; beyond whatever we are doing, there is a discernible stylistic 'hue' which is inescapable in all we are. There is thus always a sense to us, of which we are more or less aware that makes even the same universal inheritance different: it is seen differently, lived differently and discloses the world differently. What Bourdieu says of language is particularly relevant:

Language is the most active and elusive part of the cultural heritage which each individual owes to his background. This is because language does not reduce, as we often think, to a more or less extensive collection of words. As syntax, it provides us with a system of transposable mental dispositions. These go hand in hand with values which dominate the whole of our experience and, in particular, with a vision of society and of culture. They also involve an original relationship to words, reverential or free, borrowed or familiar, sparing or intemperate.   (Bourdieu 1994: 8)

Through comportment within specific, socially located sites, we inherit a habitus: dispositions that form schemes of perception and appreciation, schemes that enable cognition and valuation, thought and action. These are imbued through lasting immersion: that is, acquired rather than formally learnt, through a mimesis that involves deep identification but which isn't a form of imitation (Bourdieu 1990a: 73). Therefore, the habitus manifests a *gestalt*-like structuring of perceptions, a history distilled in being. Yet the habitus is used to describe what is there before we have the opportunity to make choices concerning what we are and who we become; and it describes our objective being, our being-for-others within the totality of the social universe. So it exists and emerges from what we have spoken of as 'the background', and it means that there is always an indeterminacy of meaning that coheres at the heart of our experience of the social. It is the nature of the world as background that makes it so difficult to recover in the lives of working people the real human consequences of their social condition. Or, rather, it is present but it is submerged in their talk, and so requires an onto-logical account of their relation to the world to recognize and to validate their experience. The relationship is one of ontological complicity:

The relationship to the social world is not the mechanical causality between a 'milieu' and a consciousness, but rather a sort of ontological complicity. When the same history inhabits both habitus and habitat, both dispositions and positions . . . history in a sense communicates with itself, is reflected in its own image. History as 'subject' discovers itself in history as 'object'; it recognizes itself in 'antepredicative', 'passive syntheses', structures that are structured prior to any structuring operation or any linguistic expression. The doxic relation to the native world, a quasi-onto-logical commitment flowing from practical experience, is a relationship of belong-ing and possessing in which a body, appropriated by history, absolutely and immediately appropriates things inhabited by the same history.

(Bourdieu 1981: 306)

Yet it is this indeterminacy of meaning that coheres at the heart of our experience of the social that makes the work of articulating that experience so difficult and it is why dominated people are so often reduced to silence in the face of that discourse of the social we all participate in known as 'common sense'. Yet it is the determinateness of the locality of learning, of coming into being, 'on the back' as it were of this naturalizing confusion through which we become absorbed in dealing with our social destiny because it is sedimented in the grounds of the versions of humanness we embody, that means we must think in terms of the personal consequences of inequality and stigma and think in terms of a:

social psycho-analysis which set out to grasp the logic whereby the social relations objectified in things and also, of course, in people are insensibly internalized, taking their place in a lasting relation to the world and to others, which manifests itself, for example, in thresholds of tolerance of the natural and social world, of noise, over-crowding, physical or verbal violence – and of which the mode of appropriation of cultural goods is one dimension.

(Bourdieu 1984: 77)

For these reasons we are better advised to see class as exemplified not pri-marily in declared opinions but in the 'immediate adherence, at the deepest level of the habitus, to the tastes and distastes, sympathies and aversions, fantasies and phobias which . . . forge the unconscious unity of a class' (Bourdieu 1984: 77). And to see sedimented in the repeated practices of labouring on the cold steel of the gym's weights, and packing oneself into too-little dark-space with a mass of other bodies, with so much noise that one has to shout at the top of one's voice to be heard and then drink a gallon of beer in order to begin the inexorable push towards the evening's teleological climax 'a fait or a fuck', the contours of a world that is lost because it is a world that working people's lives are built upon. It is within the reference points of this life that their speech circles, often without recognition because recognition involves an act of objectification which their position in the world forecloses upon, because 'what else is there?' What kinds of life could there be outside of what is known? Dispossession and brutalization are their own anaesthetic and this is the only comfort working people find and it is why they so seldom take the cultural practices that are left them neat, undiluted by drink or drugs, since escape from the inescapable requires that distancing from the immediacy of one's brute being which drink helps the common mind find, even if Monday morning brings reality rapping, relentless as hard rain, on the windows of our immersion in the world.

It is this sense of a bounded world of practicably realizable practical forms that constitutes the sense of limits that protect working people from the destruction of humanity involved in looking upon the qualities of another life that cannot be lived. It is to this lost world, that speaks from beneath the transcribed voices, that makes itself manifest without consultation with the truths of our culture, upon which our lives and interpersonal relations are 'built', that we must search for understanding. And, of course, this will seem to some as taking liberties, as 'drawing conclusions beyond the data', as though the grounds of human life were not founded in engagement, as though there were no mystery to the lives of those shrouded forever from the bright lights of human possibility, as though we should all be levelled and forced to conduct our discussion of human Being at the level of their chosen lowest common denominator, as though the mutilated vision of the sociologist-scholar should circumscribe the limits of phenomena, of vision and recognition. We must leave, break from, evacuate their pre-constituted world, their world of intellectual habits and habitual stupidities and honour the leisure our privilege gifts to us with the gift of honour to those for whom there is no suspension of the burden of necessity and a temporality that is forever now and a past of degradation that constitutes that present:

Everything that we will advance concerning the world must originate not from the habitual world – where our initiation to being and the great intellectual endeavors that have renewed it in history are inscribed only in the state of confused traces, emptied of their meaning and of their motives – but from that present world which waits at the gates of our life and where we find the means to animate the heritage and, if the occasion arises, to take it up again on our own account. We will not admit a preconstituted world, a logic, except for having seen them arise from our experience of brute being, which is as it were the umbilical cord of our knowledge and the source of meaning for us. (Merleau-Ponty 1968: 157)

Beneath the voices that speak of what is ordinary to them, of what is part of the inescapable rhythm of a week that is no longer guaranteed to be a working one, and the highlight of the Friday and Saturday nights out, we must be aware of the indivision of an experience in which each is caught with others in the same movement of time, which precludes the fixing of the experiential meaning of certain experiences, but through which the latent content of the world is manifest. We must see that the determinateness of the temporality working people live, their realization of their life-course, their sense of what is appropriate to them at this point and what is about to befall them – that these are things that are both pressing in a practical way and yet sensibly indeterminate, are invisible to them. As Wittgenstein suggested, religious belief is the paradigm human condition, and the difficult thing is to see the groundlessness of our believing except as a way of living. The relative invisibility of culture to working class people, the worldhood of their world, that it is a distinct 'world', issues out of their relation to the world as this is mediated by their economic and social position, a field of forces delineated relationally by the network constituted amidst the twin sites of primary capital acquisition, the family and the education system and the state agencies which striate economic position and mediate access to the labour market as well as one's social experience. The structures of being-in-the-world, as they are constrained by the grounds of possibility of this social space limit the extent to which working class people are able to perceive the nature and extent of the worldhood of their world. Whilst they have a sense of 'our world' and what is 'for us', the actual content of a different life, in its detail, is beyond them.

Habituated, embodied, practice is the condition of these people's entry into being,[16] and the conditions of this heavy habituation create, in experience, something akin to the 'weathering' that occurs as a river runs through a landscape. Life's experience might be a flux, but it is a flux that follows the parameters of a broad flow of life. Just as the direction of a river is the result of an evolving passage through the medium it encounters throughout its course over time, it is similar with the history of a people. Just as the swelling of a river following torrential rain might cause it to overflow creating new paths, so, too, the destruction of what stands beneath these people's habits has left a group whose displacement has dissipated that flow of life, and partially rerouted it, such that one can no longer discern clearly whether or not they remain involved in the same distinct flow. Looking at its past route allows us only to see its origins, not its future. And understanding the present demands a comprehension of how the 'inherited background', the embodied dispositions that are pre-conscious, pre-personal, antepredicative and primordial, constitutes the experience of these new conditions. The world of comportment, the realm of the habitual that is inherited cross-generationally is what constitutes the banks of experience. As Dewey put it:

Experience is no stream even though the stream of feelings and ideas that flows upon its surface is the part which philosophers love to traverse. Experience includes the enduring banks of natural constitution and acquired habit as well as the stream.

(Dewey 1934: 7)

Habit and the habitual sensuous meaning of our environment steep life with felt significance: a dispositional, enduring sensibility that is deeper than intentional knowing[17] and which acts as the banks through which the river of our experience flows. The sense we acquire through our habitual life forms the 'grooves' through which we become ontologically complicit in our environments, through which we fit into our world because it makes sense to us. As Merleau-Ponty put it, 'What is important is how they use their bodies, the simultaneous patterning of body and world in emotion' (Merleau-Ponty 1962: 189).

The meaning of the world becomes fused in sensuous awareness, what our self-consciousness stands upon and depends upon to enact with others the culture we share, *feel* and through which we generate speech and action that connects with the feelings of others who share those conditions. This is the obvious meaning in the utterance: 'Ye' feel like an Asian' and: 'well the'r not gunna understand, they an't 'ad to put up wi' 'avin' tu bi wi' the'r own kind 'ave thi?'[18] This 'simultaneous patterning of body and world in emotion' is another way of making visible how the circumstances of our lives are of consequence for our felt relation to the world. And this, while it may be expressed in our conscious ideas, is of much deeper significance to us than our conceptualizations concerning the world. The point is that there is a great stability in these conditions, circumstances and events: a familiarity in being and experience which is the setting of our experiences themselves and to which they, at least partially, refer. Yet this being that contextualizes life remains indeterminate and ambiguous, it is difficult to be explicit about it because what has formed it, is the amorphous notion of a 'whole way of life' and 'whole lifetime'. Such habitual meaning is latent in our conscious avowals and objectifications concerning the world, and it is obvious in the way one fifteen-year-old man depicts his life:

S: But ahr [how] du yer think other kids feel abaht [about] it?
X: Well I dun't know, thi's not many kids I know that like school, I mean, alrait [alright] thi's odd one, but ohnny people I know who like school is people wi' [with] a lot'a money. Thi get talked to a lot different bi' teachers, [S: Yer reckon?] Ye definitely, and them people wi' not a lot'a money thi don't giy 'em [give them] no respect, thi talk talk to 'em like the'r animals. [S: It's allous kids from certain

areas in' it?] Ye, ye, coors, [of course] like up ahr end, we're we gu at Aston Comp', thi's kids from Treeton and Catcliffe and thi talk to them like the'r not theer, like rubbish.
S: Du thi really?
X: Ye.
S: We'er a you from?
X: Aston.
S: And which areas du kids come from that thi' [they] treat different?
X: Well, Aston, Treeton, Catcliffe.
S: Du thi treat them badly or better?
X: Well, people wi a lot'a money from them areas are alrait, but it's just them that an't got a lot'a money or them that weren't very good in't little school. Thi don't encourage them to du better, thi just mek 'em worse. 'Cos [Because] thi' just, thi just, put 'em dahn [down] even more, thi don't giy 'em any encouragement to get better.
S: Ye. Ahr du yer think though, yer know kids though that yer know at school I mean a lot'a er 'em 'll gu on YT [*Youth Training Scheme*] [P: Probably ye.], du yer think thi know that?
X: Ye. That's wot'a a lot 'ar 'em se nahr [now], 'cos we're near to leaving, wi' [we] leave next May and the'r all sayin' 'Oh, I'm guin on dole', 'I'm doo'in this that and t'other', an' four or five o'r 'us a'r goo'in in't army, cos that, in a way . . . it's not an easy way aht but it's ohnny thing wi'v got for'us.

This makes clear the nature of experience's 'educating', or bringing one to a coherent set of beliefs practically attuned to the conditions of possibility that show-up in the space of one's being. This man has clearly already learnt that class and income bring respect and that, as far as institutional mediators are concerned, his own lack of capital means that he will not be respected. His speech marks a reconciliation to a fundamental relationship that his life-experience has already taught him will likely lead to further symbolic violations. Furthermore, this man's perception of injustice displays the presence of a coherent political sense, what Bourdieu calls an 'ethos': a practical way of valuing the world and 'knowing what is right' without this becoming part of a constituted political ethic. By fifteen, life has taught the basic truths of class inequality. He knows that to be poor and working class is to have no status, to be disrespected for what one is, and, with it, he recognizes that there emerges a lack of concern and of help from those charged by the state with the task of care. This framing of the world for him, in an age where ahead of him lies yet more government intervention in his working life through the discipline of the Training Scheme, is far more likely to be confirmed than challenged, and so the grounds of a rudimentary class sense of the world are laid: a sense of the world as a place full of beings of a different class who will be positioned differentially with regard to him, whose destiny will be better and yet who are likely, at points,

to interfere in a determining way with his own fate. Clearly, the circumstances and events he speaks about have consequences for the felt
significance of this man's lived time, for the total way in which he inhabits
the world, for the way that he feels his lived human potentiality, what some
would call his 'agency', the possibility of his action and his future, for the
'patterning of body and world in emotion' that Merleau-Ponty talks of, for
the way that he must live his destiny. There emerges here, through his words,
a sense of the inscription in the objective being of the poorer kids, a delineated future, a future that will come to them because of the way that the
world responds to people of that kind, of that habitus, whose world of
'being poor' has imbued in them the stigmatizing marks of being working
class, of low caste. That he has learnt to transpose those lessons of what he
has seen, that he *has* been taught through the brutality of his experience
about class emerged, with remarkable insight, later:

X: I mean, when they were little, a lotta'r ahr [lot of our] teachers se, 'we wo' brought
up in good homes' an' that. We're brought up in good 'omes it's just that they had
loads'a money and we an't, they got a rait [right] good education and they think
that we can have that when we an't got a lotta money, thi think we can 'ave wot
they'ad but wi can't.
S: Tha'r absolutely rait.
X: Cos thi's a lotta people in ahr [our] school that an't [haven't] got'a lot o' money
and it's not their fault, teachers know that but thi talk dahn . . . on [down to] 'em
as though it is . . .
S: [*Obvious sadness in the acknowledgement*] Ye I know.
X: It's not fair . . . [*pause*] . . . It's not right.

It is a comment reminiscent of one made by a young woman quoted in
Kozol:

'Well,' she says, choosing her words with care, 'the two things, race and money, go
so close together – what's the difference? I live here, they live there, and they don't
want me in their school.   (Kozol 1992: 31)

Both understand that somehow they are marked in ways that lead to their
being denied the resources of self-respect, value and inclusion, and both
exhibit a sense that somehow this is related to the way in which economic
position mediates identity. Questions of work and inequality and a desire
for respect, emerge throughout this interview. With adolescence so marked
by the sense of an impending future of yet-more-of-the-same, there can be
little wonder that adolescence has sunk into the problems that mark mature
working class life. The collapse of a pre-ordained working age of fifteen or
sixteen for working class kids has not so much prolonged adolescence, in
the way that university prolongs adolescence into young adulthood for
middle class kids; rather it has immiserated youth, forcing young working

class people to face a world of struggle, strain, economic hardship and the beginnings of what will likely be a prolonged humiliation younger. The sense of a collective fate comes through clearly in this man's speech, as well as his sense of futility and hopelessness that is manifest in his sense of the army as 'it's not an easy way aht but it's ohnny [only] thing wi'v got fo' us'. This makes clear the way in which our background sense of social conditions becomes internalized in sensibility, in one's attitudes to the world and to people and the way these conditions have consequence for what are called one's 'values'. This is an uneducated young man, as unaccustomed to speaking of his experience as he is of meeting anyone interested in him, yet his speech is marked by a sensitivity to life that is based upon a self-disciplined respect for others. Yet it is apparent that his teachers can do nothing to harness and focus what is, manifestly, an engagement with the world that is the roots of what teachers perceive as intelligence in us all. If, as J. D. Salinger commented 'You don't have to think too hard when you talk to teachers', then it is because they do not think too hard when they talk to those they do not expect to be educable. The complacent stupidity of their patronizing comments about being from 'good homes' is obvious to this young man whose speech manifests a practical sense of the economics of intelligence. He has none of the benefits of the education that they have enjoyed, and yet he is aware of the problems that economic differences create for families around him. This man's speech manifests a coherent sense of the world and sense of injustice linked to what life has already taught him. The effects of the abuse and his own powerlessness emerge, and yet he immediately connects these issues to questions of injustice, which he sees as embodied in the necessity that being forced to buy a school uniform represents to those who he knows can't afford it:

S: Du you get treated like that?

X: Naow [no], cos I dun't gu to teachers nahr.

S: Why don't yer?

X: The'r not bothered. Thi's [there is] no point. When yer gu to 'em anyway, thi talk to yer like yer not theer [there]. Most a' time thi' don't even wanna know yer. And when thi du it's ohhny [only] to shout at yer or somat [something], or put yer dahn [down]. Like we've got this new school uniform and it's eleven pound a 'T' shirt, an eighteen pound a sweat shirt, an people that an't got'a lot'a money gu to a market an' thi can get a white polo shirt fo' three quid an thi can get a jumper fo'r a fiva, an' thi not gunna pay twice as much, three times as much a thi?

S: Du you still 'ave a uniform?

X: Ye, it's not shirt and tie anymoor, it used to be that, nahr it's just polo shirt, sweat shirt and black trousers, black shoes.

S: Ahr yer. It's interesting that yer su conscious o'r poor people . . .

X: Ye, but it's totally ahta line though. If a poor family, say if thi'v got two people up at that comprehensive, thi'v got to buy two jumpers, or maybe three or four jumpers, two a piece, and it's same wi't' T shirts, it's gunna be, yer gunna bi talkin' seventy-five quid and then thi's the trousers and the'r shoes, ridiculous.

S: The'r are a lotta people unemplyed in that?

X: Oh ye. coors, rahnd us.

S: How do you notice that in kids?

X: Well in the dress an' that. Thi' can't afford trainers an' stuff. I mean some parents don't give a damn abaht the'r kids. Thi's a kid like that called XY, from Treeton, he's a sound enough kid, he's a bit mouthey, an he's got trousers 'alfe way up 'is leg,[19] I know it's not 'is fault an that, he's sound enough. He's got rait good train-ers, he buys 'is own trainers, 'is got a paper rahnd, he gets twenny-odd quid a week, I think he gets twenny three, he 'as three quid an' his Mum teks twenny quid off 'im.

This man is already intimate with the fundamental experiences of working class life; he is already wise to this world of subsisting and already partici-pates in the marginality of its economy through his milk round; he already knows the shrieking, shrill shock of being woken too early to the cold of endless frostily dark mornings that are the bane of working class life, while teachers lie in bed. Yet, stupidity and inability have been taught him from an age at which he ought to have been spared the ugliness in people's hearts. This tells us much about the experience of young working class people. We begin to see from what their world is constituted, how it is disclosed, from what the forestructures of their perception issues.

Our sense of the world is therefore a sense of our place in the world; but it is a distinctly embodied sense of where we belong in the hierarchies of social life as this mingles with our sense of the environment that we belong in. The sensuous world of our embodied being, what our avowed con-sciousness stands upon, is shot through with class experience; it is, as it were, a *place* of class. The worldhood of our world is one delineated by class processes. The talk I have quoted reveals space being encountered through the repulsions that cause disquiet and the comfort of familiar engaged coping; it is a patchwork of significances; a network of affective meaning enveloping us:

It is in this entwining of oneself and the world, in which the emotions are played out, and play a vital role, that things matter, that a conflicting, cohering, flowing, and always pulsating *locus* emerges. This is the proper sense of 'worldhood' . . . to be overwhelmed with this place of horror . . . is to find oneself within a space into which one is sunk, at odds, at depths, at flickering continuities of inhabitation.

(Mazis 1989: 264.)

One is touched by one's environment, such that one comes to recognize the solicitations of the world, and respond through the primary bodily rhythms of fear and security, the primary affective sense, through which locality and self-hood emerge from the flow of perceptual and practical sense that root us in a particular world. But the permeation of space with the primordial sense of ease or struggle, is something that results from our sense of place's foundedness amidst symbolic violence, vulnerability, dislocation and threat; amidst insult, anxiety, loss and fear. Place is hewn from amidst social and economic relations:

The objective structures which science apprehends in the form of statistical regularities (e.g. employment rates, income curves, probabilities of access to secondary education, frequency of holidays, etc.) inculcate, through the direct or indirect but always convergent experiences which give a social environment its *physiognomy*, with its 'closed doors', 'dead ends', and limited 'prospects', that 'art of assessing likelihoods', as Leibniz puts it, of anticipating the objective future, in short, the sense of reality or realities which is perhaps the best-concealed principle of their efficacy.   (Bourdieu 1977: 86)

Our sense of reality, and our embodied practical sense of the immanence of our immediate world are the pre-objective traces of the economic forces that impact upon the environments into which we are born and in which we must live; but the process of coming to take up our place in the world means that our environment is accepted in its facticity as a natural order of things and persons in which we come to accept our place.

Here we glimpse the possibility of moving beyond a model of the working class as trapped by the inability of its members; by their failure of imagination and will to readjust to economic changes. Moreover, we glimpse the extent to which necessity has the form of an absent presence, a presence that is felt in its consequences but rarely recognized, yet which has effects throughout the lives of working people. This sense that inheres at the heart of their experience of the social, is deeply affected by aspects of their environment that produce severe vulnerability, degradation and lack of self-worth. So that, while they may have had experiences which 'taught' this, that is, through which they acquired this sense, they may not be self-conscious of it, in so far as we can identify consciousness as a form of awareness 'which is transparent to itself, its existence being identifiable with its awareness of existing' (Merleau-Ponty 1962: 380).

Rather, these conditions delimit a world in which the resources for a non-alienated life are absent and in their absence we find present to ourselves only what Lawrence called:

The utter negation of natural beauty, the utter negation of the gladness of life, the utter absence of the instinct for shapely beauty which every bird and beast has, the utter death of the human intuitive faculty.   (Lawrence 1994a: 152).

This is an absence both of the instruments of culture that facilitate the possibility of a different way of life and of the resources required to adopt such a relation because the presence of necessity, at the heart of the practices of life, precludes the adoption of that relation. Moreover, the practices that have developed in these conditions, in this environment, are themselves alienated, which means that there is an absence of alternative models of possibility that do not involve borrowing from another class fraction. As Ostrow suggests:

This is just an expression of the fact that the coming into context of the world, i.e., the formation of environment, at once transcends and extends beyond any characterization of this or that physical location. Within the configurations of sense and predispositions that constitute the pre-objective aspects of experience – the variety of places we move to and from – that 'hang together, are mutually motivating and implicatory' . . . The economic and social conditions of belief are not merely ideological conditions, they are the experientially functional conditions of lived environments in the deepest modes of our habitual attachment to them. In other words, it is not enough to state the negative or repressive characteristics of social conditions *upon* the consciousness of man. In so doing we are still left wondering how these conditions are not just 'out there' exerting force, but are *human* conditions, intrinsic to the organization of experience. We do not merely 'value' and 'accept' an ideology of 'unending consumption'; consumption, as the dominant objective mode of the socio-economic environment, is a deeply funded[20] habituality.

(Ostrow 1981: 293)

Conditions of domination do not confine themselves, like unwelcome visitors, to the public spaces of the house of being. They come to penetrate and pervade the most intimate aspects of being, being part of the very processes that shape the conditions of self-hood, position and place; they haunt life from an early age and develop exponentially, leaving nothing untouched. As abuse, domination lodges itself at the heart of intimacy, affecting its very conditions.

We now have an understanding of the extent to which social structures come to inhabit individuals through the mediation of a particular place and history. Sense, then, emerges through our practical mode of being, through which we come to understand the kind of life that is ours, through which we come to appropriate the elements of our life-style. It is to this process that I now want to turn. However, before doing so, I want to look at the experience and process of interviewing. It may seem strange to do this at this point, but it helps to make the issues clear.

5

Understanding the barriers to articulation

"elp yerselves!' he said. "elp yerselves! Dunna wait f'r axin!'
He cut the bread, then sat motionless. Hilda felt, as Connie once used to,
his power of silence and distance . . . 'Still!' she said, as she took a little
cheese. 'It would be more natural if you spoke to us in normal English,
not in vernacular.'
He looked at her, feeling her devil of a will.
'Would it?' he said, in the normal English. 'Would it? Would anything
that was said between you and me be quite natural, unless you said you
wished me to hell before your sister ever saw me again: and unless I said
something almost as unpleasant back again? Would anything else be
natural?'
'Oh yes!' said Hilda. 'Just good manners would be quite natural.'
'Second nature, so to speak!' he said: then he began to laugh. 'Nay', he
said. 'I'm weary o' manners. Let me be!'   (Lawrence 1994a: 243–4)

We have now looked, in some detail, at the relation of working class people
to their environment. Through my elaboration of a set of insights concerning their being-in-the-world I have already tried to cast light on things that
one needs to be sensitive to in the treatment of the talk of working class
people. If we understand the way utterance and articulation emerge from
being-in-the-world – from comportment and engagement – then we stand
a chance of recognizing the significance that working class speech articulates. The last chapter dealt with the detail of this. However, in this chapter,
I would like to look at the consequences that follow from these insights for
my own research practice. The conditions described in this work have consequences for the way that one can access the material presented in this
work. That is, the conditions described present practical difficulties that one
must overcome if one is to gather material that can generate and ground an
account of working class culture. It was partly these problems that guided

my search for intellectual resources through which one might constitute the phenomena as well as my search for ways to embed my account in the culture around me. The practical techniques tended to be personal, embodied, gestural and postural skills that I had to produce in order not to disturb the conditions of utterance through which working people articulate their world. Clearly, issues to do with personal capital and demeanour are of importance here. It is because I am a working class person that I am able to occupy space in the appropriate manner so that I am absorbed invisibly into contexts through which the understanding exhibited in background practices is disclosed[1] and, with it, the world so constituted.

The greatest problem of this work was how I could possibly render the experience and ground it in the words of people of the town. The other main problem was then to frame a form of writing that could lay out the sense of these lives. The difficulty is shaping the medium of transmission in such a way that it is able to carry the message. The task is therefore to deploy instruments of construction that enable readers to recognize phenomena that they may know through a different relation, in my account and thus experience their plausibility. This exerts an anchoring effect upon the account, in that it must negotiate a number of fundamental stereotypical perceptions of working class life, which fail to understand the relation of working class people to their condition as well as the relation of producers of representations of working class life to that life and to producers' own conditions of production.[2] This is why my own work is embedded in a reflexive method that has at its heart an understanding of the relation of working class people to their environment and an awareness of the errors involved in the spectatorial premise. In opposition to this we have seen that we are an embodied 'point of view' (Merleau-Ponty 1964: 165), a vehicle of operative intentionality that must be understood through ideas that allow us to understand the practical realm that founds perception.

The last two chapters, tried to provide an illustration of the position Bourdieu has argued for:

Sociology has to include a sociology of the perception of the social world, that is, a sociology of the construction of the world-views which themselves contribute to the construction of this world. But, given the fact that we have constructed social space, we know that these points of view, as the word itself suggests, are views taken from a certain point, that is, from a given position within social space. And we know too that there will be different or even antagonistic points of view, since points of view depend on the point from which they are taken, since the vision that every agent has of space depends on his or her position in that space . . . No doubt agents do have an active apprehension of the world. No doubt they do construct their vision of the world. But this construction is carried out under structural constraints.

And one may even explain in sociological terms what appears as a universal property of human experience, that is, the fact that the familiar world tends to be 'taken for granted', perceived as natural. If the social world tends to be perceived as evident and to be grasped, to use Husserl's terms, with a doxic modality, this is because the dispositions of agents, their habitus, that is, the mental structures through which they apprehend the social world, are essentially the product of an internalization of the structures of the social world. As perceptual dispositions tend to be adjusted to position, agents, even the most disadvantaged, tend to perceive the world as natural and to find it much more acceptable than one might imagine, especially when one looks at the situation of the dominated through the eyes of the dominant.   (Bourdieu 1990c: 130–1)

Moreover, I have tried to illustrate the existential and personal grounds of that doxic modality; at the way in which people in Rotherham experience their world through a self-evident acceptance; as a 'given'; how one's objective position in society produces a sense of the future, immanent in the present; a 'sense of reality' (Bourdieu 1977: 164) that operates as a 'pre-verbal, taking for granted of the world that flows from practical sense' (Bourdieu 1990a: 60). In some detail, I tried to illustrate the epistemic prejudices latent in the position of observer and spectator. This in itself validates the epistemic vigilance instantiated in the precept of reflexivity. However, given that being-in-the-world is a unifying structure that underlies articulation, then this should have consequences for the way a researcher treats the people he or she relies upon to disclose their world. It is, therefore, appropriate that I address the practical issues arising from the practice of interviewing.

In the last chapter, we looked at the relation between perception and environment and at the conditions under which aspects of the environment might become present-to-hand, occurrent in perception. And we saw that this can abstract entities from the world in which our awareness of them is founded; from the totality of assignment-relations and the engaged projection of local life. This has allowed us to see the significance of certain forms of utterance, often tied to the situational, implicit meaning of the referential whole. However, on top of this we must recognize the effects of linguistic dispropriation. That is, that working class people are aware of themselves as speaking a devalued linguistic form, as lacking the authority to speak in public and even semi-formal situations. Furthermore, we must also recognize that they often simply have not had access to the conditions to acquire and become confident with vocabularies of self-articulation, especially of feelings and conditions that often lack a public dimension that might ground such vocabularies and provide the means of confident acquisition and thus act as the context of resources necessary for successful articulation of the nuances of their condition and its effects upon their lives, feelings and self-constitution. It is a problem Mulhall expresses:

the significance of the situations in which an individual finds herself, and the import and nature of her emotions, is determined by the range and structure of the vocabulary available to her for their characterization.   (Mulhall 1996: 80)

This is a serious range of issues that must be resolved practically if one is to successfully pursue a strategy of interviewing working class people. If we accept their linguistic dispropriation, then we can accept that their linguistic competence will follow the contours of their practical lives and the realm of engagement that circumscribes their existence. And we can see why interviewing is, more often than not, going to fail with many. It is these problems that I want to look at in this chapter.

A problem I encountered very early on, was that, when I asked questions which aimed at eliciting a response that isolated the specific occurrent properties of entities or phenomena as present-at-hand, people simply could not respond at all because such questions presumed a forestructure which was proto-theoretical in that, in order to respond to the question, one had to sever the phenomenon from its place in the world of practical concern and comportment. My naive questions, in effect, in their interpretation, removed the phenomenon from their practical referential domain and, in so doing, became meaningless to the interviewees who simply could not recognize the question as denoting something *in* their world. My questions, when they were bad, 'de-worlded' the phenomena and entities and were thus meaningless to individuals whose comportment and solicitation could only take place through the available network of possibilities. What, at my worst, I was doing is captured by Heidegger:

When space is discovered non-circumspectively by just looking at it, the environmental regions get neutralised to pure dimensions. Places – and indeed the whole circumspectively oriented whole of places belonging to available equipment – get reduced to a multiplicity of positions for random Things. The spatiality of what is ready-to-hand within-the-world loses its specific aroundness; the environment becomes the world of Nature. The 'world', as a totality of equipment ready-to-hand, becomes spatialised to a context of extended Things which are just present at hand [occurrent] and no more. The homogeneous space of nature shows itself only when the entities we encounter are discovered in such a way that the worldly character of the ready-to-hand gets specifically *deprived of its worldhood*.

(Heidegger 1962: 147)

However, I did not originally ask questions that embarrassed people out of my own stupidity or insensitivity. Rather, this 'de-worlding' is characteristic of the way of being of the phenomena revealed by academic work

(Dreyfus 1994: 139). The burden of proof the work involves, meant that I needed to be able to get local people to talk of the area in terms of its effects upon them and, whilst it may sound implausible to say that many are unable to describe the place and its effects upon them, this *is* the overarching experience of living here and trying to do this work. Moreover, many of those who possessed the disposition to describe their world were people for whom Rotherham had, in some way or another, been 'de-worlded', through their experience of industrialized work and the trade union or through time in prison or the army or a spell of further education in the local technical college.

However, the most frightening aspect of this work is the number of people who, even when one knows them intimately, are extremely difficult to interview and record the voices of. And, there is the further problem that the most marginal and dispossessed seem to be the least able to articulate their experience. This issue of silence is the huge mass that this work circles around. It is disturbing and frustrating to the point of anguish to see such an important phenomenon and to understand so clearly its roots: even to know how it feels and yet to be unable to capture it, make it understood, explicit. For how does one sign silence? How can one render a socially acquired condition of something akin to muteness? How does one communicate the intimate experience of loss involved in sensing conditions discovered in solicitude, of a being one is connected to in care, having been denied the resources to communicate gesturally, posturally and linguistically with those who share their position? And how does one validate an interpretation that cannot be recognized nor constituted by those whose condition it is meant to depict?

Clearly, such an account will be endlessly contested and never foreclosed upon, but, if one lives among working class people, one can begin to see the presence of this condition. Whether it strikes one as a powerful, disturbing non-human presence at the heart of persons, one demanding a phenomenologically grounded explanation, perhaps depends upon one's proximity to individuals who are thus afflicted and also upon the extent to which one's relationship to them takes place through forms of intimate association, rather than more formal social relationships. Moreover, and this is perhaps telling, it is those whose lives have been most impoverished, in whom the abuse has been the most absolute, whose lives fall, almost beyond sense, in the absurdity of an endless struggle with the 'now' of their lives, that are the worst afflicted. It is as though their absorption in coping, in the immediacy of the strategies of surviving, means their awareness is maintained in the available, in the ready-to-hand, such that the contemplative condition is foreclosed upon.

Yet even though it is difficult to embed an account in their own words, their condition is part of a general condition that one can unlock through the words of others. And even though the technique of the interview has the effect of derealizing the world, or deworlding phenomena, there are other ways of tracing the existential conditions of the world disclosed to these people. As I spent time outlining in the last chapter, talk generally reveals the totality of involvements and signification, the network of practical articulations in which understanding is grounded in the comprehending interactions of people. The talk that one comes across as a member of the town discloses the phenomena and experience that concern us because they exhibit what concerns them, in what way and what manner.

There is much transcription of conversation in this work. Most of this was taken from wherever I heard anything said that pointed-up the underlying background structure of articulation which, as we have seen, may be aspects of a domain of comportment habits that are not easily linguistically articulated. But, as well as talk that manifests the everyday coping that manifests articulations of the referential-whole, there is also much interview material. The difference is the interviews were unavoidably semiformal and in them I found myself having to try and force the people I talked to to make everything as explicit as possible, within my own sensitivity to the effects of this situation and stance. In the interviews I tried to guide the establishment of a realm of sense in which individuals would spontaneously constitute the sense of practices that do not follow the logic of formulae and which exist as systems of realized practices.[3] However, pushing them to take the position of spectator in regard to their own action, to constitute it as though it were, throughout, consciously constituted by a rational actor, often met with incredulity, embarrassment and a sense of estrangement, as though finally the books had got to my head.

Yet a sensitivity that is perhaps best characterized as 'epistemic' was not the only prerequisite for the practical dimension of this work. One's understanding of ontology must be practically realized in one's own comportment. One needs to be able to to assuage a whole range of anxieties in order to be able to carry out an interview. I would like, now to look at these issues because these are very powerful forces that act as barriers to articulation. There are severe tensions involved in asking people to speak who do not feel socially instituted to hold opinions. The people who I needed to record the speech of, were possessed of a dominated linguistic habitus, one that they were aware of as stigmatizing on formal linguistic markets. Hence, in formal situations, because they feel they do not possess the instruments to satisfy the requirements of public, official language, they experience a personal tension that tends to lead them to the ultimate euphemization of silence. And this is inscribed in a practical state, it is something they feel, even against their self-avowed will. So powerful are these social forces and so over-arching is the social structure that is the condition of possibility of such processes, that I found even in situations like the gym which might off-set the connotations of an 'interview' (i.e. a quasi-formal situation) and even with people I had known for a number of years, there was a deep reluctance and anxiety.

I never found asking people for, or doing, interviews a very comfortable experience. And not only on my part. My sense of unease was my own sense of the tensions towards hyper-tension and hyper-correction in them, manifest sometimes in smoking or in fidgeting. I was aware that interviews were an ordeal for many, something that they would not want to repeat. For many, the situation of systematic, co-ordinated, talking about particular aspects of life brought back too many of the ghosts that haunt so many working people, so much of the symbolic violence that makes us, to ourselves, what we are. Even where people were extremely sensitive and revealing in what they articulated, I could never get beyond this sense of failure that clung to the air. It was as though around us there were the ghosts of so much that had affected us all so deeply. This sense of eerie worthlessness is obviously not something one ordinarily experiences in interaction with people one knows; even among working people, it is carefully avoided. In many ways, the pervasiveness of the experience, and that it arose even with someone who is an intimate, reveals the depth of what Bourdieu characterizes:

The sense of the value of one's own linguistic products is a fundamental dimension of the sense of knowing the place which one occupies in the social space. One's original relation with different markets and the experience of the sanctions applied to one's own productions, together with the experience of the price attributed to one's own body, are doubtless some of the mediations which help to constitute that *sense of one's own social worth* which governs the practical relation to different markets (shyness, confidence, etc.) and, more generally, one's whole physical posture in the social world.   (Bourdieu 1991: 82)

It is a fact often overlooked that working class men are often acutely shy and often have extremely low self-esteem. One seldom confronts the extent of the abuses of the souls of working class people as concretely as when one tries to interview them. Even people who one knows to be articulate, thoughtful, insightful and powerfully evocative in their speech, exhibited tendencies of shy restraint as soon as one formalizes the situation, even simply through the introduction of a tape recorder. I found this a sobering experience. And, though it is one I understand completely from my own dispositions and from my experience of education, particularly university, I've never got beyond the shock, gut-level response, that it should not be so.

Too many academics care too little about any of these issues, and the process of writing often makes these processes invisible and unrecoverable. Yet the disposition to feel practically the effects of the social structure within which this kind of exchange makes sense and would take place is a prerequisite and yet academics seldom have the practical skills and intellectual proclivities to comport themselves towards 'research subjects' with the solicitude necessary for human understanding. However skilled one is, however easily one manages to avoid the institution of a more formal market, the best one can do is end up with a quasi-formal situation, in that for linguistically dispossessed groups the interview is *always* an intrusion, because, for reasons we discussed in the last chapter, it is clearly different from the interactions of everyday life and, after all, its final aim is the making of an accurate record that will be inscribed in culture. And, even in the unusual situation where the researcher and subject are formally equal, sharing the same situation, there remain imbalances in other forms of capital. All of this has a bearing on the matter of getting people to be interviewed and to speak.

Yet asking people to 'speak' about their lives immediately institutes a difference. It immediately institutes issues of linguistic competence and introduces the specters of the state education system and the normally encountered institutions in which its competent products work: the Department of Social Security, Job Centre and local council, none of which are well trusted. In this context, the very request to do an interview becomes ominous. I also found it tremendously disconcerting to my own sense of identity, in that it forced me into an objectifying relation to people who are just like me: who speak the same, walk the same, laugh the same, eat the same, spend their time in very similar ways and who are my only experience of a natural group. Moreover, there was something tragic but revealing of the depth of their humiliation, in the actual process of trying to 'gather data' about their lives. The tragedy arises when one talks to someone and listens to them talking with great insight about work or unemployment or what they thought of what was ahead for young people. Yet as soon as one asked them to 'be interviewed' their unease was palpable. One man, a highly conversational man of considerable insight, refused absolutely to say anything, insisting '*I* don't know 'owt [anything], gu an' ask X, he's bi'n [been] to college, he knows stuff. I can't talk, me.' And another insisted, 'It's n' good askin' me, Ah can't talk.' The extent to which one meets this response among working class people might be surprising if one doesn't understand the levels of their dispropriation. That is, their personal sense of their inability to do what all congenitally normal human beings can do, speak. A sense taught them through the education system as well as through other state organizations. So, often, I would do an interview and after the person would say, 'That won't any good wo' it.' Just as at the beginning they would say 'I don't really know anything', 'I don't know as I can 'elp ye.' It was these regular apologies, apologies from people taught to apologize for their lack of competence, that one realizes that these people were acting purely out of goodwill. Since they didn't feel authorized to speak, they felt that what they said was uninsightful. And this from people who have lived through great changes; some of whom have fought for their country, some for their jobs, and seen violence against their own kin. Many have simply endured the daily degradation of looking for work, being laid off and being insulted by low wages, long hours and poor conditions. And yet still, they 'know nowt': the last great paradox of domination, that those who have suffered are finally robbed of the right to be indignant.

Sadly, there were many, some of them some of my closest friends, who simply would not be interviewed. From the rest of my knowledge of them, I knew this was not mistrust, just a socially learnt and instituted sense of themselves as unable to speak. The presence of the tape recorder changed the sense of the context by demanding the adoption of a linguistic competence that was not tied to the performative situation-specific speech of the immediate context and its talk. The simple object, the tape recorder, seemed to proclaim a whole range of non-present practices that belonged to another social universe. The tape recorder seemed to acknowledge implicitly the objective hierarchy of habitus and linguistic competence and bring into their space an acknowledgement of the legitimate language[4] and the fact that, in relation to it, they speak a devalued form, 'slang', a dominated linguistic competence. This displayed a logic of their own practices in that it showed that they suspend the dominant criterion rather than contravene it and thus that they are always open to feeling its implied judgement in instances of their lives. Thus, when confronted with a formal market:

like the one constituted by a linguistic survey or investigation . . . [popular competence] . . . is, as it were, annihilated. The reality of linguistic legitimacy consists precisely in the fact that dominated individuals are always under the *potential jurisdiction* of formal law, even when they spend all their lives, like the thief described by Weber, beyond its reach, so that when placed in a formal situation they are doomed to silence or to the broken discourse which linguistic investigation also often records.   (Bourdieu 1991: 71)

This 'annihilation', therefore, was something that I often never managed to surmount, even with people who trusted me and knew me. And it was something I had to negotiate during interaction with people. What Bourdieu describes is something always present, something that always threatened to break through to the surface, the triumph of humiliation and degradation, of the social institution of incompetence, over the biologically normal and universal personal ability of speech. And to see this strange effect of power, of the socially learnt fracturing damage to people who are often astute and incisive speakers, was like an instantiation of the central themes of the whole work. Yet it was a deeply disturbing experience and something I have never really felt I have done justice to. It was as though beneath us, exerting an influence from which we can never quite break, was a great abyss of silence that threatened to silence the speaker. At one point, one person broke into an extended pause and said 'can yer turn it off, cos I can't 'andle this'. My own desire to articulate the nature of life, here, somehow seemed to embroil those whom I needed to speak in an impossible burden that I have felt was something not proper, something wrong. Something distasteful. Yet, also, it somehow re-affirms the need to understand the processes that make individuals unable to speak of their own lives, condemned by their own deep sense of the impropriety of their own articulation, to silence. An opposition to the cheap words of so many who are authorized to speak and do so with unselfconscious impropriety:

The authorized speech of status-generated competence, a powerful speech which helps to create what it says, is answered by the silence of an equally status-linked incompetence, which is experienced as technical incapacity.   (Bourdieu 1984: 413)

It is that experience of 'technical incapacity', that is an experience, that demands an effort to articulate it and which interviewing working class people makes manifest.

Yet there was a problem of recording interaction and speech. I felt it most acutely at those times when I had been particularly struck by instances of lucid, highly creative, often comic bits of interaction that articulated precisely the circumscribed nature of their lives and yet this was often in situations where it was impossible to record, like the street, gym or nightclub. At these times I have done my best to commit the interaction to memory and I have written it down at the earliest possible moment. This was important not only because of the impossibility of recording but because the same people, if they consented to be interviewed, when asked questions, did not produce speech that was as revealing as their communication in particular contexts. We have already looked at why this might be so, but it does mean that much of working class life is invisible because the spokespeople it does produce, even in towns like Rotherham, seldom live out the life of the class as such and many academic writers simply never see (or never see as relevant) many of the most important sites that reveal the conditions of working class existence. It is as though the working class are condemned to live always through moments, because their wit, insight and intelligence are produced, practically, for the situations through which they live. But much of what they are is lost to those moments since their cultural conditions go unrecorded and unarticulated. An important aspect of this is that, even within the realm of culture, there are very powerful forces to enforce euphemization and to refuse to recognize the issues involved in the conditions of working class life. It is something enshrined deep in the practical political sense of working class people. As one person put it:

X: Ah [I] read what yer gev [gave] mi' an' Ah can see why thi' dun't like it. Tha [you're] tellin' truth. Tha' ses it exactly ahr [how] it is an' thi' waint [won't] like that. Tha ca'(n)t tell the truth.

In the university climate it is possible to narrate instances of working class life and to have this held against one, personally. The same dynamic towards euphemization that the working class feel, intuitively, around middle class people, operates within the academic field against those who try to understand working class life in its detail. Those 'lost moments' that working class people live through are lost because they are hidden, concealed in social space because working class people know they cannot be acknowledged in the dominant public discourse because of propriety and its newest radical form, political correctness. And anyone caught trying to bring these topics into the gaze of the academic risks facing all the consequences of heresy. Yet such is the invisibility of working class life that this itself just seems inconceivable.

I have tried to capture the sense articulated in those moments. The burden of proof falls heavily, particularly since I must commit to paper not only people's words but the world that makes their words not only sensible but cogent.

There were times when I succeeded in establishing the kinds of conditions in which individuals would focus in their speech about their lives in Rotherham. It was a matter of capturing some of the insights that one hears around working class people. I found that there was a good deal of knowledge about precisely what had happened to areas like this: a powerful political habitus, a deep political sense, an embodied set of values through which people spoke of 'right' and 'wrong', often through the actual examples of family and friends. However, this is a political sense that operates more as a moral code concerning friends and family, and, whilst there were distinct themes of class running through their attitudes, people would often be disconcerted if pushed to formulate overtly political conclusions. It was more an issue of right and wrong based upon a practical class sense of what kinds of behaviour to expect from individuals, and not really a political sense. It is a propensity to produce answers to political questions that only on occasions rises to the level of explicit utterance. Bourdieu suggests a reason:

In short, whereas one might naively say that people are more politically informed, more politically competent, to the extent that they are more educated, in my view one should say that those who are socially designated as competent, as entitled and required to have political competence, are more likely to become what they are, to become what they are told they are, that is politically competent.

. . . The sense of political orientation can govern some practical political choices without rising to the level of discourse, and it will be disconcerted and disarmed by situations in which an answer is required at the level of discourse.

(Bourdieu 1993a: 162)

The book demanded that I elicit answers at the level of discourse. Moreover, it became clear that readers had a taste for certain kinds of 'evidence' and have a predilection for stories that demanded a certain kind of sympathy. It was almost like the category of the 'deserving poor', those in whom the effects of poverty and dispossession can be contemplated. One is always aware that there is too much that cannot be brought into the political light. And we cannot forget that this piece of writing began life as part of an examination of its author, which means that the demands to 'substantiate' and 'legitimate' the account were pressing. And I knew that what would qualify as proof would be excerpts of material of a specific form. Bits that were articulately tragic, not the silence of those most lost. In this regard the book shares the demands of the culture that it was, of necessity, written for; it bears the hallmark of a class whose relation to language is that of the scholar, the person free to treat language not as an instrument of practice but as an object of contemplation and who use language contemplatively to constitute objects. Because of this, I knew that I had to try and push the people interviewed to objectify their own culture, to treat it as a 'landscape', to describe it as present-to-hand, occurrent, a position that involved a break with their primary experience. Despite what I have written, I found myself, at points in interviews, simply feeling a very powerful compulsion to try and find some way to elicit from the people interviewed utterances that would communicate their experience without the reader of their transcribed words having the background required to understand.

During interviews, I felt the pressure of having to push these people to take up an objectifying distance, to make explicit some of the things that they accept simply as 'there' and unalterable. It became clear, in such a situation, that their lives of enforced engagement with the world that is left them does not lead them to the perceptual techniques of objectifying their environment. This was why questions like, 'How do you see Rotherham?' or 'How do you find Rotherham?' got one nowhere. The problem was that people simply didn't understand their lives in these ways: they lacked the instruments and, more importantly, they lacked these perceptual techniques because of the relation to their experience that the necessities of their lives mediated.

The overwhelming similarity of the life-styles of the people with whom they live acts as a closure to their perception. Their experience of the social world is that of an immense similarity, and the reactions and communication of others reinforces this primary experience of the social, so that they are unable to take up a gaze upon their life as though it was an object that might be in some way determined and different from any other people. They are accepting of their experience, as a fate, as life. Moreover, these kinds of questions, to the extent that they presumed a subject-position of distance produced through a constituting gaze, were too similar in form to, and thus experienced as resembling, a scholastic situation. Therefore, what I had to do was to obey the logic of the fields that the people themselves establish and in which their utterances have value. That way, if the social field established gave value to their linguistic productions, their reason for participation would be the pursuit of respect that characterizes the protected markets they establish among themselves. What was practically effective in this enterprise was my bodily hexis and my education, which I found I could use together to make the persons interviewed feel 'instituted', authorized, to speak: to legitimate their linguistic competence as best I could. I had to thus destroy the linguistic artefact produced when 'incompetent' speakers meet a 'competent' speaker. So what I had to do was to try and give people a sense of what my work was about; to show the meaning of the work in terms of their lives in concrete situations. This was hard work, and sometimes my imagination would simply fail and I would fail to give the person a sense of what the work was about.

Because the problems generating the questions were from a different social space, one structurally higher, I consciously emphasized the extent to which my own life followed the contours of their own by talking to them about our day-to-day experiences. This also gave me the concrete examples to begin to introduce some of the ideas that were generating my work and which I wanted them to comment upon. I was trying to get them to talk about their experience in the context of the work I was doing. This was a kind of embedding of the ideas against the touchstone of their experience. This technique also emphasized my own immersion in the same conditions, and this helped to alleviate tensions accruing from differences in linguistic and symbolic capital. Trying to involve them in the work, trying to share a sense of the intellectual problems with individuals, went some way to counter-acting some of the damage done to their sense of linguistic competence in the formal education system.

Getting working people to feel comfortable with speaking and authorized to speak in the face of so much of their experience which dispossesses them of their own instruments of expression, demanded a constant monitoring, on the spot, of the effects of the social structure that frames all social interaction. I found my first task was one of persuading the person that they had something of interest to say. But this was difficult when they themselves cannot imagine how anyone could be interested in their lives. Getting someone to be interviewed is *almost* a paradigm example of getting somebody to do something for nothing. What I had to do was to render the work meaningful and hope that they would then participate. Getting them to believe that they had something to say that I was going to relay, something that I myself wanted to say but couldn't say without their help, was the way of getting them to feel enough self-respect and self-importance to speak. This meant that I had to try and make the work theirs, to try and suspend the sense of the dominant market and to re-establish the criteria that create value in the spaces they inhabit in order to involve them in exchanges through which they could feel recognized and recognize their own experience and thus become involved in 'striving to recover a meaning that was both their own and alien to them' (Bourdieu 1990a: 3).

What this amounts to is a kind of engaged, committed interaction in which one helps the other to articulate the pieces that have contributed to the totality of their experience, the conclusions that life has brought them to. It is a technique that Bourdieu describes as 'a relationship of *active and methodical listening*' (Bourdieu 1996a: 19). This demands a deep attentiveness to the person, a willingness to immerse oneself in the narrative that emerges of a singular life history, and yet from this position of shared thoughts and feelings to be able to sensitively respond in affirming ways that exhibit a precise practical understanding of the objective conditions in which their life and the lives of this group belong. For all the difficulty in getting people to be interviewed, this is actually very similar to what in the penultimate chapter we will see as a characteristic of working class speakers, so that once the interviews were under way the person interviewed often experienced the same solace that is a characteristic of their friendships. Through this method it was possible to establish the kind of talk that working people normally participate in, but under informal conditions. I found myself trying hard to get people to talk with the casual accuracy that normally characterized their linguistic productions; whilst being careful to control the interaction, to monitor my own levels of speech as well as verbal and non-verbal signs, in order to guarantee the engaged participation of the people being interviewed.

However, because working class people do not feel authorized to speak and seldom get the opportunity to articulate their own experience, much of their social experience is repressed, even avoided, and an interviewer has to try to get them to talk freely, to help them to say what is repressed. The task of interviewing, therefore, is one of getting living, moving experience to express its own meaning, and then not to lose its sense in formulations that abstract that sense from its conditions of possibility. Interviewing is not simply a matter of recording responses to questions, it is about enabling the truth to emerge, about enabling people to speak who have spent a lifetime experiencing their lack of importance, whilst listening to an ever-growing number of spokespersons who misconstrue their experience. In order to establish a relationship of enquiry, therefore, one needs first to establish the importance of the experiences recounted in a way that signifies the experiences. The interviewee can only give a response, properly speaking, if they can appropriate the position from which it matters, and this was what I worked to establish. One way in which I tried to make the issues explicit and to bring the background of our lives into view, was by trying to describe life in a different place, in order to give another sense of life in which the sense of our lives might be cast into relief.

Underlying all my interviewing strategies, then, was my sharing this space, culture and life. Bourdieu captures the importance of this:

Social proximity and familiarity in effect provide two of the social conditions of 'non-violent' communication. For one thing, when the researcher is socially very close to her respondent she provides her, by virtue of their interchangeability, with guarantees against the threat of having her subjective reasoning reduced to objective causes, and those choices that she experiences as free made to seem the effect of objective determinisms revealed by analysis . . . When . . . an unemployed worker [*questions*] another unemployed worker . . . with whom she shares virtually all the characteristics capable of operating as major explanatory factors of her practices and representations, and to whom she is linked by close familiarity, the rationale for the questions is found in her dispositions, which are objectively attuned to those of the respondent herself. Thus the most brutally objectifying questions will no longer appear threatening or aggressive because her interlocutor knows perfectly that she shares with her what she is inducing the other to divulge and, in the same way, shares the risks that the speaker exposes herself to by speaking about it. And the interviewer can never forget that by objectifying the respondent, she is also objectifying herself, as is attested by the adjustments she introduces into certain of her questions, moving from the objectivizing 'you' to 'one', which refers to an impersonal collective, and on then to 'we', in which she clearly states that she herself is involved in the objectification. (Bourdieu 1996a: 20)

This relation of familiarity meant that there was the possibility of establishing a sense of mutual involvement in the conditions and situations being discussed, which meant that interviews could become quite vivid mutual expressions of life and of some of the deepest, most troubling experiences of our culture which would generally be glossed over or heavily euphemized because of propriety. The situation thus became:

a two-handed socio-analysis, in which the analyst is herself caught up and examined, much as the person she is submitting to investigation.   (Bourdieu 1996a: 21)

In these conditions what occurred was an objectification by participants in which the participants would struggle to articulate the hidden principles of their lives, the externality that they experienced and which their practice accommodated. In these special conditions, in which the participants are playing a socially extra-ordinary language game of trying to use language to state the usually ignored conditions of their experience, an often repressed set of truths would emerge about the dissatisfaction they felt with their lives and position. In these conditions, their sense of who and what they are emerges, it is given voice.[5]

A feature of these exchanges, indeed one common to working class people's interaction, was that, even where there was latent sadness within the content of speech, it was relayed with a kind of joviality intent on hiding the deep sources of pain and the deep resignation to a world of sadness that speaker and hearer both know is immanent in their narrations. Hence, so much of the depth in the content of what is exchanged in these interactions is masked by a sad fatalistic laughter that is paradoxical in nature because it amounts to a publicly acceptable way of recognizing a personal agony arising from shared fate. The forced laughter underlines the pathos of recognizing what life amounts to within this realm of possibility. People would finish talking about something that they could simply not resolve, like being stuck on the dole knowing there was little escape from the cycle of their lives in this context, and they'd laugh, knowingly, and acknowledge things understatedly. It was as though the magnitude of the impossibility of their lives ever being qualitatively different made them ashamed of what they are and they'd say 'It's a good job I'm not a manic depressive' or 'It's a good job wi' not suicidal, Sime', and smile. At times the whole situation seemed to resonate with the absurd hopelessness of the fact that human existence is founded upon meaning, that our worlds are always meaningful, yet instead of the pleasure of fascination and the fruition of absorption in a realm of personally experienced value, what we have is the counterfeit of this inalienable human capacity in the ugliness of a brutal realm and the triumph of a meaningless valuelessness. And the everyday misery of these people is so ubiquitous, so utterly mundane, so much a fabric of the ordinary lives of ordinary people that it barely seems worthy of remark as people live their lives of quiet despair. As one young unemployed woman described her feelings:

> Yer just feel like yer left out. I just don't know how to put it into words. It's shit really but yer can't moan, that'll not mek [make] life better, tha just 'as to ger'on wiy it [get on with it].

Sat listening to these people talking about experiences that I knew so well, I was struck by how isolated so many are, how alone, and how the feelings are subordinated, repressed, in order to go about our daily lives amidst the severe anonymity of lives bereft of shared experiences: that is, experiences enmeshed in a public world of collective life which particularized personal time, fixed existence in a moment of shared space. We share an experience of struggle, and in the interviews great swathes of common experience emerge, but the condition of living this is, all too often, alone. Like the Protestant Weber describes, alone before God, so many struggle to experientially efface the wasting of life with whatever available experiences there are. It is a paradoxical witnessing of a common experience, rooted in the social but based upon a profound denial of the possibility of the social and, particularly, of the civic. The interviews manifest the common pain of lacking a viable connection to others, and yet also proclaimed the impossibility of founding life upon such connections. Many spoke of their difficulty finding friends, of their mistrust of people, of their wariness of people and of the nastiness around them. All of this shows the decay of elementary solidarities. The interviews were like a miracle, some flaw in the logic of this world: people communicating amidst the white noise of denial and confusion. Through one another, for a moment something important was established; what Merleau-Ponty expressed beautifully:

> We witness every minute the miracle of related experience, and yet nobody knows better than we do how this miracle is worked, for we are ourselves this network of relationships. The world and reason are not problematical. We may say, if we wish, that they are mysterious, but their mystery defines them: there can be no question of dispelling it by some 'solution', it is on the hither side of all solutions. True philosophy consists in re-learning to look at the world, and in this sense a historical account can give meaning to the world quite as 'deeply' as a philosophical treatise. We take our fate in our hands, we become responsible for our history through reflection, but equally by a decision on which we stake our life.
>
> (Merleau-Ponty 1962: xx)

Even in conditions of atomization, in which selves lack the grounds to found meaning in one another, even where all we have are fractured lives torn from a coherent centre of experience, we witness this network because of its absence. Even amidst the most acute isolation, we share common experiences and we find in the despair the need in ourselves for 'this network of relationships'; a network whose social impossibility preoccupies many of these people. For how much longer one wonders?

Listening to the intimate dramas and ordinary misfortunes of these lives; hearing in their words and in the very timbre of their voices the sanctions of the education system and the state bureaucracy that mediates access to labour and housing markets for so many, one senses, in one's heart, the deep social wounds visited upon flesh that wears itself inappropriately, that the 'main mechanism of domination operates through the unconscious manipulation of the body' (Bourdieu and Eagleton 1992: 121). The suffering, like the domination, goes from body-to-body with all the invisible power that the objective has to inscribe itself in our most personal sense-of-the-world. This sense that the body has of itself as 'at home' or estranged, and the body's capacity to respond to gestural and verbal resonances, the body's capacity to feel the urgencies of those in whom it finds itself, became a problem for me whilst transcribing at university. Somehow, facing the problems of these conditions, which I have always had to return to, demands being among people who share that fate. I found listening, alone, over and over to the voices of people I had interviewed, soul-destroying. When I had been with them, that pain had not arisen because I had experienced some solidarity in our shared personal history, but alone I was simply consumed by the injustice and human wastage, and yet the very conditions of dislocation proclaimed the futility submerged, half-knowingly in people's summation of their personal predicament. It was something that I tried to explain to one of my friends:

S: Yer know when I'm do'in mi interviews and am wi' people, I feel fo' what the'r sayin' but it dun't [doesn't] affect mi as bad as when I'm on mi' own 'ere 'cos thi's like a solidarity in talkin' abaht [about] ahr [our] lives, whereas when I'm 'ere, it just kills me. I sit in mi' room and Ah'm do'in' mi interviews and listening to the' voices and it just upsets me s' much. Cos, I'm 'ere wi' all these people who 'ave good lives, it just seems s' wrong and s' unfair and it's worse cos I'm on mi own, kind'a re-livin' it.

X: Ye, but yer shun't let it get to ye' like that cos us who yer interviewing, that's ahr lives and it's not as bad for us cos we don't know owt [anything] else. I mean, fair enough, it is wrong and us lives are shit and money's shit but we 'an't seen wot you've seen and it's all we've known. So don't get upset abaht it cos them that yer interviewing, they can live wi'y it. We 'ave to, so it's not as bad.

This woman is effectively saying that the social conditions people live in inscribe in them dispositions that ensure they do not experience their situation as being as dire as it seems to someone who has come to see it through the eyes of the dominant aesthetic. She is therefore acknowledging exactly what Bourdieu believes to be the basis of the sociological gaze: distance from these types of conditions. A distance which makes the comprehension of working class life such an inherently prejudicial enterprise.

Therefore, the desire to create the conditions in which experience can begin to be articulated by interviewees and can accede to consciousness, to explicit discourse, and in which the truth can emerge, is a careful skilled labour for the interviewer. One based upon a deep practically instantiated sense of all the subtle minutiae of the un-representable background manifest in their experience and articulations. It depends upon establishing conditions of care in which people who know these things better than any academic, but in a different mode, can be helped to make explicit what is manifest in their embodied, sensuous, feelings of what exists pre-personally and pre-objectively for them. The goal of truth must be actualized through the craft of sociological method. But this is a craft learned not through the application of an abstract formalizable technique but through the researcher having extended his/her practical sensitivity by deepening his/her understanding both of the conditions of existence of the people interviewed and the effects of the social structure on the interviewing relationship itself:

This craft is a real 'disposition to pursue truth' . . . which enables one to improvise on the spot, in the pressing situation of the interview, strategies of self-presentation and adaptive responses, encouragement and opportune questions, etc., in such a manner as to help the research respondent give up her truth or, rather, to be delivered of her truth.   (Bourdieu 1996a: 30)

I hope that throughout I have given the reader the grounds to adopt a 'feeling' for the people's words that provides them with their sense; that restores, as far as possible, the context from which the speakers' sense of the world emerges: the peculiar necessity of the life that they speak of; that common world I share with them, that has come to inhabit us, that shared experience of culture, that mutual possession by the same world, that affinity of being. It is to this that we now turn more directly.

6

Necessity and being working class

There is a terrible beauty in some of these girls – terrible, I mean, because it is ephemeral, foredoomed. The language that our children speak may not be standard English but there still is wisdom here. Our children have become wise by necessity.
(Kozol 1992: 34)

And dimly she realized one of the great laws of the human soul: that when the emotional soul receives a wounding shock, which does not kill the body, the soul seems to recover as the body recovers. But this is only appearance. It is really only the mechanism of the re-assumed habit. Slowly, slowly the wound to the soul begins to make itself felt, like a bruise, which only slowly deepens its terrible ache, till it fills all the psyche. And when we think we have recovered and forgotten, it is then that the terrible after-effects have to be encountered at their worst.
(Lawrence 1994a: 49)

Living in Rotherham, one cannot help but be struck by an underlying coherence in the life of the place; a collective experience; a distinct sense that seems to recur throughout conversations, an emergent theme. Moreover, as one encounters life in this way, it soon becomes clear that much everyday expression is rooted in people's experience of insecurity and an inability to secure for themselves the things they need in order to live. Moreover, one realizes that these people are in this predicament because of a particular relation to the institutions of English society which they inherited at birth. But, when one has got that far, then listening to people's speech, one begins to realize a pattern of change that has occurred quite rapidly and which has affected these people deeply, acting to reconstruct their lives in many different areas simultaneously, and yet connected to the same central condition of their lives. And, furthermore, there is another very powerful experience that characterizes such areas: people seem depressed, pessimistic, unhappy. Even the ways they have fun seem touched by the desperate conditions of their lives. And, once one knows people in an area like this, something else emerges: the ones who have somehow managed to develop a sensitive and enquiring relation to human life suffer quite deeply and in many different ways for doing so. And this, if one lives among working class people, is what indicts their condition: those people who develop a human relation to the world, who are thoughtful, sensitive – for want of a better concept – 'non-alienated', are, at best, frustrated and, at worst, miserable. They live like this stoically and, on the whole, without much criticism of the individuals among whom they live. Indeed, most see it as their fault, as a personal failing that they feel as they do, rather than as part of a general social condition. This may seem a trivial matter, but when one lives with people who are decent, ethical, sensitive, astute and, often, knowledgeable; who are helpful, generous and, often, skilled (if uncertified), and yet whose conversation is so full of a needless self-depre-cation born of abuse; who present themselves in terms of the limitations they have learnt are their own; in terms of their innate uselessness and inability; then one senses a hidden tragedy in their barely spoken of, and uncertain, pain. A few examples of conversation might give some small insight:

S: We'er [where] do you work?
M: Retail . . . (pause). . . .or Ah [I] did. I got laid off abaht [about] three month agu.
S: Did ye? Ahr yer findin' it on dole?
M: It's not much fun. When yer workin' ye' think if ye' 'ad time ye'd du this an' that but it's not very good. Ye'v got to hang on to whatever w'k [work] ye'v got, n' matter ahr [how] bad it is 'cos ye dun't know what kinda hole yer gunna end up in once yer on dole.

Well, I'm a builder rait [right] an' truth 'r [of the] matter is that if yer want a livin' wage, ye'll [you'll]'ave to work abroad 'cos [because] thi's no decent wages 'ere, even if tha travels fo' work, it's all same, thi' know that thi'v got us rahnd [around] the'r little fingers an' thi know thi' an't got to pay no bonuses anymore . . .

. . . We're all in the same boat, yer heads fucked up every day of the week . . .

W: The future fo' ma kids, it's bleak, not just fo' mine but fo' all young kids, thi just don't know when it's gunna end; all thi's 'avin' nothin' an' du'in nowt [nothing], an' bein' nowt, it might bi w'se [worse] in ten, fifteen years might it?
S: God I'ope not but I know, yer feel like that dun't yer?

J: Ah wo' married young an' wi did struggle at f'st, wi' t' [with the] little 'uns an' M [*husband*] ohnny [only] an apprentice but wi expected things to get better an' t' bi able to relax a bit an' enjoy life nahr [now] but it's all bi'n tekken away nahr an' it? Instead'r bein' all right wi' gunna 'ave to struggle rest'r 's lives.

F: It's allous [always] bin' an 'ard w'kin town this, w'k [work]'ard, play 'ard, that's ahr [how] it's allous [always] been. All wi ever expected wo t' leave school, to gu' t' w'k in steel w'ks, like mi father befo'ore me, look at 'im, born t' w'k, straight in after school, that's all he expected an' all he got.

Readers may be sceptical that such comments are representative of the feelings and experiences of working people and this work began as an attempt to begin to record, and then to understand, the sense of the world such articulations emerge from. Whilst working people do not continually produce such utterance throughout their daily lives, since life is something their practical philosophy insists be gotten on with and not dwelt upon, the number of such comments that one comes across is considerable and exhibits remarkable consistency. So, these quotations are not exceptional and nor are they from people who were conscious of being particularly revealing about themselves. Indeed, anyone who lives among working people must know that such utterances are very common in response to things like newspaper articles, television programmes and the everyday experiences of people in these places, indeed to anything that draws attention to the vulnerability that makes their condition one of anxiety, such that anything that focuses upon their insecurity can elicit such manifestations of the prolonged strain involved in their position.

For now, I do not wish to consider the detail of these quotations, except to say that these people's speech emerges from a distinct sense of the world and the excerpts do give us a sense of the content of everyday speech in places like Rotherham. And yet, as one listens to these people, at a time when self-development through education and training has been so aggressively toted by politicians and managers as a means of self-development that will transform individuals into employment assets, why, in these conditions, could a process of self-development make any sense since it is likely only to increase their capacity to suffer *in these conditions?* Without economic change, an economic problem will not be solved by educational action. In these conditions the contradiction involved in education – that it might well turn out to be a waste of effort – is something that is becoming clearer to these people as they see so many on yet another training scheme, and yet another graduate fail to do very much more than they might have aspired to do without incurring the debts of education. If any have a right to cynicism and misanthropy, then many of these people do, because their daily experience teaches them the emptiness of the injunctions that have for so long sustained so many to, as the new-managers might say, 'better themselves'. Their experience has taught them the uncertainty of work, and yet they are told that training and education are the way to an income and security. They learn that this is a road to nowhere;

one that never seems to end, and that, no matter how far they walk along it, their condition does not appear to alter. There seems only more uncertainty and the resolve of another plan or scam to get through the problems of the immediately pressing future. There are, then, uncertain expectations, which cynicism helps resolve the anxiety of, conjuring a feeling of autonomy and the appearance of control from a context of compromise that approaches futility. These are some of the greatest problems that human beings face: how is one to find a route within a society that will allow one to participate in the forms of experience one learns are important to human life? How is one to avoid being consigned to living out a stigmatized identity that can be lived only with a degree of bad faith? And, for many of these people, how is one to acquire the forms of capital that will allow them to avoid the terrible problems affecting so many at the bottom of these societies? For many of the least endowed with symbolic and cultural capital, it is a paradox that they must solve at the price of their dignity, through a restructuring of their comportment that reaches to the deepest aspects of self-identity and personal autonomy. The paradox is highlighted by Bourdieu:

> The logic of adjustment of dispositions to position allows us to understand how the dominated can exhibit more *submission* (and less resistance and subversion) than those who see them through the eyes, i.e., the habitus, of the dominant . . . that is, less than intellectuals would envision . . . when they go in the direction of a sort of spontaneist populism, theories of resistance . . . often forget that the dominated seldom escape the antinomy of domination. For example, to oppose the school system, in the manner of the British working-class 'lads' analysed by Willis (1977), through horseplay, truancy, and delinquency, is to exclude oneself from the school, and increasingly, to lock oneself into one's condition of . . . [domination]. On the contrary, to accept assimilation by adopting school culture amounts to being coopted by the institution. The dominated are very often condemned to such dilemmas, to choices between two solutions which, each from a certain standpoint, are equally bad ones.   (Bourdieu and Wacquant 1992: 81–2)

Under present conditions, the price of resistance, of standing by the dignities of an older order in which working people had some worth, has become huge. When one has little, it is easier for everything to be taken away, and, as the impact of new welfare measures bites more deeply, it is clear that working people must learn to hide their dispositions towards resistance and learn the dutiful jig of acquiescence. Here, therefore, there is a distinct experience because there is a distinct economic and, more importantly, political condition. It is this that, often unknowingly, binds working people in a shared experience of commonality.

Therefore, I want to ask the question 'what is at the heart of working class people's experience?' It is a question the intellectual climate has made problematic. For many within the university, the issue of class is one that they simply do not have to care about, except in ridicule and scorn, and even amongst academic sociologists the term, as far as they are concerned, can have no unambiguous meaning. This has always puzzled and confused me. How could this be? What has happened to our intellectual culture? Why has it been so blind and so silent when so many have lived through so much turmoil and watched the results of generations of struggle being given up without even a statement of surrender? We are taught from an epistemically early age that class is a vague and even unhelpful concept, that there are many different class fractions, which make my question analytically meaningless. Yet if one engages with working people one finds a profound sense of the centrality of a common experience of their living conditions and of the society in which they live. This experience is obvious in every constitutive moment in which the society is made and remade and in which the conditions of exclusion and marginality, of hardship and humiliation, are achieved through all the totality of affinities and repulsions that modulate the contours of English social structure.

Yet, we are taught to scan for difference, to trace the differences between groups, to find what separates those working from those not, to find the differences between age cohorts and the like; but what if the truth of a series of lives was one of a similarity beyond difference, of an identity of kind that is fundamental beyond differences between that kind? Of a shared plight; a destiny dominated by the uncertainty of work and by a life constituted amidst a space of possibility delimited by the constant mediating presence of state agencies like the Department of Social Security (DSS) and Job Centre. Moving from the first principle that class is a problematic concept and that changes in society have rendered it less important than in previous periods, it is easy to reach the conclusion that working class people are no longer a group who experience distinct cultural conditions, conditions which shape the realm of personal possibility and destiny. So, over the last thirty years, class has moved towards the bottom of the hierarchy of objects of study: a sort of treason of the intellectuals, British style.

The academy invites us to participate in the sense of a world freed from the practical urgencies that invest it with the sense it has for those who must know it through vulnerability and insecurity. Entry to university ushers a break with the fabric of the world, and we are invited, if we are to hope for success to beckon with its elegant fingers, to come to feel a repulsion to the politics of the poor. Reality gets lost in the race for the hyper-coherence of politically correct opinion and in the games of good-conscience that are the dominant motif of the conversations of radical intellectuals. In place of the fundamental issues of dispossession that this society is built upon we discover that working *men* are sexist and racist and part of a group responsible for the world's oppression: white imperialist, heterosexual males. The embodied ethics of a silent group, unrepresented in the spaces of delicate discussion, are never recognized, nor are the racism and intolerance, the deep processes of abjection and uglification that are the very condition of the experience of elite university-space that the bourgeois across the world are willing to pay so much for. There is little that one can say in the face of the denial of the importance of the most fine-grained of human interactions in the face of the petty grand-narratives that pass so much muster among the radical intelligentsia who occupy the arts faculties, gaining huge symbolic rewards for what amounts to a social parody obscuring the grounds of their own privilege and investment-strategies. Moreover, too much of their radical agenda, whatever its rhetoric, amounts to a stigmatizing of some of the most powerless sections of society and ends in the grotesque nuances of an exclusion of those already excluded who have clawed their way to share their space. It is a state of affairs Ros Coward is to be admired for having the honesty to acknowledge:

The economic guts have been ripped from large areas of the country. In less than a generation, many men have watched an entire edifice of everyday life, built on steady work and a regular wage, crumble . . . The price of this is huge, not for some nameless horde but for individuals whose hopes and frustrations have been written out of the political agenda . . . It is known that young men, perpetrators of much crime, are also its main victims . . . But the media is wedded to the image of the yob because it seems to encapsulate the real and imaginary fears of our times. The yob is carrying the weight of masculinity which, for a variety of reasons, middle class society finds increasingly unacceptable, and rhetorically dumps onto the men of lower class. He is a classic scapegoat: lugging around the sins of our culture while the rest of us look sanctimoniously on.

For centuries, poor men and crime have been connected in the public imagination, particularly in periods of economic hardship. But contemporary fears have a new element. There's a growing belief that there is something in masculinity itself which inclines poor young men to anti-social behaviour. In fact, this is a recent twist to an old story. The yob is not a new phenomenon . . .Contemporary theories of a social underclass draw on this long history of male-outcast groups. The 1990 image of the council estate, with its gangs of alienated youths, abandoned mothers and violent homes, drug dealing and drinking, and chronic crime, is an update of an earlier vision of the dark side of Britain's social landscape.

These images would not work unless legitimated. Two discourses have provided them with a respectable gloss – underclass theory, and a quasi-feminist critique of masculinity . . . Hatred of yobs has become entangled in a wider hostility towards men, a hostility fuelled by a quasi-feminist critique of masculinity. It is the maleness of the yobs, and particularly the hyped-up machismo which they represent, which is often seen as the main problem . . . Indeed decrying men and macho values has become a favourite media pastime. And no doubt some of the less pleasing aspects of masculinity should be mocked. But when this disparagement of all things male gets linked to the poor, in fact to those who are most disadvantaged in the current economy, the result is much more problematic . . . A critique of masculinity, which was originally intended to undermine traditional claims to male power, has now become a way of attacking the least powerful men in our society. That critiques of gender can be used in this way should warn us that they are not necessarily progressive. Women's protests against male dominance have, at times, intersected with, or even reinforced, middle-class efforts to subdue and 'civilise' the male 'underclass'. And the history of this link between feminism, and efforts to 'reform' lumpen masculinity, serves as a contemporary warning.   (Coward 1994)

And in the same piece she captures the effects of this in the popular press and the respectable middle classes:

'Yob', once a slang insult, is now a descriptive category used by tabloid and quality newspapers alike . . . Yob is a species of young white working class male which if the British media are to be believed is more common than ever before . . . The yob is the bogey of the Nineties, hated and feared with a startling intensity by the British middle class. Janet Daley describes such men as 'drunken Neanderthals', while Jeremy Kingston, also in the Times, reckons they are 'crapulous louts'. Simon Heffer of the Telegraph claims, like Peter Lilley, that not even women of their own social class can tolerate such ghastly specimens: 'Nobody wants to marry a yob because he is boorish, lazy and unemployable.'

The language in which such young men are described – louts, scum, beasts – can be heard across the political spectrum. It appears in an extreme form in Sun editorials and in a modified version in sombre discussions of youth culture, as well as in some feminist writings on contemporary masculinity . . . This insistent view of the 'yob' as morally delinquent – idle, criminal, unemployable, and (a very Nineties inflexion, this) unmarriageable – would cause outcry if used to refer to race or women.   (Coward 1994)

An example of this genre is Tony Parsons' piece, 'Thick on the ground thick in the head' where we are told that Parsons 'ventures into the tattooed jungle, where a new breed of slothful, parasitic animal has chewed up and spat out the dignified values that once made him proud to be part of Britain's working class'. Parsons' position is indeed fascinating, considering his origins, and it is worth quoting because it illustrates the personal distinction that can be garnered by what is effectively racial caricature; an inability to recognize the processes whereby individuals come to bear the marks of stigmatizing conditions upon the flesh. Parsons begins:

Something has died in the working class – a sense of grace, feelings of community, their intelligence, decency and wit. The salt of the earth has become the scum of the earth, a huge tribe of tattooed white trash . . . now they are impoverished in their heads and in their hearts. They are post-literate. They can read. But . . . they don't . . . With their distended beer bellies, dyed blond hair and pale tattooed flesh, they belch and threaten their way through life. They contribute nothing. They spoil everything. They are lost in a cultural wasteland that I call the tattooed jungle . . . As their brains have shrunk, so their bellies have ballooned . . . These people wouldn't know self-respect if it bit them on the backside of their shell-suites . . . Auberon Waugh . . . asserts that the distinguishing feature of the working class today is their viciousness, their lack of any Christian compassion – certainly God is dead in the tattooed jungle . . . The love of a good time is now a mindless gluttony. Where there was once a thirst for knowledge, there is now only a celebration of ignorance. Despite their surface aggression, the working class are horribly passive. Afflicted by cultural lethargy, their flabby minds are as undiscerning as blotting paper, willing to soak up any rubbish that prime time trash culture decides to pump out . . . In the tattooed jungle they are happy to advertise their creed. Say it aloud: I'm plebeian and proud. All notions of social mobility or cultural aspirations are suspect. In the tattooed jungle they cling to all those bogus clichés about the working class – that they have no airs and graces, that they lack pretension and are honest.

(Parsons 1992)

What is interesting about this kind of presentation of working class people is that it makes no attempt to understand the phenomena it describes. It is easy to overlook the processes of subjectification involved in being positioned in a stigmatizing way. The shell suit, like track-suit bottoms and T-shirt can be purchased extremely cheaply and are uniquely fitted to the lives of people with no public life (i.e. the unemployed, those condemned to a life in the private space of the home) and who thus, denied the symbolic profits of public life, are condemned to make an elective affinity of what is a social destiny that they are powerless to change and which they can enjoy some revenge over by wearing garments that create an effect of negative distinction or stigma. Condemning people to be what they are has the dangerous effect of making them embrace what they are perceived to be. Like the ugly, you leave them no place for dignity, and they build a world upon their abjection. In a world in which such slight differences of comportment carry such savaging judgements, one can perhaps understand the logic that compels individuals, lacking the means to be other than they are, to fail to exhibit the shame appropriate to charity. Parsons' characterization of the destruction of the traditional values he associates with working class people interestingly focuses upon the appearance of working people, on their bodies and manners, on the most visible signs of class life-style emblematized in the flesh like stigmata. That his intuitive account fixes upon these features as signs of social decay is itself revealing. It illuminates the forms of classification through which bodies are perceived, as well as the roots of misrecognition through which the social conditions necessary for the acquisition of forms of bodily hexis are misperceived as natural, individual, moral dispositions instead of socially mediated forms that relate directly to cultural relations of domination and exclusion. Such features may themselves be emblematic of social conditions in which the conditions of acquisition of traditional modes of comportment and related forms of association have been destroyed, leaving anomic groups whose lives are characterized by a kind of abject human existence that their comportment has to manage and of which it thus bears the traces. In a sense, if class is embodied, corporealized, and if the conditions of the working class have become untenable, to a degree anti-human, then we should expect this to be manifest in changes in comportment and in the patterns of responses which manifest what matters to people. The process at work, here, involves the death of an ethos, the decay of a morality made flesh. It is in this light that we might see Parsons' focus upon style, deportment and manners, since these are the primary signifiers of speciation. Parsons' piece, however contentious, is a response to changes in the social fabric of British culture. However, we would be well warned to consider Gareth Stedman Jones' comment:

I was not trying to suggest that these people were lovable or that they were easy to feel solidarity with. But then, as now, the discourse created them, as a sort of 'other' whom no one respectable could identify with. That creation serves a conservatism born of fear. The main difference is that this 'other' was seen as degenerate and pathetic rather than violent. But they were still seen as a menace right across the political spectrum.   (Quoted in Coward 1994)

The problem is that Parsons makes no effort to locate the reasons for these changes in the destruction of the cultural locations in which young working class people once came to embody the ethos, the forms of comportment in which working class self-respect and the ethical decency characterized the working class when its communities were built on mass employment. Yet, in regions like South Yorkshire, the reasons for the decay are obvious, and many older local people are only too aware of the causes of the loss of dignity and security that they grew up in. For them, it is clearly the destruction of work and the culture that surrounded it, and its replacement with non-unionized, low-waged work and periodic unemployment. Work and the presence of the union were fields in which working people could come to experience forms of dignity based in the sense of an ethical life beyond the world of consumption. Moreover, traditional industries fostered forms of association through which working people could experience a sense of personal value beyond the fight for distinction through consumption which now tends to characterize the lives of the atomized communities of current conditions. Without the sites that operated as social fields in which working class people could come to experience their own value and grow up to embody forms of comportment that brought esteem, their culture has tended to collapse into a morass of confused and fractured forms. Living in a world in which the horizon of secure, well-paid employment has been replaced with the uncertainties of a life lived within the constitutive horizon of an uncertain world of itinerant, low-waged, low-skilled, atomized work, with the ever-present threat of intermittent unemployment, has left many working class people with fragile identities and low self-esteem. Their sense of reality impaired by a life of privation they barely recognize as injustice. A quality of life so bleak that it confines being to a pathological degree. Such conditions of scarcity amidst affluence, of severe vulnerability amidst images of security, of dislocation without movement, have led to the creation of a class in which many have come to appear 'odd', abject, because they have been unable to participate in spaces in which they could learn, mimetically, body-to-body, the manners and styles of deportment of the accomplished adult, attuned to the respectable world of a civilized realm in which there exists, practically and dispositionally, a civic culture oriented to public civility. In the context in which they grow up, amidst too much insecurity and insult, the grounds of a public realm of respect are lacking because the grounds of self-respect are too often denied. For many, living in semi-isolation, in conditions that encroach upon sensory deprivation, lacking a public context and role, their relation to any public realm beyond that of state agencies has become tenuous, with the result that their comportment has become haunted by insecurity and self-doubt. A socially mediated condition of carelessness producing people who couldn't give a shit because there is so little for them to care about that cannot lead them to a punitive relation to themselves and others. This insecurity leaves many unable to feel able to appropriate the schemes of postural and gestural organization that belong to a world they do not feel authorised or justified to belong to. For many of the poorest and most dispossessed, this leaves them unable to appropriate the socially valued forms of comportment through which individuals come to exhibit competence, and for some the whole social-physiognomic process that Goffman captured in the notion of 'exhibiting presence' (Goffman 1971), becomes problematised, their being-for-others becoming 'not quite right': exhibiting in the moment-to-moment achievement of their posture something absent in healthily socially embedded, human beings. This fracturing of their embodied powers, their corporeal prowess, this becoming partial in the forms of humanity they learn to embody is like an embodied metaphor for their social condition because, in these conditions, they are, in a very real sense, only partly alive. They may be biologically alive but they do not have access to the resources, symbolic as well as economic, to have a life. They are the zombies that British culture has created by condemning them to the living death of a stigmatized, abject, being. That such people are part of the co-ordinates of life in such areas, is made clear by a woman whose comment shows that the objective being-for-others of such people obeys the logic of stigma (Goffman 1990):

X: Ah [I] saw these kids other day an thi [they] looked like retards an' as I went past 'em Ah thought to miseln, 'Oh, no, the'r not retards, the'r just poor' an' it occurred to me that a lot'r really poor people look retarded.

It is the context in which individuals come to embody the forms of comportment that they do, and the relation between the exigencies of a social environment and the patterns of possibility and response exhibited in posture, that are overlooked by Parsons and those who bemoan the death of any civilizing process occurring among the industrial working class. It is the economic changes and the social conditions they ushered in that have consigned these people to a life of marginality which, naturally enough, manifests itself in their comportment, manner and style. Their being exhibits their exclusion from forms of respect and their condemnation to stigmatized forms that ensure that it makes no practical sense for them to invest their being in modes through which, finally, they cannot achieve respect. The words of one tattooed man are testimony to the conditions that create the sense of abjection Parsons describes:

X: I mean A'm unemployed an' A've got tattoos an that, so I'm one'r them but thi' dun't think wi' 'ave feelin's an wi dun't care abaht [about] us kids, thi dun't think wi worth owt [anything] du thi? Yer know, wi want best fo us [our] kids an' that. Ah mean, I've tried 'ard an' that . . . through mi life, like, an' Ah dun't consider miself to be a bad person or nowt, I've just 'ad n' luck . . . mi gran ses I must'a killed a robbin or sumat [something] 'cos Ah just 'ave 'ad nowt but 'ard luck . . . yer know wi' that job an' wi' that lass. [*Pause*] I mean Ah [I] try nahr [now], I'm tranna [trying to] get this taxi thing off grahnd [ground], but Ah need fo'ty quid fo' that. Tha knows [you know]. . . .Tha gu's on dun't tha? Ah get up some times an' it's just too much fo' mi, yer know, it creeps over yer, it just gets too much an' tha can't tek no' mo'ore, [S: 'Ah know . . .'] yer know, Sime I wan'a job, Ah want to work, I wan'a bit o'r money in mi [my] pocket so as ah [that I] can gi [give] some to ahr lass [girlfriend] an' fo' kid [their child] an' that but Ah'm stuck, Ah dun't know what Ah can du except this . . . Yer know, Wi've 'ad some 'ard times lately, really 'ard, wi an't 'ad n' food, wi' an't even 'ad money to buy some milk to 'ave wi' us cereal, an' wi'v bin like that fo' weeks. It's heartbreakn', it's just a strain all time an' tha just wants t' not live, tha just can't see n' point in thi' life . . .

This man's insistence upon his 'bad luck' and his desire to work show that he shares many of his parents' motivations and sense of life, but what he cannot share with them is that life of work that was the backdrop to their sense of life. With that economic context gone, this man, like many others, has not had the opportunity to become part of a way of life through which he would have imbued those dispositional schemes and postural sets whose disappearance Parsons laments. Moreover, in his exclusion he has become, in a sense, as deeply lost as a human being can become, because he cannot found an identity of value. Instead he must simply confront the daily misery of his position in which there is so little for him to found self-esteem. To use a religious term, these people are condemned. Denied the grace, or even the hope, that consists in acceding to valued forms of social existence and they live as sinners: walking reminders to the saved that outside of the games of respect we compete in, there is not just nothing, but the hell of being nothing.

Yet perhaps there is, obscured in Parsons' response, another significant and related cultural shift. It seems that any concern, within the university, with the lives of working people has declined with the progressive rise of a generation of academics, now in control of the university sector, many of whose careers depended upon the post-Robbins expansion of that sector and yet who seem, shamelessly, complicit in the ceding of resources so fundamental to their own careers. The accession of this generation to positions of authority and cultural legitimacy has coincided with the challenging of heroic representations of class. The key organizing locations of labour were based upon the only form of power that working people have historically had – the possibility of withdrawing their collective labour in order to assert what amounts to a negative economic power – and this was tied to the industrial sector, particularly to the male-dominated industries of coal, steel, rail and the docks.[1] Yet, as economic change weakened these workers, as the working class declined as an economic and political force, and this tells us much about the academy, it seems that any interest in the working class as an *object* of interest declined. From here, given English academic culture's deep antipathy to the working class and to thinking very deeply, it was a short step to the kind of unacknowledged contempt that surrounds the topic and particularly male members of that class. Certainly, from the late eighties, to be a working class man within the university has been to confront a steady drizzle of veiled contempt and indifference based in the culture of stigma Coward describes so well. Whilst women within the university are still not as powerful as their male counterparts, they have successfully constituted themselves as a group who suffer discrimination. Clearly, the role feminism has played in the reconfiguration of academic culture has been an important aspect in the emergence of this climate.[2]

Women writers, like Beatrix Campbell in *Wigan Pier Revisited*, have been concerned to counterpose heroic narratives of class with the fact that working class communities are based upon the patriarchal exploitation of women:

> Ashington man was the archetypal proletarian, the archetypal patriarch . . . As in the Army and the Stock Exchange, men's companionship did not produce social cohesion; it fostered power and privilege for men within their own class and community . . . No day matched Sunday for desolation. Up with the children, the woman kept them quiet while the man had his lie in, made the dinner while he sank a skinful at the pub, kept the kids quiet while he slept it off, made the tea, put the kids to bed while he ended the day down the club . . . Miners' clubs along the north east coast were the cathedrals of their communities, the space where men had their pleasure and their politics. Their homes, however, remained some of the worst in Britain.
> (Campbell 1984)

In this process of realignment the communities of the great manufacturing and industrial areas of Britain have come to be represented as relics and the issues the problems facing them raise are seen to belong to an older order of debates that that generation of academics settled and transcended. More importantly, those issues offer little symbolic profit to a group whose status depends upon the distinction of their opinion. And into this new order of discourse a growing interest in ecology has meant that such communities have become associated with pollution and the ruin of the environment. The issues of poverty, and inequality fundamental to English society and culture have been degraded, down-classed as part of the endless shuffling for correct opinion that so preoccupies the chattering classes. Issues of class have gradually descended into the realm of cliché and stereotype at a time when for many the problems of urban poverty, unemployment and the problems connected with the new criminality of drug abuse have come to be a daily practical exigence. Alongside this shift in the intellectual field, there has been an equally important move within the political field in that throughout the 1980s the Parliamentary Labour Party moved towards the right and away from its natural, traditional constituency. These areas were the heart of support for the Labour movement and the 'old' Labour Party. The connected destruction of the unions and the industries to which they were connected, epitomized by the 1984–5 miners' strike, left these communities abandoned in a landscape made desolate by industrial dereliction and its human costs, the decay of the social fabric of these lives. As the grounds of a foreseeable future were erased, and the conditions of a continuity that supported the traditions of decency that were at the heart of the industrial culture of these area were never established, the sense of personal lives became serialized, episodic, that of an atomised, never-ending present, bereft of past co-ordinates or progression, and without the connections of a public realm of value, there emerged, to fill the gap, the anonymous aggression characteristic of spaces devoid of a public culture of inclusion and mutual purpose. In a world as radically absurd as this, in which individuals are unable to experience the mutual affirmation involved in respect and competence, as people weave their rhythms from the very stuff of comportment, drink and drug abuse have become the only way to nullify the human faculties sufficiently to make life bearable.

For anyone trying to write about the working class, then, there are clearly tremendous problems, because the notion itself is at stake in the struggles of professional groups who are themselves invested in the production of opinion about the social world. We can see from this discussion that the struggle over the correct representation of the social world is itself a stake in the struggle between the classes.

At times of severe economic and political realignments of the kind that Britain has gone through in the last twenty years, this struggle over the truth of the social world becomes exceptionally important, not just in the political field but in personal lives. The transformation of the British economy has profoundly affected the lives and life-chances of working class people, and has had particular consequences for the traditional industrial areas of the north of England, Scotland and South Wales. Firms have used the deregulation of the labour market to enforce ever more casual, often part-time, 'flexible' working practices, which have radically changed ordinary people's experience of work and with it their sense of their life. The casualization and deregulation of labour markets, with the added effects of great uncertainty of employment as well as a decline in overall safety standards, alongside the levelling of wages in the public sector, has had profound consequences for the quality of life of ordinary people.

Only around 40 per cent of the work-force enjoy full-time, tenured employment or secure self-employment; 30 per cent are insecurely self-employed involuntary part-time or casual workers; and the bottom 30 per cent of society either work for poverty-level wages or are unemployed (Hutton 1996b: 14). Alongside these changes to working people's lives the economic context of their lives has been deeply touched by changes to the welfare system; by changes in the tax system, notably the reducing of the top-rate in income tax, which has shifted the burden of taxation downwards; by growing inequality and increasing poverty as benefit levels, access to benefits and the value of pensions have all fallen and all of this at a time when the wages of working people have been falling. If we look to the government's own figures, throughout the eighties the distance between rich and poor has clearly widened with the income of the poorest 10 per cent falling from £73 a week in 1979, the year that Margaret Thatcher came to power, to £61 in 1991 (in real terms, after allowance for housing) according to a study by the Institute for Fiscal Studies (quoted in Hutton 1996b). If one looks at the European Union's definition of poverty – that is, the number of people who live on less than half average earnings – this number was 5 million in 1979 and 13 million in 1990 (Hutton 1996b). There can be little wonder that illnesses related to nutritional deficiencies, in a word, malnutrition, are returning to areas where people are expected to live on such meagre incomes, little wonder that it is once again common for mothers to go without food and for the cupboards to be bare. As one young woman described it:

> X: I've allous [always] got to se' 'no' to mi kids, an', A've [I've] got to du wiyaht [without] food an' A've [I've] got to bi 'ungry a lot, so I eat bits o'r stuff that an't [are not] good fo' yer, sweet stuff, yer know . . . Ah dun't eat right an', wot's w'se [worse] is that wi't [with the] kids A'm not 'appy wot A feed them, Ah know thi dun't get enough . . . an' Ah worry that it'll affect the'r 'ealth an that. Can yer imagine bein' completely on yer own? . . . Yer know, well on yer own it's really ard in it an' . . . that's wot bein' poor is, like. Ah just an't got enough an thi's nowt else I can giy up.

The consequences of these conditions are that mortality rates in the most deprived areas of the north of England are now as bad for some age groups as they were in the 1940s, and are four times higher than in affluent areas. This primary relation to necessity, its consequence, is perhaps most evident in figures of mental and physical ill-health; but, as doctors in these areas know, the figures are merely the tip of a very large iceberg. The most personal aspects of human existence have been touched by these economic and political conditions and working class culture has had to deal with these personal effects and social conditions.

Merleau-Ponty suggests 'I say that I *know an idea* when there is set up in me a power of organizing around it words which make a coherent meaning' (Merleau-Ponty 1962). Life has taught this woman the real meaning of necessity, that it means looking in her children's eyes as she registers the effects of conditions of privation in the natural expressivity of their bodies, seeing the disappointment in their eyes, the deprivation in their posture, the relation of 'going-without' setting into their ways. Her words are organized around the coherent centre of an experientially deep sense of the world emerging from the primal encounter between her perceptual life and these conditions. A perceptual realm whose horizons emanate from this state of being 'without'; of saying 'no' to her children, of being undernourished, of worrying about the effects of this state on her children and of her own lone-

liness amidst this strain. Whilst, all the time, being haunted, in the very condition of their existence and practical being, by the incessant need to give
up still more and thus living constantly within the realm of the desolation
involved in there being nothing else, within one's means, to give. The ulti-
mate affirmation of one's personal failure, a terrible acknowledgement of
the futility of one's personal capacities, the complete affirmation within
one's system of needs, of one's powerlessness. Condemned to a life in which
one has so little power to help one's children, where one feels the absence
of self-determination to such a degree, where one has been sacrificed
without one's knowledge, or consent, how can one begin to cope or to
empower one's children? It is easy for middle class people to talk in general
terms of loving one's children and giving them one's attention, but economic processes need the intervention of a political will before any individual is empowered.

Working people know this well, having witnessed the use of the political
and judicial institutions of the state to 'improve labour relations', that is, to
take away workers' rights: a process of pacification that was aided by the
creation of structural unemployment. Official unemployment figures,
changed at a rate that it has been difficult to record, are notoriously inac-
curate, and yet remain alarming: thirty-five million across the industrialized world. These are changes that have touched working class life deeply,
indelibly, to the extent that for those who have lived through this process,
who have lived with its effects on the only culture they have ever been
allowed, such changes have created a gnawing sense of confusion, vulnerability and insecurity that will live forever in the people who have come to
be persons within this context. Will Hutton captures the general condition
well in his overall summation of *The State We're In*:

For two decades unemployment has been a grim fact of British life, bearing particularly hard on men. As well as those included in the official count who want to work
and can't find it, there are millions more who are marginalised – prematurely retired
or living off inadequate savings or sickness benefit. One in four of the country's
males of working age is now officially unemployed or idle, with incalculable consequences for our well-being and social cohesion. The number living in poverty have
grown to awesome proportions, and the signs of social stress – from family breakdown to the growth of crime – mount almost daily . . . One in three of the nation's
children grows up in poverty. In 1991 one twenty-one year old in five was innumer-
ate; one in seven was illiterate. The prison population is the highest in Europe. The
British are failing.

Above all we live in a world of us and them . . . The country is increasingly divided
against itself, with an arrogant officer class apparently indifferent to the other ranks
it commands. This privileged class is favoured with education, jobs, housing and

pensions. At the other end of the scale more and more people discover they are the new working poor, or live off the state in semi-poverty. Their paths out of this situation are closing down as the world in which they are trapped becomes meaner, harder and more corrupting. In between there are growing numbers of people who are insecure, fearful for their jobs in an age of permanent 'down-sizing', 'cost-cutting' and 'casualization' and ever more worried about their ability to maintain a decent standard of living.

The rot starts at the top.   (Hutton 1996b: 1–3)

What this makes clear is that there have been fundamental and far-reaching changes in the economic life of British people, and that this has been a story driven as much by the powerful motivations of class interest as by the economics of the free market.

The issue of the representation of class can never be more contested than during a period in which the object to be depicted has itself been severely politically contested: that is, during a period when state institutions have been used to try and alter the nature of working class culture itself, to change the way working people experience their lives. In Britain, then, these economic changes have acted to undermine the working class's ability to contest decisions made in the political arena and as such the changes have affirmed the conditions of their dispossession. Frank Field, MP, has been a figure vilified by the Left[3] and yet he has acknowledged that:

You could say that we have Workhouses because the poor now are heavily concentrated in certain areas. Huge ghettos, in a sense, are like Workhouses where people are gated geographically, many of the people in those streets will be those who are now caught in that Welfare trap.

These conditions, like the years of the Great Depression, have virtually quashed the possibility of working class resistance. With work so difficult to come by and to keep, and conditions so hard, many working people have come to feel a job is the limit to which they can aspire. However, once, these people lived and worked together and were bound by the rhythms of work, but now they share only their collective decline, a decline, moreover, that is encountered as personal fate, separated as they now are from a public life capable of investing them with the dignity of an identity embedded in a social function. A sensitive person can see all around the misery of people condemned to a life devoid of the legitimacy of objectively assured qualities, robbed of any human right to competence, and one can feel the confused anger born of fear and insecurity that such conditions produce. There can be little wonder, therefore, that in their intermittent commuting through working class areas, the English intelligentsia has made its decision to follow the German model, *circa* 1930, and just pretend its ghettoized peoples are doing meaningful work and are being remunerated sufficiently to keep them from the door.

Throughout the 1980s, government policy effectively undermined the conditions that embedded and reproduced the traditions that gave life to trade union struggles – perhaps the one 'genuine principle of a counter culture' (Bourdieu 1984: 395) – and laid the foundations for a political orthodoxy that represents the interests of the educated, organized electorate whose votes they must secure to form a government. As Bourdieu has suggested, 'The products offered by the political field are instruments for perceiving and expressing the social world' (Bourdieu 1991: 172) and, throughout this period of realignment, both major political parties have conducted political discussion through discourse that effectively disavow class. In this respect perhaps one could say that Margaret Thatcher achieved her desire to destroy socialism in England, a desire that carried her to refuse to recognize the existence of 'society' itself. It is telling because her policies effectively destroyed, for many, the social fabric of a civic culture in which the more colloquial meaning of that word was experienced. For those without steady work and the experience of inclusion and consecration involved in elite education, it might well have seemed that Margaret Thatcher was right, that there were, indeed, only individuals and families.

This discursive shift, among the generation of politicians and academics now in ascendency, can be seen as part of a generational process of individual self-investment (and self-forgetting). At a time when working people have most needed the compassionate interest of persons with the institutional position to represent them in the symbolic struggle,

which sets professionals against each other . . . for the conservation or transformation of the vision of the social world and of the principles of di-vision of this world . . . What is at stake in this game is, on the one hand, the monopoly of the elaboration and diffusion of the legitimate principle of di-vision of the social world and, thereby, of the mobilization of groups . . . It thus takes the form of a struggle over the specifically symbolic power of making people see and believe, of predicting and prescribing, of making known and recognized, which is at the same time a struggle for power over the 'public powers' (state administrations).   (Bourdieu 1991: 181)

In order for government policy to be shown for what it is and for there to be the hope of policies framed through an accurate understanding of their position, working people needed these processes to be brought into the public realm through which intermediaries might have been involved. At a time when working people have been struggling with endless bureaucratic and state recategorization; an endless reclassifying of the phenomena of unemployment and inequality; with being renamed by public powers and by a state bureaucracy that has played an important role in the realigning of working people's expectations and with the reconfiguring of their sense of the limits of life; the intelligentsia, when finally it might have had a national public role, was busy career-building and consolidating its own privileges.

Obviously, the instruments of classification available are social products that emerge from these contexts of struggle, and we have to confront the peculiar problem that this struggle, over the legitimate representation of the social, is one of the key stakes in the political field. Furthermore, the object of research is itself at stake in the everyday struggles that people participate in over the nature of their lives; indeed it emerges from this context. It is this which makes the representation of class such a highly contested and loaded enterprise, such that many of the words that we use to talk about the social, in general, and class, in particular, are located somewhere between euphemism and insult. Hence, any piece of writing on class 'lives' within this network of pre-established meanings through which any writing on the topic will be understood, and this makes difficult the reclamation of sense and experience necessary to my work, but it is, nevertheless, an inescapable condition of writing about class. Moreover, the gap between the audience who are likely to receive this text and the nature of the experience that it tries to constitute, makes its reception problematic. So, what, then, given the unlikeliness of my writing being received and understood, has driven me to this effort to constitute a distinct experience that the scholastic gaze disavows as a possibility?

It is my sense of the need to express an experience that is contained in so much of the incidental detail expressed in working class people's speech and which strikes me throughout daily life. The lives of these people and the problems of rendering the sense of their lives, illuminates many of Merleau-Ponty's insights and of particular relevance is what he called the 'primacy of perception' (Merleau-Ponty 1964). It is as though conditions of abjection and vulnerability create an unmediated relationship to perception that roots these people in a telling experience of the society in which they live; and a relation to themselves that, by calling them back to a primal experience of a perceived essence, one that their lack of status cannot alter in the perceptions of others, draws them back to a fundamental truth about the conditions of positive identity, of self-fruition and the very possibilities of love, intimacy, family-hood, friendship and mutual respect. That is, their social position creates an unmediated, primal relation to the conditions of existence that circumscribes their culture and expressivity, and this relation is manifest in perception, as our kinaesthetic lived-bodily presence to the world. In order to understand the phenomena of the sense of these people's lives we must begin with a philosophy that understands the primacy of perception: that is, the ways in which the shared culture imbued through comportment and practical, habitual skill are the grounds of possibility of the sense we find sedimented, without reflex or consideration, in perception. As Merleau-Ponty expresses it:

> By these words, 'the primacy of perception', we mean that the experience of perception is our presence at the moment when things, truths, values are constituted for us; that perception is a nascent *logos*; that it teaches us, outside all dogmatism, the true conditions of objectivity itself; that it summons us to the tasks of knowledge and action. It is not a question of reducing human knowledge to sensation, but of assisting at the birth of this knowledge, to make it as sensible as the sensible . . . Thus, although we are always immersed in the world and perceptually present to it, yet the idea of truth itself is an ideal implied in the least perception.
>
> (Merleau-Ponty 1964: 25)

We must realize what Merleau-Ponty called the ambiguousness of the perceptual world. The world discloses itself through perceptual perspectives constituted through the meeting in us of our position and trajectory, the flesh through which the felt sense of our world is acquired. Yet from this ambiguity there emerges a world so determinate that, for working people, it can resonate with anxiety and ring with misery. To understand this we need to recognize the reciprocity of perception that emerges from a primordial realm of engagement and response acquired in a shared form of life that has determinate conditions of possibility given in the cultural relations implied in one's economic position. In the end, our perceptions involve us in a lived relationship with the world: a relation that only derivatively is one of thought and yet which is the primary realm of our sense of the world. Our relationship to the world is thus manifest in the spontaneous reactions through which the world is disclosed. Perception is part of the initiation to the world that is involved in coming to inhabit it through the habitual realms of practice and the expressive styles of the people among whom we live. If we accept this corporealization of experience, that it founds consciousness and experience through a sensuous awareness that involves the flesh as a totality of self-realizing form that undergirds, in unequal societies, the grounds of possibility open to groups of individuals, then we can begin to accept the sociological possibility that not all groups will share experience that is as rooted in the primordial brutal being of the body. That is, that powerful, affluent groups will be able to realize themselves through symbolically mediated forms of experience which demand acts of cognition that appear to weaken this thesis. And, more importantly, these ideas are particularly suited to the illumination of those lives which by social conditions are confined to realms of existence conditioned by an inability to distance the world through the resources that affluence secures. Without the cultural and economic resources to found some security and without the symbolic resources to create a frame of secure and positive self-interpretations, trapped in a world of trying to get by and the injunctions involved in this status-less vulnerability, in conditions of material and symbolic deprivation, one's perceptions of the world become ever more threatening, and seem to bite deeper at the core of self-hood, violating the realm upon which one's status as a moral being for oneself depends. In these conditions, the thesis of the primacy of perception, has particular relevance for an understanding of the lives of the urban poor in an age of economic rootlessness and a state that has become so expert in the management of the dispossessed.

It is as though the conditions of working class life create conditions in which the phenomenal body's anchorage in and bond with the pre-objective world is more complete, as though this realm encompasses the greater part of their existence, touching all aspects of life, as though these conditions of perception create a horizon encompassing the percept, and as though this fundamental context and condition is manifest not only in what they do but in the style in which it is done and which is exhibited in much of their speech. When the solicitations of the world around us involve the subject in a coercive world of what *has* to be done, with little pleasure or remuneration, and of a bleakness of possibility, then the primacy of perception must become a problem for people whose experience this is. The deep primacy of perception of the everyday experience of working people amounts to a continuous emerging sense; a shaping, undeniable force that destroys for them any possibility of being other than they are; setting parameters to their ways of dealing with the world. It is a sense of the limits of their lives that one hears clanging around their speech like the tolling of a bell. It haunts everything that working people think and say, every choice they make; their lives take place in the long shadow freedom's light casts across the obstacle that necessity represents to them. Bourdieu suggests that the life-style of working people, the choices they are able to make about the environment in which they live, emanates from an inescapable deprivation of necessary goods, that their culture is a virtue made of necessity, a resignation to the inevitable, a sense of the limits of life which is also a forgetting of those limits as limits, a forced contentment with one's lot which, as bad faith, yet one emanating from an absence of volition, produces throughout working class life tension-points, forms of individual and group pathology that working people must negotiate in these times. Bourdieu suggests:

Taste is *amor fati*, the choice of destiny, but a forced choice, produced by conditions of existence which rule out all alternatives as mere daydreams and leave no choice but the taste for the necessary.

The taste of necessity can only be the basis of a life-style 'in itself', which is defined as such only negatively, by an absence, by the relationship of privation between itself and the other lifestyles. For some, there are elective emblems, for others stigmata which they bear in their very bodies. 'As the chosen people bore in their features the sign that they were the property of Jehovah, so the division of labour brands the manufacturing worker as the property of capital.' The brand which Marx speaks of is nothing other than life-style, through which the most deprived immediately betray themselves, even in their use of spare time; in so doing they inevitably serve as a foil to every distinction and contribute, purely negatively, to the dialectic of pretension and distinction which fuels the incessant changing of taste.   (Bourdieu 1984: 178)

The accuracy of Bourdieu's insight is reflected in the comments of an unemployed man of eighteen:

X: Like, A'm [I'm] from a council estate, in K, an' A've [I've] done time, rait [right] in young offenders places an' community service an all kids doin' that shit ahr [are] from council estates an' wi'v got nowt guin' [going] fo us aht [out] the'er, yer know what I mean? We've got no money, we've got no jobs, thi's just nothin' fo' us to do, we've got nowt, yer know what I mean? We'eras you look at kids, se', up M [*Middle class area which provides students for the old grammar school, now a sixth form college, which serves the wealthier areas*], or W, wi' money, or whose parent's 'ave got money; they've got a life an't thi? Ye' see 'em rahnd tahn 'avin' a good time wi' the'r trendy clothes an wot not, thi'v no need to gu' aht thievin' . . .

What is striking in this man's speech is his articulation of the absence of a 'life' in terms of an absence of income and, importantly, a difference of status and identity involved in forms of symbolic capital ('trendy clothes'). It is remarkable how far this man sees his own problems as emerging from the shared conditions of others in the area who are like himself, and how he presents their plight as emerging from an absence of the material resources that would render their lives culturally meaningful and which would allow them to ascend to the (human) status of 'having a life' – and one might add, following Charles Taylor, personhood. This man articulates clearly the extent to which having a life and being a person are dependent upon a certain basic level of income through which individuals can partic-ipate in consumption which, in these societies is one of the main ways in which individuals place themselves, experience social participation and inclusion and, through the adornment of the body with the necessary consumer signifiers, accede to a recognized form of social existence, even at this minimal level. From conditions of scarcity, with the absence of material resources, their position of exclusion comes to dominate their experience because it is the fundamental condition in relation to which their existence is constituted. That their lives issue from this inescapable deprivation of necessary goods is powerfully attested to in the connection this man makes across different domains in his deliberate but unselfconscious repetition of 'nowt . . . no . . . no . . . nothing . . . nowt' in: 'got *nowt* guin' fo us . . . *no* money . . . *no* jobs . . . *nothin'* fo' us to do . . . we've got *nowt* . . .'

Merleau-Ponty suggests that we distinguish between 'an authentic speech, which formulates for the first time, and second-order expression, speech about speech' (Merleau-Ponty 1962: 178). If we see perception as embedded in a sense of the world that emerges from this primordial meeting of the phenomenal body and the pre-objective world, then we can recognize a type of speech that is a kind of originating expression emerging from the amorphous silence that envelops the dispossessed in so much of their experience. This offers us a way of describing speech which is formulated on-the-spot, 'in the thick' of life: which is expressing ideas that are emanating from the density of lived-through perceptions for the first time. Obviously, not new concepts or new ideas, but descriptions and self-descriptions by the subject that are being formulated for the first time, by them, about themselves and the world that impacts upon them. It is using speech to incarnate the meaning, and thus express the sense they are aware of in the conditions and relations that delineate their objective being. This type of speech, close to that required in therapy, is different from 'second order expression', or what Merleau-Ponty calls elsewhere empirical language, the stock-in-trade of speech acts we use to go about our daily lives.

Merleau-Ponty insists that the philosophers never use the empirical language as it is given but use it in such a way that they transform the staid meanings of the words into something vital, so that they become authentic words. And the people whose testimony is used here are doing exactly the same. It is for these reasons that I have always felt a certain reverence for such unselfconscious articulations of what, with a different register, vocabulary and dialect might easily pass for profundity. The young man speaking of 'nowt' in his life, deploys concepts that emerge through his lived experience that approximate to the same sense of necessity that Bourdieu uses. Looking at the testimony in this chapter forces us to consider the nature of our framing and using of concepts. These people are clearly, in their stories about saying 'no' to children, of 'gu'in wiyaht', seizing upon and using expressively conceptions of their lives as emerging from a primary encounter with necessity, that gives to their existence a dispositional hue issuing from their social conditions. Wittgenstein remarked that:

Life can educate one to a belief in God. And *experiences* too are what bring this about; but I don't mean visions and other forms of sense experience which show us the 'existence of this being', but, e.g., sufferings of various sorts. These neither show us an object, nor do they give rise to *conjectures* about him. Experiences, thoughts, – life can force this concept on us.
So perhaps it is similar to the concept of 'object'.   (Wittgenstein 1980: 86)

It is as though involvement in a certain kind of prolonged encounter with the world has brought them to apprehension of a sense of their existence immanent in the generality involved in a certain kind of experience visited upon their lives as part of the fabric of their living in the world. Some idea of necessity is inescapably necessary to their understanding of one another and their place in the world: it is part of the constitution of their interaction, part of the 'working principles' that guide their responses without being consciously formulated; part of their learning the form of life in which they grew up: part of the myth of their life, impressed upon them in the course of interacting with the world. It is knowing that world as the primary, affective space of being, of knowing it as an inarticulate home of responses, resonances and proclivities that produces in one this sense of the authenticity of these people's speech, knowing what is involved beneath the expressions, what the expression emanates from, what Heidegger called, 'the wordless joy of having once more withstood want' (Heidegger 1977: 163), the essential excess of meaning involved in the incarnation of sense involved in their expression, as though their world is speaking through them, as though they were formulating the world afresh in these moments in which, some for the first time, individuals were consciously formulating a formal narrative of biography. Yet even slavishly transcribed testimony loses that quality of presence and incarnation,[4] that expressive value involved in the natural meaning that cannot signify apart from the context in which they occur.

It is difficult to render the powerful sense of that experience of authenticity contained in the physiognomic perception that flashes instantly through bodies which share the same conditions of existence, in what is 'second order expression'. It is unavoidable that this writing will be received apart from the conditions that produced it, whereas the recorded testimony, as speech, 'smells' (Barthes 1986: 309) to borrow an expression from Barthes; it is an embodied practice suffused with the embedded significances of its conditions of utterance. The difficulty is to give enough

of the 'background' of reference and expressive sense, enough that is constitutive of the way of being-in-the-world, for the reader to feel the meaning
with some sense of the force of being and not merely to be involved with
the text as a diagnostic exercise of characterization. However hard a writer
tries to imbue the work with the engagement of lived time, written sense
and the sense of practice are distinct, and writing only achieves the illusion
of their coherence. Moreover, one can't aspire to produce the kinds of
writing that would deliver such an experience of presence or immanence to
the densities of experience given, say, in the works of D. H. Lawrence or
Toni Morrison. However, it is important that the reader read with the same
sense of charity that was part of the moment of testimony and transcription; a moment Bourdieu characterizes as:

The sustained, receptive attention required to become imbued with a sense of the
singular necessity of each personal testimony, and which is usually reserved for
great philosophical and literary texts, can also be accorded, by a sort of *democrat-
ization of the hermeneutic posture*, to the ordinary accounts of ordinary adventures.
It is necessary, as Flaubert taught us, to learn to bear on Yvetot the look that one
affords so willingly to Constantinople: to learn, for example, to give the marriage
of a woman teacher to a post office worker the attention and interest that would
have been lent to the literary account of misalliance, and to offer to the statements
of a steelworker the thoughtful reception which a certain tradition of reading
reserves for the highest forms of poetry or philosophy.   (Bourdieu 1996a: 33)

Listening to the young man talk of the nothingness that his life is; of the
way his situation renders his existence passive; a passivity reflected in the
desperate, brutalized humility of his inflexion; apprehending the immanent
significance of his manner, one feels present to oneself, intuitively, the conditions of acquisition of this oratorical style and one feels, through the postural impregnation involved in sharing kind, the immediacy cloying the
body's sense of the immediately pressing urgencies involved in his life's
encounter with necessity. His speech not only concerns the experience of
passivity violating his experience of the world; his expressive being, his
posture and tonality, are possessed by the necessity that infects his being-
in-the-world. This is part of the totality of the expressive act, part of the
peculiar multi-dimensionality of human communication, and it communicates the urgency of the despair, the abjection of this way of life, to listen-
ers who feel and grasp the powerlessness and vulnerability. And this is often
what working people need in order to feel at home in communication. The
expressive style denotes an intimacy with social conditions born of absolute proximity. It is verbal exclamation manifesting the effects upon the
subject at a primordial level of these conditions; it is something akin to pain
behaviour. An extension into the linguistic domain of a more primitive level

of response that as a form displays the depth of the violations involved in this lifestyle. It is a manifestation of a primordial level of disturbance manifest in expression, it is as far from the euphemization of middle class speech as the primordial emissions of the beaten body of the boxer are from the triumph of form over substance of the ballet dancer.

Many writers have focused upon the centrality of a vocabulary of self and of the emotions in the constitution of our moral status as persons; yet what does this man's speech tell us? For him and for those like him, it is as if he is possessed by nothingness. This possession of self by the effects of an economic condition, this transference of the deadness of things, through the nature of social relations, into human culture and into the life of being, takes place through the medium of practice, through engagement in communities characterized by purposelessness.

The power of this man's speech involves the fusion of thought and word, their intervolving which creates that magical communion between sense, cognizance and the life of the body. This is what gives working peoples' speech its remarkable prosody. Emerging from direct solicitations from the world, it seems to be gripped by that determinacy, delivered over to the vibrancy of a world so directly encountered; and such speech seems to have assimilated its meaning to excess such that it seems, to those sharing the conditions, to register the truth of these conditions in what to middle class speakers might seem simple, formulaic, unpenetrating formulations of direct experience. It is speech that works on the real problems of existence because they press daily upon these individuals and in relation to it, one is not meant to position oneself oppositionally as rational ego, but as feeling-subject. It is often an invitation to *feel*, to be inhabited by the conditions that produce the sense, the fatigue, the hopelessness, the despair, the fear, the anxiety, the anger and, alongside those, the humour and the tragedy. It is an invitation, buried in a way of being, born of a form of life, to be inhabited by a common way of being bothered by the world, of its making itself matter in a shared way, to care about the world in a characteristic way. The problem here is that whilst these persons' self-hoods are clearly located amidst 'webs of interlocution' (Taylor 1989a: 36), they are embedded in a culture that is itself socially disengaged, in the sense of atomized; empty, in the sense of devoid of positive valuations, both of personal activity and of the sense of life revealed by life amongst the group to which these individuals belong. These are the effects, subjectified through processes of corporealization, of social domination, of class dispropriation, of the milieu created by a government that, with their historical role in the industrial process no longer necessary, has effectively taken steps to produce the invisibility of these social categories, the disappearance of the dispositions these people once had to imbue in order to live: the extinction of this class of people. And the results are forms of personal misery and confusion rooted in the social effects and costs of economic policy:

Whereas the old system tended to produce clearly demarcated social identities which left little room for social fantasy but were comfortable and reassuring even in the unconditional renunciation which they demanded, the new system of structural instability in the representation of social identity and its legitimate aspirations tends to shift agents from the terrain of social crisis and critique to the terrain of personal critique and crisis.   (Bourdieu 1984: 156)

Moreover, this sense of confusion and crisis; of nothingness, of abuse, of fracture, of damage; demarcates the fundamental space in which working people exist. I am not suggesting that *all* working people are *as* gripped by this sense as the most vulnerable, but that it is part of the primordial realm, the background referential-whole, of practical reference, that they feel underpins their existence. Even the highest paid working people exhibit a sense of their good fortune embedded in certain knowledge of what has befallen so many and which lies all around them in any trip into town. And this sense that vacillates between existential confusion and anger at the certainties of inequalities embedded in such a primal encounter with necessity is true not only of the unemployed, the working class without work, but of the working poor:

I w'ked fifty-three hours last week fo' 'undred an' fifty quid. It's disgustin'. An' that wo on' jack-hammer. That's *'ard* labour that is, I'll tell yer, it's *fuckin' 'ard* w'k. Whoever said money in't everythin' wo' a liar. It' gets thee everythin' . . . [*Pause*] . . . Wi wo just unlucky, to be born wi' nowt [nothing].

The question 'what is at the heart of working class people's experience?', in this context, has a pressing sense because one hears it represented daily in such talk, which makes manifest the tensions and worries that press upon these lives. One hears conversations about the price of a cup of tea; about where is the cheapest place to buy a baked potato for dinner and an earnest and considered discussion of whether it actually represents value for money against the cost of the basic ingredients bought separately. One often hears talk like the following:

X: Ah [I] ses to 'er, yer just freezin' space, if Ah wo you Ah'd [I'd] buy some cheap bread an' stick that in. An' shi ses, 'Oh, Ah'm not du'in' that . . .
Y: Oh, shi's silly, shi's just wastin' money . . .
X: Ah know but shi wain't [won't]'ave it.

It is very hard to imagine the classes whose privilege is bought with such insecurity being possessed by the needs of so little. But these are people who have been levelled. The lack of economic power, the lack of an ability to stand above necessity with comfort and grace, is a levelling experience, and like all levelling experiences it brings with it a profound sense of vulnerability and insecurity; these establish both bonds of commonality as well as the conditions for estrangement, enmity and envy. Vulnerability and insecurity cast their own particular hue over a human life, a hue that is present throughout most of the scenes of an area and something that permeates the bodies and souls of those involved.

Lawrence wrote, in *The North Country*, of the 'Moans and booms, the soul of a people imprisoned'. Lawrence understood the ghastliness of the working life and it was perhaps natural for him to focus upon industry as the culprit for the everyday misery visited upon working people. One suspects that he must have understood that, even with the dreaded pits gone, little would have changed in the fundamental delineation of their condition. Behind the gloss technology lends to the perceived finish of contemporary society, the undercoat upon which its sheen depends remains the same. The same fundamental relations are managed through new technologies as the powerful assimilate the fruits of an abundant society in which for too many the present resembles the past and the future never seems to arrive. The words of Malcolm X must ring true for many, as he describes the rage involved in continually being made to encounter, endure, live-*through* a sense of one's abjection, as stuff of no use, and to the life-casting determinacy involved in being subject to such perceptions:

it could make me a very vicious and dangerous person – knowing how they had looked at us as numbers and as a case in their book, not as human beings. And knowing that my mother in there was a statistic that didn't have to be, that existed because of a society's failure, hypocrisy, greed, and lack of mercy and compassion. Hence I have no mercy or compassion in me for a society that will crush people, and then penalise them for not being able to stand up under the weight.

(Malcolm X 1992: 22)

Yet this experience, like many Malcolm X describes, must be familiar to anyone whose trajectory was not through elite universities into the well-remunerated, worthwhile careers to which they lead, but from school to training scheme, lower-end tertiary college training and low-paid work and intermittent unemployment. A life-style the existential roots of which begin to be experienced, as the pull of trajectory immanent in one's position, in secondary school in one's early teens: a pattern of life established in perception and habit based in the flesh's awareness of the effects of its objective categorization, that in these societies lasts throughout one's life, sedimented, for all to see, in the conditions of acquisition of all the cultural acquisitions one subsequently incorporates. The sense of soul-destruction involved in such fractured, damaged trajectories and of being known to oneself as part of a mass of people reduced, in their social existence, to the realm of statistics, comes through in what one man in his early forties said:

> I wo a builder, an as yer know, thi's [there is] too many o'r [of] us an' not enough w'k gu'in rahnd [round], thi'v tekken [taken] bonuses away all ovva place, so nahr Ah'm [I'm] on dole du'in [doing] odd fiddle but thi's not much'a that abaht [about] an' tha [you] ohnny [only] meks enough for a ne'et [night] aht o'r sumat . . .
>
> S: Ahr du yer feel about your time on the dole?
>
> Well nahr tha askin' mi sumat [something]! Well . . . [*pauses*] . . . despair, but it dun't se' enough that. Sad, arr, it's like ye'r on't bottom an tha can't gu no lower. Yer know, tha just a number an' yer feel it, when yer sign on an' that . . .
>
> S: Can't yer see yerself gettin a job?
>
> Yer must bi jokin'! Ah can't see a way out, not no 'ow. I'm fuckin' 'undred percent certain thi's no way aht: just look arahnd yer. I mean thi's s' [so] many young people aht [out] on w'k, an the'r cheaper to employ an all. I mean look at people . . . tha knows, twenny to thirty, thi's nothin' thi'v got nothin'. Thi's nowt on offer fo' em at all. I guess when I left school I at least 'ad a few good years wiyaht [without] all this shit . . . I mean tha gets what, forty nine quid a week. What the fuck can yer do wi' that?

For these people, like Malcolm X, there is a primacy in their perception of a powerful experience that they have undergone, in different ways, together: each experiencing the same, if from a different perspective; like different views, from the same level, of the same object, except that the object itself is part of us and we are part of it.

The primacy of this perception is exhibited in this 'authentic speech', this expressive act through which a meaning emerges that is lived through mutely, stoically as one's life conditions, what 'goes without saying'. There are many ways for human beings to be conscious, and this is a form that '*feels* itself rather than *sees* itself' (Merleau-Ponty 1964: 22). It is not the speech of an objectifying subject concerned to break from practice, it is the work of expressivity of a cogito that is 're-integrated into the transcendental process of the "I am", and consciousness into existence' (Merleau-Ponty 1962: 383). It is speech about the primordial grounds of their life, the experiences upon which their conscious life is constituted and which their speech registers without problematizing. It 'reveals to us the permanent data of the problem which culture attempts to resolve' (Merleau-Ponty 1964: 25). It is speech that reflects a practical state of belief, of implicit faith, that emerges from the inherence of subjectivity in a sense of temporality acquired through forms of comportment that involve habituated ways of relating and responding to the world, such that a habitual setting is projected which has a general structure which outlines prior to reflection an anonymous, pre-personal, shared environment that the subject's responses emerge from and aim at, and which is the deepest seat of identity and understanding, but which it is more appropriate to deal with as a state of the body's socialized, kinaesthetic awareness, a corporealized sense of existence that takes us beyond any decision to believe. Such testimony manifests this sense, most notably in the sense of entrapment and pessimism that is such a deep aspect of the experience of being for the poor everywhere.[5]

What is manifest in such speech is our primary relation to a pre-objective world which solicits our sensibilities such that our perceptual field is already, always, before reflection begins, laden with values that govern our experience and the conscious orientations we take when we reflect from these grounds upon issues of personal or social justice. It is clear that such speech does not just consider the effects of certain living conditions upon a person, but exhibits a coming-together of values and judgements sedimented in the experience. As though, over time, through sharing certain experiences one finds a sense of coherence being formed, in which a sense of the world configures itself for the subject, a form of practical knowledge that we might see as wisdom, a sense of where one stands because of certain aspects of one's experience that have cause to make one loyal to what one knows in virtue of what one has been through. This is what the world has bid us to know, a calling to order by virtue of the nature of experience; an understanding of the effects of certain fundamental structures and relations that have directly influenced one's existence and which become sedimented in the grounds of practical sense and action. It is that truth that we cannot betray because it is the truth of our lives; it is a truth emergent from the grounds of the place that fate cast us upon. Such testimony has the form of originary expression, because it emerges from an involvement in the world 'which carries us beyond subjectivity, which gives us our place in the world prior to any science and any verification' (Merleau-Ponty 1964: 395), an experience of the fundamental structures immanent in the sense of place and position and which is disclosed through comportment; what we experience most emphatically in perception. As Merleau-Ponty puts it:

Natural perception is not a science, it does not posit its objects, it does not distance itself from them for the purpose of observation, but it lives with them; it is the 'opinion' or the 'primary faith' which binds us to the world as to our native land, and the being of what is perceived is the antepredicative being towards which our whole existence is polarised.   (Merleau-Ponty 1964: 371–2)

Perception gives us the lived world, and where our perception of that world takes place through forms of comportment that issue from conditions of vulnerability and entrapment we might expect it to manifest a radical polarization towards the native land in which one finds oneself limited by limitations of existence that remain beyond one's power to change.

It is as if social space consisted of phenomena that always bear the mark of motive and value upon them, such that the very element in which we move and act is always possessed of intention and value such that we are always part of a realm of sense that has an effect like gravity in natural space, modulating existence with pulsions of attraction and revulsion that seem immanent to the world. These are aspects of sense, of the meaning of our environments, that interpenetrate our being as part of the ground of the sensible which orient us in social space and they are aspects of experience that we fore-ground in consciousness only under certain conditions. We need then, with Merleau-Ponty, to see perception as a phenomenon of the lived body and recognize the extent to which we come to know a world and to discover our interconnectedness with the world through our embodiment and thus through our immersion in a particular way of life and context and, more importantly, come to appreciate that this knowledge is sensuous and perceptive before it is conscious: that our primary experiences throughout childhood and our ongoing lives are determining before questions of choice arise for us. If we consider existence in this way, then we have a way of appreciating levels of sense that take place as vague, partially formed knowing, practically orienting, responses rooted in a pre-conscious awareness of the world akin to the learning of a continuous aspect that constitutes a horizon within which things, people and spaces show up with a particular luminescence. This sense is rooted in the deepest experiences of one's primary milieu and operates as a system of spontaneously realized preferences for people and things; it is most forcefully felt in the feelings of elective affinity spoken of in the language of love, and is powerfully enforced in feelings of abjection, the immediate revulsions that are so important to the reproduction of abject people's abjection. This practical sense which modulates interactions is a form of embodied sensitivity capable of eliciting psycho-somatic effects in the nervous system and emotional life of individuals. The astute satirical drama *Auf Wiedersehen Pet,* written by Dick Clement and Ian La Frenais, provides an example of the interplay of this level of aversion and its somatic effects in a scene that captures the feelings that permeate English class relations. The story involved the group of workers mistakenly taking a break from the Spanish heat in a swimming pool owned by a retired English businessman who discovers them and disciplines the group for trespassing:

Bomber [*Overlooking a Spanish villa*]: It'd bi nice to think you could retire to some place like this. 'Suppose the best I can 'ope for is a caravan . . . overlooking the Bristol Channel.
Nev: At least people would talk to yer there Bomber, ye'd have neighbours an' friends. Move out here you'd prob'ly wind up next to the same people that hauled us out 'a the pool today.

Oz: Ah know wi wo trespassin', like, but, pho'or soon as I seen his face I 'ated 'im. He's just the sort'a person makes yer ashamed to be English.
Barry: In all fairness Oz, he prob'ly feels the same about you.
Oz: What, well he shouldn't should hi, 'cos . . . every time I see 'is sort, the' hairs on mi back curl up. Ach!
Moxsie: The bourgeoisie.
Oz: eeh, a prick in my language. He's the sort'a bloke that'll sit in the golf club all day moanin' an' groanin' or writin' letters to the papers abo'ot [*Imitates posh English voice*] 'How people don't pull their weight', an' then what does he do when hi cops his pension, eh? Sheeo't! Body swerve down to Spain so hi dun't get collared fo' any tax.

This makes clear that one's relation to the world in perception, as a subject, is one of engagement, involvement, of our being situated by our bearing distinctive marks which lead the flesh to know the world through the consequences of acts of categorization that confine individuals to lives in certain spaces and distinct positions within culture. Oz's feelings are based on the pre-reflective, affective significance of class that situates this relationship. Our relation to the world, in perception, is one of 'internal communication', or a 'rootedness in the world', it is that of a *'pre-objective view* which is what we call being-in-the-world' (Merleau-Ponty 1962: 79).

If we accept perceptual experience as a pre-objective, primordial, milieu from which linguistic use and meaning emerge, then we have a way of recognizing how experiences can be deeply marking to the point of being life-constituting whilst also being inchoate. This allows us to see why certain aspects of our primary world will have formative consequences for our being-in-the-world without being fixed-on and clearly articulated. An environment might be one in which people grow up suffering what one might loosely call, 'sensory deprivation', an absence of developmental stimulation and the conditions for adequate self-development; and yet one might be unaware, in consciousness, either of the extent to which one's life issues from such a context or even of the negative effects within one's life.[6] A peculiar effect of domination is that many of the most dispossessed seem unaware of the extent to which their life is circumscribed by such conditions. Conditions of dispropriation mean that people do not have access to the resources; the instruments through which their understanding might begin to constitute a concrete sense of the limits of life and, paradoxically, the more fully the limits of life enforce themselves, the more powerfully people inscribe a sense of this life as the *only* life possible. Furthermore, living a life within strict confines, or a life in which life is simply awful, there can be little incentive (there could be no interest) in developing other forms of consciousness beyond those of the 'mindless' everyday coping skills through which it makes sense to *live* such conditions. In such conditions it makes sense to maintain one's being at a level of straightforward everyday coping, to dwell in the background, circumspectively, within the range circumscribed by the cultural conditions of the life around one. To begin to develop forms of consciousness that make the world consciously problematic, something to be thought about; to move away from the efficiency of habits attuned to life in this world would be to invite a slide from semi-conscious frustration to absurdity and transform ordinary unhappiness into misery. Living life in the context of minimal expectations, the only strategy that makes practical sense is to maintain an ignorance of anything better, to kill one's hopes. James Agee captures this beautifully:

This arduous physical work, to which a consciousness beyond that of the simplest child would be only a useless and painful encumbrance, is undertaken without choice or the thought of chance of choice, taught forward from father to son and from mother to daughter; and its essential and few returns you have seen: the houses they live in; the clothes they wear: and have still to see, and for the present imagine, what it brings them to eat; what it has done to their bodies, and to their consciousness; and what it makes of their leisure, the pleasures which are made available to them . . . I have said this now three times. If I were capable, as I wish I were, I could say it once in such a way that it would be there in its complete awfulness. Yet knowing, too, how it is repeated upon each of them, in every day of their lives, so powerfully, so entirely, that it is simply the natural air they breathe, I wonder whether it could ever be said enough times.[7]   (Agee and Evans 1969: 289)

And this is why anyone in Rotherham who seems to have any inclination to think or care in ways other than those that are generally realized in these conditions, seems to suffer. To be a normal human being, with a degree of civility and concern for one's fellow creatures seems to lead to varying degrees of depression, suffering and misery. This must indict the conditions in which these people live out their lives.[8] There is little wonder that the humanity of these people seems to be withering, as though human decency is a cloth that has been stretched too thin, as though it were a joke told once too often, as though liberties have been taken for too long, making such a practical morality absurd. Whatever does survive, in working people, by way of humanity survives in spite of their present conditions. Anyone who lives with working people quickly hears this philosophy of self-willed ignorance and emotional refusal, like a refrain to the naive who still hope for a quality of life:

X: I think rahnd [round]'ere thy 'as to just try thi' best to enjoy thi'seln [yourself], gu 'aht an get pissed on weekend wi' lads, smoke a joint. I mean it's *no fuckin' good* been serious all time an' thinkin' abaht [about] it. Let's face it, if wi all sat an' thought abaht it all, rahnd 'ere, abaht us lives, we'd all top' us'selves. Tha's *not got to be* serious.

This expresses a mode of intentionality, a way of projecting being, a technique of absorbed distraction that is here being advised as a technique of coping, since abstinence and a beholding of the world is a one-way trip to palookaville, to the hell of being consumed by the desires that belong to an absent world and, effectively, another class or to the nothingness of no public existence embedded in the companionship, pleasure and concerns of others. As another man expressed it: 'Tha best not aimin' s' high, like, else tha'll never get the'er an' bifo'ore tha knows it, thi' life'll bi gone.' It is advice of the most practical kind; to be circumspectively absorbed in the world that is left us; to be content with a form of life so impoverished that the collective sense deposited in common sense involves an understanding of the required ways of being, and counsels an effort to actively acquire and nurture the techniques and modes of being that allow one to exist amidst the painful existential consequences of this life with a minimum of regret.

This philosophy of life is typical in a town where unemployment officially stands at 14.7% and which over the last fifteen years has seen gross domestic product per head reduced dramatically from over 92% of the average for the United Kingdom to only 79%, with average earnings declining by 15% in the period 1980 to 1992. A trip around Rotherham's Job Centre reveals jobs which pay as little as £1.44 per hour, a problem that is worsening as poor wages drive down the market rate. If at an economic level there is such a link between employed and unemployed, then why should there not be such a meeting at the level of their experience? Even those who have kept their jobs have witnessed massive redundancies among fellow workers, and these economic conditions confront all families in one way or another. As one man expressed it:

X: Eh up, Ah've just realized that most'r mi family are losin' the'r jobs! I wo' at' mi parents' 'ouse last night an' [and] an uncle'r mine cem [came] rahnd to talk to mi fAther abaht losin' his job, 'cos mi father's already lost his job an' mi' uncle's losin' 'is nahr so he wants to know abaht DSS an' wot to du wi' [with] 'is redundancy. It comes as a shock to 'em, yer know, just ahr [how] unfair it all is. I mean, thi'v w'ked all the'r life an't thi'?
Y: Ye, not like us who grew up wi DSS an all that shit as a way'r life!

And yet, alongside my first question, 'what is at the heart of working class people's experience?', another seems to arise: 'What does 14.7% unemployment mean?' That is, what do these economic conditions actually mean: what are the consequences for individuals and communities? What does the uncertainty of present and future and a continual lack of money, mean? What are its consequences? Furthermore, what impact have the agencies of the state made upon people's lives, over the long-term, with all the subtle changes that have gradually impoverished the poor even further until we have reached the present point where the idea is to make life so unbearable for the unemployed that they will take any kind of work, no matter what the conditions or the wages? What has all this meant? How does it manifest itself? Not in the sociological and economic co-ordinates of professional social commentators, but to those whose lives have been forged in this context and who have seen an increase in violence, an increase in drug use, a growth in poverty, in begging, in stealing and a general increase in the hostility latent in their social environment: a decay of the culture that in living memory was theirs?

It is what low wages and high unemployment mean to these people that I am trying to understand and communicate and I believe that listening to these people as they talk reveals the truth to us. There is a sense in which statistics and social research seldom capture the sense embedded in the cultural relations that are felt throughout the surface of social life. Yet it is individual lives that manifest the problems created by socio-economic phenomena and their responses affect the cultural realm that humans spin around them and, as such, such phenomena have a significance that is their human truth. These things are, at the least, experienced through the coherence-initiating life of people as subjects, and we must preserve the unity of human life which deals with, makes sense of, suffers, phenomena that the academy breaks up and in breaking up, corrupts and impoverishes.

Returning to my question, 'What is at the heart of working people's experience?', and the connected one, 'What do unemployment and insecurity mean?' it is important to remember that these are questions about a condition of life that people deal with and have to resolve practically. Whilst I have posed these questions as a means of opening a space in which to try and explicate lived experience, there is something artificial in posing questions which do not themselves exist in the world as queries awaiting answers. And, clearly, these issues are, for many working people, problems without solutions, which, nevertheless, they have to live through as best they can. What for specialists are technical problems, dealt with through specialized, euphemizing languages, for these people impact directly on the most personal realm of their lives, in the realm of the immediately sensible and they deal with its effects in perception, our primary source of awareness.

So, why write, at this time, about a topic that has become so unfashionable that most publishers would not consider reading the manuscript? And why in a manner that raises the spectres of all those dead figures and clichéd images that a professionalizing sociology profession want to forget? Because those 'Old young men' of the depression of the 1920s are with us again, as the ravages of ill-health, poor diet and a life led in the endless uncertainty of the nether world of unemployment have taken their toll on the bodies and thereby the souls of working people. Perhaps, for professional social commentators, it can never seem quite as bad now: after all, it all happens in colour now. And so people will persist in misunderstanding the nature of working class experience and fail to recognize the extent to which there is a powerful and distinct experience that cuts to the core of identity and separates these people from other class groups from a young age. A divide something like that in America over Vietnam between those who had to go and those who didn't. In our society it is between those whose experience is government schemes and unemployment and those with elite qualifications from traditional universities, those whose economic and especially cultural capital is protected from the inflationary effects that are bound to occur as a government uses all the tendrils of the state welfare and education system to deal with the problem of unemployment and thus of labour supply.

It is this experience of position, of hardship and estrangement from the possibility of belief in a valued position in society, and, on top of this, of a struggle to maintain self-respect in the face of institutions like the Department of Social Security that lead to the hatred and bitterness that Malcolm X articulated regarding the very idea of a realm of civil society within the public sphere. For these people, there is extraordinarily little by way of simple human recognition, let alone anything approaching a sense of their value, that is part of the everyday fabric of their lives. It is this sense of the teaching of an attitude towards the world that is contained in the experience of a people situated in relation to certain fundamental structures, like the labour market, the education system, the state apparatus of the DSS and the political system itself, that I have suggested grounds working class existence in something that is originary for it, something that has great primacy for their subsequent experience and what they go on to become. There is a primacy to these perceptions because they define a world which must be negotiated. Something that would contradict any desire to euphemise or misconstrue one's experience. The availability of this sense of the world emerges from perceptions emerging from concerned absorption in the everyday practical world in which we encounter the sedimented expression of these class experiences embodied in the comportment of others. The words of one woman illuminate the way these issues come to be involved in one's sense of life:

X: Young people nahr, thi dun't look 'appy at all.
S: Du yer reckon, different from se twenny year back?
X: Oh aye, Thi' look sad, when yer look at 'em in town an that. Thi look miserable . . . thi' ave a kind'a 'opelessness in the'r faces . . .'specially when thi get to the'

teens, it's like thi' [they are] thinkin' to 'emselves 'we'er du a gu after school . . . next?', ye' know, [*Voice rises for emphasis*] 'what is the'r fo' mi?'. Whereas when we wo' young, wi could get a job anywe'er an' not just that, wi knew wi could get a mortgage fo' a place we'er 'as ahr [our] kids nahr [now], thi' dun't know if thi'r ever gunna 'ave a 'ouse an a place. [*Pause*] Oh it affects everythin' dun' it, family and future an everythin'.

What is interesting here is the way she fixes upon the effects of such conditions on the demeanour of individuals. As though demeanor displays the primal effects of these conditions. It is as though this woman has come to be aware, through her own experience, of the fundamental existential ramifications of such social conditions because these conditions are imbued in the forms of comportment through which individuals, as part of a distinct culture, deal with, and respond to, those very structuring conditions. Furthermore, this woman is aware of the sense carried in the continuous, mindless, dispositional patterning of reactions and responses which exhibit a world experienced, felt, seen, showing up, within the light of a certain form of being, held within the confines of a highly circumscribed space of possibility. The bonds of the flesh that are common class origin and life style allow her to feel, body-to-body, the sense of this response to the world as it exists for those she knows have grown up without hope or choice. Her expression makes clear that within the phenomenal field of her immediate perception, that is, her naive, spontaneous perceptions, she feels gripped by a sense of the 'social necessity turned into nature' (Bourdieu 1990a: 69) carried in the demeanour and forms of comportment of the young people she describes. She articulates the relation between the demeanour of the young people and the relation to the future inscribed in the relation to themselves and the world that their responses, their comportment, instantiate, and this adds the sense of pathos that is so pronounced in this woman's sense of these people because, as far as she is concerned, it is as though their future is manifest in the present condition that she sees exhibited in demeanour, knowing the conditions of acquisition of those muscular patterns, postural sets and forms of gestural response.

We need to be aware, considering the significance of this woman's testimony, of some of the insights of *Gestalt* Psychology. Merleau-Ponty discusses the importance of the notion of *Gestalten* in understanding the phenomenal field and perception, which consist of *Gestalten*. The basic idea is that perception depends upon configurations or structures of interrelations of parts, yet it cannot be reduced, for its sense, to the parts, because the whole seems to us *essentially* organised, such that we spontaneously perceive a meaning that absorbs us without perception of isolated aspects and their interrelationship. One finds this phenomenon exhibited powerfully in regard to the human capacity to recognize other people. A face is a paradigm example of a *Gestalt* in that we need the whole face to trigger recognition, because the face only has the features it has in terms of its being-perceived as an organized whole. Yet it seems that deeper aspects of the perception of human dispositions, of moods and intentions, depend upon quite prolonged acculturation and the imbuing of perceptual techniques that are neither consciously learnt nor taught. The cues that one picks up on here, are not only immensely subtle but they form part of the background structure of comportment upon which human interaction and understanding are based but of which people do not need to be conscious in order to carry-off existence and consciousness. Wittgenstein characterised these phenomena as 'imponderable evidence', and included 'subtleties of glance, of gesture, of tone' (Wittgenstein 1958: 228) And, as he suggests, 'I may recognize a genuine loving look, distinguish it from a pretended one . . . But I may be quite incapable of describing the difference' (Wittgenstein 1958: 228). The point here is that we are immediately aware of the sense of faces and bodies and this arises not from the static body caught in still-pictures but from the continual play of movement and gesture from which significance is spun, the fabric of intersubjectivity human interaction weaves. Wittgenstein remarks:

Think of the recognition of *facial expressions*. Or of the description of facial expressions – which does not consist in giving the measurement of the face!

(Wittgenstein 1958: 285)

Recognizing facial and gestural expressions involves understanding the significance of a person's look and gesture. And one learns this through a slow, imperceptible, prolonged and intimate involvement in the life of a culture in which one interacts and learns to comport oneself with the full range of expertise, both appreciating and producing, 'on the spot' and 'right on cue', the appropriate significances and expression that make one a competent individual. As Wittgenstein put it:

Is there such a thing as 'expert judgement' about the genuineness of expressions of feeling? – Even here, there are those whose judgement is 'better' and those whose judgement is 'worse'.

Correcter prognoses will generally issue from the judgements of those with better knowledge of mankind.

Can one learn this knowledge? Yes; some can. Not, however, by taking a course in it, but through '*experience*'. – Can someone else be a man's teacher in this? Certainly. From time to time he gives him the right *tip*. – This is what 'learning' and 'teaching' are like here. – What one acquires here is not a technique; one learns correct judgements. There are also rules, but they do not form a system, and only experienced people can apply them right. Unlike calculating rules.

(Wittgenstein 1958: 227)

That is, the skills one needs are an aspect of the overall awareness involved in our becoming accustomed to comport ourselves within a specific form of life. This is perhaps why people are better at recognizing faces of their own race, and partly why one finds people of the same race or group share a coherent sense of the system of relevant differences constituting the expressions of people of their own culture and why individuals can recognize what are felt to be the most salient characteristics of their own culture. Hence, in a sense, there is no definite answer to the question, how is the meaning of a gesture learned, since it is not a question of learning, but of the acquisition of the referential-whole of background comportment through which we come to participate in and feel the significance of patterns of action and response that are part of the communities in which we live. This is why Dwyer concludes:

> The *Gestalt* provides the model of that which is primarily the bearer of sense. Its bearing sense is a matter of its expressing sense. This is why sense does not transcend that which has or expresses sense, and why understanding is the understanding (the perception) of the actual bearers (actual signs, gestures, etc.) of sense . . . Understanding must start somewhere. The basic (natural) kind of sense perception is the perception of sense. In part II of the *Investigations* Wittgenstein speaks of 'fine shades of behaviour' (p. 203). The obvious analogy is with fine shades of meaning. Our perceptual capacities are such that we can spontaneously discriminate such fine shades. (Dwyer 1990: 121)

Sense, therefore, does not transcend that in which sense is immanent; and understanding consists in perceiving the sense of demeanour, gesture and comportment. Thus, our most natural forms of sense-perception are inextricably perceptions of sense, because we never cognitively inhabit the world prior to its being sensible for us. Such capacities to perceive 'fine shades of behaviour' (Wittgenstein 1958: 207) and the meaning they manifest may be spontaneous; but the sense we perceive is not always equally available, nor always perceived by all. Rather it is our situated, engaged comportment that makes certain senses available, and the sense or practical belief associated with conditions is a state of the body, a 'relationship of immediate adherence that is established in practice between a *habitus* and the field to which it is attuned, the pre-verbal taking-for-granted of the world that flows from practical sense' (Bourdieu 1990a: 68). It is as though the woman quoted earlier's situated existence and her experience of her own life within the context of this decline make such perceptions available to her, that is, attune her to the significance that the demeanour of the poor is often trying to obscure. No one wants to look poor, 'like a right scrubber', but nevertheless some do. The woman quoted earlier is aware, not merely, of something carried in the outer form of clothes; she is possessed of an inner sense of the abuse and vulnerability that the comportment of the people she describes is meant to efface. Her own engagement in this form of being, of living the body, and understanding what processes constitute that form of comportment as a necessary form of being – something that had to be taken up in the face of social processes in order to live amidst them – are the basis of her perceptions and awareness of this sense. It is a form of understanding of being in which phenomena – things and people, as well as processes – show up; are perceived within the phenomenal field, or the world as it is perceived in immediate perception; and it shows how the everyday way of being discloses the world in particular ways that presume our being in specific circumstances. This is why Heidegger talks of being as a 'clearing', the German word involving an allusion to light – the suggestion being that things show up in the light of this understanding of being involved in perception.

It is because social processes lead to the adoption of certain forms of comportment and demeanour; influence the relation to being and the understanding involved in forms of life, that the social universe consists of constellations of sense that we can see in the barely perceptible, often almost unspeakable details of manner and gesture that led Wittgenstein to suggest that 'What is most difficult here is to put this indefiniteness, correctly and unfalsified, into words' (Wittgenstein 1958: 227) and yet such details betray a whole attitude to the world and human beings. It is because the inescapable context of coming-to-be is so marked by inequalities of power and resources that individuals, as they imbibe the comportment of their culture, inscribe within their flesh a sense that, within the objective hierarchy of the social universe, contains 'the most fundamental principles of the arbitrary content of a culture in seemingly innocuous details of bearing or physical and verbal manners, so putting them beyond the reach of consciousness or explicit statement' (Bourdieu 1990a: 69). Individual comportment thus involves, through its expressive realization, a coherent, tacit sense of the cultural whole within which it takes place and which its performance enacts. Posture thus 'recalls' the sense of that realm and of the relations that constitute the space of sense[9] which comportment emerges from and realizes. Hence persons, as the expressive beings they are, are the bearers of sense, which is why Wittgenstein insists that 'The human body is the best picture of the human soul' (Wittgenstein 1958: 178).

The woman speaking about the misery she sees in the faces of the young clearly has an intuitive grasp of why what is manifest in their demeanour is so deep and so tragic, that it cuts to the heart of their existence and exhibits the lamentable condition of their soul. She perceives in the whole of the expressivity that makes the concept of person incompossible, irreducible, 'logically primitive' (Strawson 1959: 101); in their bodies perceived as sums of dispositional patterns, muscular and postural schemes of continually instantiated organization, the sense that they bear before the world, a sense that is not something like a style that they enact but which flows from the very grounds of their being and possesses them.

Yet from the grounds of this woman's insight, there arises a problem that is at the heart of English society. If perceiving the nature of their condition is based upon an awareness based upon shared conditions, then people who do not share the conditions will perceive their condition differently. And this is what makes these people's predicament, politically, so futile, because recognizing the pain that indicts the society, depends upon being able to perceive the 'numb imperatives' (Bourdieu 1990a: 69) made body during the long process of acculturation of position involved in growing up in places like Rotherham.

In response to this phenomenon, one can simply be struck by the abjection of the poor, or one might simply find them ridiculous, good for a cheap laugh, or one might recategorize the phenomenon in different ways. However, this woman's situated life has made available to her, the forms of sense, the sensitivity, that she engages the world through; and these perceptions reveal the wisdom involved in her sense of the world around her and in response, it is all too plausible to refuse to see her world under the same aspect,[10] 'in the same light', and thus to remain unable to see. She recognizes that the bodies of those around her manifest a condition that has extorted what is essential and left only insignificance. 'Just like a schoolboy whose head's like a tin can, filled up with dreams, then poured down the drain'.[11]

We need to recognize that working class people's lives are lived against this background which obtrudes, creating for them a sense of despair that is akin to an aesthetic response, in that it is part of a learned form of perceiving the significance of their environment, a form of spontaneously perceptually realized 'reading' of their world based upon an immanent sense, practically acquired, of that world. It is a state that we are used to recognizing in photographs of the past, the sense that poverty and vulnerability create, the down-and-out bleakness of black and white photo-journalism; yet too many are insensitive to the similarity in the wasted lives of those with whom they share the country. Yet many working people's lives negotiate this despair and the effects of the social decay of their environment. Listening to working people speak, one thus needs to appreciate the conditions from which their immediate, primary sense of the world issues, and be sensitive to how this is inflected in their manner and way of speaking. As Merleau-Ponty elaborates:

Here the meaning of words must be finally induced by the words themselves, or . . . their conceptual meaning must be formed by a kind of deduction from a *gestural meaning*, which is immanent in speech. And as, in a foreign country, I begin to understand the meaning of words through their place in a context of action, and by taking part in a communal life.   (Merleau-Ponty 1962: 179)

And later, he continues:

We find here, beneath the conceptual meaning of the words, an existential meaning which is not only rendered by them, but which inhabits them, and is inseparable from them.   (Merleau-Ponty 1962: 182)

This inhabitation is manifest in the speech of the woman quoted earlier. It shows that the situation impacts upon the affective grounds of her life, even though she herself is relatively secure, by virtue of her age, from the acute conditions that face those younger than her. Her words emerge from the thickness of being; from the grounds of a social and historical condition, and this general condition is the broad context of sense that her words communicate. This condition is the medium through which the stream of her life washes, and, given the difficulties encountered in her daily confrontation with these conditions, it is as though her consciousness finds the flow of life difficult: it eddies here, forms ripples and whirl-pools there, like water across a rocky terrain, and these conditions are what her thought encompasses by touching. The wash of life across the contours of this medium constitutes perceptual existence, the openness to being that her speech manifests. And the speech manifests a form of care in its concern, an engagement that registers a passing away of previous social and historical conditions but conditions known only directly, in perceptual existence, as a form of life, as a space of possibly realizable goals.

The deeper sense of her speech manifests the background of a phenomenal space, of an internally related context shared with those around her. The sense of despair she sees embodied in the young is like a theme of the town, a theme manifest in people's existence, in the relation to life that their comportment manifests. Perception opens up this fuller context of practical sense, and our words manifest the deeper ambiguities and important human aspects of the phenomenal field that being opens upon. This field of perceptual phenomena is what our language games get a hold of: it is, as it were, the nip-and-tuck that we engage language, both as tools of sense and as bridges in being, to give sense to – the sense that we live through and feel, the meaning that we feel life has given to us, what we feel is determined, that which we could not ignore, which moves us to fight for our say and sacrifice ourselves to its truth. It is a realm of sense: of our *ethos*, our lives, existence itself, individually invested in the fate of our immediate category and people. Yet this 'theme' exists at the pre-objective level of somatic being; it affects this woman's sensibility, it obtrudes upon her awareness mimetically, through her deep sense of the significance of comportment. This hopelessness that she sees in the faces of the young affects her; finds its place in her perspective upon the world. Sadness, pessimism and despair are for her, knowing these conditions, infectious through the logic we share for knowing a way of life. In his *Remarks on the Philosophy of Psychology*, Wittgenstein makes the suggestion, 'When a theme, a phrase suddenly says something to you, you don't have to be able to explain it to yourself. Suddenly *this* gesture too is accessible.' And what he says of gesture is true of demeanour: it is a *Gestalt*, a matter of perceptual organization, of pre-objective coherence, of our perception of the sense of the phenomenal field, of our unknowing discernment of a pattern, a process at the heart of all forms of depth-association. The possibility of this form of perception clearly depends upon an ethical relation to these persons. A form of care born of intimacy with their conditions of acculturation constitutes in her gaze a horizon that mediates apperception constituting an affinity, or empathy born of a shared form of being. It is effectively a side-taking, whether it knows itself as such or not; it is an affinity embedded in a comportment born of shared conditions of existence. And, moreover, it is a form of sight that is not itself dependent upon the objectifying gaze of a linguistically constituting subject; rather it is a form of sight, at once ethical and human, which has emerged from a continuing and life-long contact with necessity, that levelling relation that negates pretension and possibility. It is a perceptual realm revealed through shared patterns of comportment embedded in shared conditions of existence. It is this form of perception we have to reclaim from working people's speech if we are ever going to understand the sense they have of the world, and this requires us to extend our sense of the phenomena of the world.

If we look at some more excerpts of personal testimony, Merleau-Ponty's insights become more clearly grounded. Merleau-Ponty tried to replace our understanding of perception as an attribute of a subject that thinks its world: shaping perception through ratiocination; with a model in which perception emerges from the engagement of a body-subject. That is, with a model of reflection based on a pre-personal, antepredicative consciousness; a consciousness which is incarnate subjectivity; making our concrete inherence in the world, the horizon of knowledge opened by perception, the basis of a form of knowing that is also a way of being. This is peculiarly suited to dealing with people whose being-in-the-world is over-determined by an inability to distance the world in perception because of an absence of economic and symbolic power which confines them to a life

of the body dominated by the immediacy of extreme insecurity and vulnerability. This condition is one in which the subject must, daily, endure negative experiences that operate like sanctions, delineating a sense of the world
that amounts to an 'unconscious' which comes to frame, practically, their
relation to the world. It is a relation that is manifest in the following
people's words:

X: A've got four kids an' thi's a lot'a families like us, an' if they all feel like we feel,
an' yer can bet yer life thi' du, then that's a lot'a [lot of] worried people an' a lot'a
people who'r [who are] just gettin' by. I mean, if thi' cut back anymo'or, else I
s'pose prices 'll gu up, then God knows, wi will be strugglin'. I mean, all ma
money gu's on 'ouse, kids an' food, that's it an' [*Voice rises*] I an't got enough nahr!

X: Ma kids, thi' see us strugglin' the'r mam [mother] an' me, every day an' thi' see it
nahr [now], like, that thi's nowt [nothing] the'er fo' em. I mean, ma [my] eldest,
he's eight an hi thinks instead 'r [of] gunna [going to] w'k fo' money, hi thinks yer
gu' tu' post office fo' it! An' it's bad nahr, what's it gunna bi like in nine year or so
when hi leaves school?

X: I've bi'n rait depressed this week. I 'ate winter. I got up at 'alfe five an' it wo' pitch
ahtside an' tha [you] w'ks an' then when tha comes 'ome it's dark again. Thi's a
name fo' it in't the? That kind'a depression we'er yer dun't get enough sunlight.
Tha' gets up in dark and get'ome in dark, Ah dun't know.

What is clear in such testimony is that the world given in experience to these
people is one mediated by an economic necessity given in their social position that is part of the network of relations they find themselves in.
Moreover, this world is given in perceptions that arise from the meeting, in
experience, of body-subject and world. That is, the sense of perception
arises from the patterns of comportment that form the pre-personal, anonymous background, that economic and class position shape through their
primary impact upon the conditions of existence through which we are sen-
sitized to forms of awareness and forms of explicit understanding. As
Langer puts it, 'the subject's way of living its body is decisive for the manner
in which it apprehends the world' (Langer 1989: xvi). What emerges from
these people's speech is that their primary experience of existence is of a
concern over necessities and conditions that impact upon them so severely
that it curtails the possible ways for them to realize their way of living. This
establishes for them a lack of modalities through which they live the body.
This background has a severely anchoring effect upon self-descriptions and
the meaning of the world; it has an un-deniability that transforms itself in
being. Taking Langer seriously, then, if the pre-personal manner of engaging the world carried in comportment – the subject's way of living its body
– is constrained by, and absorbed in, non-self-realizing modes of being,

then we will have communities which exhibit forms of personal suffering, socially rooted, which will likely be expressed in various forms of personal and group pathology.

What is clear in these people's speech is that unemployment-figures and statistics of poverty do not capture their experience, because for them these social relationships are phenomenal, part of their lived world and their life in it. What we have to do, to overcome the alienation involved in the academic understanding of these phenomena by their being written about, mainly, by people whose professional life means that their understanding is, at best, of a second-order nature, is to look to the way the phenomena are constituted in the everyday ways of being of the people whose practice emerges from an engagement with the phenomena themselves. Too often, the discursive instruments offered by the academic and political fields, are derivations, which presupposes the primary perceptions, the originating sense that these people's speech details. As Bourdieu concludes:

It follows from this that social science cannot 'treat social realities as things', in accordance with Durkheim's famous precept, without neglecting all that these realities owe to the fact that they are objects of cognition (albeit a misrecognition) within the very objectivity of social existence. Social science has to reintroduce into the full definition of the object the primary representations of the object, which it first had to destroy in order to achieve the 'objective' definition.

(Bourdieu 1990a: 135)

Economic and social policy descriptions are products. The phenomena they designate exist, at a primary level, as aspects incorporated into the being-in-the-world of those whose lives are touched by the conditions that academic analyses depict; they are part of the phenomenal field of body-subjects, and possess a sense which, even when inarticulate, is rarely simple because it emerges from and involves the deepest aspects of human being.

This is why I have discussed at such length the significance of the words of the woman who describes young people as ' . . . miserable . . . thi' ave a kind'a 'opelessness in the'r faces . . .'. For her words express the transmission of a deep sense of the condition of her class which is sensible to her through her situated perceptions as a person in this culture. And it is a sense gained from an awareness of the sense manifest in gesture and demeanour, exhibiting an embodied sensitivity, a tactile intelligence that transmits, 'body-to-body', as it were, the truth in the being of others, of low wages, high unemployment and vulnerability. It is important to notice the link between this practical sensitivity which is a developed form of intelligence (though uncertificated and of no objective value) and a form of despair, through human connection and personal quality, that comes from developing humanly, individually, in this culture. This sense of unease is a daily reality for this person, something she has been made sensitive to because she can see the starkness of the contrast to her own life, the decay of the co-ordinates of partnership, co-habitation, family, home. And this is a sense all the more profound for being unarticulated, unspoken: a sense that is latent, felt as obtruding within the realm of the particular projects of life but which is usually heard only indirectly and seldom dwelt upon when articulated. It is what is lived-with, what is unsaid, the great morass that life is a struggle to break from.

The world that these people's testimony emerges from is one that resists efforts to ignore it, one that obtrudes, constantly pressing into the phenomenal realm, like a problem that must be dealt with, accommodated to in comportment. Yet this is a world they belong to, and can see the deeper aspects of, because of the way that they have grown to live their bodies as part of a particular class group, and it is experience embedded in the wider significations involved in being the bodies that they are. These are some of the wider ramifications of our being incarnate subjects: the kind of phenomenal field that is constituted for us is affected by the meaning of the embodiment we make incarnate. These people are talking about a realm of immediacy that is whole, saturated with immanent significance. This immanent significance is what 'the primacy of perception' involves, and I have argued that the perceptions involved in being positioned as these people are, makes one open to the world in a certain way, it teaches one to be engaged with the world, habitually, in distinct ways: 'From this phenomenological perspective, bodily experience is not reducible to an actual momentary interoceptivity occurring in a particular instant of the present' (Langer 1989: 32). Through the pre-objective, habitual world that working people live in there comes to be lived a 'global' or bodily intentionality that amounts to a distinct pre-objective orientation that touches all manner of engaging with the world of objects and with institutions and persons.

It is this that constitutes what many middle class people find the deep cynicism of working people's humour, the callousness that can characterize their attitudes to the world. But it is the power of the experience of degradation described, the sense of fracture that constitutes the primacy of working people's perception, a power in experience that teaches them what might be called 'lessons' about the nature of life and of society that their attitudes and practical affinities emerge from. It creates an 'expressive interest' in their lives that can be a very powerful force in bringing working people together in the spaces in which they live, making them feel comfortable around one another, through the fulfilment of this expressive need. And this explains why, as a people who have lived through very particular social conditions, who have a very particular, unambiguous, even marking, experience, they feel a deep estrangement in the company of people of a higher class whose lives do not bear this mark in every aspect of life, whose distance from necessity makes them better able to maintain the pretence of life itself. The pretence has been shattered for working people. This lack of distance from necessity makes working class people's experience more determinate, less amenable to euphemization, more shaping, and it leads them to need to talk about life in a way that is more personal, critical and, to the extent that it is less euphemized, more honest; but it is this experience of the primacy of their social conditions that characterizes the warmth and decency of their companionship.

Living in a working class area, therefore, it is impossible not to confront the presence of a powerful force touching all of our lives; whether it be a force that drives one to steal, be violent, use drugs, suffer mental illness or be quiet, resigned to misery, or, the most usual response, going out to forget one's problems, there is something at work in our society that has affected the working class very deeply, that has created fear, insecurity and disillusionment. Around them working people see a loss of the basic things they once relied upon, and they are acutely aware of what faces the young, that their parts of the world have indeed become 'meaner, harder and more corrupting' (Hutton 1996b: 3). These changes have had a profound effect upon the sense of life in working class areas. Few aspects or areas of life have gone untouched, and the cynicism that has so much come to characterize working people's lives, the disdain with which they have been treated, has come to mark them, to be an aspect of their experience that has fostered that same attitude in them. Why should they care about a society that has refused to care about them? A man in his fifties suggests, 'We worked all our lives an' now . . . well . . . You're the dirt on somebody else's shoes.'

Yet, at the most fundamental level of sense-experience, what have been the consequences of the wasting of the traditional co-ordinates of these cultures? Thinking about the testimony that I have used here and of the experience that I have been a part of, I am drawn to Bourdieu's insights concerning the projection into the future involved in our everyday practices. Taking this Heideggerian insight seriously, then we see that, when the grounds of the present are taken away, people's projective absorption ceases, and they are left with a debilitating experience of malaise that damages their sense of existence at the very deepest level. And this is an experience that is virtually uncapturable through the position of the scholar who retreats from the world in order to think life. As Bourdieu puts it:

Science has a time which is not that of practice . . . Scientific practice is so detemporalized that it tends to exclude even the idea of what it excludes. Because science is only possible in a relation to time which is the opposite of that of practice, it tends to ignore time and so to detemporalize practice.   (Bourdieu 1990a: 81)

Moreover, from this position, there are critical aspects of phenomena that cannot be appropriately rendered. Yet, for those from the most dominated sections of social space, those condemned to a life of meaninglessness through unemployment and endless training schemes, or the never-ending cycle of poor work and the same terrible employment conditions, it is as though they are in a position akin to the one that Bourdieu describes as a:

sudden reduction to the present, that is, to the past, the abrupt severing of the commitments and attachments to the future which, like death, casts the anticipations of interrupted practice into the absurdity of the unfinished.   (Bourdieu 1990a: 82)

Many in such areas have been reduced to the same endless present which leaves them little to anticipate; rather they experience such an inability to alter the course of their lives that they come to lack the sense of themselves as having a will to affect life at all. It is as though the sense of existence that comes from involvement, the experience of initiative that comes form being able to affect one's life and satisfy one's needs or desires, becomes so eroded that individuals no longer feel any urgency to their existence. I'd like to consider the testimony that closes this chapter in relation to this insight of Bourdieu's:

Urgency, which is rightly seen as one of the essential properties of practice, is the product of playing in the game and the presence in the future that it implies. One only has to stand outside the game, as the observer does, in order to sweep away the urgency, the appeals, the threats, the steps to be taken, which make up the real, really lived-in, world. Only for someone who withdraws from the game completely, who totally breaks the spell, the *illusio*, renouncing all the stakes, that is, all the gambles on the future, can the temporal succession be seen as a pure discontinuity and the world appear in the absurdity of a future-less, and therefore senseless, present, like the Surrealizts' staircase opening on to the void. The 'feel' (*sens*) for the game is the sense of the imminent future of the game, the sense of the direction (*sens*) of the history of the game that gives the game its sense.   (Bourdieu 1990a: 82)

There are many who live in a condition akin to this. Their lives are absorbed in the effort involved in coping and getting by and in the stress of dealing with an unfulfilling world and they are possessed of a sense of the absurdity of this endless present which seems to be the inescapable context of life. If it is the 'history of the game that gives the game its sense', we can understand why these lives seem possessed of so little sense, because the history that the tradition that their lives instantiated has been interrupted and altered, and it has left them going through the motions of a form of life grown old. Their hearts still beat, but their sense of 'inner time', the pulse of time in their veins, the temporality they live, has gone awry. There is little opportunity for them to exercise choices, to change their lives and they see, through the vision of their children, only more of the same. What has been destroyed for these people is the sense of the conditions of their time as something they can use, through their action in the world, to realize themselves. Instead of the future being a field that stretches beyond them, it has become a vertical face they cannot begin to conquer. Their lives try to obey the logic of working life, they try to impose, artificially, the rhythms of working culture through voluntary work and visits to the gym, but employment is in a condition of scarcity and the only thing they can do with their time is waste it. In this context, dreaming becomes pathological because it means feeling the weight of necessity more cruelly. It is a life of the absurd where hard work and self-development lead directly to a more painful experience of this condition. It makes most sense to deaden the self, one way or another. As one person explained the process:

At first it 'its yer 'ard, when yer lose yer job, an' yer bo'ord [bored] stiff an' miserable an' yer strugglin' 'cos'r [because of] money but after a while, yer brain starts to work differently, yer don't do it deliberate, like, but if yer din't start to change yer thinkin', yer cun't [could not] live . . .

This man presents the effects of changed conditions as effecting a change in the architecture of the mind, a change he sees not as an act of self-will or conscious choice but which he feels is necessary, like anaesthetic for an operation, if he is to go on living a life in which the feelings, the *sense*, of this malaise are not so acute as to completely nullify his capacity to cope. It displays the embodied situation of consciousness, the extent to which our conscious life is located in and thus affected by a more primordial, pre-objective phenomenal realm of the lived body entwined in a world that encroaches, affecting me, moving me, leading me to feel, at the heart of me, what is given to me in perception of the world. That is, in perceptions given to the lived-body, which are infused, not merely, with the sense of the world, but of myself and my position. This man's words illuminate the process whereby individuals struggle to deal with impoverished existences by never developing into certain possibilities, learn to refuse the soul's endless pressing into its possibilities. It is like an unconscious activity of self-curtailment; of accommodation to the necessary carried out through the practical mediation of being throughout one's daily life. Yet this process is based on conditions of deep alienation from the sources of recognition, presence and value that can animate the flesh with the gleaming sense of people of objectively assured value; those possibilities for life given whose condition is a valuing public context that most, in these societies, find in the realm of work and the companionship and position it ensures. This man's condition excludes him from the possibility of human connection and respect, and what he describes is a process of alienation from his own self-actualization; the presence of otherness at the heart of subjectivity; an invisible dispossession of the ordinary initiative of existence; a state brought about by his changed relationship to the source of the ability to alleviate necessity, the source of life for working people that the wage represents. The words of Rainer Maria Rilke seem strikingly appropriate:

... we are alone with the alien thing that has entered into our self; because everything intimate and accustomed is for an instant taken away; because we stand in the middle of a transition where we cannot remain standing.   (Rilke 1993: 64)

What was most intimate for these people, the customs of the culture that was theirs, have been washed away, and this man's voice hails from amidst a transition that has left many behind and many unable to stand with any security. However, this transition is historical and economic, and it involves a transition for a whole category of individuals, all required to remain standing through the transition. And their problem is that the 'space to stand', so to speak, is contracting. It has left many growing to despise their human capacities because they have been dispossessed of the conditions in which they might experience their humanity positively, in which they might fulfil their potentiality. Hence, they cannot understand their capacities nonnegatively and come to hate what they see as the faculties responsible for their inability to 'be happy'. As one unemployed man said of his time at college, 'Ah regret it nahr. All it seems t' 'ave done is med mi mo'ore aware a ahr bad life is 'cos Ah'm still in same position as when Ah went.' Another man expressed it even more poignantly: 'Ye'v got to bi brain dead to live in Rother'am.' This is a state to be aspired to because so many people are now experiencing their desires and human capacities as things that only bring them suffering. The more they develop, the more accustomed they become to the pleasures that an income allows, the more, potentially, they will suffer, because their culture is a culture of necessity, of 'going without':

We're allous [always]'avin' to calculate what wi' need, yer know, if wi buy one thing, then wi' 'ave to gu wiy'aht sum'at [without something] else, an' then it's w'kin' up that time again at w'k [work]: somehow, gettin' that money back an' startin age'an [again].

The more they become, the worse they will feel; the more their sensitivity connects them to others, the more they will experience the suffering around them, a suffering all the more poignant and severe for its being a shared condition, their suffering, a suffering they live with, that obtrudes issuing from the background of their culture, manifest in the lives of those among whom they live. This is something that marks working people very deeply, it characterizes their lives, and in so doing becomes part of their characteristics and hence character.

This is what makes them recognizable, from above, as figures in a landscape; it gives them their 'realism' and 'cynicism'. Many of the pathologies of their culture stem from this, but here I want to concentrate on why a philosophy of self-fulfilment can make little sense for these people, and why the force of their perception forces them to characterize their lives as 'doing nothing'. The pain involved in living in conditions in which one's life lacks an embedding in a public world of reference and self-respect was well expressed by one man who was unusual in talking about himself as 'depressed', a remark he was asked to confirm in what followed:

S: Du yer feel depressed, then?
B: . . . Ye, I feel guilty fo' not w'kin' [working]. An' Ah [I] started to feel depressed early on [S: Ahr early?] er . . . abaht [about] a month, when tha's bi'n [you've been] through lookin', an' dole an that, . . . [S: Can yer describe yer feelin's?] fuckin' boored, a sort'a bein' totally bored . . . thi's now't 'ere is the? . . . [*Pause*] . . . Ahr lass comes 'ome an Ah feel terrible [*voice rises*] 'cos shi's bin to w'k an' shi'll se', 'what 'ave yer done today?' An' Ah 'ave t' se', 'well nowt'. An' w'se [worse], Ah just dun't seem to 'ave ' will anymo'ore to du 'owt [anything], stuff that Ah used t' du, and yet Ah feel restless, right pent-up, in mi'self but I can't settle to du owt [anything] . . . [*voice trails off*] . . . [*Pause*] . . . an' him that dun't [does not] work, dun't 'ave no money, either! [*laughs*]

Questions about the nature of happiness in working class people's lives are worth considering because what this man is articulating emerges from a way of life that he knows has always been heavily circumscribed, such that what satisfactions there were, the happiness that might be expected, was of a particular form, and yet even that has gone. This man described to me how he had lost interest in fishing and his garden, two things that, in the context of the world of work, he had enjoyed; but now, the loss of will he describes has taken these pleasures away from him. What has gone is the overall, habitual context that gave his life its sense and meaning; and the pain and despair are just other ways, barely conscious ways, of his realizing that his cultural 'lot' in life, his fishing, gardening and boozing, were not really life-sustaining. But, in the absence of the resources for the reproduction of life, there is little but the restless contemplation of a condition ever more subtle in its effects, as life leaks away into the sterile grounds of a dying way of life. In this light, it seems that Bourdieu's formulation of the question is insightful:

I think this question of happiness is very important. The doxic attitude does not mean happiness; it means bodily submission, unconscious submission, which may indicate a lot of internalised tension, a lot of bodily suffering . . . I have discovered a lot of suffering which had been hidden by this smooth working of habitus. It helps people to adjust, but it causes internalised contradictions . . . One may be very well adapted to this state of affairs, and the pain comes from the fact that one internalises silent suffering, which may find bodily expression.

(Bourdieu and Eagleton 1992: 121)

This internalised tension and silent, barely expressed, suffering, is evident in much of the testimony which reveals individuals struggling to alter their expectations and to accommodate to a realm of much frustration and little humanity. What is manifest is the tension involved in trying to change one's embodied sense of the world, to re-learn how to *be*, but to learn how to be *less* than one formerly was; to give up the pleasures that one had become habituated to; to foreshorten one's taste for existence, to give up the immediacy of the chase of life; to live, as it were, in the shadow-world of unsatisfied need. This 'smooth working of habitus', which accommodates people to changes in their social conditions whilst minimizing their awareness of suffering, is captured by Walter Brierley, writing about a similar time of despair for working people:

That agony-day once a month, he dreaded it, more for Jane's sake than his own; it almost killed her every time. And he was so helpless, had to see her suffer and couldn't say anything comforting. And this was a pointless, hopeless existence. He suffered one way, she another. He opened his eyes, turning to look at her. She was lying on her back heavy in sleep . . . about her nostrils was a pallor like death. Lines beneath her eyes and on the forehead cut into the soft, smooth flesh; it must be upon these that folks based the assertion that the past three years had aged her. Unless, of course, they had seen that she, like him, had lost the spiritual vigour they once had. He turned back to the world of fire again, struggling against an impatience tinged with hate and anger. But there was no fire in the emotion, it was merely a faint emphasis of the general attitude of mind which had come to be part of him. Always now something pressed him down, holding him below a level which he ought to be on, which his being was rightly fitted for. If he could forget this, if he could tune himself wholly to this lower level, his existence might be smoother, he might move freely again. But he could not, he knew he could not, and therefore the attitude of mind must continue, the impatience, the anger, the hate, the concrete unhappiness.   (Brierley 1983: 3)

What were once called 'the appetites' have become things of shame because they bring, in the absence of the means of their satisfaction, only a bitter frustration and a deep cynicism. And these matters involve forms of sense that require us to move beyond the model of the conscious-subject linguistically constituting experience; they involve the totality of being that language and sense emerge from. They are existential, to do with these people's being-in-the-world; to do with the heart of their being human. 'What is there?', 'What can I hope for?' and when these are answered: 'Is this because of what I am?', 'Is this misfortune mine?' These are questions that delineate the deepest confusion. As one person confided to me: 'I'm scared. I spend most of my life being afraid and I try and say to myself that I'm alright but I never feel it.' These are ontological questions; they are matters deeper and more important than the usual questions that are asked about working class life. For it is a world in which issues of income and education are only the most basic indices of life in a class-divided society, which indicate little of the sense arising from what they indicate. Moreover, we must realize the fundamental sense the world has, even the world of objects that we perceive with least ambiguity, because of the ways that world comes to be meaningful through the forms of shared comportment through which we come to inhabit the world as a place immanent with a sense we cannot ignore. Through our coming to live our comportment as the very basis of our sense of the world, we exist in space that is permeated by a lived sense that 'binds me to the things which count and exist for me, and links them to each other' (Merleau-Ponty 1962: 285) which makes the objective world a world of intertwinings, of resonances emerging from one's position. This is why Bourdieu writes:

The world of objects, a kind of book in which each thing speaks metaphorically of all others and from which children learn to read the world, is read with the whole body, in and through the movements and displacements which define the space of objects as much as they are defined by it. The structures that help to construct the world of objects are constructed in the practice of a world of objects constructed in accordance with the same structures. The 'subject' born of the world of objects does not arise as a subjectivity facing an objectivity: the objective universe is made up of objects which are the product of objectifying operations structured according to the same structures that the *habitus* applies to them.   (Bourdieu 1990a: 77)

The order of things subsumes the hierarchy of bodies because the bodies themselves are patterned according to a logic of use that marks all things, bodies and objects, along a continuum between the distinguished and the vulgar, grace and condemnation. Hence we can now see the task of this chapter more clearly and realize that our task 'means trying to name, even if one cannot really hope to make it felt, this collective experience of powerlessness which is at the basis of a whole view of the world and the future' (Bourdieu 1990a: 97).

7

The culture of necessity and working class speech

> Their conversation is like a gently wicked dance: sound meets sound, curt-
> sies, shimmies, and retires. Another sound enters but is upstaged by still
> another: the two circle each other and stop . . . The edge, the curl, the
> thrust of their emotions is always clear to Frieda and me. We do not,
> cannot, know the meanings of all their words, for we are nine and ten
> years old. So we watch their faces, their hands, their feet, and listen for
> truth in timbre.   (Morrison 1990: 10)

In attempting to understand working class experience, Bourdieu warns that
we must be careful not to 'leave out the relation to class condition which is
part of a complete definition of that condition' (Bourdieu 1984: 372). And
Bourdieu goes on to say that intellectuals usually apprehend 'the working
class condition through schemes of perception and appreciation which are
not those that the members of the working class themselves use to apprehend it'[1] (Bourdieu 1984: 373). Rather, we need to understand the habitus
which is 'normally (i.e., with a high statistical probability) associated with
that position' (Bourdieu 1984: 372). We have already established how this
is to be rendered and considered the resources that allow us to understand
their relation to their condition. Here, the insights of Merleau-Ponty concerning the nature of pre-reflective, antepredicative experience are helpful.
What is needed, is a description that captures the sense of practices that are
often construed negatively from the standpoint of the dominant position.
We have to remember that, for a large number of working class men in this
country, their relation to the written word has been reduced to writing their
name on cards their girlfriends and wives buy for relatives. As Bourdieu
captures their position:

At best, they are at the mercy of their own spokesmen, whose role is to provide them
with the means of repossessing their own experience . . . The dominant language

discredits and destroys the spontaneous political discourse of the dominated. It leaves them only silence or a borrowed language, whose logic departs from that of popular usage but without becoming that of erudite usage, a deranged language.

(Bourdieu 1984: 462)

It important to look at their own articulations and at what processes influence the style of their articulation in order to be aware of what their manner displays about their social condition. This allows us to recognize in a different and critically important medium, the extent to which, in their sensibility, they feel a sense of their class position which they perceive as written in nature because they are 'not clever' and thus condemned to work 'wi' mi' 'ands'.

Moreover, the way in which their position mediates their being-in-the-world, means that their comportment is constrained by the possibilities constituted by the forms of engaged coping that their world requires them to be practically involved in, in order to exist in this space with any respect. Their social conditions encourage forms of comportment that emanate from a realized dealing-with which ensures that the derivative mode of revealing of conscious perception occurs in terms of the absorbed non-self-referential openness (Dreyfus 1994: 58) that is characteristic of human comportment in most of what it does. It is openness to a particular world, disclosed through a practical, engaged form of life, upon which the derivative experience of looking depends. It is this directedness towards the world involved in comportment, the implicit intentionality and understanding embedded in our form of life, the way that everyday activity discloses the world, that one must be particularly mindful of when dealing with the experience of working people. The boundedness of one's world, its specificity and parochialness are less obvious to those who spend life among their own. It is a point Bourdieu makes:

The extreme narrowness and homogeneity of the space of life, which means that one's adult life is spent in the same environment as one's childhood, excludes alienation, that attenuated disorientation that leads to the act of looking. The tourist or outsider can cause astonishment by photographing everyday objects or local people at their habitual occupations . . . The familiar environment is that which one has always seen but never looked at because it is 'taken for granted'.

(Bourdieu 1990b: 34)

This work tries to manifest this phenomenon through illuminating perception as an aspect of our everyday being-in-the-world.

Perception is mediated by the sense that coheres throughout the horizon constituted by the background of involvement-relations realized in the uncapturable ground of comportment skills that disclose this world and make possible our engaged regulated realization of possibilities given in the realm of the possibilities available to us as the beings we are. As Sartre put it, since 'meaning came into the world only by the activity of man, practice superseded contemplation' (Sartre quoted in Cooper 1990: 49). As a mode of perception, the gaze involves the relation of a group of people to the world, and this, I am suggesting, is affected by the totality of processes that establish the conditions of their comportment and way of being-in-the-world. This is heavily circumscribed by the forms of capital that one has access to such that being is highly mediated by the distance individuals can create (or cannot create) from aspects of their environment which impact upon them. Vulnerability and powerlessness affect relation to environment in innumerable different ways. Experience emerges from the concrete ways of living the body we inherit in the comportment of the immediate culture whose sense we carry deposited in the corporealized subjectivity, others see realized in the glances of nuances and stance which are all positioned (and thus position individuals) within the hierarchies of the society in which we live. The forms of comportment and the most obvious stylistic aspects of this as we perceive them in deportment and gesticulation and manner are circumscribed for working people by their social position and experience which, I will argue, lead them to have a primary sense of the world actualized in their comporting-responses to the world of others which their comportment is itself a response to.

We must begin to appreciate the social consequences of philosophical insights concerning the primacy of a form of comportment that underlies perception, thematic awareness and intentional action. That is, that these modalities are subtended by a way of being in which they are disclosed through the horizon of our form of life such that being is antecedently understood in our pre-ontological, pre-epistemic dwelling with others and our world. If we accept this as the deepest embedding of human beings in the world, the deepest, most general aspect-grounding experience of being, then we need to ask whether this has sociological consequences for the study of dominated and impoverished communities. Such ideas, with their corporealization of the sense of human existence move away from the primacy of the linguistic-constituting subject narrating transparent social experiences, offer forms of insight into the modes of subjection and entrapment of the most dominated members of human societies. These ideas are important in allowing us to understand the profundity of processes that affect a form of life as that historical form instantiated in comportment is left to wither. These ideas offer us a way to understand what is socially and personally at stake when the cultures of the dominated are sacrificed because economic policy demands there is no alternative. Moreover, it

offers us a way to recognize other fundamental aspects involved in the relation of the urban poor to the world. It allows us to glimpse the consequences of living in a realm the background structures of which are
alienated, antipathetic to human self-realization and unable to support
viable, human, forms of association such that the field of available, realizable, possibilities reproduces alienated, socially dis-embedded forms.
Forms based in patterns of responses that disclose the human realm in a
manner befitting the object domain, rather than the concernful solicitude
appropriate to dealing with sentient beings. What happens to those who
have a sense of human decency, who feel the need for mutual respect, when
the inherited world is negating? And what follows when one's pre-objective
sense of place and world, of the familiar, prior to intentional positing or
judgement, has become eroded such that one is unable to feel that one can
rely on its day-to-day continuity, nor be guaranteed the pervasiveness of the
infinitesimal details taken for granted in the background structure of the
form of life that is the very condition of one's everyday life? In conditions
of progressive decline, the sense of personal life becomes racked by a fear
immanent to the conditions of being. An anxiety manifest on one twenty-
five-year-old's comments:

X: C's, that chippy at bottom a ahr [our] road, 'is tranna [trying to] develop custom
an' mek [make] it a place to 'ang aht [out] but it's attractin all these headcases an'
the'r the'er [they are there] till three, thi' park the'r cars on ahr [our] street, it's bad
enough wi' taxi rank cars parked up. But yer look at it nahr [now], it's just gettin'
worse an' worse rahnd [round] 'ere. Rother'am's just dog rough nah [now], it's
fuckin' *dog rough* man. All ye' get all time is people eyein' yer all time an' a lot on
'em an't 'ard at all, 'cos [because] 'ard dun't 'ave to bother. Thi's no wonder that
people wi' any intelligence, wi any appreciation ahr [are] just gettin' aht. 'Cos who
wants to live wi' every time yer gu aht'a a do'or [out of the door] some fuckers
lookin' at yer. Thi's [there is] thi's bloke on ahr street nahr, parks his Sierra the'er
an' hi eyes mi aht all time. One'r these days his gunna catch mi in a bad mood an'
A'm gunna gu up an' ask 'im what his problem is. Trouble is, thi's mo'ore an'
mo'or guns nahr. Tha needs t' watch who tha [you're] fallin' aht wi'. Look at X,
he's got a gun, his muther keeps a shotgun fo' 'im, his brothers 'ave both got guns.
An' like, Y, his brother's dealin' nahr (S: 'Is hi?') His bin [been] rahnd today an
beat one'r 'is smack heads up. Took knuckle dusters, 'cos he wo a big lad, hit 'im
an' split all his head open an' said, 'Ah'll bi back fo' mi money on Thursday: 'ave
it' an' all these young lads 'angin' abaht on streets actin' 'ard, that's all thi'v got
to do, thi's nowt else fo' em to think good abaht 'emselves so all thi du is attack
us, it's us innocent people wi' families that's sufferin' all time. A'm, tellin, yer man,
get aht. Ah mean, tha's 'ad to w'k an' tha's 'ad it 'ard an' bin through a lot'r shit
but if it gets thi aht'a this shit 'ole it'll a bin w'th [worth] it. Ah mean, 'as tha'
[have you] seen them dahn river, all them fuckin' drop aht's fishin'? (S: 'Ye, I 'ave.')
Thi's sumat wrong wi' 'em, the'r not rait in 'ead. Thi's just mo'ore an' mo'ore

fuckin' weirdo's abaht. Tha's got to keep thiseln fit an' strong, an' tha's fuckin' got to bi able to fight because mo'ore an' mo'ore nahr it's comin' dahn to that 'cos it's ohnny thing these wankers respect. Ah mean if thi' know yer 'andy an' thi know ye'v got 'ard friends, like X, he's popular just cos ih's s' fuckin' 'ard, his respected an' it's all the'r is fo' us nahr. Thi walk past yer an' thi' stair at yer an' f'st to look away is the weaker one an' once thi' see yer as weak, then yer a target to 'em. Unless thi' know ye'v got 'eavy friends. Yer know, ahr know people, like W's brothers, they do hits on people, really serious violence that the'r paid fo. V's bin dahn yer know, his ohnny just settled dahn, well thi's last four years an' got that business sorted out. (S: 'What did hi gu dahn fo?') Gang violence, judge just said, 'ye, send 'em dahn'. (S: 'What did thi' du?') Attacked this bloke, thi ad baraclav-ers on an' lot, baseball bats. But hi's quietened dahn a lot after his spell in prison. It's fuckin' rough. Ah'r remember 'anging abaht on Wellgate as a kid an' nahr look at it! It's fuckin' orrible. All them women sittin' drinkin' waitin' fo' one'r them boy-racers t' come rahnd fo' a quick fuck. An' the so fuckin' rough, yer listen to 'em, thi'd rather suck yer dick than talk to yer. It's fuckin' depressin'. . .

In a world in which the last ten years have brought noticeable change, in which even the relatively young have an experience of decay, people can see the emerging tendencies and they fear the future they see emerging in the present. The decay of the dimension of personal respect and civility, par-ticularly in public space, is well expressed by one woman:

X: It is just getting worse all time rahnd [round] 'ere. Ah can't stand it. Last night next-door neighbours were F'in' and Blindin' it at each other an' the'r kids wo' cryin'. An' mi an' Y [*Husband*] could 'ear 'em. An' it med me feel invaded. Ah did, Ah felt violated.[2]
S: Ye, it's like that in town, yer walk abaht an' yer can't ignore ahr bad it is.
X: I 'ate it wi' E [*daughter*] cos ye'll bi walkin' along an' yer can' 'ear lads an' lasses talkin', swearin' abaht sex, 'cos yer know wot the'r like nahr, [S: Ye.] an' Ah' [I] 'owd [hold]'er close t' mi an' se', 'Come on love', 'cos Ah don't want it touchin' 'er. If Ah could Si, Ah'd send mi kids to a public school t' protect em from all this. Owt t' get 'em aht. Ah mean it's t' late fo' us in it?

What both these quotations show is that human beings' most general ways of being-in-the-world, through being circumspectively absorbed in the world, are in these conditions actively frustrated and they are being forced to take up stances of consideration of who and under what circumstances they can be solicitously absorbed in the being of others. The pressing into the present involved in comportment, is frustrated by the decay of their form of life as it is embodied in the pervasive responses of those they gen-erally encounter such that the ethos they engage others through is becom-ing situational and forced ever more into the domain of consciousness. The world that they encounter requires 'a more precise kind of circumspection, such as "inspecting", checking up' (Heidegger 1962: 409). The frustration of the world these people's comportment 'expects'; changes to the referential whole, the *Gestalt* of expectation that would remain invisible unless unfulfilled; have begun to impinge and they are forced to take up the stance implied in depiction, a representation the motive of which is the frustration of their everyday sense of dignity. The world, as background, is obtruding and the world of a deliberating subject emerges from the background of absorption in the world because the world of everyday absorption deposited in their comportment no longer awaits the fruition of its competence. The longer first quotation, particularly, displays what Heidegger describes as:

Being-in-the-world, as concern, is *fascinated by* the world with which it is concerned . . . When concern holds back from any kind of producing, manipulating, and the like, it puts itself into what is now the sole remaining mode of Being-in, the mode of just tarrying alongside . . . This kind of Being towards the world is one which lets us encounter entities within-the-world purely in the *way they look*.

(Heidegger 1962: 88)

These quotations display the extent to which this world is encountered through the primordial realm of disconcerted affective concern and a kind of alienated living-amongst which is not that of solicitation. Rather, these people are disturbed by the inhumanity of the world around them. Projecting into the present, forms of comportment oriented by the traditional ethos, these people are concerned by the threat of personal violation. These people are describing a condition and their relation to it, in which concerned absorption has become problematic, in which they have to consciously ignore aspects that break-up their circumspective comportment. These people's talk is emerging from a frustrated need to deal with a daily ignoring of aspects of a world that break-up the practical relation of circumspective coping with the background of their lives. We might see this obtrusive disturbance of the practical attitude as a kind of involved deliberate attention, one emerging from anxiety initiated by the decay of the form of life in which these people grew up, a decay they see manifest in comportment and expression, both of which display a different way of being, one based upon a different interpretation of the value of existence. Differences manifest in everyday skills, discriminations and practices that indicate that the people they describe dwell in different background practices. In the world in which they live, the comportment they share and the form of solicitation they embody, have become conditional; and so, often, they find their own decency refused, unrecognized, rebutted. Through this, and through their on-the-spot recounting of their sense of anxiety, their world is revealed. These people's interpretation of life in terms of the matterings with which their life is practically concerned has been undermined, and what they describe with a frustration that would be bitterness if they felt there was a realm of value upon which to ground indignation, is the breakdown of the moral way of life that they would never have been aware of articulating through a discourse based in a practical ethics, unless their lives had not, of necessity, become separated from the everyday way of life they now see as so problematic. The concern about life-plans, exemplified by the point about people of appreciation leaving and the wish to educate children privately, reveals individuals who are made to confront daily questions of the deepest significance and to confront the economic basis of human dignity and appreciation. That these issues have arisen so starkly reveals how completely the form of life as the form of life of damaged people carried some humanity and respect which has decayed with the fracturing of the life of the town into forms that are based in disconnection and aggression, into forms of abjection through which people are encountered as present-to-hand. Both quotations make explicit the extent to which we are creatures for whom the kind of life we are able to live is an issue, that our being is one of *care*. Given that we inhabit the world as being-there, through forms of comportment that disclose a clearing of what matters to us, a realm of involved dealings-with, then if aspects of the public world of everyday comportment change, the referential-whole will be affected and aspects would begin to obtrude. Moreover, if comportment is critical to this process of disclosure, then we might expect the kind of social decay described to be accompanied by a somatic experience of personal disjunction, a general sense of malaise as the body experiences an absence of the grounds of value. What is being taken away here is the very possibility of on-going, practical belief in the network of relations through which one took up, through the silent communication of bodies in comportment, the ability-to-be that disclosed the world as inherently meaningful. Life for the economically marginal and unemployed is a condition in which absorption in a public domain all but ceases and possibilities recede. This condition reveals the extent to which being-in-the-world is a unitary structure, that our form of life is dependent upon a system of public significances amidst which we appropriate, unconsciously, our being, yet, as a condition, the life of the economically marginal, infrequently employed, and long-term unemployed, involves exclusion from that realm of realized, embodied significances, drawing the affective-somatic realm of personal being into crisis.

Taking phenomenological insights seriously, we can begin to see why aspects of the most profound significance can be less than transparent and yet manifest in humans dealings in everyday life. We can see why, in a context of such alienation, amidst the aimless aggression of such public spaces, as well as the decline of the forms of comportment traditional to working people, one would expect the body to be affected by the background with which it has to engage and cope. It seems to me that this is why there is so much illness in these areas and so much talk of mental illness and recounting of what is clearly pathological behaviour. The phenomenal body roots us in this disturbed world which affects the field of the personal we struggle to achieve around us. This world which envelops us, touches us through our perception, whose meaning we *feel*, even when we try to ignore its ugliness, infects the phenomenal body, making sense, that aspect of being rendered magical in the musings of great poets or musicians, becomes a pollutant marking the poor in the simple act of knowing what from childhood innocence they cannot ignore. The phenomenal body, the *locus* of the field of being-in-the-world, is subject to an unfolding of meaning grounded in perception that can, at times, consume the primordial domain of affectivity to the extent of explosion and illness. To be vulnerable, is to be powerless to rescue oneself from the immediacy of a meaning based in one's inability to distance oneself from this relation to the world; it is to be to the social world what the foot soldier is to battle and to be unavoidably affected by the trauma of a world that is unremitting in the negativity of its solicitations; it is to be infected with this knowledge of the world and thus to endure the marks of that knowledge. The corrosive personal affects of this vulnerability and the traces of its affective resonances are manifest in the words of one man:

I've bi'n [been] really down lately, feeling ill and depressed, just wi' job situation as it is an' I've bi'n to doctors and thi'v gi'd mi' some anti-depressants and ahr [our] lass's not well and she's bi'n tekkin' [taking] it aht [out] on me and wi'v just 'ad a big bust up. Shi's stormed aht'a 'ouse an' gone to 'er mates . . . I think I've found another job, like, but it's not what'a want, it's low paid and shitty. [S: Is it?] Oh aye. It's a filthy fuckin' job, Ah'll be comin' home filthy an' thi'r in't a canteen or 'owt.

With the experiences recounted in personal testimony in this chapter in mind, with their acute sense of the abjection of the world around them, it is worth considering Dewey's observation:

The world we have experienced becomes an integral part of the self that acts and is acted upon in further experience. In their physical occurrence, things and events experienced pass and are gone. But something of their meaning and value is retained as an integral part of the self. Through habits formed in intercourse with the world, we also in-habit the world. It becomes a home and the home is part of our everyday experience.   (Dewey 1934: 104)

What it is to have a world as a 'home', that leaves as its traces a meaning that disturbs and violates the moral self; in which self-respect, instead of being founded in a realm of spontaneously realized human value, is something one must struggle to achieve; is manifest in the quotations we have looked at so far in this chapter. We can see that the medium of this familiarity is the lived body which experiences an intensity of experience, a being-there, trapped in time, in *this* history, sensuously enmired in a pre-given world such that each moment 'is driven into time like a wedge and stakes its claim to eternity' (Merleau-Ponty 1962: 393). Just as their social position regionalizes their being-in-the-world, affecting their sense of space, it also affects their sense of the span of their lives, their experience of periodicity. Just as they feel trapped by the progressive encroachment of the worsening cultural conditions, many feel trapped in an eternal present of the current rhythms of their existence. Their experience of the drabness of the same is one thing, but interwoven throughout it is the hauntingly unevocative yet powerful experience of debilitation that time itself adds through a stagnant duration in which the body experiences the reproduced eternal moment of its own ineffectiveness, its own impotence. In lives bereft of public contact and the unconscious gestural markers of appreciation; life becomes pervaded by a certain dread and the immanent sense that one is unable to help oneself, that destiny depends upon others, and these fuse in the body's sense of a world at an end. The futility comes through in the understated expression of one man:

S: Ah you still on't busses?
X: Naow . . . I've bi'n finished eighteen months.
S: What've yer bi'n do'in?
X: Nowt. I've bi'n on't dole all't time, I'll likely nivver [never] work age'an.
S: Ahr do yer find bein' unemployed?
X: Terrible! It's fuckin' shit.
S: Ahr do yer mean?
X: I nivver feel rait. I feel rait depressed all time and ill, like. I think it's shit. It gets me dahn [down] rait bad, I'm just rahn' [round] 'ouse all't time, 'cept [except] fo' if I cum dahn 'ere. [*Pauses*] Still, tha can't grumble can yer? Life gu's on and all that, eh? Tha just 'as to mek best yer can and 'ope fo' best.

This man makes clear that the future towards which he is oriented is one of the foreclosure of possibility, that the future immanent in his condition is one in which he will be in the grip of this present. His experience of time is tied up with his experience of his social condition, with his powerlessness to render both meaningful. This incapacity of the normally human result of embeddedness in a social realm – that we experience our existence as meaningful, even through the management of damaged identities – leaves the unemployed subject to a general, continuous and repetitive world whose totality is a general malaise of unrooted nausea, expressed in 'I nivver feel rait', the common acknowledgement that their sense of well-being is eroded. As another man expressed his feelings:

S: Ahr [how] long tha [have you] bi'n unemployed?
X: Too long. I'm pissed off. At f'st tha [you] thinks it'll be a good crack but after a
month tha's 'ad enough. I find I can't get up. I mean, thi's nowt to get up fo' in't
day, nowt that can't be done in't afternoon, so tha stays in bed so as day's shorter.
The little things get tu yer an all. Tha' knows, tha' teks it aht on your lass or't kids.
S: Ahr dus it mek yer feel?
X: I dun't know, it scares me I think. I dun't know. I dun't mean like rait frightened
but I just seem to be scared nahr [now] at times. Like signing on an that, tha scared
all time. I wish thi wo somat I could du.
S: Wo' abaht yer kids?
X: I just 'ope it's better fo' em. But it's fuckin scary. I mean, it's bi'n shit fo'a long
time nahr an' it?

Such expression, like much of the transcription in this book, marks this
'class sense, hidden away deep in the body' (Bourdieu 1993a: 166), yet,
because of the very conditions of this experience, these people are dispossessed of hope. They retreat to the domestic realm, 'the site of last resis-
tances' (Bourdieu 1979) to search there for a sense of worth that can only
be grounded in a public realm and, finding only the ghostliness of their own
impoverished self-respect, they 'tek it aht on your lass or't kids'. From such
a sense of powerlessness and vulnerability the political realm seems ever
more remote, which leaves the root causes of this malaise to a realm of
political specialists. The problem is that the dominated cannot recognize
their plight in the discourses supplied by politicians and specialists, and this
seems to disqualify what they know from their ordinary experience because
it seems to belong to the domain of ordinary life and not to the domain of
'politics', as it is constituted. Lacking the competence to constitute their
experience through the instruments of expression of the political realm,
they ignore that realm. Political representation depends upon a transition
from the deep-seated, corporeal sense of the world revealed in the transcribed speech, to the self-conscious representation of their interests. It is a
difference that Bourdieu draws attention to:

There's a whole analysis to be done of the ways in which a group is able to constitute itself as a group, to constitute its identity, symbolize itself, to move from a population of workers to a labour movement or a working class. This transition, which
presupposes *representation* in the sense of delegation, but also in the theatrical sense
of *mise-en-scène*, is a very complicated alchemy in which the specific effect of the
'discursive supply', the range of already existing discourses and available models of
action (demos, strikes, etc.), plays an important part.   (Bourdieu 1993a: 166)

As things stand, the people interviewed are reduced to a practical state of
making political choices from amidst schemata of perception – a realized
political taste – that they have inherited as part of their cultural traditions,

between two options that offer them little. A move towards political organization would require a changed relationship to the world, one required in order to effect a change in their consciousness. As we have seen, too many processes constrain the horizon of being to the circumscribed limits through which life takes place. This, we have seen, is part of the working class relation to the world. This problem of political representation is intimately connected to the political efficacy, the legitimacy, of the dominant language and to the institutions that inscribe in bodies the dispositions to speak and perform it and, conversely, the dispositions to feel its legitimacy and authority. Language-use, speech, emerges from a relation to the world and a social position and condition. The transcribed material that we have looked at so far in this chapter has provided useful indications of the extent to which working class speech issues from its context of production, yet it is important to go on and look at the experiences that define that context to individuals and lead to their embodiment of the sense they go on to instantiate in their comportment and articulation.

The problem, it seems to me, is deeply embedded in the relation of working people to language. This itself is part of their relation to the world as it is mediated by their specific immersion in a pre-objective realm that their language-use must forever negotiate and express. Bourdieu expresses this relation:

I think that one cannot fully understand language without placing linguistic practices within the full universe of compossible practices: eating and drinking habits, cultural consumptions, taste in matters of arts, sports, dress, furniture, politics, etc. For it is the whole class habitus, that is, the synchronic and diachronic position occupied in the social structure, that expresses itself through the linguistic habitus which is but one of its dimensions. *Language is a technique of the body*, and linguistic and especially phonological) competency is a dimension of bodily *hexis* in which the whole relation to the social world expresses itself. Everything suggests, for instance, that the bodily schema characteristic of a social class determines the system of phonological traits that characterize a class pronunciation, via what Pierre Guiraud calls the 'articulatory style'. This articulatory style is part and parcel of a lifestyle that has become embodied, *fait corps*, and stands in linked relation with the usages of the body and of time that properly defines this lifestyle. (It is no happenstance if bourgeois distinction invests its relation to language with the same distancing intention it engages in its relation to the body.)

(Bourdieu and Wacquant 1992: 149)

Conversation takes place incidentally, it is part of the performance of producing other actions, part of the field of the night out and the market in partners; part of the field of work, part of the field of the gym: but it is not the object of action in a pure, disinterested way. Language is seldom used contemplatively as an end in itself; there is no neutralizing distance adopted to language nor the things it is used to designate. Language issues from and is tied to the world as it is revealed through the lens of a way of life. It is thus infused with the sense mediated by comportment and the endless interplay between comportment, or habitus, and the social and economic structures which impinge upon immediate life. The bourgeois relation to language is intertwined with an ingestion of the world through security and economic power, of the gradual sense the body has of its position; a habituated *sense* of the world guided by the freedom that spending power buys and the unconscious security of those whose status cannot be questioned: the conditions of possibility of the schemes of perception of a world that doesn't 'bite' in perception, in which friends and lovers are free of the degrading effects of the severely circumscribed limits of life that condition the deprived. The speech of working people is embedded in the urgencies of a world whose solicitations demand a constant readiness which impinges upon consciousness and the way the world is constituted, felt, lived. Just as they are immersed in a reality that is constantly resistant to forms of non-alienated being, so their speech carries the marks of a world in which, to use an appropriate cliché, life is cheap. It is as though, at all times, domination forecloses the possibility of adopting a neutralizing distance even in self-presentation. In a world that does not operate in terms of etiquette or formality, individuals negotiate their social identity quite directly – that is, with minimal concessions to styles intended to impress. It is a world in which one is likely to be reduced to one's 'objective social essence', either by state agencies like the Department of Social Security or by others. In a world so dominated by processes that threaten and cajole a person into perceiving themselves through the conditions in which they live, money becomes a continuous undercurrent of the surface of social life. What one is or does, as an indicator of income, has taken a fetishized bent in these conditions, a condition perhaps exemplified by the figure of the drug dealers who have increasingly become almost mythical heroic figures: 'Drug dealers are like excitin' people. Yer know, fo' women, thi' live in the shadey-margins, thi' 'ave money, nice car, free drugs . . .'

The markets of working class speech value a bodily hexis and articulatory style based upon a refusal of euphemization, a demand that persons be open, not-guarded, and exhibit an involvement in the speech that mirrors involvement in the urgencies and exigencies of a common world that refuses formalities and is uncomfortable with second-names and 'small talk'. A practical injunction for honesty and expressivity, that propels participants to outspokenness that might shock were it not part of the logic of the spaces working class people claim as their own. Hence 'How's work?'

might be met with a matter-of-fact, 'Fucking 'orrible; Ah 'ate it.' Expressions like 'Nah then Shag'; 'Nah then shit-head'; 'Ahr [Our] shit-fo'-brains'; 'Nah then ugly'; 'Nah then yer slapper'; 'Nah then yer tart'; 'Nah then yer slag' and 'Nah then, cunt' are welcomes shared publicly between the very closest friends to denote the kinds of friendship the mutuality and proximity of which allows the ritualized public declaration of derogatory terms that are the class's slang acknowledgement of its objective position and lack of value. This kind of what was once called, 'pit talk', in its revelling in the deep slurring of words and reliance upon a certain coarseness of the voice, is like a mimetics that at the level of expressivity reproduces the depth and physicality of the experience that it issues from. Such expression conveys an intimacy with conditions of acquisition that make such speech such an effective, and also un-maskable, signifier of class origins. Yet, it is an articulatory style that is linked to the experience of class and degradation. It is the speech of people who are excluded from the spaces whereby they might acquire instruments of euphemization and who occupy positions in which their speech is not valued, so that what they say has no consequences which means they have no sense of what they say as mattering or as having consequence, such that they feel they can say what they want and, certainly, the contexts in which they speak freely are ones in which they can say, virtually, whatever they like without social effect or cost.

Working class men's speech is marked by a suspension of modes of euphemization, a kind of linguistic anarchism that makes them able to say almost anything.[3] Moreover, speech circles around the practical touchstones of working class life: work and shifts; so many of the exchanges that go on between working men begin with 'What shift thy on?', or else 'I'm fucked this week, it's Zombie shift'; or in the absence of work, disgust at unemployment and bad treatment by the Department of Social Security; or else sport, the weekend's nights out, and the opposite sex.[4]

The extent to which necessity remains the structuring condition of working class life is surely manifest in this vernacular landscape where people find solace in an immediacy of relation to one another and find in that immediacy a proximity of relation that life in difficult spaces demands. This is part of an ethos that demands a freedom of expression that might be experienced as 'honesty' but which is better characterized as forthrightness, a willingness to volunteer more than is required, to indulge in a surplus of meaning that is often seen as weakness and simplicity by the petit-bourgeois. However, this is clearly a disposition that is taught. As one man put it: 'Mi grandmother allous told me "Be honest even if it offends people. Even if thi dun't like it, tell truth." That's 'ow I wo' brought up.' It is a point expressed with even more poignancy by another, 'Ah'll tell yer sumaht [something] nahr [now], mi fAther allous [always] teld [told] mi, never try an' impress anyone an' never lie.' That this is a powerful aspect of the habitus of these people, of the dispositions and expressive style demanded, is made clear in the following conversation:

J: Ye see rest on us 'd se' sumaht [would say something] if hi wo' tranna bi clever an' usin' wrong word, one'r us 'd *se'* 'Shur'up yer daft fuck'. Ye' see that's your trouble. Like wi'y all get on, an' wi like t' bi corrected like that, but you wun't du that would yer?

S: Naow, I wun't. It's not right fo' mi t' du that anyway, cos Ah've got benefit o'r a privileged education an' you lot an't.

J: Yer too fuckin' nice a bloke. Ah mean tha must bi one'r most decent men Ah've ever met but if Ah se' sumaht wrong Ah'd want yer t' se', 'naow yer silly cunt, tha's got that wrong, tha means this', yer see. It's better if tha just honest.

This forthrightness, which is seen as a mark of respect to the other person, is a form that is demonstrated in postures and gestures that contravene the petit-bourgeois order perceived as 'poshness', and any form of 'aloofness' which working class men and women tellingly equate with teachers, librarians, council workers, Social Security officials and politicians. As another man warned, 'Never trust men in suits, men wi' silly smiles, like fucking Tony Blair and never trust anyone wi' blue eyes. I've never met anyone wi' blue eyes who wo' honest.' The cautionary note concerning being 'too nice', in the earlier piece of testimony is usual and revealing. What precisely is it that it is possible to be 'too nice' for? What is it that causes them concern in someone manifesting such dispositions? Clearly, it is their practical knowledge of this economic and social realm in which they can see that decency threatens to lead to abuse. As one man put it:

X: Tha's got t' know who yer can bi rait wi' [right with]. Ah' [I] mean, Ah'm like this wi' you an', one or two others, but no mo'ore than an 'andful an' when Ah'm in street, or gym, or at w'k, Ah'm different. Tha's got t' let people know thi' can't tek [take] advantage o'r yer, else thi'll walk all ovva [over] yer. Ye'v got t' save ahr yer ahr fo' them people yer can trust but fo' others, just se' 'Fuck you'. Thi'll respect yer an' thi'll watch yer space. That's thi only way rahnd 'ere [around here]. It in't a nice place. Tha ca(n)'t be all respectin people an' shit.

And as another man expressed it:

X: What tha's [you've] got t' du [do] is react wi' aggression t' these people. Like wi' that, if someb'dy asks yer 'what's that?' tha just ses 'What the fuck 'as it got t' du wi' you?' an' tell 'em t' 'Fuck off'. Tha's got t' let people know that thi' can't mess wi' yer. Thi's no niceness in society nahr, tha' ca(n)'t bi decent, Ah get it all time in taxis, people are tryin' it on all't time, *all the fuckin time*, an' Ah just 'ave to bi' [be] 'ard wi'y 'em. Tha'as [you have] to show no weakness t' 'em [to them] or else the'll tek advantage o' yer. If Ah wo' like you an' respectful t' people an' a nice bloke, like, Ah'd get n' fuckin' fares paid. Tha' gunna 'ave t' develop an' 'arder way wi' people, Sime.

As another man counselled, 'Tha too nice, Sime, tha wants to try insertin' the words "*Fuck off*" int' thi' vocabulary.' It is as though this world solicits hardness as a way of avoiding having to deal with threat and actual violence; as though a certain comportment and expressivity is called for in order to avoid ingress into one's personal existence. It is as though life in such areas is too condensed, too compacted, too overwhelming, such that personal space must be projected by the body in a way that nullifies the possibility of potential conflict: 'dun't gi' none o'r that [*taps side of forehead at eye level with right forefinger*]; no eye, if tha passes a group'a lads, dun't look dahn, keep thi' 'ead straight ahead, and walk past standin' thi' grahnd, dun't shuffle or twitch, bi calm an' tha'll bi rait' as one man advised. Self-respect imposes this form of comportment as a condition of respect, even though as a mode of comportment it proclaims the decay of that realm of civic honour. These forms are linked to economic dislocation; as another man put it: 'Thi wo' none'r this, "Ah' walk 'ere an' Ah'm not gunna move aht'a nob'dy's way an' if tha moves tha weak" shit till jobs in industry started t' gu.' These modes of comportment through their attempt to assert a respect that can only be grounded in life among others, display the extent to which, for many, life is dis-embedded and lacking any viable integrative force that would lift the burden of an individuated path to self-worth from their shoulders. As a stance towards life, an attitude towards others and oneself, these 'guides to being' instate a relation to the future immanent in the conditions of those who have little to expect from their present which is a way of feeling the annihilation involved in a future that is pointless in terms of any possibility of establishing a network of relationships through which one might found a sense of human, and self, value. As Bourdieu puts it:

[this] is undoubtedly just one of the ways of making a virtue of necessity. The manifestation of an unreasoning commitment to realism and cynicism, the rejection of the feeling and sensitivity identified with feminine sentimentality and effeminacy, the obligation to be tough with oneself and others . . . are a way of resigning oneself to a world with no way out, dominated by poverty and the law of the jungle, discrimination and violence, where morality and sensitivity bring no benefit whatsoever.   (Bourdieu 1991: 96)

This is like a morality in that it is based in modes of comportment, and its concern is respect; but it *sounds* like an active disrespect for others. To recognize something deeper in this, one needs to appreciate the alienation involved in the background that makes this world what it is for these people; the totality of negative injunctions that have gone, daily, into making these people perceive the world through the modality of absorbed coping that they have had to adopt in order to deal with it. One also needs to appreciate the extent to which having to engage the world through these forms of comportment is something that must be permanently sustained, and that this can only be done through extreme tension. However, as the testimony shows, it is a way of being that working class people have no choice but to take up, in order to cope, through absorption, with the world that they find and which creates them.

This lack of distance from social conditions, the naturalization of the world into which they were born, is never more obvious than in the vernacular landscape present in their speech and their articulatory style. Their speech reflects the background that has come to inhabit them. As the world has levelled them, so too the world is levelled by them. There is little space for the luxury of euphemization in a world that impacts upon them so directly and which in its sanctions is so negative; so dominated by ugliness and which so often denies the possibility of human recognition, without it being stood for, maintained in an active labour of self-presentation. Living in these spaces, it is impossible to neutralize the world through the adoption of a distance to oneself, the world and others. These people are in the midst of a world that is too often brutal in its detail, too often degrading, too often reduced to the basics of human life. Even where this world foregoes upon an immediate assault upon oneself, one witnesses the degradation of others, a degradation in which one is implicated. Working class people's speech issues from a world that is brutal; it is part of a dealing with this world which so often defiles us, and hence it tends to be unselfconsciously brutal. I say 'unselfconsciously' because the speakers are simply rendering a world that is the background without which there would be no world for them. That it is, effectively, an alien world in which one seldom ascends to humanity and its associations, is something which occasionally comes to the surface in working class people's speech. It is the impact of this alienated world with which the speech of articulate working class people is often suffused, which leads the petit-bourgeois, whose existence is based upon a self-distancing from this kind of expressivity and from all 'extreme' avowals, to see in the brutality present in working class speech and, particularly, though not exclusively, working class *male* speech, a personal disposition towards inhumanity rather than the rendering of a world that is itself callous. For the middle classes, who have (never quite) grown to maturity in the protected enclaves of the university, free to assert themselves with regard to many kinds of principle and with an integrity bought at the price of the exclusion of many within that space, this is what they find so abject and objectionable in working class speech about the opposite sex and sex itself; though their class racism focuses upon working class male speech under the guise of political correctness and radical chic. Yet working class people's speech about sex, alienated as it is, emerges from the brutality of the markets which working class people enter in order to negotiate their sexual lives.

These kinds of differences, the system of patterns and phenomena constituted by working class people's speech, issue from the way the comportment or bodily hexis of working class people is impacted upon by the constitutive power of this background frame of necessity and ill-will that roots them in a world of so little value and a struggle that has become so habitual; against necessity, worthlessness and condemnation, that they no longer have a sense of a goal. Moreover, what is manifest in a preference for hailing someone in the street in the manner described to me by one woman: 'I allous know it's X 'cos I'll be walkin' along and I'll hear some'dy shout: "Na' then yer fuckin' bastard!"' is based in a 'morality which converts transgression into duty' (Bourdieu 1991: 96) a refusal of the 'submissiveness and docility implied by the adoption of legitimate ways of speaking' (Bourdieu 1991: 95). It emerges from the deepest levels of acculturation and implicates a whole social universe. It emerges from the primary experiences of family and school and is part of the complete cosmology that is learnt through these spaces. It is part of a complete experience of the body that is rooted in these sites of primary acculturation and it is then progressively confirmed through the position individuals occupy and experience. As an articulatory style, this transgression and refusal to euphemize displays a kind of valiance, a sort of honour, a dignity in the face of the experience of position that working class life is. It is best revealed in working class humour which in its coarseness, its vulgarity and bitterness exhibits a shared understanding of position and its experience. As an oratorical style and mode of comportment, it is transgressive: it proclaims someone with a certain attitude to authority and a certain relation to the English social universe. As Bourdieu has suggested, the concessions of politeness always contain political concessions (Bourdieu 1990a: 69). Welcomes based upon swear-words are ways in which the stigmatized proclaim their difference and experience a spontaneous affinity inscribed in their affective being by their objective predicament. When one woman shouts to another 'Nah then yer fucking bastard!' or 'Nah then slapper' she instantiates a practical morality, an ethos, that is radically different from that of one middle class woman who described Rotherham men as 'vulgar, crude and they swear too much'. And, in using such an expression, the first woman locates herself within that universe that makes her appear, from above, as vulgar and crude.

Yet what do these differences amount to, and what do they tell us about the culture of England? At the base of these differences of response are different schemes of evaluation; a different set of tastes which are opposed. Different social groups instantiate a different priority of values which then act as embodied emblems through which they are recognized.

Obviously, the lives of different class groups are situated in different spaces and take place through different sites. In the sites that groups use, they assimilate the space through their own dispositional schemes and they thus establish conditions in which their own locutions will have value; that is, participants will collude to establish criteria of appreciation favourable to their own products. And, since the linguistic habitus is an aspect of the overall generative powers of the habitus, these linguistic markets will be distributed in social space in accord with the differential fields constituted by the different classes. However, the education system enshrines the culture of the dominant class as the national culture; it elevates one form of linguistic habitus to the status of legitimate, as the form of speech befitting those who are appropriate for senior and professional positions. Underlying different linguistic markets, there is thus a practical knowledge of a unified linguistic market: the models of pronunciation and bearing, of manner and etiquette of the English bourgeoisie. This means that between social fields there are objective relations that are irreducible to the interaction occurring within them. This helps us to understand the meaning of working class people's experience as that of a dominated group because the lives of working people take place through modes of comportment that are based on accommodation to symbolic hierarchies that mark them negatively. Such hierarchies have constituted the realm of their lives and are inscribed in the context of their experience, and are thus absorbed within comportment as part of the being-there of the way of life into which individuals are socialized. It is as though the hierarchies are present through the acts by which individuals try to absent themselves from their jurisdiction. The objectivity of these processes, the very generality of the hierarchies that are the very structuring possibility of the public and civic life of the English nation-state, ensure that the only strategy available is the one they adopt, which is to emblematize the characteristics that they know, practically mark them. This means that, in their own personal space, they must continually efface the legitimacy of the institutions and manners of the dominant culture and make of each field through which they move a field in which they can influence practically the criteria of value. What is characteristic of working class space, therefore, is a suspension of the laws of price formation that operate in the fields of the dominant; an effacement of the legitimate competence. Thus, the spaces of Rotherham, and especially the leisure spaces – places like the gym, the nightclubs and pubs – are protected markets in which the competence of the people who inhabit those social fields can exist positively, in which the social properties they possess can be said to be capital and not simply a series of deficits. So that within these spaces they can be attractive, charming, eloquent and funny. The site of these personal interactions is used to construct a series of spaces, markets, in which the laws of price formation which apply to more formal markets are suspended. As Bourdieu suggests:

In these private exchanges between homogeneous partners, the 'illegitimate' linguistic products are judged according to criteria which, since they are adjusted to their principles of production, free them from the necessarily comparative logic of distinction and of value. Despite this, the formal law, which is thus provisionally suspended rather than truly transgressed, remains valid, and it re-imposes itself on dominated individuals once they leave the unregulated areas where they can be outspoken (and where they can spend all their lives), as is shown by the fact that it governs the production of their spokespersons as soon as they are placed in a formal situation. It would be quite mistaken, therefore, to see a 'true' popular language in the use of language which obtains in this oasis of freedom, where one has licence (a typical 'dictionary word') because one is among friends and not forced to 'watch oneself'.   (Bourdieu 1991: 71)

Working people thus spend their lives having to pursue a strategy of seeking out spaces in which they can accede to existence in the face of a unified market in symbolic and cultural goods within which their bodily hexis and speech patterns are hopelessly stigmatized. And one sees these processes even within working class towns, where one has areas inhabited by middle class people whose children make certain spaces their own through the kind of subtle imperialism that consists in shifting the criteria of evaluation upward, which immediately alters the sense of social space in such a way that working class people become suddenly reduced to an absurd status, where, through the subtle insinuations of glances and the positioning involved in stance, they feel a need to exempt themselves from that context in search of spaces in which they might feel comfortable. That is, in spaces constituted by their own in which the laws of price formation befit their own capital. This is most evident in sexual relations which are the realm in which the mediation of relations in terms of the forms of capital inscribed in bodily hexis is most clearly exemplified. Because of the minimal amounts of capital that sections of the working class have, they have to pursue strategies that involve frequenting places that operate as protected enclaves which they can retreat to and avoid, with the help of drink and friends, the direct effects, upon the body, of valuelessness. Participating in a night out with working class men, one can see this practical negotiation of social position being mediated, through spaces and the categories of bodies that use them, and see the way in which people's dispositions disclose a world of determinate value in relation to which these men are situated. As space is disclosed through the positionings comportment spontaneously achieves, one can feel the emergence of a realm of sense which participants are aware of in various ways and in regard to which they achieve their own personal situatedness within that space. For working class men, this practical sense, makes them subtly aware of an absence of required capital. An absence that they feel in practical terms through the differential that they are situated in relation to others who are enjoying the fruits of a better position, namely the forms of simple recognition that pass between humans when equals. Hence it makes sense for them to turn to enclaves which operate as protected markets in whose terms they can feel free of the invisibility or stigmatization that haunts them when around people who instantiate the criteria of dominant markets. This is clear in relation to the spaces that Rotherham people frequent in order to meet each other for the purpose of forming sexual relationships. Rotherham is close to Sheffield, and Sheffield is the place where most middle class people go when they go out. Moreover, the market for partners in the centre of Rotherham is one that exhibits the characteristics of a protected enclave, which has its own laws of price formation,[5] and which thus protects local people from the devaluation that would occur if the 'products' which circulate in these markets were suddenly made to participate in markets governed by the general and dominant criteria of evaluation. Placed within other markets, with the dominant criteria of evaluation, viewed with eyes attuned to the dominant aesthetic, they would slide into obscurity and become objects of fun.[6] With this in mind we can see working class leisure practices as part of a realistic hedonism (Bourdieu 1984: 394) that issues from these cultural conditions, and yet which is also a break from the extreme tension involved in this life – a defence of the self from the injunctions and misery of this position. This seems to me to be what working class solidarity amounts to. It is a solidarity of commonality that they recognize one another through, and it is a strange phenomenon to capture because it is at once powerful and yet inexplicit, instantiating the living part of leisure as opposed to the world of work which demands a different attitude to existence. It is the generosity of poor people, anxious to give in order to accede to existence, to live for a moment away from the nagging calculations of every moment of conscious worry, anxious, for brief times, to be free of the continuous anxiousness involved in a present one hates but cannot change, aided by drink and companionship to 'have a good time', refusing the relation to self thrust upon one by economic conditions. To reach beyond the degradation of penny-pinching to do what is right and do the work of friendship that friendship demands in the ways that life has taught you are most necessary and readily needed, to 'throw your money about like a man with no arms' as the saying goes, and try to affirm the only medium of being that might help provide the illusion of a life that is something beyond abject. An illusion that for moments drink and drugs may realize but the truth is, until the next time, there is only the emptiness of the conditions of the culture that spawns such forms. The ritual of the night out affirms a form of relation that their conditions require yet which those very conditions ensure cannot exist. The economic conditions facing these people are too hard and too isolating for the solidarities of labourism to ever exist. And these people live compensating, as best they can, for what is not there, trying desperately to conjure fun, as a duty of the young, to not show seriousness or concern about their life, to simply 'have a good time' as the end of a life in which it is clear there is so little of quality. The eeriness of such a tranquillized hedonism, so concerned with pleasure as an anaesthetic rather than aesthetic experience, the real desperateness it betrays beneath the shallow avowals of love and friendship, Bourdieu captures:

There is still a sort of economic calculation in the unwillingness to subject existence to economic calculation. The hedonism which seizes day by day the rare satisfactions ('good times') of the immediate present is the only philosophy conceivable to those who 'have no future' and, in any case, little to expect from the future . . . the being-in-the-present which is affirmed in the readiness to take advantage of the good times and take time as it comes is, in itself, an affirmation of solidarity with others (who are often the only guarantee against the threats of the future), inasmuch as this temporal immanentism is a recognition of the limits which define the condition.   (Bourdieu 1984: 183)

It is a philosophy of life articulated by one woman:

Yer just want t' get thiseln [yourself] aht wi' thi [with your] mates an 'ave a good time. Yer ohnny [only] young once; yer spend most'r yer life old. It's n' good thinkin' what's gunna 'appen' just get thiseln aht [yourself out] an' enjoy yerself.

And, again, by a man:

I mean, tha's [you've] got thi [your] mates and tha [you] comes dahn gym. I mean, that's wot life's abaht in' it? Tha gu's [go] to w'k and earns some money and then thi's [there is] training and seein' yer mates and then your lass but tha's got to gu aht and 'ave a good laugh. Life's too short kid, tha can't worry all't time, tha's gott'a let thi 'air dahn and get yerseln in club and 'ave a bit or'a boogy and mek [make] a fool on thiseln [yourself] chattin' to all't nice women. Thi blow thi'y aht [you out] and tha' walks 'ome wi' a bag 'r chips on thi' own but so wot? That's life. Tha's got'a gu aht [out] wi thi mates and 'ave a good neet [night], it dun't matter if tha pulls a bird or not, fuck them, tha' wi thi mates f'st and 'owt else is a bonus.

The extent of the highly circumscribed limits of this life-style emerge in these quotations, which reveal the extent to which this attitude amounts to a realistic hedonism that is an adaptation to and defence against conditions of cultural dispossession and economic marginality. Yet this solidarity is one that is confined to spaces of relative anonymity used by people embodying the same practical ethos. I say 'relative anonymity' because public spaces like the pub of the working class have suffered with the erosion of the industrial culture of these areas. The general social decay has had such a profound affect upon the elementary solidarities of public life that the dispositions towards personableness on which 'the local' was built have disappeared. Whilst the old still frequent such spaces, the young, even when they are poor, have become absorbed in a culture of calculating hedonism based upon display which has eroded all but the vestiges of the primary solidarities of previous generations. It is something alluded to by one woman:

Ye' see wi' us thi' wo' none'r this beein' nasty t' people 'cos thi' an't [haven't] got right stuff. We wo' brought up not t' ever stare at anyone an' not t' tek piss aht on [out of] people who din't 'ave right clothes because none'r us 'ad 'owt. But it in't like that now. Ah never wanted 'owt, an' 'ave been 'appy wi' mi life 'cos Ah knew Ah cun't ever 'ave 'owt else.

This woman is marking an important change. To accede to existence one must adorn the body with the appropriate consumer signs. Yet, even where working class people are buying expensive named clothes, there is still a manner to their consumption that marks them as unmistakably the children of industrial culture. There is a huge homogeneity of style, a powerful standard of dress worn to places that are full of people wearing the same kinds of things. And these codes are subtly enforced in terms of advice and criticism. As one man put it:

If yer gu aht rahnd 'ere it's all same anyway in't it? It's all pastel shirts an' black trow or jeans fo' lads an' then skirts up 'ere an' tops dahn 'ere fo' lasses.

As one woman put it:

Me an' mi friend X, wi' wo' walkin' t' Z [*nightclub*] an' wi' saw these blokes walkin' along wi' the shirts tucked in an' shi ses, 'Oh, they must bi married 'cos thi'v got the shirts tucked in, 'cos all young 'uns wear the'r shirts aht dun't thi?

Even with the current vogue among the working class for 'named' clothes, it is still a culture of extreme similarity through which one distinguishes oneself through wearing clothes of a highly restricted type. Dressing outside of these norms would mean paying the price of invisibility. It is as though the large number of bodies crammed together wearing variations on the same theme permits a kind of anonymity and acceptance within a general sense of distinction. Even though there has been an erosion of the dispositions of a public culture, the spaces working class people frequent still operate as protected markets in which they can feel some value away from the general culture and its daily injunctions.

This realistic hedonism, as a practical sense of solidarity with those who share one's dispositions, space and fate, is tied to a social logic; an unspoken set of practical choices that lie behind the choice of places to go. Choices constituted amidst a sense of space, a set of attitudes to places that are 'full of students' or 'Weekend millionaires'. In the face of a market in which they can have no value, they will absent themselves, choosing a place where they don't face the degradation of having little value.

These processes are seldom articulated, rather they are latent in the on-the-spot decisions people make on the night out, and they are processes that operate practically, impacting upon the phenomenal field of the lived body, prompting action to be taken. Yet, as Bourdieu astutely remarks,

> The most fundamental principles of class identity and unity, those which lie in the unconscious, would be affected if, on the decisive point of relation to the body, the dominated class came to see itself only through the eyes of the dominant class, that is, in terms of the dominant definition of the body and its uses. (Bourdieu 1984: 384)

Given that most working class people live out their lives in such spaces, they have little awareness of their objective being, and they deal with its effects only indirectly as it is inscribed in the spaces they inhabit. They have little awareness of the perception of their objective being which one finds in the socially innocent language of likes and dislikes as that is used by other class groups to constitute themselves in public space. And they are spared a knowledge of the contempt and ridicule the educated classes have for the industrial working class, a scorn manifest in popular culture, in songs like the comedy duo, Hale and Pace's 'Northern calypso', with its chorus 'I'm a big fat northern bastard'; and perhaps its female equivalent, the 'fat slags'. This works simply by caricaturing the habits associated in the popular imagination with working class men and women: obesity, misogyny, inarticulateness. This produces a body of common reference points for practical orientation in space in British culture which is itself based purely upon a mis-recognition of the social conditions that have produced the characteristics the song parodies.

The spaces that working class people inhabit, therefore, exhibit a distinct quality, they have a certain 'feel' that is related to the dispositions of the individuals who occupy the spaces and to the universe of social relations that have contributed to the system of dispositions and the patterning of social space. Unlike the formalized world of the petit-bourgeois, the spaces working people use have the characteristics of *free markets* in which the 'politeness' and hyper-correction of petit-bourgeois manners are practically effaced. As Bourdieu suggests, 'two antagonistic world views, two worlds, two representations of human excellence are contained in this matrix' (Bourdieu 1984: 199) and the working class world is one that is organized around the reality principle: that things are real and real in their consequences so that they demand that individuals 'get real'; address themselves to the world in a manner that does not deny, in its expressivity, the experience that the deep-rooted dispositions of the habitus emblematize. It is a world in which being is prioritized over seeming (Bourdieu 1984: 199):

nature and the natural, simplicity (pot-luck, 'take it as it comes', 'no standing on ceremony'), as against embarrassment, mincing and posturing, airs and graces, which are always suspected of being a substitute for substance, i.e., for sincerity, for feeling, for what is felt and proved in actions; it is the free-speech and language of the heart which make the true 'nice guy', blunt, straightforward, unbending, honest, genuine, 'straight down the line' and 'straight as a die', as opposed to everything that is pure form, done only for form's sake; it is freedom and the refusal of complications, as opposed to respect for all the forms and formalities spontaneously perceived as instruments of distinction and power. On these moralities, these world views, there is no neutral view-point; what for some is shameless and slovenly, for others is straightforward, unpretentious; familiarity is for some the most absolute form of recognition, the abdication of all distance, a trusting openness, a relation of equal to equal; for others, who shun familiarity, it is an unseemly liberty.

(Bourdieu 1984: 199)

This obligation to be natural, expressive and open, is exemplified in unself-conscious speech about topics that would normally be vulgar and taboo in formal markets. So, for example, one gets examples of speech like:

Ah can't stop shittin' at moment. I cun't get off ('t) pot this mornin'. And I got off and went back dahn [down] stairs and Ah needed to gu back for another shit.

As well as conversations like the following which can go on for fifteen or twenty minutes:

X: Ah wi' gu'in aht then lads? [Are we going out then lads?]
Y: If tha [you] wants a night'aht [out] yer can come wi' [with] us. Wi'r [we are] gu'in' aht from w'k to B Hotel but tha'll 'ave t' sup Guinness, it's all thi' 'ave.
X: Guinness! It meks [makes] mi shit black next day.
Z: Ahr, tha [you're] pissin' from both 'oles. It's like wAter aht on a scaffoldin' pipe. It's like thi's a flock o'r [of] sparrers in' bog [toilet].
Y: When Ahr [I] sup the stuff it dun't get chance to come aht, Ah throw it all ovva f'st when Ah get in.

Z: What abaht you Sime; dun't it mek you shit thiseln'?

S: Ahr never lose control a' [of] mi bowels when Ah'm drunk.

Y: It's cos tha dun't drink enough!

Z: Ahr, [yes] on 'oliday one'r lads wo sat bi' pool, then he got up an' started runnin' to lift, like 'Get aht'a [out of the] way! Get aht'a way!' an' hi ran to bog an' hi' missed and shat all o'er floor an' bidet!'

Y: Ahr [I] got up in night once, an' someb'dy'd thrown up in sink. It stunk awful an' Ah wo like (*Imitate gipping and feeling nauseous*) an' Ah' gu's back to bed an' a weks Ahr [our] lass up an' ses 'A's *thar* thrown up in sink?' an' shi ses, 'Ye . . . I ave.' Ah ses, like toilets this far from sunk (*Holds hands up to show a distance of about a foot*), 'Why din't tha do it in toilet?', Shi ses, 'It smells in toilet [*laughs*]. S' next day Ah wo pushin' coat 'angers dahn sink to clear it.

This kind of transgression is part of a proclamation against the docility implied in the acquisition of the dominant manner and it is also part of a labour of representation, a theatrical presentation which acknowledges lack of dignity and fulfilment in many of these people's lives.[7] It is a style that is shared by working class women, if one woman's opinion is anything to go by:

Women are wose than men fo' stuff like that. Ma friends 'll [will] see a bloke at eleven an' se' 'Ooh, 'is a right ugly bastard' an' then at 'alf past one thi'll se' 'Where's that ugly bloke from earlier', 'cos thi want someone t' gu back wi' an' ye'll se', 'Ye' but yer said hi wo' ugly' an' the'll se' 'Well Ah wain't notice when Ah'm sat on 'is face.' Or 'Hi's got a knob an't hi? Wi' can do it doggy style, Ah shan't 'ave t' look at him then!'

This shows not only that slang is a key characteristic of working class speech; 'the form *par excellence* of "popular speech"' (Bourdieu 1991: 94); but that a central trait of working class speech is the transgression of dominant censorships, especially in sexual matters. These are men and women who have grown up knowing that they speak an illegitimate form, and yet who reject the docility involved in euphemizing to produce what they know they can never produce a competent form of: the legitimate ways of speaking.

It is this relation to an ever-present, deeply internalized sense of the cosmology of the social through which the body, marked through the inescapable processes of comportment that are the very possibility of being-in-the-world, is aware of itself as part of a total, contextualizing position that is a relation to culture, the world and the realized social categories that persons are. Furthermore, this sense, present through the 'looking glass self' contained in the responses of others forms the always present background, the horizon of possibility, in which working class experience takes place. This context inhabits the body, individuals understand themselves in

terms of its horizons because it is the context from which they must negotiate the world; it constitutes the place from which they must work within
the world. This context makes itself manifest in the styles and 'attitudes'
that individuals adopt towards the specific strategies they adopt in living.
For working people, it means their experience of the world is shaped by an
accommodation to the inescapable exigencies of the world that is 'there' to
be dealt with because they lack the economic and cultural capital to
exchange a losing position for something better. The choices that they make
take place in relation to a necessity that their practical social life negotiates
so as to reap some simple pleasures, even if the simple pleasures they enjoy
are as unmeasurable as a kind of tough, cynical, realistic manner of talking
which human self-respect imposes and yet within which there is a strict sense
of decency. Moreover, these forms of speech do allow the expression of
affection, love and friendship and, in operating as neutralizing conventions,
they do allow for the public proclamation of an affective world. This is clear
in the working class tradition of using the word 'love' as a mark of respect
in locutions like: 'Alrait Duck! Nah then, Duck: ah' yer alrait love?'; 'Alrait
'owd love' or 'Nah then mi 'owd friend it's good t' see yer.' Such conventions
do allow working people to speak with tenderness, sensitivity and openness
about matters of love and friendship and manifest affection and sensitivity,
as the following example makes clear:

S: Ah dun't know why people 'ave kids, me.
X: Ohr Simon! Ahr [how] can yer se' that! Tha [you] can't beat 'em! Tha' can't beat
'avin' a little girl come an' sit in yer lap an' put 'er arms rahnd yer an' se' 'Ah love
you daddy' an' sayin', 'I love you too dear'. This mornin', Ah've got up an' 'ad t'
'ave sugar *frosties* wi'y'er [with her] an' then Ah [I] 'ad to watch Grange Hill
wiy'er. Tha can't beat it. An' this mornin' Ah wo runnin' rahnd 'ahse [house] cos
'ave 'ad posh spice (S: Ahr she's fuckin' nicest, Ah could 'ave a thing abaht'er) she
ses, 'Mummy you're like Victoria', cos ahr [our] lass's hair's like hers, tha can't
beat 'em.

It is part of a way of acknowledging the fundamental relations of personal
life and part of an openness in personal and sexual matters that contrasts
starkly with the evasive non-public nature of bourgeois communities where
public displays of affection are often frowned upon as lacking self-control.
It is part of a way of speaking that acknowledges the relations upon which
individuals lives depend. It is perhaps clearest in relation to possessives like
'Hi's one'r ma' lads' with its roots in the apprentice-system and most clearly
with the expression 'Ahr lass' to denote a wife or girlfriend. For example:

I mean, I'm lucky, Ah've [I've] got a good lass and she's a good mother and looks
after ahr [our] little'un, and shi's great really, I'm lucky to 'ave 'er.

Such expressions recognize the importance of the individuals they denote without being over-familiar. Whilst they do avoid the embarrassment of too-open a recognition of the importance of these relationships, they also enable individuals to be open and expressive about the existential roots of their personal lives. This openness is part of a general exclusion from the means to develop the linguistic competence that would make working class speech obey a more formal logic of production. Which is a way of saying that forms of speech that follow the logic of bourgeois competence are:

Linked to this higher degree of censorship, which demands a consistently higher degree of euphemization and a more systematic effort to *observe formalities*, is the fact that the practical mastery of the instruments of euphemization which are objectively demanded on the markets with the greatest tension, like the academic market or the high-society market, increases as one rises in the social order, i.e. with the increased frequency of the social occasions (from childhood on) when one finds oneself subject to these demands, and therefore able to acquire practically the means to satisfy them.   (Bourdieu 1991: 85)

The openness of working class speakers is, in a sense, a result of their structural position which means they do not have access to the acculturation of the forms of euphemization, the tools of being able to censor oneself and still say, in an acceptable form, what one means. Their comportment thus tends towards a practical refusal of the dominant manners of speech and practice. It is this difference in comportment that makes working class men such an easy target for those simple distinction strategies that operate by ridiculing the 'macho-ness' of working class men. There is a tendency to represent the openness of working class people as simplicity and the outspokenness of working class speakers as invasive.

We must, therefore, recognize this linguistic habitus as a wider aspect of a class ethos that openness and outspokenness ('speaking one's mind'; 'saying what you think') as one of the organizing principles of an embodied cosmology of the social. This is part of an attitude to the world carried in comportment; part of a world disclosed in bodily hexis; part of a coherent system of respect, esteem and honour, which itself is tolerant and extensive and yet which operates purely practically in the distances marked between people, the way space is marked out for others and in the control of non-verbal personal cues like the control of the gaze (for example, not staring) and in things like the sharing of necessary items.[8] This bodily hexis, as far as men are concerned is characterized by a way of walking, of moving in space, of gesticulating, of swearing, joking, 'bantering', of laughing, eating, drinking and 'being a lad', of being 'straight as a die', a 'rait lad', of being open to talk about the problems of life but which rejects excessive sentimentality. It is a personality characterized by solidity and earnestness rather than niceness, a nature that harsh conditions demand, because 'If tha' dun't learn t' bi 'arder tha'll gu under.'

It is also an identity that working men are duty-bound to embrace in relation to its opposite, the female, which is sensitive and changeable and which they experience as contrary, 'Ahr, she's a woman yer see, the'r a strange species women tha knows?'; 'tha'll never understand women. I've gi'd up tryin'', 'the'r a different species' and 'a breed on the'r own' . The nature of the linguistic markets that Rotherham men establish is part of a much deeper and inter-penetrating set of cultural relations all of which are mediated by necessity. All ways round, it is a world of harsh realities. We must remember that the 'fortunate' in this world work, and yet the work itself is boring, demeaning and often physically uncomfortable, with little financial remuneration. The harsh externalities of life, the way this world impresses itself in perception, demanding forms of expression that render the sense of these conditions, are exemplified by the words of one man describing his feelings about work:

Fucking ell it wo' cold this morning! I fucking 'ate it gettin' up and runnin' fo't [for the] bus in mi hobbies[9] and thi' [you're] scruffy clothes. Tha feels a rait *fucking* plank. I wo late last week an' I'ad to run fo' bastard bus and I fell ovver, cos'a mi boo'its. [*laughs*] I nivver got that bus age'an! [*laughs at the humour of his embarrassment*] Fucking ell . . . [*pauses*] . . . but when it's cold I fuckin' 'ate it. When tha gets to w'k and tha sits on't site and it's laggin'[10] it dahn, tha just feels like cryin' some mornings. I'm not kiddin', tha dus [you do]. Sometimes I feel rait sick gunna w'k and I'll sit on some'at [something] and all't bricks arahnd yer a wet and *tha'r* wet and tha just wants to fuckin' howl. Everythin's cold when tha touches it and it seems to cut thi [your] skin and all thi hands gu numb, then tha fucking cracks thi'seln' [yourself] wi' an 'ammer cos tha can't feel thi'ands. Ye, I fuckin' ate it in winter, tha weks up in't morning and tha snug in bed and tha dun't want to get up. Naow . . .

If we consider the body as a network of lived-through meanings, a configuration of concrete conditions, such commentary exhibits the starkness of incarnational consciousness for those whose body-subject-hood is mediated by their having to engage with the world through the absolute proximity to the worlds materiality that being a manual worker involves, what Lawrence described as a relation to the elemental. These people's being is reduced to being a tool, an instrument, a being that must hump and shift materials as the condition of its own existence and this way of comportment reveals the world in determinate sensuous-affective ways:

Ah wo' [was] at w'k today an' gaffa teld mi that wi' wo' 'avin' a delivery ah' [of] gravel t' put dahn on this job. Wi like du'in' this big drive way at this gret posh ouse. Fuckin' trouble is at ahr place, the'r in't enough workers on site an' ahr gaffa's got mi on this job on mi own. So, Ah'd bin [I had been] diggin' aht [out] this patch an' barrerrin' [barrowing] it rahnd t' back o'r [of the] 'ouse. Anyway, Ah'd bin [I had been] w'kin' abaht [about] an 'our an' this lorry arrives an' Ah gu's aht an', anyway, wi' cun't dump this stuff near 'ouse 'cos'r these cars so hi dumps it. Tha should'a seen size on this fuckin' heap 'a gravel. Anyway, Ah thinks to miseln', it'll not shift itseln [itself] tha better get w'kin' an' so Ah wo' stickin' it in barrer an' tekkin' [taking] it t' site an' smoothin' it all dahn [down]. An' tha should'a fuckin' seen ahr far Ah 'ad t' barrer this stuff. Ah w'ked mi fuckin' bollocks off, Ah did, t' get job done. Ah wo' s' [I was so] fuckin' fed up wi' job Ah thought ohnny thing t' du is get the bastard done. Anyway, Ah'd just got last bit done, it wo' abaht three o'clock, an' mi fuckin' arms wo' killin' mi an' Ah sat dahn fo a rest. Ah wo' fuckin' lathered, mi top wo' wet through an' Ah sees this lorry comin' up road an Ah thought to miseln', [*Voice rises inself-mocking irony*] 'Oh, someb'dy else must bi 'avin' some w'k done, Ah'm glad some other fucker's got t' shift it!' An' this lorries gettin' closer an' closer an' then it pulls up an' driver gets aht an' reads mi (t') delivery details an' Ah'm sayin' to' 'im, 'No mate, no, [*Again voice rises*] wi'v 'ad ahr delivery *this mornin*' an' this lorry driver ses 'Naow, that wo' ohnny f'st 'alf, wi' wo' deliverin' it in two runs'. Ah could'a fuckin' ro'ored. Ah stood an' watched 'im dump it all dahn again an' Ah went an' sat on top'r it. Ah wo lookin' rahnd an' it all seemed s' fuckin' empty apart from this fucking' heap Ah'd got t' move an' ah wo' lathered an' knackered, all mi back' 'urt an' mi arms. Ah just wantd t' gu 'ome. But Ah got miseln back t' w'k an' Ah just managed t' get it all shifted in time t' gu' 'ome.

Through a life of these kinds of physical demands, demands which shape inescapably forms of comportment and hexis through continuously structuring the body's powers, an original mode of projecting existence is founded in intersubjectivity, and individuals find themselves bound to others through structures of knowing deeper than cognizance and self-awareness, a deeper way of knowing the world, founded pre-personally in the common way of life of the body situated by class. These pieces of testimony emerge from the primordial body of feeling and perception, from an unmediated encounter with the world that is manifest in an expressive style rooted in this bodily hexis which refuses linguistic form and elegance in preference for a phonetics and deportment that render the sense of the urgency and annihilating alienation involved in the constant violations of a primordial realm based upon continuous discomfort. It is as though the physicality of their experience, the hard labour and physical discomfort as well as the immediacy of oppressive work relations, leads them to take refuge in a kind of pleasure of immersion; in an involvement in their own description, in the deep-mouthed slurring of their speech, in the harshness of the consonants, in the non-euphemized sexual words, that, like the conditions they experience, connote an unmediated, primal relation to body and to one another. Brute being, stripped of the very possibility of formalized symbolically mediated relations; of a social identity that depends upon a distancing and conscious self-presentation, that demonstrates a respect for forms and thus for forms of respect that the primal relation of necessity disavows. It is as though the basic, primal nature of the swear-words contains the greatest charge of significance, as though contained in the syllables is a long-buried wealth of meaning, a surplus of meaning that emerges from the pre-conceptual matrix of sensuously felt meaning of lives spent in a mainly passive mode in which experience is confined to the vulnerabilities of work and unemployment. Alongside the harshness of work, we must bear in mind that another form of subjection haunts working class experience, in the figure of the 'gaffa':

Gaffa's at ahr [our] place, the'r [they are] right bastards. Thi' fucking come rahnd every hour to see what w'k tha's [you have] done. An' tha's bi'n luggin' thi bollocks 'aht and thi' 'ave fuckin' cheek to tell ye' that ye'r not working 'ard enough. Owd M, [*Work mate*] he teks [takes] piss aht [out] on 'em rait bad, he tells 'em to 'fuck off' when thi cum rahnd, *he dun't fuckin* care.
S: Don't bosses du owt?
Naow, thi just ignore 'im. Minds ye, thi fucking deserve it. Thi' think wi' fucking slaves . . .[*Pause*] . . . Mind's ye, on wages day we all tell 'em to 'fuck off'.
S: Why's that?
'Cos 's fucking wages ah [are] su bad!

These examples of speech, taken from informal spaces in which working class men talk with one another, show why there is a habituated sense of brevity, a habit which rejects sentimentality, and which despatches obvious discomfort and anxiety through a guttural slang which, in its brevity and terse unsentimentality allows them to speak about the over-arching existential problems contained in a life's duration ungraspable by people not from the working class, who, therefore, simply find such speech vulgar, not looking to the depth that the surface hides and thus missing everything:

which belongs to the art of living, a wisdom taught by necessity, suffering and humiliation and deposited in an inherited language, dense even in its stereotypes, a sense of revelry and festivity, of self-expression and practical solidarity with others (evoked by the adjective 'bon vivant' with which the working classes identify) . . . there is the efficacity of a speech which, freed from the censorship and constraints of quasi-written and therefore de-contextualized speech, bases its ellipses, short cuts and metaphors on common reference to shared situations, experiences and traditions.   (Bourdieu 1984: 395)

This sense of revelry and practical solidarity is obvious in the following humorous exchanges:

X: (*On being given a coffee*) Fuckin' 'ell, Ah [I] know Ah like mi coffee strong but this bastard's offerin' mi aht [out].

X: 'Ah used to work in this warehouse, it wo' a borin' job, but wi'd all bi dahn [down] different isles stockin' up an' someb'dy'd [somebody would] shout, 'I'm Spartacus!', then another'd shout, 'No, I'm Spartacus', an' then everybody'd join in, like that scene in't film, yer know?'

X: Eh up! (H)I's tranna [trying to] tell mi abaht owd [old] films nahr! Hi's bin tranna tell me abaht Katherine Hepburn fo' last ten minutes an' hi means Audrey Hepburn!

S: Yer know that film shi got an' oscar fo' we'er she's bin trav'lin' and at end thi' ask 'er which place in world wo best an' shi ses 'Rome', cos shi met Gregory Pech the'er.

Y: Ahr [yes], it wo' [was] a sex film that wer'n' [wasn't] it? Shi wo gu'in' rahnd world sein' who wo' best lovers an' thi' ses to 'er, 'Which men wo' best lovers?' an' shi ses, 'Well Red Indians 'ave got longest cocks in World an' Scotsman 'ave got thickest . . .' an' thi' ses to 'er, 'what's your husbands name?' an' shi ses 'Tonto MacTavish'. That wo one wer'n' it?'

(X doing exercise on floor. Y watching.)
Y: Hi dun't look s' fat layin' dahn does hi? Hey up X, thi' shapes comin' on! Yer' shape 'er a sack o'r shit, nahr: a sack o'r shit tied in middle!
X: Shur 'up yer fat bastard!
(Y lies on bench flying. X watches.)
X: One day, Y someb'dy's gunna come dahn them stairs wi' a bucket o' fish an' start throwin em at yer.
(Y finishes exercise and X lies on bench and does flying)
Y: Ahr but X, least Ah can gu sun bathin' by pool wiyaht [without] people keep gettin' ahta an' tranna' roll mi back in water!

X: Did thy 'ave a good Christmas Y?
Y: Ahr, one'r best A've 'ad but A'm payin' fo' it. Did thy 'ave a good Christmas X?
X: Naow. A'm not much bothered abaht it . . .
Y: Tha' not one'r these tha thinks fAther Christmas's a fat bastard ah tha'?

These kinds of exchanges, spin pleasure from an otherwise banal world, they make the dullness of work or unemployment recede for a short moment in the pleasure involved in the mnemonic consonance carried in the resonance of voice and situation. As Merleau-Ponty suggests:

to understand a phrase is nothing other than to fully welcome it in its sonorous being. (Merleau-Ponty 1968: 155)

To understand the warmth and self-deprecation in such humour, one must have some felt-sense of what passes by a sort of 'postural impregnation' (Merleau-Ponty 1964: 118) between them; the expressivity and consecration involved in gestures rooted in a shared way of being and relating. As Bourdieu puts it:

> The joke, in other words, is the art of making fun without raising anger, by means of ritual mockery or insults which are neutralised by their very excess and which, presupposing a great familiarity, both in the knowledge they use and the freedom with which they use it, are in fact tokens of attention or affection, ways of building up while seeming to run down, of accepting while seeming to condemn.
>
> (Bourdieu 1984: 183)

Listening to such speech, one is struck by the ingenuity of it, the endless forms of banter that go on, often about situations of acute anxiety. Such speech operates upon the basis of transgressing the rules of cultural legitimacy, of recognizing nothing as sacred, of profaning all things as a means of establishing and affirming a common ethos whilst also de-sacralizing, refusing to recognize the legitimacy of institutions from which they are excluded.

This disposition to profanity is a key aspect of the habitus of dominated people. It is perceived as an aspect of sincerity and strong feeling which, in being voiced openly, displays the characteristics of one who can be known and thus be relied upon to take a certain stance; as opposed to one who remains silent, secretive, a 'dark horse' that cannot be known and thus who cannot be relied upon. Such blunt speaking is seen as being passionate and therefore a mark of engagement, of a lack of distance which makes a person non-manipulative; it is an aspect of a kind of honour. It is an aspect of an organization of self based in a public realm of comportment habits through which working people recognize one another. As one man counselled:

> Dun't bother wi wot anybody else thinks. So long as tha honest wi people an' tha gets thiseln in order, yer know, yer 'ave some honor abaht yer, then never bother wot anybody else thinks.

This constellation of dispositions and oratorical style, a preference for straightforwardness and profanity as opposed to etiquette and fine words, is part of a practical discourse of the social that acknowledges the destiny of the group. It is a destiny acknowledged in the realm of common reference involved in the repeated description of shared predicaments and experiences. A destiny based upon a shared relation to the major social institutions of British culture. Institutions which form a matrix within which the bourgeois and petit-bourgeois can acquire symbolic capital and legitimacy. In a word the benefits of positive existence guaranteed by being on the right side of that line that separates winners and losers. An effect of economic and cultural dispossession is that individuals are divested of the material and cultural resources for them to found a life of self-value.

Moreover, in relation to key institutions of legitimacy, the main guarantors of the bourgeois sense of self-value, like the education system and the positions to which it leads, working people are negatively marked through a lifelong denigration of their primary capital and milieu. Yet such institutions, and the cultural configuration they serve, ensure the internalization, in varying degrees, of the norms of apperception which ensure that working people are possessed of the dispositions to perceive and recognize the system of significant differences without also having access to the instruments necessary for them to understand the illegitimacy of the social conditions of the legitimacy they grant in their perception of others and themselves. In these conditions, it makes sense for the excluded to elect to exclude themselves in an attempt to exercise symbolically a volition effectively denied them. Yet this is an assertion of cultural identity that is always in bad faith, in that the disposition itself emerges out of an implicit sense of oneself as devalued, as fractured and damaged, as 'not clever' and thus condemned to a life of insecurity and hardship.

Articulatory style is thus an aspect of bodily hexis; an aspect of a group's relation to the world as this economically mediated relationship is inscribed in the comportment of groups who share a common location and condition and thus who mutually habituate each other as part of being in a culture and world. As Bourdieu outlines:

Strictly biological differences are underlined and symbolically accentuated by differences in bearing, differences in gesture, posture and behaviour which express a whole relationship to the social world. To these are added all the deliberate modifications of appearance, especially by use of the set of marks – cosmetic (hairstyle, make-up, beard, moustache, whiskers etc.) or vestimentary – which, because they depend on the economic and cultural means that can be invested in them, function as social markers deriving their meaning and value from their position in the system of distinctive signs which they constitute and which is itself homologous with the system of social positions. The sign-bearing, sign-wearing body is also a producer of signs which are physically marked by the relationship to the body: thus the valorization of virility, expressed in a use of the mouth or a pitch of the voice, can determine the whole of working class pronunciation. The body, a social product which is the only tangible manifestation of the 'person', is commonly perceived as the most natural expression of innermost nature. There are no merely 'physical' facial signs; the colour and thickness of lipstick, or expressions, as well as the shape of the face or the mouth, are immediately read as indices of a 'moral' physiognomy, socially characterized, i.e., of a 'vulgar' or 'distinguished' mind, naturally 'natural' or naturally 'cultivated'. The signs constituting the perceived body, cultural products which differentiate groups by their degree of culture, that is, their distance from nature, seem grounded in nature . . . Thus one can begin to map out a universe of class bodies, which . . . tends to reproduce in its specific logic the universe of the social structure. It is no accident that bodily properties are perceived through social systems of classification which are not independent of the distribution of these properties among the social classes. The prevailing taxonomies tend to rank and contrast the properties most frequent among the dominant (i.e., the rarest ones) and those most frequent among the dominated. The social representation of his own body which each agent has to reckon with, from the very beginning, in order to build up his subjective image of his body and his bodily hexis, is thus obtained by applying a social system of classification based on the same principles as the social products to which it is applied. Thus, bodies would have every likelihood of receiving a value strictly corresponding to the positions of their owners in the distribution of the other fundamental properties.   (Bourdieu 1984: 192–3)

Articulatory style is thus linked to a whole cosmology of the social world and is an aspect of our deepest relation to the social universe. It is inescapably an aspect of our location in the social universe because as an aspect of the habitus it is linked to a whole system of dispositions acquired, initially imperceptibly, through a process of mimesis. It thus cannot be studied in isolation from that habitual world and its relation to the social universe. Speech is an aspect of the way in which the whole body responds by its posture, in its deepest reactions, or 'instincts', to the tensions of the social fields through which individuals move. We thus learn to speak as part of a total assimilation of habitual skills that allow us to comport ourselves towards the world in a knowing, intentionalist, way. Language learning is thus an aspect of the training and shaping of our bodies. In learning to speak in determinate ways we absorb, quite spontaneously and unconsciously, somatic techniques that function socially as patterns. So, we learn to hold our eyes and face in specific ways, we acquire a sense of how to position our hands during speech, we acquire a sense of how to modulate our listening and speaking with the appropriate gestures and we learn to use the mouth, tongue and voice box in particular ways and how to regulate our breathing in accord with the modulations of the dialects we all speak. We learn to do this delicate, melodious dance of being through appropriating, quite unconsciously, appropriate gestures which are acquired as habits of the flesh, a somatic know-how, part of a dynamic bodily structure through which we produce the gesturing sonority characteristic of human beings. This is why Merleau-Ponty felt it important to recognize that:

Like crystal, like metal and many other substances, I am a sonorous being.
                                                        (Merleau-Ponty 1968:144)

In speaking, we incarnate a sonorous field of expression that in its complexity and range establishes a realm of possibility and difference that is rooted deeply in the structures that mediate communities' acquisition, use and stylization of their sonority. One man once described to me how he felt the rhythms of the dialect he spoke were affected by the time they spent at work around the thresh-thresh of the machines of the mill. Yet the rhythms of dialect, and particularly the phonological traits of speech, are part of a sensuous pleasure of the body. The sounds one produces in speaking are not only heard by one's own ears but *felt* through the jaw-bone and skull.[11] Hence we feel at home among certain rhythms and 'at sea' among others. We feel a deep affinity, a spontaneous and deep ease, among those categories of beings whose sonority is the same as our own. This accounts for the experience of prosody we feel around the speech of those like us, as though our self-investment in the sociosomatic, 'physiological', structures of being renders some forms of expression and certain words *more* meaningful, loaded with a significance embedded in the sensuous grounds of our being. Our speech is thus part of a habitual way of living our motility. To speak a particular dialect, to be able to generate its particular cadences and accompany this with its characteristic gestures and inflexions, is to be possessed of a form of life; it is, through possession of a certain bodily schema or hexis, to be open to the world of others in a way that summons forth the expressive gestures and sonorous resonances; the vibrant energies that can, for dominated people, under particular conditions, be therapeutic, a refreshing and replenishing of the generative capacities denied, thwarted and frustrated in the world. We can thus better understand what Merleau-Ponty meant when he wrote:

My body discovers in that other body a miraculous prolongation of my own intentions, a familiar way of dealing with the world. Henceforth, as the parts of my body together comprise a system, so my body and the other person's are one whole, two sides of one and the same phenomenon, and the anonymous existence, of which my body is the ever-renewed trace, henceforth inhabits both bodies simultaneously.

(Merleau-Ponty 1962: 354)

That 'anonymous existence' consists of a totality of habitual, embodied, skills and dispositions, the background frame of comportment that we all utilize in innumerable ways, practically, as inescapable guides to practice.

The articulatory features of a people's speech thus express the deep-rooted dispositions of the habitus. Articulatory style is an element of an 'overall way of using the mouth (in talking but also in eating, drinking, laughing, etc.)' (Bourdieu 1991: 86), and for working class men articulatory style is part of a relation to the body that is dominated by the refusal of 'airs and graces', the refusal to stylize through the imposition of a dominant form, being wedded to a version of naturalness in speech and bearing manifest by talk about the basics of life and a pleasure in the things of the body, either as sensuousness or as an aspect of a humour that celebrates ingestion and defecation, as in the following examples:

X: Fuckin' ell that lad could drink beer fo' England.

X: I like a load a beer, a good gab, a barrer [barrow] full o'r food an' then [*tosses head back on one side and closes eyes imitating sleep*] a good kip.

X: Ah 'ad a rait good shit this mornin'. Ah like a good shit, it du's yer good, cleans thi' aht.

This articulatory style is part of a relation to the body that emphasizes strength and straightforwardness as part of a refusal of censorship, deviousness and haughtiness which thus renders someone reliable, 'one of us'; a 'natural' person around whom one can 'be oneself', 'natural', and not have to obey formalities, 'stand to attention', 'watch what you say', be self-conscious and formalize one's speech and practices in accord with the formalities of dominant forms. This articulatory style designates a kind of worldliness, a temporal attitude, misrecognized as cynicism, which is a form of dignity and self-projection based in the strength of the voice, a sort of pleasure in the strength and coarseness of the voice, which alludes to a potential for violence.[12] As far as men are concerned, it is part of a relation to the body wherein the body is valued for its size and strength and carried through the world with shoulders open, head up, with torso ambling like the shoulders of a great cat. Bodies that work take the easiest and most relaxed course between two points. No excess tension is lost on the pointlessness of a posture that functions as a form aimed at respect.[13] Moreover, as all fighters know, one must achieve a way of structuring posture and generating strategic movements that conserve as well as expend energy and the fastest way to respond is from a tension that is based in a relaxed awareness of the muscles, lest one is to tire in the later rounds. Moreover, this distinct articulatory style, and the habitus to which it relates, issues out of conditions of life that it then signifies or emblematizes. Both the articulatory style and the bodily hexis to which it is linked in the system of differences constituted by the space of class life styles become identified as the 'seat' of personal identity.

This is natural, given their economic and cultural conditions. For they are the bearers of a form of identity that has its roots in the physical manipulation of things rather than the processing of symbols; in a kind of near illiteracy in which they dare not write, and live *through* a speech that hugs the ground of their practical existence. And this is where their relation to the educational system and the position it mediates becomes critically important:

we must . . . stop to consider what is perhaps the best-hidden effect of the educational system, the one it produces by imposing 'titles', a particular case of the attribution by status, whether positive (ennobling) or negative (stigmatizing), which every group produces by assigning individuals to hierarchically ordered classes. Whereas the holders of uncertified cultural capital can always be required to prove themselves, because they *are* only what they *do*, merely a by-product of their own cultural production, the holders of titles of cultural nobility – like the titular members of an aristocracy, whose 'being', defined by their fidelity to a lineage, an estate, a race, a past, a fatherland or a tradition, is irreducible to any 'doing', to any know-how or function – only have to be what they are, because all their practices derive their value from their author, being the affirmation and perpetuation of the essence by virtue of which they are performed.   (Bourdieu 1984: 23–4)

Educational processes constitute consecrated groups, individuals who are perceived to possess a dignity which is part of a manner of deportment, an essence informing the style of practice but which is not perceived as an aspect of the practice; it is something beyond the mere technical competence of performance. However, for those possessed of 'skills', condemned to dexterity rather than intelligence, the status of their competence is more problematic because technical competence is liable to decline through loss and even obsolescence through economic and technological change. This has many consequences. It means that, as periods of unemployment extend, an individual's competence is seen to decline, making him less 'skilled', less marketable; and it means that skills are seen to depreciate with age so that status declines as one ages. Furthermore, the competence of industrial workers is also open to reclassification. In England the replacement of the old *City and Guilds* training with the National Vocational Initiative has meant the invalidation of a whole generation of skilled men's competence,[14] meaning that they have had to retrain. Most importantly, however, as holders of uncertified cultural capital, they understand themselves through the nominations carried out within the public discourse of the state agencies, something they are encouraged to do from an early age by agents like careers advisors and, then, through adulthood, by the Department of Social Security, that construct the class in attempts to increase economic utility through finessing the 'fit' between the technical competences of the working class and the positions that are available for them to fill (or the construction of these spaces through 'training' schemes). This essentialist understanding was manifest in much of the testimony of the last chapter and comes through strikingly in the following:

X: . . . it's like wi'r [we are] a burden simply by existin'. Ah mean, them 'r us what an't got jobs cheapen wages an' thi's too many on us to ever bi any fucking use. It meks yer feel like yer shun't bi 'ere.

S: What yer mean, if yer an't got a family, like?

X: Yeh, if yer single like us an' all the'r is is this.

Clearly if one is only what one does, then if one does nothing and is not integrated via a partner, then the context of qualitative significances, the space of distinctions through which one can locate identity is something like a singularity a force that collapses the forces of the field that normally shape space as possessed of sense. If one understands oneself through doing, then being becomes nothing when one is excluded from employment. This relation to self, we have seen, is manifest in identification with beliefs about the naturalness of expression and in an identification with the body as the site of powerful compulsions that are the seat of identity and which must be expressed as an aspect of a 'natural' integrity, 'that's just the way I am', and 'whole-heartedness'. An allegiance exhibited in possession of the competences that mark the condition because they issue form it. This identity is thus a product of the working class's relation to culture in general where, even to the family, value is determined by capacity to work, to bring home a wage and to reproduce the family.

If we want to glimpse how the understanding involved in this comportment comes to be lived, we need to consider the processes that mediate the formation of a relation to self instantiated in comportment that is based around essentialist understandings of intelligence and abilities. The words of a fifteen-year-old offer us some insight into how this understanding comes about:

S: Yer know teachers, right, du yer feel as though they direct yer in a way, du thi mek yer feel as though there are things that yer could or couldn't do?

X: Arghh, *definitely*. Arghh, cos them people that aren't brighter, like me, I'm ohnny [only] in Blues fo' maths and I'll get in mi maths group and if yer in a lower group teachers 'ed se 'Oh yer thick anyway, what yer coming fo?' or 'What du yer come for, yer can't du it.' That just med, that just 'oh I'm not doo'in it then'.

S: It's demoralising in it?

X: Ye.

S: Thi used to du that to me. Du yer think that affects yer outlook to work and the decisions that yer mek?

X: Err . . . Well . . . it dus in a way cos yer think that yer can't du'owt and that yer can't learn nowt and yer thinkin' that yer boss's gunna se' that and if yer boss ses that then that's it, yer out'a work, then yer on dole queue. So . . . yer think yer 'ave to just stick wi' wot I can do: I an't got much of a brain, so, I might as well use mi body, wot I 'ave got.

This is a young man speaking from 'forest-ways radiating from and arrowing towards an unwavering centre' (Steiner 1989: 34): a clearing circumscribing itself through a constitution given in the nominating power of teachers who define him to himself. Through their mediation he comes to understand his competence as belonging to the realm of nature, to his body; the realm of the physical, the technical skills his socially defined competence demands he acquire so that he can achieve a relationship to the opportunities left him. He thus exhibits an awareness of himself as given to a destiny of labouring with his body, as he puts it, what 'I 'ave got'. There is a kind of dualism operating here – working people talk of 'not having a mind', they occasionally joke about their stupidity ('If I 'ad a brain cell Ah'd bi' a cabbage') – a dualism that leaves them the body and materiality as what cannot be denied them (it can only be devalued). They thus must find expertise in the realm of competence they are constituted as possessing, be inherited by their heritage, to work, even in spare time to be committed to the project of exertion without end in the pointlessness of a work which reproduces the materialities of existence but never the generative structures of human association required to inhabit the world as more than a stranger. Moreover, what is clear in this man's speech is that the life of the body is all that he feels is left to him. He has possession of his body, at the price of having to adopt a relation to himself as that of a tool, and his coming to relate to his body as a kind of mechanism which wear and tear will destroy, 'ten mo'ore y'r Ah labourin' an mi' body'll bi fucked, an' thi's s' many unemployed that thi can just sack yer an' get someb'dy younger' as one man put it. Their social and economic position, then, mediates their encounter with the world and encourages the adoption of a certain way of treating their body, of tending for it, of producing it as a body fit for the reality that it must deal with, and they do this within the confines of the horizons of their social expectations of personal decay and future hardship ('what will I do when I can't work'). But the role of state education and the appalling economic conditions that were constructed for young working class people at the end of the nineteen seventies, in the formation of this horizon of possibility, emerges clearly in the following testimony:

S: What kinds a things mek yer not like school?

X: Teachers, way thi treat yer, way thi talk to yer, treat yer like kids instead o' adults, thi treat yer like yer five, and not fifteen and that bugs mi.

S: What kind'a things in particular?

X: Well, keepin' yer behind and giyin' [giving] yer loads and loads o'r 'omework. I know its a GCSE course but thi gu rait ovverboo'ard.

S: What abaht ermm, du thi like talk dahn to yer?

X: Ye thi' du, rait bad. Thi don't 'ave no respect fo' us.

S: What other things mek yer not like school, in particular?

X: I used to like school, I don't know, I just don't like it anymoo're, I just an't got no interest in it, thi's just nowt theer fo mi.

S: When did yer start to feel like that?

X: erhh, end o' third year. Cos I'm in fifth year nahr, end o' third year.

S: So it's last, since what? How ow'd a' yer, nahr?

X: Fifteen. Since Thirteen. I don't like it at all.

S: Du yer think it's cos yer feel adult nahr?

X: Ye. I don't like be'in treated like a kid.

S: What would yer rather be doo'in nahr?

X: Boxing, working and earnin' money.

S: Are yer serious abaht earning yer livin' as a boxer?

X: Ye. I can do that, it's somat I can do that I dun't 'ave to gu on a scheme fo.

S: What do yer see, like, looking ahead o' yer? I mean, how do yer feel about the job situation now?

X: Well, jobs that we've got choice on, aren't very good. For starters, if we gu on a Y.T. [*Youth Training*] that's wot, twenny, thirty-odd quid a week. Wot's that to us? [S: Ah know.] It's not a livin' that. So, I'm thinking abaht goo'in, in army nahr.

S: Which regiment?

X: I dun't know. I dun't know whether to gu in marines or not. I think 'am gunna go'o in marines.

S: I think it's probably a good thing cos yer can, like train, and like, the other thing is that yer want to aim fo' is like tryinn'a get to be an officer and things like that, pick up a trade and stuff, and I think probably that'd suit yer cos yer could use yer boxing and if yer like, fight fo'r 'em an that thi don't treat yer like a normal squaddy, so it might be a decent living.

X: Ye, that's wot mi Dad said to mi. He ses thi's not much aht 'ere. He ses, yer can gu to yer gym an' that but I think best bet is to gu in army and get in them competitions cos they'll get yer a fait every week, an that, so I think that's wot I'm gunna do.

We find in this young man's speech the interrelation of two sites, the working class family and the school, which together establish the horizon of possibility of individuals' existence. School teachers, lacking any sense of such people as educable, treat these kids as uneducable, and reflect these judgements as the 'considered opinion' of specialists to working class parents, who, working with the same practical understanding as their children and lacking any other authority with which to oppose the teacher's opinions, carry out further confirmations of the initial symbolic violation of their children's dignity by insisting that the child, who they often want out of the house and independent anyway, follow a career which, in contemporary conditions, can only reproduce conditions of acute social vulnerability. This process was reflected in the concerns of one man for his younger brother:

X: Ah felt fo' ahr Y [*fifteen-year-old brother*] other day. [S: Ye?] Mi Mum an' Z [*partner*] went up to 'is school, it wo' like an open-day. An' a lot'r teachers were quite negative abaht [about] him. Thi wo' sayin', 'Oh, his easily distracted'; 'Hi' dun't concentrate'; 'Hi's not academic', 'hi likes to du things wot are practical'.

An' when thi got back mi Mum wo' 'avin' a gu at ahr [our] Y abaht it all. An' I
tried to tell mi Mum that shi shun't [should not] listen to these teachers, that thi
often wrong wi' kids, that it dun't mean 'owt but shi just wun't [would not] listen,
shi wo' sure that 'cos thi' [they are] teachers, what thi' se' is right.

S: So what's appenin' wi' your Y; what's thi Mum tellin' 'im t' du?

X: Well that's worst 'r [of] it. Shi's bin sayn' that hi' ought not t' try an' foller like wot
Ahr [I] did, Ah wo' quite academic at college, after school, an' shi reckons ahr
[our] Y ought t' du someaht [something] more practical. But Ah think thi' [they
are] wrong. Ah mean, hi's a nice lad. Hi's got a nice temperament, hi's not a bad
lad, Ah think hi' needs some 'elp an' encouragement, Ah think hi's confused. Yer
know, hi wo' sayin' to mi, 'X, teachers se' Ah'm not very good at school, what can
Ah du?' an' 'Du yer think Ah'll bi able to get a job or Ah'm a just gunna bi a
doley' an things like that an' Ah feel fo' 'im cos nahr [now] hi think his not gunna
[going to] bi any good at owt. What wo' worst though wo' when Ah went t' bed,
Ah [I] could 'ear 'im in bed cryin' an' Ah went in an' gev'[gave] im an hug an' hi
wo' 'eartbroken, poor lad an' it meks mi angry. Ah've tried talkin' t' mi Mum
abaht it but shi's from that generation when teachers were somebody, yer know?

This again makes clear the extent to which the twin sites of school and
family operate together to encourage working class people to become what
they are initially perceived to be. What starts life in the class–racist
responses of teachers to the primary signifiers of class in the body, manner
and speech of working class kids, is transmitted to parents who experience
academic classifications as neutral and, importantly, as guaranteeing a kind
of dignity beyond mere technical competence, the absence of which thus
becomes transposed into a lack of personal value of their children. The
insistence in the testimony of the older brother that his brother is 'not a bad
lad', is an affirmation of a sense of the personal value of the brother which
he feels is denied in the teachers' judgements. This exhibits a good deal of
the silent, unspoken pain, that working class people[15] feel because of their
educational failure. This reveals something it is easy to overlook about educational classifications. That is that they are:

not experienced as purely technical and therefore partial and one-sided, but as total
hierarchies, grounded in nature so that social value comes to be identified with 'personal, value, scholastic dignities with human dignity . . . so that privation is perceived as an intrinsic handicap, diminishing a person's identity and human dignity.
(Bourdieu 1984: 387)

Being told that one is not clever is like being told that one is fat or ugly; it is
not something about which one can achieve indifference because it is likely
to play a deciding role in one's destiny, particularly in the possibility of a
worthwhile life and happiness. Thus we end up with people defined to their
families, through acts of nomination that effectively shape apperception,

give perception its sense and reality its hue, as 'useless', 'unable', 'stupid'; lacking in the dignities given to the privileged. A kind of individual destiny shaped by the collective perception of the truth of a way of being. In these ways the being-for-others of an individual comes to exert a powerful influence on their being-for-themselves. It is a process, the tragic extent and full force of which is captured by Bourdieu:

> Because everything inclines them to judge their own results in terms of the charisma ideology, students from the lower classes regard what they do as a simple product of what they are, and their obscure foreboding of their social destiny only increases their chances of failure, by the logic of the self-fulfilling prophecy. The essentialism implicitly contained in the charisma ideology thus reinforces the pressure of social determinisms. Because it is not perceived as linked to a certain social situation, for example, the intellectual atmosphere of the home, the structure of the language spoken there, or the attitude towards schooling and culture which it encourages, academic failure is naturally imputed to a lack of gifts. Children from the lower classes are indeed the appointed consenting victims of the essentialist definitions in which clumsy teachers (disinclined . . . to relativize their own judgements sociologically) imprison individuals. When a pupil's mother says of her son, and often in front of him, 'He's no good at French,' she makes herself the accomplice of three sorts of damaging influences. First, unaware that her son's results are a direct function of the cultural atmosphere of his family background she makes an individual destiny out of what is only the product of an education and can still be corrected, at least in part, by educative action. Secondly, for lack of information about schooling, sometimes for lack of anything to counterpose to the teachers' authority, she uses a simple test score as the basis for premature definitive conclusions. Finally, by sanctioning this type of judgement, she intensifies the child's sense that he is this or that by nature. Thus, the legitimatory authority of the school system can multiply social inequalities because the most disadvantaged classes, too conscious of their destiny and too unconscious of the ways in which it is brought about, thereby help to bring it upon themselves.   (Bourdieu and Passeron 1979: 71–2)

In the testimony from the young man who wants to be a boxer, it is clear that there are powerful tensions between the two sites of school and family, that the conditions of the primary milieu are not synchronized with the school. The forms of dignity – the stoical maturity demanded by the world that this person encounters, a world of urgencies and struggles – are deficits in the realm of school whose exercises seem pointless, especially in relation to the economic future that the teachers' classifications lead such people to prepare themselves for. In relation to the world that he encounters, education seems not only pointless but absurd:

> X: No. What's point in us learning about World War Two. Alrait it's nice to know what yer country did fo' war an that but what du we wanna [want to] learn abaht,

oh, what wo' thing we wo doin' other day? Oh in science we wo' learning abaht watching paint dry, that wo us title, I mean, what du wi need that for? Or what du wi need to know abaht [about] sewer works for. That's not gunna get us far in life is it?

S: It'd be alrait if thi offered yer somat wun'it? I mean, knowing abaht sewer could be really important if yer wo gunna be an engineer an' if yer wo gunna be working dahn theer.

X: Ye. Tha rait. If I could see some point. I think ye should 'ave different kinds . . . It's a waste o'r time gunna school, I hate it, it's borin' An' mi brother wo even worse: he 'ated every minute on it. An I used to, I loved little school, cos all mi old mates wo' theer, first mates I ever met, but when yer get up to comp, yer get split up from 'em an' that. Yer meet new 'uns an' yer meet all idiots an . . . [*voice trails off*]

The more aggressively the social realm impacts upon people from dominated groups, the more absurd become the scholastic exercises which, being exercises for exercise' sake, such people find it difficult to see the point of, in reference to the practical realm of their lives, especially given their sense of the future immanent in the lives of those around them. The problem[16] is that the conditions of practising the techniques of disinterested contemplation, a fascination with questions rendered speculative, conspicuous, posed purely for the pleasure of the fruition of the process whereby one satisfies oneself of the correctness of a solution or interpretation as opposed to a practical working out of a problem in the world, seems to have no sense to people too wedded by necessity, urgency and position to the principle of 'reality' and a world that brooks no interpretation, which is always simply, 'there', insisting to be dealt with. The problem for this man is that the culture of the classroom and the understanding it requires are existentially foreign in that they belong to a form of existence to which he has no primary, domestic access. Instances of school or academic culture are cases of mediated decipherment, and, without possession of the cipher, mastered through a long and slow process of familiarization with the gratuitous exercises of the school, the experience of learning is reduced to one of the conspicuous perception of objects in their simple phenomenal state; a state manifest in his not being able to 'see a point' which, without possession of the instruments to decipher and perceive the meaning, is literally true for him. It is a problem Bourdieu characterizes:

In their current form, experiments at bringing people into contact with cultural works follow a rule which is familiar to experts in acculturation: a technique can be learned and understood perfectly and then forgotten because the conditions of practising this technique have not been provided, and because it is not integrated into the total system of attitudes and customs which alone can give it a foundation and a meaning . . . In the same way, the first primary school teachers in Kabylia, at the end of the last century, continually deplored the fact that their pupils seemed to forget everything they had learned as soon as school was over, whether it was the height of trees or mathematics, which are techniques bound up with a whole attitude to the world which, in any case, schooling did not, or could not, convey by itself.   (Bourdieu 1990e: 104)

The familial milieu is part of the overall context that we have been looking at, and its pressures are too often those which make labouring communities want offspring economically active or, at least, independent, sooner rather than later. Parents lack the resources to ensure educational success. With so little to offer, against a context of youth training and unemployment, boxing and a fight every week are the limit of this man's father's aspirations:

X: Ye, mi grandad wo' in army, i' fought in royal airforce, but then'he'ad to get stopped doo'in' that cos thi' weren't enough miners so he 'ad to gu' an' work in't mines.
S: Is that wot yer grandad wo, a miner?
X: Ye.
S: What du's yer Dad du?
X: He dun't he du's a bit o'r fiddle, that's all he dus really. Hi used to work in't shovel works, yer know mekkin' shovels and garden forks.
S: Yer got brothers and sisters?
X: Ahrr Lee's a joiner, he's a qualified joiner and he's goo'in on a course to become . . . [Pause] . . . and ahr Dean's at Sotherlands, a big Foord factory up ahr way.
S: What fascinates yer su much abaht boxing? Why du yer enjoy boxing?
X: Ahr just like physical side on it, gettin' 'it, 'ittin' people. Ahr love building mi'seln up, ahr love all sport. I find't spoort interesting, it's not just that I like 'ittin' people, I like gettin' 'it, I like learnin' abaht it.
S: It is interesting, it fascinates me.
X: It's like 'em, it's like a will thing, yer know, gettin' 'it and knowin yer can tek it, an that. It gi's [gives] yer a rait good buzz. I mean, yer know ahr fit yer are, cos if yer weren't fit yer cun't du it, tek it, tha knows . . . mi Dad ses. Even if yer can't mek it professional or if yu do mek it professional and yu dun't mek it very far, at least ye'v got it fo' streets, so that yer can lose, but yer don't lose as much.
S: Du yer enjoy things nahr or du yer feel that yer ready to move on? And start se, gu'in aht drinking an' livin' an adult life?
X: Ye, I 'ate school and thi's nowt fo mi to do much 'cept mi boxing.

Like so many, even with the good intentions that are rarely sincere in these conditions, this man's family, do not establish around him the conditions for the long, slow process of acculturation that is demanded for the acquisition of the forms of competence that render education meaningful. The extent to which such familial contexts render literacy absurd comes through in the words of one young pregnant woman:

X: Ah get sick'r [sick of the] telly [television] on. Ahr Y, hi just sits wi' telly on all day. Ah'd rather sit an' read or write or sumaht. Hi 'ad telly on other day an' Ah went an' sat on mi own an' sat dahn [down] to write sumaht an' hi cem through an' ses 'What's that?' An Ah ses. 'It's a pen an paper?' an' hi ses, 'What are you du'in'?' an' Ah ses, 'Ah'm tranna write sumaht' an' hi ses 'Yer mad you! Yer argh, thi's sumaht wrong wi' yer!' An' it's same wi' mi Dad, hi' wain't gi mi any quiet an' his never took n' interest an' hi cun't giy a toss but when Ah fail hi'll gu up wall wi' mi' (S: 'Ah know, Ah understand X') Yer can't win. Yer just think *what's it all abaht*! An' Ah try but Ah've done two weeks solid in 'ere, standin' in fo' every body. Doctor 'll gu barmy if hi finds aht, hi teld mi Ah wo' du'in' t' much when hi knew Ah wo' doin' sixteen hours an' mi A levels.

This makes clear why Bourdieu suggests:

> The aesthetic disposition, a generalized capacity to neutralize ordinary urgencies and to bracket off practical ends, a durable inclination and aptitude for practice without a practical function, can only be constituted within an experience of the world freed from urgency and through the practice of activities which are an end in themselves, such as scholastic exercises or the contemplation of works of art. In other words, it presupposes the distance from the world (of which the 'role' distance' brought to light by Erving Goffman is a particular case) which is the basis of the bourgeois experience of the world. Contrary to what certain mechanistic theories would suggest, even in its most specifically artistic dimension the pedagogic action of the family and the school operates at least as much through the economic and social conditions which are the precondition of its operation as through the contents which it inculcates.   (Bourdieu 1984: 54–5).

The very possibility of accommodation to the process of education, the plausibility of pursuing a strategy of social climbing using the hierarchy of certificates and institutions as the ladder, can be effectively curtailed by the deepest existential structures that delimit an individual's life.

What is clear in these pieces of testimony is that the school institutes – certainly as far as these people are concerned – a unified market, a dominant, distinguished criterion of practice value and worth, in relation to which these individuals' primary culture and familial milieu become deficits. In contrast, the primary culture of dominant groups, their way of deportment, their manner, the way they look, move, gesture and speak is deeply confirmed because congruent with the educational system and the positions to which it leads. This means that the habitus of these groups, in relation to dominant institutions, acts as a multiplier of capital, leading to their experience of themselves and the whole social realm as one of 'quasi-divine' grace, of comfort, ease and self-respect. What we see in the case of the young boxer is that, through his primary milieu, of home and locality, he has learnt to embody a form of dignity which sets him apart from the teachers and which he equates with maturity; and, in the testimony from the woman, we find a practice that is equated with the school, writing, meeting with derision from a family member. In different ways both of these people experience a conflict between education and their own primary location within the society in which they live. The activities and comportment of the young man, which have arisen as ways of coping and managing some self-respect in the world that faces him, are met with derision and condescension by those who taught him.

The examples of testimony that arise in relation to the experience of school make clear the sense of violation involved in essentially bright, decent, and even considerate, individuals coming to imbue a sense of themselves that they must live up against: a fracturing, damaging sense of self learnt through 'all the judgements, verdicts, gradings and warnings imposed by the institutions specially designed for this purpose, such as the family or the educational system'; that have through 'the meetings and interactions of everyday life', come to inscribe a powerful, and experientially profound, sense of the social order that makes visible the extent to which: 'Social divisions become principles of division, organizing the image of the social world'. Through this complex but indeterminate experience of the world, 'Objective limits acquired by experience of objective limits' amount to a 'sense of one's place', which lead individuals to exclude *themselves* from the things, persons, places and experiences from which they are excluded. So, we can see here the only response that is possible in the face of this social experience: to become what one has already been quietly and subtly told that one is; to take up the being, reflected to us in the reactions of others. The testimony shows the extent to which individuals are aware of the space of possibilities, the objective opportunities, ahead of them. Such communities began to deal with this trajectory, with the personal effects of their prolonged decline, in the early eighties. Since then, the choice of employment schemes, unemployment (an experience gradually being organized into work-training and thus employment schemes) or the possibility of more humiliation in a classroom, has been set. It is an experience summed up by an ex-miner in his mid-forties:

X: Thi'v [they have] brought back school fo' adults nahr [now].
S: Ahr [how] du [do] yer mean?
X: Well look at these schemes an that, things like E.T. an that an the'r not jobs, the'r just things we'er tha gus [go] an' thi tek [take] a register, it's just like school Ah'm [I'm] tellin' yer. An tha [you] feels like tha did at schoil [school], it's not like w'kin'. An' nahr, it dun't matter wot age thy are, thi in't no end to it, we're all just like bein' at school.

And the duration and cyclic nature of these solutions to the problem of mass unemployment come through in the words of another man in his mid-forties, reflecting on his experience:

X: . . . so after'r seventies thi' brought in these trainin' schemes, nahr [now] YTS's an employment trainin schemes were preceded by TOPS courses an' things like that, ye? But Ahr [I] did one'r those as well.'
S: What wo they like?
X: Well thi' wo' a load'r fuckin' shit.
S: Thi' wo like YTS's?
X: Ye. It wo' a six months apprenticeship.
S: Wo' it 'as badly paid as YTS's?
X: It's exactly same. Exactly same, in fact YTS's wo' better off. Not on YTS sorry, on Employment trainin', on Employment trainin yer get ten pound over an' abover yer 'mm, yer 'mm, income support, well when yer went on TOPS courses yer din't get anythin' over an' above, what you actually got was dinner money an' travellin' expenses. So Ahr made four pahnd odd ovver an above beco's thi' wo [was] a free bus run from Rotherham aht [out] to Remploy an' Remploy wo' on same site as TOPS course, so wo' all I 'ad to do wo', I din't 'ave to gu in to Sheffield so I wo' claimin' bus fares to Sheffield but I wo ohnny [only] guin' to Rotherham, nah [now] this wo' befo'or bus devolution so that it wo costin' mi' twenny pence to gu to Rotherham, we'er'as it wo costin mi' like thirty-five to forty-pence to gu to Sheffield on top of that, on top of that, I got dinner money, so if I took sandwiches, an' if I took some, an med a few pence a day on t'bus fares, I came aht, I cem aht, I wo mekkin' abaht four quid a week. Four pahnd odd a week,[17] over an' above, over an above, what dole money were then. [S: 'What wo dole money then?'] I can't remember, twenty pahnd. Twenny odd pahnd.

These people thus exist amongst a matrix of institutional sites which mediate their relation to the social and which render them docile, having to carry out the self-disciplines of filling in their 'back to work' programmes, as a condition of their ascension to utility. It is a disciplinary matrix whose aim is:

directed not only at the growth of its [i.e. the body's] skills, nor at the intensification of its subjection, but at the formation of a relation that in the mechanism itself makes it more obedient as it becomes more useful, and conversely.

(Foucault 1977: 137–38)

This disciplinary matrix has been the context for a progressive rationalization of work itself, but the result of this cultural shift in the space occupied by working people is obviously chronic vulnerability and confusion. In a world in which the qualitative space in which self-respect is founded has become so compressed, so contested, in which the resources for a mediated relationship to oneself and others must be fought for because they are not given, then we might expect self-identity to be reduced to the equally reduced possibilities of a public existence left to the denied, to take up the domain of a form of being that cannot, finally, in the immediate present, be denied, the body and the life of a fighter:[18] 'I can do that, it's somat I can do that I dun't 'ave to gu on a scheme fo.'

When people's lives are reduced to this, robbed of a public context of relations through which they can reach positive evaluations of themselves and others, and, moreover, when one belongs to a group which is denied access to the instruments, as well as the forms of comportment that in our society mark the accomplished person; that mark intelligence and one's belonging to the realm of mind; when one is consigned and consigns oneself to the realm of the body; when one's livelihood is dependent upon one's practical, habitual, generative capacity to learn competencies rooted in the motor-skills; then it is little wonder that the body should become the 'seat' of personal identity to oneself, when these very conditions instil forms of comportment that refuse euphemization and which signify to others a condition of mindlessness and crude physicality that is disgusting. And here we might pause for a moment and consider Ortner's suggestion that nature is 'something that every culture devalues, something that every culture defines as being of a lower order of existence than itself' such that categories of person who are perceived as 'being more rooted in, or having more direct affinity with, nature' (Ortner 1974: 72–3) are themselves deval-ued. The lower orders themselves are interpreted, within the dominant tax-onomies, as being lodged in their animality, tainted by the materiality of many of their tasks and the utility of their service function. This condition illuminates 'the paradox which defines the 'realization' of culture as *Becoming natural*. Culture is thus achieved only by negating itself as such, that is, as artificial and artificially acquired, so as to become second nature, a habitus, a possession turned into being' (Bourdieu 1993b: 234); a somat-ization of relations of domination. For the young man who wants to be a boxer, this is truly social destiny become fate, culture become essence, in that he has been persuaded, not of his capacity to utilize the generative capacities that we all possess as normal healthy human beings, nor of his capacity to extend himself, *exist*-himself through the range of possible being that being-human opens us all onto, because the field of his being is so heavily circumscribed by the realm of possibilities delimited by the ulti-mate condition of his existence, such that he has learnt that his being is dys-functional, that his natural ability is to be *unable*, and that he is condemned to wander the world within the parameters of a sterile way of being born of a barren, excavated world. As another man said:

I've got no brains me. Mi brother wo good at school but not me. He got all't brains in 'ahr [our] family. I've got to w'k wi mi 'ands, labourin's ohnny [only] thing Ah can du.

S: 'ave you never thought of goo'in to night classes?

Tha must bi joking! It's no good mi goo'in in't class room, I'm thick, I allous 'ave been, ahr kid got all brains in ahr family. Naow. It's buildin' sites fo' me, I mean, I 'ate it, som'a shit we 'ave to du and it fucks me up, but it's work.

And as another woman expressed it, 'It might bi alrait fo' you' tha's got a big brain, but I an't.' What is fascinating, is that it is obvious that working class people see intelligence as in some deep and determining way genetic, as an aspect of genetic endowment: the size of the brain or as a 'strain' that, once bestowed upon one family member, dissipates. It is a model that extends to any culturally prestigious competence, as the following conversation makes clear:

X: Ahr [our] Y [*grandaughter*] plays clarinet. Shi's just started. Aye, well shi gets it from mi Dad who wo [was] really musical and nob'dy' else in family wo ohnny [only] mi an' Ah [I] ended up in Marines killin' people, but then it's skipped a generation an' come back in ahr Z's [*daughter*] young 'un. Ahr, it's smashin!

This is why cultural dispossession is seen, even by those whose life-condition it is, as 'a state of "nature" in danger of appearing as if it is part of the nature of the people condemned to it' (Bourdieu 1990e: 110). Moreover, in the conversation where I suggest going to night class, what the transcription does not fully reveal is the vehemence, the strength of the belief in his natural inability and the acceptance of the destiny it involves. As a site of symbolic violence and varying degrees of abuse, there is little wonder that working class people forever equate the notion of a classroom with humiliation, when one considers experiences like the one narrated to me by a twenty-six-year-old taxi-driver:

X: Well, Ah never teld [told] yer did ah? But Ah cun't [could not] read till Ah wo fourteen an' then Ah ohnny [only] learnt so that Ah could read road signs fo' when Ah started drivin'.

S: What 'appened at school then?

X: Well, most'r teachers learnt that Ah cun't read an' thi'd just leave mi alone, 'cept [except] fo' C, he wo a bastard. Hi 'ad us read this fuckin' book called *White Fang* an' Ah used to dread gunna school, an' Ah used to try an' remember it, them bits that Ah'ad to read, but then when Ah stood up to read Ah cun't remember [*Laughing*] so Ah used to just stand up an' se', 'White fang wo' a fuckin' dog' an' hi wo' stupid', so he used to cane mi, so Ah wo gettin' stick every fuckin' day [*Laughs*], yer know, an' so, Ah never learnt to read, hi wo 'appy to stick mi but never actually helped me learn.

S: Ahr did yer learn then?

X: Ah learnt miself from boxin' magazines an' porno mags an stuff like that.

S: What abaht writin' then?

X: Well, Ah can't write nahr, Ah dun't even like writin' mi name on checks. It's like wi' date, I 'ave to ask what date is when A'm writin' checks aht, that gets yer some looks, A'll tell yer.

S: What abaht essay plans, din't thi teach yer ahr t' du them?

X: Well, I din't even know what a sentence wo' till you teld mi, an' nob'dy ever taught mi abaht any o'r that.

S: Not even abaht ahr to use dictionaries?

X: Naow, honestly, nowt like that.

Bearing such experiences in mind, to say nothing of the social logic we have been considering, there is little wonder that many working people suffer a kind of post-traumatic stress in regard to their experience of education. For many, going near an educational institution involves a kind of hyper-vigilance, accompanied by intrusive recollections and the kind of intense psychological distress that is characteristic of disorders like agoraphobia. This is the obverse of the miracle of education as it is experienced by the bourgeois. Whilst for them their experience of acculturation is one of a permanent, quasi-messianic enhancement; for working people, their experience of acculturation is one of violation, of reduction and stripping away; a process of symbolic violence that leaves them lacking the resources of confidence to feel comfortable doing very much, but what they must learn to do in order to survive in the world that is left to them. It is no coincidence that the man who left school being unable to read, learnt in order to drive and thus to be able to work as a taxi-driver. So many working class men leave school and only learn to read and write through work, with mothers and girlfriends helping them fill in their first time sheets until gradually the routinized tasks and limited competence they demand, allow them to become comfortable with this highly circumscribed realm of words. The words of a man in his sixties confirms many of the processes we have been looking at:

X: Ye see, Ah [I] wo nivver [never] very bright at school, it weren't in mi, Ahr [our] M [brother] could but he got mi fAther's ways but fo' me, Ah nivver picked up readin' rait. In them days thi' used t' come rahnd [round] an' if thi' saw yer stuck wi'y [with] a word, thi'd [they would] bang yer like that (*imitates crack on head with knuckles*) on 'ead an' se, 'Tha thick', an' then when A'd gu 'ome, t'owd man'd [father would] se' 'What's that bump on thi 'ead?' an' ye'd tell 'im teacher gev it yer an' t'owd man 'd think tha'd got it fo' cheakin' teacher so 'id [he'd] giy [give] yer some mo'ore knuckle. That's ahr it wo in them days, thi' weren't no other teachin' ways. So, Ah left school wiyaht [without] beein' able to read and write an' it wo' ohnny [only] when Ah wo' in Royal Marines that Ah' learnt. Ah'd sit an' Ah cun't [couldn't] write 'ome to mi Mam an' so one'r lads, owd YZ, hi wo an

Edinburgh lad, lived on S street, his a grandfAther nahr [now], hi took mi to one side an' hi learnt mi to read an' write so Ah could send a letter 'ome t' mi Mam an' Dad. Ah wo grateful to 'im. But even when Ah finished in Royal Marines an' went in Steelw'ks Ah wo still havin' to foller each word wi' mi finger an' it wo' ahr [our] lass whot 'elped mi then.

The insistence that brightness 'weren't in mi' exhibits the reasoning that Bourdieu's characterizes so well:

By awarding allegedly impartial qualifications . . . for socially conditioned aptitudes which it treats as unequal 'gifts', it [the school] transforms *de facto* inequalities into *de jure* ones and *economic and social* differences into *distinctions of quality*, and legitimates the transmission of the cultural heritage [the elite habitus]. In doing so, it is performing a confidence trick. Apart from enabling the elite to justify being what it is, the *ideology of giftedness*, the cornerstone of the whole educational and social system, helps to enclose the underprivileged classes in the roles which society has given them by making them see as natural inability things that are only a result of an inferior social status, and by persuading them that they owe their social fate . . . to their individual nature and their lack of gifts.   (Bourdieu 1974: 42)

And this testimony also shows that, in the thirty-five years that separate the two men, little has effectively changed, for many. There is little wonder that working class kids fare so badly, when school teaches them so completely that they lack ability and gifts, and reduces them to the essential traits through which they are perceived in the first instance: 'thick', and with it the other adjectives through which they comprehend their social essence: coarse, rough, low, vulgar:

X: Well working class do swear a lot, we are rough, what du thi expect us to be. It's no good gu'in on't' building site when tha drops sum'at on thi' foot an sayin' [*in posh voice*]'Oh dear'. Fuck that, I'll talk 'ow I want.

And this reduction of individuals to a pre-defined essence is the hallmark of racial and gender oppression, yet it is a process that is not consigned to the perception of racialized minorities,[19] it stands at the heart of society, particularly English society. As Bourdieu puts it:

the privileged classes of bourgeois society replace the difference between two cultures, products of history reproduced by education, with the basic difference between two natures, one nature naturally cultivated, and another nature naturally natural. Thus, the sanctification of culture and art . . . fulfils a vital function by contributing to the consecration of the social order. So that cultured people can believe in barbarism and persuade the barbarians of their own barbarity, it is necessary and sufficient for them to succeed in hiding both from themselves and from others the social conditions which make possible not only culture as a second nature, in which society locates human excellence, and which is experienced as a privilege of birth, but also the . . . legitimacy . . . of a particular definition of culture. Finally, for the ideological circle to be complete, it is sufficient that they derive the justification for their monopoly of the instruments of appropriation of cultural goods from an essentialist representation of the division of their society into barbarians and civilized people.   (Bourdieu 1990b: 111–12)

When the man in the previous testimony says 'what du thi expect' he connects conditions of existence and manner. He is, in a sense, asking that it be remembered that these people exist purely through markets in which they exist as sets of capacities, as agglomerations of motor-skills to do tasks that companies can't afford computers to do, as labour power. They have little to fall back upon except their capacity to work: this is the mode of practice through which they have some value as persons and which locates them in a network of working people. It seems therefore that the family and the school, which mediate a specific relation to certain forms of habitus, produce a relation, not only to certain forms of economic life, but that they reproduce a whole relation to the body that is part of the history of working class life. These primary conditions are the conditions of acquisition of the corporeal schema from which and in relation to which individuals must negotiate the world. As Merleau-Ponty puts it:

> to the extent that I can elaborate and extend my corporeal schema, to the extent that I acquire a better organized experience of my own body, to that very extent will my consciousness of my own body cease being a chaos in which I am submerged and lend itself to a transfer to others.   (Merleau-Ponty 1964: 118)

This corporeal schema is a 'conduct, a system of behaviour that aims at the world' (Merleau-Ponty 1964: 118). In perceiving a glance or an acknowledgement, we spontaneously realize an appropriate response which is brought forth from comportment, from the modality of our practice, from the patterning of our corporeal schema. Thus perception and comportment, or what Merleau-Ponty calls 'motility', are rooted in one another and root us irreducibly in one another, in particular communities. Spontaneous affinities arise from the deepest roots of the social processes of individuation and sociation. As Merleau-Ponty suggests:

> It is this fundamental correspondence between perception and motility – the power of perception to organise a motor conduct that *Gestalt* theorists have insisted on . . . This is what would be the function of mimesis, or mimicry, in its most fundamental and irreducible form.
>
> Sympathy would emerge from this. Sympathy does not presuppose a genuine distinction between self-consciousness and consciousness of the other but rather the absence of a distinction between the self and the other. It is the simple fact that I live in the facial expressions of the other, as I feel him living in mine.
>   (Merleau-Ponty 1964: 146)

The point about mimesis is that through performance we produce a postural schema that reproduces an already organized totality that renders a meaning, the performance of which we *feel* – 'sense' – incorporate into our repertoire of sensation; yet which we also spontaneously use, with varying degrees of consciousness, to weave sense into the personal and public space through which we move, comporting ourselves sensibly. Hence comportment has the character of physiognomic perception; it is an incarnate knowledge of feeling and sensation that, in a way, precedes conceptualization, subtends articulation. Through this, there are the grounds of a kind of pre-communication, which passes by 'postural impregnation' (Merleau-Ponty 1964: 118) from person to person and which influences our experience of comportment by providing the space of possible styles of corporeal schema, and, thus, our experience of the world as the determinate place of a determinate subject. The grounds of this pre-communication, of this initial sympathy, are ingrained in that delicate, unknowing dance that being plays upon the somatic grounds of personal existence, that mystical meeting place between individual incarnation and collective life, the 'total continuum made up of all the lived relations with others and the world' (Merleau-Ponty 1964: 140–1). It is through our coming to command progressively a more developed range of gestural and postural sets that we acquire a deepened capacity to appreciate the immanence of sense in the sensible as it emerges from an interplay on the border between being and the world, in the flesh as it assimilates humanity. This is why Merleau-Ponty says it 'is characteristic of cultural gestures to awaken in all others at least an echo if not a consonance' (Merleau-Ponty 1973: 94). The immanence of sense coheres for us through our primary sensory experience of the specific grounds of acculturation, and we *feel* the deeper sense of human significance in accord with our primary position. Through it, things, people, experiences, resonate within a range located by the poles of comfort and security and an anxious vulnerability born of estrangement and threat. Hence certain spaces and modes of address mortify, leaving the flesh cold, gripped by its fixedness in an objectivity born of the gesturing comportment of other. Whilst among our own we experience gestures which seem to consecrate and we feel pulled, momentarily, towards the shores of the islands of existence in which our humanity has its possibility. We need to be aware of the founding of individual experience in the intercorporeality of embodied subjects who, living through the same conditions, come to share a way of being that has a certain generality (which may be out-run by the grounds of individuation that it also permits), that shapes, fundamentally, their relationship to the world and to others. As Bourdieu suggests:

the social relations objectified in familiar objects, in their luxury or poverty, their 'distinction' or 'vulgarity', their 'beauty' or 'ugliness', impress themselves through bodily experiences which may be as profoundly unconscious as the quiet caress of beige carpets or the thin clamminess of tattered, garish linoleum.

(Bourdieu 1984: 77)

Primary conditions of existence, social relations objectified in places, objects and individuals, are insensibly internalized and become part of the attitude to existence that one's comportment shows. Position, the totality of relations that constitutes each individual's perceptual existence is sedimented in the body, not only through certain tastes, or incorporated schemes of perception and appreciation which result in objectively classifiable practices and distinctive signs that manifest a perceptible 'life style', but also at the deepest and most primitive levels of the body's need for certain forms of physical experience, for certain forms of 'pure practice without theory', in Durkheim's sense. Through the practical interactions of the primary milieu, the life of the phenomenal body is gradually acquired and it is generatively, though often unknowingly, productive of the world which it presupposes and aims at through the range of the habit-body and the particular motor-gestural skills that are the body's conditions of comportment and its immersion in a meaningful world. This is why Merleau-Ponty suggests:

What 'precedes' intersubjective life cannot be numerically distinguished from it, precisely because at this level there is neither individuation nor numerical distinction. The constitution of the others does not come after that of the body; others and my body are born together from the original ecstasy. The corporeality to which the primordial thing belongs is more corporeality in general.

(Merleau-Ponty 1995: 174)

Our individual needs and desires emerge from a shared pre-personal realm that is assimilated through intimate familiarity with dispositions we acquire through the postural impregnation involved in the locations in which we live. As Levin puts it:

bodily attitudes of others gradually inhabit my own body simultaneously shaping me in their own image and carrying forward my body's own implicately ordered needs.   (Levin 1990: 39)

This mimesis, 'always contains . . . something ineffable . . . something which communicates, that is, from body to body, like the rhythm of music or the flavour of colours . . . falling short of words and concepts' (Bourdieu 1984: 80) and it roots us in a familiar world through the generative dispositional schemata, embodied, through which we realize our existence. The body is connected, rooted to its own conditions of production and acquisition and by this to cultural realms and the categories of flesh that realize and embody those experiences. Through those realms and those people, through the re-connection felt in physiognomic perception – the consecration of our gestures, postures and tastes – we experience the deep sense the body has of the familiar, and of its need to feel certain states because they are part of its felt, moment-to-moment sense of its place in the world, part of its deepest origins in primary relations that give to our perceptions that deep texture of affective hue that makes the sense of life both personal and social.

This 'great unending experience, which is given us, a knowing of the world' (Rilke 1993: 36) that perception is, is structured by what we are as agents and this is given in the phenomenal field as it is constituted through comportment which is incorporated through the social fields through which we move, along the life-course, and this is inescapably mediated by the influence of structural phenomena on the constitution of the spaces in which we live. This sense the body has of the familiar and the acquisition of tastes is a primal underpinning of cultural life, yet it operates, for the most part, purely practically; an orienting system of valuation, of persons and things acquired as a sense of a native world based in the indelible marks of infancy and childhood. It is a familiarity realized in dispositions so deep that it is how the body feels its way through the world, attracted here, repulsed there (liked here, rejected there), partaking of this and not that. Tastes and forms of pleasure, that are acquired with a relation to the body that issues out of a socially mediated relation to the world, are part of the phenomenal body's sense of itself, a sense forged in the mutual intercorporeality of agent and immediate community that amounts to a pre-conscious membership of a group condemned to finding pleasure in the pure, unmediated pleasures of the body; to pure practices because their relation to the culture enshrined in the education system means their exclusion from the instruments of perception that would make possible the founding of an intersubjective realm that enjoyed a greater freedom from the fundamental phenomenal meaning of occurrent objects. However, this pleasure in the domain of the phenomenally primordial, almost purely somatic, this incorporation of the being of technology into the treatment of the body as mechanism, is manifest in the need to treat the body ascetically in the routinized, repetitive, disciplined manner reflected in articulations like, 'Oh Ah just love to lift big weights', 'Ah need to feel tired at end o' day', 'Ah love that feeling o'r aching in thi muscles when tha's trained', and 'Ah'd rather 'ave a job, like, using my hands, and my body than just mi mind. You feel like ye'v earned thi money mo'ore when tha's cum 'ome wi thi shoulders aching an' wot 'ave yer. That's 'ow Ahr think.' This is class as flesh. A desire for the musculature of the body, for the tissue and sinew, to feel a certain way; a sense of the body that relates to the social context that is the referential-whole, the grounds of possibility of this deep-seated experience of this desire that is learned through a multitude of insignificant calls to order exhorted by an originating milieu in which habits towards leisure, time and tastes are learned and progressively confirmed. Expressed here, is a class condition transmuted into desire, into a need for the experiences that reproduce the conditions of acquisition of these dispositions. This circle is most clearly manifest in friendships in which dispositions are mutually reinforced. This is history living itself out. Even in changed financial conditions, the deep forms of the habitus remain. As the words of one unemployed Rotherham man who won £1.5 million on the lottery illustrate: 'It's unreal. You can't know what it's like. There's not a buzz in drinking now because us haven't earned it. It's taken some sinking in, 'as that.' Moreover this man went and worked on scaffolding to earn £120 and when asked why he would bother to work answered 'It's the buzz. I could lie here drinking all day and there's no buzz in that. But if someone comes up with work, I'm going to do it 'cause I must do something. I'm like a kid with the buzz of it' (Garner 1995). It is a revealing paradox that working people come to long for an experience that they find deeply alienating: 'fucking 'orrible'; 'I 'ate work'; 'look at me, I'm stuck in't steel w'ks fo' next thi'ty year. I wish I could'a bin better mentally, so I could'a gone to college or somat' and 'I fuckin' 'ate it in pit. Ten mo'ore years an I wanna be out, buy an house wi' mi redundancy. It's fuckin' me up.' Bourdieu explains this objectivity of the subjective as issuing from:

the dialectical relationship that is established between the regularities of the material universe of properties and the classificatory schemes of the *habitus*, that product of the regularities of the social world for which and through which there *is* a social world. It is in the dialectic between class conditions and 'class sense', between the 'objective' conditions recorded in distributions and the structuring dispositions, themselves structured by these conditions, that is, in accordance with the distributions, that the continuous structure of the distributions reappears, now transfigured and misrecognizable, in the discontinuous structure of hierarchised life-styles and in the representations and recognitions that arise from misrecognition of their objective truth. (Bourdieu 1990a: 140)

I have tried to illuminate how it is that conditions of existence enter into the grounds of subjectivity as part of the intercorporeal basis of our individuation within communities built on a pre-personal similarity exhibited and experienced through perceptions which are infused with the affective sense of the world as it shows up for these people through the ways that world is mediated by position. I have tried to show that working people's relation to the body is the basis of a range of dispositions, covered by the notions of 'attitudes' and 'values', that are manifest in the modality of their practices, in their way of talking or laughing, eating or walking; a whole cosmology that is expressive of the class. Moreover, the foundations of this relation are the conditions of cultural dispropriation that I have tried to describe in this chapter; in which their culture is devalued, and where they are excluded from the instruments of perception and expression through which they might realize and objectify their condition and secure for themselves a life in which they could exist as more than useful bodies. As those speaking of their lack of intelligence demonstrated, in the absence of intellectual 'gifts' they are aware that they have to reconcile themselves to a future of hard work and extreme vulnerability. A vulnerability one man captured with great force:

Thi finished us at w'k today.
S: Yer joking!
Naow. We wo w'king away and gaffa's cem [came] in and said, 'rait lads, get yer coats an' stuff and gu to canteen, yer not coming back to shop floor again.' So we got 's stuff and went to canteen and the just said 'that's it lads, yer finished. Don't bother coming in tomorrow, ye'll be paid for it but yer done nahr.' So that's it.
S: We're so fuckin vulnerable nahr . . .
Oh aye, that's ow it is nahr, nowt's fuckin' safe, nobdi's secure. Thi just play wi' yer life. It's freetnin' really. It's third bastard job I've had that's folded in last five year. I mean ahr [our] union man's tried to get this and that for us bu thi just walk all ovver yer. Thi' walk all ovver everybody nahr. Thi's nowt we can do at all. I mean, if yer working class tha's gorra w'k, thi's no other way. We've just gotta w'k, it's ohnny way we can get a livin'.

In these conditions there can be little wonder that working class men's[20] comportment seems to emblematize a form of rugged masculinity that shuns physical pain and sentimentality and which values the hardness and strength of the body.[21] In their conditions, they have to be able to turn their hand to as many manual jobs as they can in order to survive in a labour market in which they are just 'hands' and infinitely replaceable. The strategy behind getting 'a trade', as an adaptation to present economic conditions came through in one man's words about his advice to his twenty-five-year old son:

X: I mean, ahr Y, 'is got nowt to look forrard [forward] to all hi's life nahr. I asked 'im if he got a pay rise. He ses thi' got two per cent. I've told 'im to get a trade, to gu [go] an' du plumbing at college, I mean that way if anybody ses 'I need a bathroom puttin' in', he can du it. I mean, fair enough, it's not good work n' nowt [nothing] but it's cash in 'and [hand] befo'or tax man get's 'is [his] 'ands on it an' it's sumat i' [he] can du if i' loises 'is job. Ah mean, if tha loses thi' job, if tha like thee[22] tha fucked, tha ca't gu t' w'k; tha ca't get n' money but if tha's got'a trade, if tha' can turn thi' 'and t' different things, tha' can allous get by on bit's fiddle jobs. Tha'll not mek much, Ah know, enough fo' a ne'et aht, or kids a pair o'r shoes but it's money. Tha knows?

The point is that prestigious jobs require access to the prestigious spaces, an access 'bought' with symbolic and cultural capital. Being working class, even with elite qualifications, one's capital may be devalued by one's bodily hexis. This man's point is that whilst the ubiquity of the skills devalues them and ensures economic vulnerability, they are also skills that can, in these cultures, bring in some 'pin money'. Bearing in mind the reliance of the bourgeois and petit-bourgeois family on the education system and the ideology of giftedness for their social reproduction, we might see in the working class's dispositions of toughness and 'handiness', an equivalence to the reliance of the bourgeois fractions upon their 'intelligence' and cultural goodwill. Growing up working class and effete is like growing up petit-bourgeois and stupid. The working class family, given the referential whole that frames its cultural conditions, follows the social logic embedded in their position and transmits a culture that values what is seen as an innate capacity to labour, the essence of a being that labours – 'Tha's gorra be born to graft' as one sage remarked. The following exchange, where one man points out another in the near distance, makes clear the essentialist, innatist model of competence and being through which those born to work understand their fate:

M: Tha sees that lad the'er wi' 'is back to yer, 'im wi' flat cap on?
I: Ahr [yes].
M: That lad 'is one'r the world's grafters. Bahr! Fuckin' ell, *ahr*! When God put 'im on Earth, hi med [made] 'im as a worker. Hi wo' one'r 'ardest w'kin', strongest lads 'ave ever seen or w'ked wi. Fuckin' 'ell, ahr! That lad *could* graft! Ahr, hi *wo'* a grafter.

As this exchange makes clear, 'that lad could fucking graft' is praise indeed.
It is too easy to pathologize such dispositions and find them ridiculous. One needs to remember that a species of capital, a source of respect, depends upon the existence of a field in which possession of the relevant characteristics and competences allows one to be respected, '*capital does not exist and function except in relation to a field*' (Bourdieu and Wacquant 1992: 101). Many working class men exist in a world in which 'not pulling thi weight' will mean derision and the sack. One man told me a fascinating story, passed down from his father who was a miner, that illustrated the historical rootedness of this desire to be a 'big strong lad':

X: Ah can't remember whether mi Dad went dahn [down] at thirteen or fourteen but i' [he] went straight down. He din't gu to Manvers fo' six months training or anything, he wo dahn. And pullin' the weight, as well, within a week or two. And it weren't anything like it was nahr [now], or it wo a few years ago, with like, you know, little trains tekkin' [taking] yer two and three miles out, yer 'ad to crawl it, that wo it, no messin' abaht [about] and thi wo workin' with picks and shovels. But it sounds horrific and it sounds as if yer makin' it. When yer talk about it today it sounds as if yer makin' it [S: Ye it does. Ye, absolutely.] yer can't tell the story of just 'ow hard it wer' but mi Dad'd tell yer that they'd do those things and at weekends, in the holiday time what thi'd do is, er . . . Maltby Craggs is actually well known as a holiday area, cos [because] ye'd ohnny [only] get one or two days, yer din't get a week's holiday, ye din't get two weeks holiday an things like that, ermm, ye'd get me'bi [maybe] odd day or a weekend me'bi an' thi'd [they would]'ave like a sports day and all compete against each other. So thi wo just as physical, in fact even more so, on the' holiday days because they actually 'ad somethin' to prove, so once thi got past the'r teenage years, so once thi got past twenny five and goo'in up to thirty thi'd stop, right and that's when thi din't want to do anything but prior to that, what thi ad to do was to prove that thi [they] wo up to it because, as young men, they 'ad to prove that thi wo physical enough and fit enough to do the job because the men who wo working down the pit would say 'no, he cum last in every race, he allous cums last in every race' so he can't be phys-ical enough to keep up wi' us, cos they earned money on ahr [how] much thi [they] dug out. Thi din't get a wage, they earned the money on 'ow much thi dug out so wot thi wo looking for is who wo winning all races, so the race and the holiday thing was and all this physical thing wasn't about [S: Y said that last night.] and in those days, fifty or sixty years ago it was about proving yer worth. Cos if you wo winning races what wo 'appenin' was that the top team wo tranna buy yer. They wanted the young chap, the little lad, who wo winning all't races, thi wanted a fit young lad, cos they wanted 'im on't shovel, the more thi shovelled aht [out] the mo'ore thi got paid and thi also din't get paid thi din't work to a wage counter thi used to. What 'appened wo that the gang leader got paid and't gang leader then paid everyone else aht, do yer see what I mean?

If we bear in mind what Bourdieu tells us about the habitus, that in it, past, present and future intersect and interpenetrate one another so that the past remains sedimented in the life of the socialized body, then we can see that here we have social conditions structured by necessity producing a lived tradition, a tradition that lives on through the desire to build a strong powerful body, a necessity that produces a pleasure in the strength, endu-rance and stoicism of the body, and which fosters an instrumental, quasi-mechanistic relation to the body. The body as medium for producing effects in its own structure, its tissue, muscle and sinew, the body as tool of a labouring intent rather than the body as an end of pleasure-in-itself.

This relation is expressed most clearly in the two great proletarian pas-times of weight-training and boxing. The first works on the physiology of the body to create the strength of the labouring body, the other trains the body to know its space through a medium of offence and defence: in order to effect a transformation in somatic knowledge that realizes the body as a potential weapon. These forms of producing the body, of *existing* oneself *through* a mode of comporting the socialized body, is a way of instating, unconsciously, forms of capital attuned to the fields to which one's existence is tied. These are existential practices, ways of incorporating and instating schemes of classification, which the body's comportment is attuned to, and which allow one to exist in the living look of others: that is, to leap into existence through the benefits that accrue from being possessed of effective forms of capital, what we colloquially call 'having a life'. Being a 'big strong lad' or 'a good grafter' is a sure mark of people who have been reduced to little because only in conditions of scarcity and the absence of other forms of competence could capacity to work with one's body be a form of capital, a difference that made a difference. That it is, is testified to by one man speaking about what it meant to be known as a 'good grafter':

X: Na' thi' other thing abaht [about] bein' a good grafter is that it was actually a ticket, no it won't a ticket it wo a status [S: Ye, well that's wot Y wo on wi.] and it wo' actually valuable. It wo valuable status bein' known as a good grafta cos you could be favoured in all sorts of ways socially, so people e'd se, 'Ahr, but 'is this and 'is that' and 'he did this' and 'he did that' and 'yer'll never guess wot 'e did last week' but *'he's a good grafta yer know'* [S: Ye, that's wot J wo gettin' at.] and it actually depended, and it allous tops off, 'a good grafta' and a 'good lad' and a 'good grafta' and a 'good lad' are synonymous really, but the 'good lad' has extra but it always tops off, it actually seems to cancel out a lot'a the negatives. So this guy might'a been a bastard, he might'a bi'n an absolute bully, he might'a bi'n an absolute sort of totally insensitive person but [*voice changes to imitate the meaning of the phrase*] *'he wo a good grafta'*. Now the good lad is something different altogether. Now thi's a lot extra that gu's into being a 'good lad' [S: What do yer think gu's into bein' a good lad then? Cos yer still get a lot'a that dun't yer?] A good lad gi's yer a quid when tha's got nowt. Ye? Good lad gi's yer a lift when he knows that yer stuck. Good lad remembers that . . . ermm, that your lass 'as bi'n in fo' an operation 'Ah did tha get on then?' cos he wun't se, 'ah did yer missus gu on wi operation?', good lad'd se: 'Ah did yer gu on wi kids while your lass wo in hospital, eh? It must'a bi'n a pain in arse.' Na that's a good lad.

Clearly, here, identity, the lived categories realized by these people, the forms of value that show-up in this world, emerge from a constant encounter, across the dimensions of their lives, with work and lack of money. Bourdieu speaks of 'the countless acts of diffuse inculcation through which the body and the world tend to be set in order' (Bourdieu 1990a: 78) and he goes on:

Everything takes place as if the *habitus* forged coherence and necessity out of accident and contingency; as if it managed to unify the effects of the social necessity undergone from childhood . . . In a society divided into classes, all the products of a given agent, by an essential overdetermination, speak inseparably and simultaneously of his/her class – or, more precisely, his/her position and rising or falling trajectory within the social structure – and of his/her body – or, more precisely, of all the properties, always socially qualified, of which he/she is the bearer; sexual ones, of course, but also physical properties that are praised, like strength or beauty, or stigmatized.   (Bourdieu 1990a: 79)

In this milieu, the physical properties required, historically, by this position have clearly become part of the embodied cosmology of the social; part of the taxonomies of value and experience, in the midst of which individuals negotiate a way of being and existing. The dispositions they inscribe and embody, are the very conditions for the generation of the forms through which they realize themselves and these are, at point of origin, touched, influenced and affected by the social conditions of this position, relationally defined in terms of the processes we have looked at. Symbolic violence, the '*violence which is exercised upon a social agent with his or her complicity*' (Bourdieu and Wacquant 1992: 168) is thus at the heart of these people's acceptance of the being they inscribe, because they understand themselves in relation to a position that they see themselves as biologically, innately, essentially, given to do. In relation to the social fields through which they come to this understanding carried in comportment, felt and lived at the very deepest levels of affective-somatic being, the fundamental relations of this nation-state are naturalized, corporealized and able to be unknowingly actualized throughout the social world simultaneously.

This is why rights and duties seldom touch the lives of the dominated, because even where they do not acquiesce comfortably, which they never do, they are present to less than they know, and they give up more than they have a right to, because in the end no one can take what can only be given freely. The demands of the social world are such that to survive, the dominated must take up, realize, embody, categories of perception (understood as an already acquired bodily skill) that are constitutive of their identity and yet which have life-long effects for their experience of social presence, personal intimacy and the full extent of all that is meant by the idea of 'quality of life'.

How could being known as a 'good grafter' be anything other than a dominated identity; a form of being realized in the flesh and dependent upon a permanent daily incarnation of the grim duty of 'luggin' thi bollocks aht' in order to satisfy the exigencies of punitive work-relations and demands upon companions; that is, the taking up in one's physiognomy of an identity that economic conditions demand one must be? Deprivation, inequality, domination, poverty, are processes based in the way that social categories are realized, embodied, actualized through the being-in-the-world of body-subjects. Anyone interested in such processes would do well to labour after understanding the depth and terror involved in what ought to be insignificant details of manner and speech, and try to understand what is really involved in the realm of invisible, unsaid, never-constituted silent injunctions that call so many bodies to order, back to their objective social being as this is inscribed through the realized hierarchy of tastes, life-styles and body through which we all know our deepest truth and value. As Bourdieu puts it:

nothing is further removed from an act of cognition, as conceived by the intellectu-alist tradition, than this sense of the social structure, which as is so well put by the word *taste* – simultaneously the 'faculty of perceiving flavours' and 'the capacity to discern aesthetic values' – is social necessity made second nature, turned into mus-cular patterns and bodily automatisms. Everything takes place as if the social con-ditionings linked to to a social condition tended to inscribe the relation to the social world in a lasting, generalized relation to one's own body, a way of bearing one's body, presenting it to others, moving it, making space for it, which gives the body its social physiognomy. Bodily hexis, a basic dimension of the sense of social orien-tation, is a practical way of experiencing and expressing one's own sense of social value. One's relationship to the social world and to one's proper place in it is never more clearly expressed than in the space and time one feels entitled to take from others; more precisely, in the space one claims with one's body in physical space, through a bearing and gestures that are self-assured or reserved, expansive or con-stricted ('presence' or 'insignificance') and with one's speech in time, through the interaction time one appropriates and the self-assured or aggressive, careless or unconscious way one appropriates it.

There is no better image of the logic of socialization, which treats the body as a 'memory-jogger', than those complexes of gestures, postures and words – simple interjections or favourite clichés – which only have to be slipped into, like a theatri-cal costume, to awaken, by the evocative power of bodily mimesis, a universe of ready-made feelings and experiences. The elementary actions of bodily gymnastics, especially the specifically sexual, biologically pre-constructed aspect of it, charged with social meanings and values, function as the most basic of metaphors, capable of evoking a whole relationship to the world, 'lofty' or 'submissive', 'expansive' or 'narrow', and through it a whole world. The practical 'choices' of the sense of social orientation no more presuppose a representation of the range of possibilities than does the choice of phonemes; these enacted choices imply no acts of choosing. The logocentrism and intellectualism of intellectuals, combined with the prejudice inherent in the science which takes as its object the psyche, the soul, the mind, con-sciousness, representations, not to mention the petit-bourgeois pretension to the status of 'person', have prevented us from seeing that, as Leibniz put it, 'we are auto-motons in three-quarters of what we do', and that the ultimate values, as they are called, are never anything other than the primary, primitive dispositions of the body, 'visceral' tastes and distastes, in which the group's most vital interests are embedded, the things on which one is prepared to stake one's own and other people's bodies.   (Bourdieu 1984: 474.)

This relation to one's body as mediator of our relation to others and the social realm is manifest in the testimony. Even though the daily events that constitute the everyday existence of the social structures through which we exist are seldom objectified in consciousness, the testimony shows from the silence that engulfs these lives, a silence emerging naturally from lives bereft of the co-ordinates and culture to describe itself. One can see something of what Wittgenstein might have meant when he suggested, 'the unspeakable is – unspeakably – *contained* in what is spoken' (Wittgenstein quoted in Barrett 1988: 392). The transcription is haunted by the effects of a symbolic violence that has been the very condition of these forms of self-hood, even where the narration doesn't situate the speaker as victim or subject. Yet the testimony makes clear that the conditions of becoming what one has to be are conditions of humiliation, struggle, degradation and shame. Becoming unemployed, or doing any of the jobs that working class people do, involves coming to inhabit one's position amidst an all-pervasive symbolic violence that means one comes to live amidst an obscure forboding founded in the insecurities and stigmatization of a fractured form of being, a life-course that, to varying degrees is, damaged.

In the context of a comportment that negotiates the conditions of its value on the basis of utility and not upon any essential dignity or value of the person in the flesh, one would expect working class life to be suffused with a moral texture felt and lived in the insignificant invisible details of bearing and in aspects of speech. Traditionally, this has always been so, and, although the decline of the public rituals through which respect was marked has gone hand in hand with the decay of the form of life that was tied to the dispositions of mass employment in traditional industry, one can still sense the marking of respects that belong to non-respected groups and hear around one, as the testimony shows, the attempted resolution of issues that emerge from this location in the moral space of a social structure. However, this does not take the form of a topology of rank, but of a practical sense of one's *type* of being, of the conditions of life (vulnerability; that one will do certain types of work and not others; that one belongs in certain spaces and not others; etc.); a felt sense of belonging to a certain world, and yet, within that, of there being obligations to others: an ethos that values certain characteristics in speech and action that embody honesty and a commitment to values that the group embodies; values of commonality, that meant, even if one were blessed with a well-paying job, one should not seek to distinguish oneself and, instead, should maintain this style of being as a mark of respect to the form of being and the conditions that produce it.

Charles Taylor has suggested that we understand selves as beings that exist amidst a space of concerns or questions that form part of the framework or constitutive horizon in which they must orientate themselves: 'To know who I am is a species of knowing where I stand . . . our discussion of identity indicates . . . that it belongs to human agency to exist in a space of questions about strongly valued goods' (Taylor 1989a: 30). And he goes on to emphasize the need to make sense of life as a narrative: 'this sense of the good has to be woven into my understanding of my life as an unfolding story. But this is to state another basic condition of making sense of ourselves, that we grasp our lives in a *narrative*' (Taylor 1989a: 47). In order to recognize the self-hood of these people, the moral contours of the social space in which they orient themselves, we clearly need some way of understanding how their self-understanding is constrained by the cultural conditions that we have looked at. Moreover, to the extent that the constitutive horizons of their self-hood are given in naturalistic understandings of their self and competence, and whilst the sense of their world is experienced through menial work and powerlessness, we need forms of thought that allow us to understand damaged lives. If selves are moral projects, then conditions which lead to damaged self-understandings must also be moral violations. And one would expect the results of such violations to extend beyond straightforward perceptions and to lodge themselves at the heart of the phenomenal body, at the heart of the body-subject, and for the repercussions to have a kind of cumulative existential significance throughout the dimensions of individuals' lives. And this is surely what one sees in working class areas. It is present throughout much of the testimony in this work which is witness to the uneasy, unreconciled understandings that diminished selves produce in the face of the confusion involved in being located in this way. As I have tried to show, even in such stark conditions, the resources and conditions for reaching a narrative resolution of their condition are absent. And we have seen that the sense of the space of intelligibility in which self-hood is constituted is part of a moral space that is inseparable from a social structure of bodies, properties, practices and objects in which their location leaves them negotiating daily with a structure of value in which they exist towards the negative pole. In the face of these, we thus have a duty to remember that life in the moral universe of personhood and civil society is not simply about locating oneself in a space of qualitative distinctions in which one settles one's worth, but that, for many, identity is given in terms that are not negotiable, or in terms that are negotiable only in someone else's terms. That for the most dominated, the essence they are understood to possess mediates their social presence and existence in ways that are far more powerful than any personal characteristics. That issues of personal worth, for others and to ourselves, are tightly connected to the position we occupy in the social universe (and to what that occupation means in terms of comportment):

Doomed to death, that end which cannot be taken as an end, man is a being without a reason for being. It is society, and society alone, which dispenses, to different degrees, the justifications and reasons for existing; it is society which, by producing the affairs or positions that are said to be 'important', produces the acts and agents that are judged to be 'important', for themselves and for the others – characters objectively and subjectively assured of their value and thus liberated from indifference and insignificance. There is, whatever Marx may say, a philosophy of poverty, which is closer to the desolation of the tramp-like and derisory old men of Beckett than to the voluntarist optimism traditionally associated with progressive thought. Pascal spoke of the 'misery of man without God'. One might rather posit the 'misery of man without mission or social consecration'. Indeed, without going as far as to say, with Durkheim, 'Society is God', I would say: God is only ever obtained from society, which alone has the power to justify you, to liberate you from facticity, contingency and absurdity; but – and this is doubtless the fundamental antinomy – only in a differential, distinctive way: every form of the sacred has its profane complement, all distinction generates its own vulgarity, and the competition for a social life that will be known and recognized, which will free you from insignificance, is a struggle to the death for symbolic life and death. 'To quote', say the Kabyles, 'is to bring back to life'. The judgement of others is the last judgement; and social exclusion is the concrete form of hell and damnation. It is also because man is a God unto man that man is a wolf unto man.

  Especially where they are adepts of an eschatological philosophy of history, sociologists feel socially mandated, and mandated to give meaning, to explain, even to set in order and assign aims and objectives. Thus they are not the best placed to understand the misery of men without social qualities, whether we are talking about the tragic resignation of old people abandoned to the social death of hospitals and hospices, about the silent submission of the unemployed or the desperate violence of those adolescents who seek in action reduced to infraction a means of acceding to a recognized form of social existence.   (Bourdieu 1990c: 196–7.)

The 'misery of man without mission or social consecration', the silent, uneasy worthlessness of people objectively assured of their subjective worthlessness, of their lacking recognized, valued capacities that would make of them people worthy of more than they have to put up with, lends to such groups the referential-whole, the 'inherited background', that working class life issues from. This is the unspoken space they share; the totality of conditions they share in experience and which they recognize (as revealing the same apprehension or sense of the world) in the embodied responses of others. Responses that may have nothing to do with respect but which reveal a commonality that is all that is demanded as a form of respect because it amounts to a stand on what existence is within this country, an unconscious form of honour.

This is a practical sense carried in comportment, an inter-corporeal subjectivity, dense with an affective sense that emerges from the structures that we have looked at, and which continually generates manners of interaction, a way of practising the practices that characterize these people's lives. This is a grounding of moral 'intuitions' in practically operative patterns of response and gesture; 'values', for want of a better word, 'made body' through experience of this structural position and locality. This sense is not well rendered by Taylor's insights. What is apparent is that it is inappropriate to analyse these people's coming-into-being, through a vocabulary that emphasizes the role of discursive consciousness in a process whereby a self comes to orient itself to questions of categoric value. Rather, these people grow up amidst a sense of values inscribed in the comportment demanded by the exigencies of a world which demands of them a certain relation to embodiment and humanity. A world in which it is best to maintain a purely practical orientation in order to foreclose on the potential for pathological relations to self that may arise if the seat of identity becomes too extensively linguistically constituted. It is this that gives working class areas a coherent sense, so seldom articulated, though one finds it exhibited throughout the spaces that they inhabit.

These embodied values amount to a set of practical commitments, a coherent sense, that operates purely practically, through a sense of initial sympathy or distrust, of what, where and who is appropriate that is manifest, for instance, in their distrust of students and alternative identities generally, which they practically understand the symbolic logic of. One man explained his dislike for college as: 'Just, I dun't know, the freaky types, purple hair and the'r scruffy clothes and I couldn't handle them.' A deep-seated distrust and discomfort that is based in a recognition of the distinction-strategies generally pursued by students, as well as in a recognition of the privileged position that students occupy. This dislike was well articulated by one former nightclub doorman:

X: Students, Ahr dun't fuckin' like 'em. Ahr remember student night up at Y's [a nightclub]. Ah mean, Ah've w'ked do'ors all ovva Sheffield an' worst night's t' w'k wo student nights. Ah've never in mi born days met a group a people more ignorant, arrogant as what they are. Normal punters 'll queue up an' the'r rait civil to yer. But them, the'r *pushin'* an' *shovin'* all bastard time. Ah once saw one woman fall ovva an' thi' wo tramplin' on 'er, thi' nivver tried to 'elp 'er up. Ay 'ad to gu' an' get mi baseball bat aht'on back to fuckin' mek 'em behave an' 'elp er up. An' what fuckin' gets me is thi' get all this cheap entrance and cheap beer just cos the'r students an' normal punters 'ave to pay full price at weekends. An' students allous seem to 'ave mo'ore money, thi' get cheap travel an all so'orts what, se' [say], unemployed people can't get an' the'r miles better off than them . . .

Such utterance exhibits the practical mastery:

of distributions which makes it possible to sense or intuit what is likely (or unlikely) to befall – and therefore befit – an individual occupying a given position in social space. It functions as a sort of social orientation, a 'sense of one's place', guiding the occupants of a given place in social space towards the social positions adjusted to their properties, and towards the practices or goods which befit the occupants of that position. It implies a practical anticipation of what the social meaning and value of the chosen practice or thing will probably be.   (Bourdieu 1984: 467)

The sense of place is exhibited in articulations like this from one young woman:

X: Ah know it's shit rahnd 'ere but Ah'm a Rother'am person, Ah cun't [could not] live anywhe'er else Ah dun't think. Ah know thi's nowt 'ere but it's where Ah belong, gu'in' dahn [down] local t' watch match, Ah dun't know why, but Ah can't imagine livin' any other way.

There is, then, a class sense, part of a relation to the body and world that emerges from this position, which is a relation to class deposited in the deep-seated corporeal dispositions in which the working class lives without necessarily articulating itself as such. This sense pervades the surface of social life and is something of which individuals' bodily, practical sense is immediately aware; it orients individuals in social space. This sense is manifest throughout all the dimensions of their lives and is most obvious in the judgements that make it articulate. This sense, acquired through the prolonged, situated incorporation of the fundamental structures of the society manifest in the sites of their primary milieu, means that individuals come to share schemes of perception and appreciation, embedding:

what some would mistakenly call *values* in the most automatic gestures or the apparently most insignificant techniques of the body . . . and engage the most fundamental principles of construction and evaluation of the social world.
                                                                         (Bourdieu 1984: 466)

So that it can be sufficient to sit and say: 'Thi' used to be fifteen thousand men w'kin' at ahr place. Thi's less than two thasand nahr', without ever needing to argue over the ethical principles of the judgement. They share the injustices of this world and little needs to be explicated in consciousness; speech emerges from the relation to the world their body mediates and from the injustice involved in conditions that inscribe this relation within the corporeality they intersubjectively realize.

Hence the immediacy of a world that is so urgent in its exigencies is contained in the immediacy of speech constituted around an expressive need to articulate the frustrations and humiliations of this life. A need emerging from the deep primary sense the flesh has of its indignity and injustice that renders euphemization and an interest in the heightening of intermediate values inappropriate to the expressive interest embedded in their position. It is common in exchanges for this involvement with the sense of the world to be exhibited in a kind of perspective-taking; a reciprocity of empathy that is based in a reversibility of perspective that originates in the shared position that the position-taking affirms. This position-taking and the reversibility that it manifests are part of a sharing of the primal sense the world has for these people and it is condensed into a wisdom, practically taught through the situations narrated in speech about work; unemployment; the Department of Social Security; family and personal matters. All of which manifest a coherent ethical sense through which individuals can come to inhabit or dwell in the world in a particular way. It is as though the tales of everyday injustice invite one to realize and share the system of classification and appreciation that generates the moral of the stories; such that individuals can come to share the fundamental judgements of the group. Yet the power of the tales comes from the fact that they emerge from the on-going rounds of life, and in their force they contain a normative surplus of meaning which is constantly referring beyond the individual narrator, as a solitary person, to the position they share with those who participate in the narration and who share the sense of injustice that the story highlights.

In this light, we might see much of the testimony of this chapter as illustrating the need to resolve in some way a personal need that Rom Harré highlights: 'the basic problem for a person in society is to be recognized as of worth' (Harré 1979). He continues by suggesting that human beings are consistently 'seeking out occasions for acquiring respect while risking pity or disdain, and they may find these occasions in almost any social activities' (Harré 1979: 25). Human beings thus live with the constant risk of 'loss of dignity, of humiliation, and expressive failure', and all of our lives are punctuated by 'success and failures in coping with occasions of hazard' (Harré 1979: 24), where 'an occasion of hazard is a social event in which persons can gain respect by risking contempt' (Harré 1979: 312). Yet, as Bourdieu demonstrates, we are not situated equally with regard to the key institutions and locations that are valued, and many risk far more from an already degraded position and confront hazards in which there is much degradation and loss of dignity with little or no opportunity for self-esteem. For too many, life is a daily encounter with hazards in which they internalize much contempt, and in which there is nothing to be won in a society in which so many are excluded from socially consecrated forms of being, from life-styles that allow for something more than the degraded forms of those with no objective value. In Harré's terms, many exist excluded from the dominant sources of value, and its natural result is a downward 'moral career' and unexemplary biographies through failure in hazardous situations. Harré suggests that failure 'is defined reciprocally to the success from which one gains respect and dignity, and it is marked by humiliation. The experience of humiliation is the reciprocal of the maintenance of dignity' (Harré 1979: 25). Yet, as Bourdieu's work demonstrates, the relation is not simply logical and internal, it is worked out in the social world between the distinguished and the vulgar; between the two relations to culture that produce esteemed people of wealth and culture and the abject vagrants who emerge so naturally from these processes of abjection that have for generations produced the English working class.

In the context, however, of a life which involves daily hazards in which one's self-esteem is strung between precarious and generally degrading work and the social limbo of unemployment, repeated conversations about the events of the week might be seen as attempts to resolve perplexity and ambivalence; as attempts to find some peace through the shared description of events and interactions, in which one knows that the people present will position themselves by imagining being in one's position. Importantly, they share the forms of experience, understood in terms of biography and trajectory, and thus understand the anxiety involved in this relation to the situation. They are part of a matrix that works like a touchstone to reality, so that the confused can find reassurance that their experience is not simply their own; that they have not strayed too far beyond the passable limits of sanity; that their perceptions are grounded in the obscure processes of a disembedded social realm. The exchanges are a way to seek solace, a way of momentarily absolving the self of the burden of Class's daily hidden injuries. It is a practical discourse that is, at its root, moral in that it is about fulfilling the desire for presence, for existence to others as an end in oneself and not merely a means for the fulfilment of others' ends or the anonymity and gentle harassment of life on the dole.

The moment of empathy, the reversibility of perspective, is manifest in the involvement of participants in the situation narrated. Watching working class people speak, one sees that they exhibit presence through interruptions that instate an unambiguous relation to the person and situation. A lack of ambiguity that is obvious in the following woman's response:

X: Thi'v just tekken mi Dad off dole, said his not lookin hard enough fo' a job.
Y: Ahr [how] owd [old] is he?
X: 59, w'ked shifts all 'is life.
Y: That's disgraceful. It is 'onestly, it's wrong, an' unfair and unjust. Thi mek yer sick. I mean 'is paid in all his life an that an' hi should be entitled to wot's owed 'im. I tell yer, yer both young, thi's nowt in this country, ger'at while yer can, cos it's guin dahn' nick fast . . .

An involvement in others' stories manifest in injunctions like 'Ah'd a done this', 'Ah'd a said that . . .', 'Ah wun't 'ave 'ad that', and a pooling of advice concerning rights at work and with regard to the benefit system, the sharing of practical resources, phrases and ideas. Through this labour to confront a life of small denials and little affronts, what is left of self-respect is massaged and a protected market of limited value established through a practical discourse that is not quite about ethics as such; more part of an ethos in Bourdieu's terms:

I've used the word *ethos* . . . in opposition to *ethic*, to designate an objectively systematic set of dispositions with an ethical dimension, a set of practical principles (an ethic being an intentionally coherent system of explicit principles) . . . we may have principles in the practical state, without having a systematic morality, an ethic . . . people may prove incapable of responding to ethical problems while being quite capable of responding *in practice* to situations raising the corresponding questions.   (Bourdieu 1993a: 86)

Talk about such situations, played out in dialogue, is a way of coming to command the instruments to respond in dignity-preserving ways to the hazards life in this position ensures one must meet. Through such interaction, people articulate the ethos around which their comportment is organized. Through this practical ethos they learn the morality they make flesh in relation to a world that in its symbolic aggression and material resistance teaches their flesh the value of justice.

We have seen, in this chapter, what amounts to the social production of individual essences. As we have seen, the educational system is of the utmost importance in the production of individuals who feel themselves to be fit for a life of the common, difficult and unrewarding. In the education enterprise we must thus recognize an 'authority of consecration that, through the reproduction of the technical competences required by the technical division of labour, plays an ever-increasing role in the reproduction of social competences' (Bourdieu 1996a: 116). The education system is thus a critical part of that central social process of producing differences from the social continuum through that specifically social magic that transforms individuals by telling them, with authority, that they are different, constituting difference by designating it. Designating someone as competent imposes a propensity to acquire competence:

It is currently the school that has the responsibility for performing the magical action of consecration (often entrusted to religious authorities in other domains) that consists in effecting a series of more or less arbitrary breaks in the social continuum and in legitimating these breaks through symbolic acts that sanction and ratify them, establishing them as consistent with the nature of things and the hierarchy of beings by making them official through public, formal declarations.

(Bourdieu 1996a: 116)

The position of these people is such that they are perceived as possessing technical competences; the capacity to work and to train, perpetually, for this task. As holders of educationally uncertified cultural capital, their competences are perceived as skills which are, in principle, universal and infinitely reproducible. This is clearly very different to the blessed children of the privileged whose elite qualifications and academic titles, 'a legitimate juridical act of categorization, through which the undoubtedly most determinant *attribute of one's social identity* is conferred' (Bourdieu 1996a: 117), function as titles akin to nobility, conferring a dignity. The consequences of this for the holders of uncertified forms of competence is critical:

While technical competence is always in danger of decline, through loss or obsolescence, dignity, as the canonists used to say, does not die, or at least only dies with its possessor. It does not age; it is protected, like royal dignity, from the vicissitudes and failures of human intelligence and memory.   (Bourdieu 1996a: 118)

It is in this sense that the working class are only what they do and why unemployment bites so deeply at their souls. Possessors of already stigmatized competence and abject being, their relation to any means of personal and social reproduction has become problematic. People whose cultural condition has led them to see work as their reason-for-being and yet for whom there is unemployment, low-pay and retraining. No wonder so few care anymore, when, like Sisyphus, they are condemned to feeling a purposelessness they can never know the resolution of, because from birth their destiny was to be defined through the practices through which they momentarily find absorption and the mockery of a valueless remuneration. Theirs is a competence they must perpetually perform in a specific social relation, employment, and through which there will neither be consecration nor freedom from the conditions of necessity that initially produced the trajectory that work confirms and then reproduces. It is in this sense that working class people are defined, forever, in terms of an essence they must perpetually perform as a stigmatized identity in the face of their own abjection. This abject essence pre-defines them. Whatever they become, their status, like Cyrano's nose, will precede them; they will forever be an ugly people, 'plebeians, mass products' (Lawrence 1994a: 183), 'incarnate ugliness, and yet alive' (Lawrence 1994a: 159). There cannot ever be redemption through the social magic of grace. Value is a product of use; whatever they consume, whatever its value, their perceived essence degrades the act. There is no way beyond the negative aesthetics of a dominated group, no way individuals can revalue themselves amidst a class structure in which they are the lowest common denominator, the foil from which all distinction strategies distinguish themselves.

8

Conclusion

She was washing dishes. Her small back hunched over the sink. Cholly saw her dimly and could not tell what he saw or what he felt . . . The sequence of his emotions was revulsion, guilt, pity, then love. His revulsion was a reaction to her young, helpless, hopeless presence. Her back hunched that way; her head to one side as though crouching from a permanent and unrelieved blow. Why did she have to look so whipped? She was a child – unburdened – why wasn't she happy? The clear statement of her misery was an accusation . . . Guilt and impotence rose in a bilious duet. What could he do for her – ever? What give her? What say to her? What could a burned-out black man say to the hunched back of his eleven-year-old daughter? If he looked into her face, he would see those haunted loving eyes. The hauntedness would irritate him – the love would move him to fury. How dare she love him? Hadn't she any sense at all? What was he supposed to do about that? Return it? How? What could his calloused hands produce to make her smile? What of his knowledge of the world and of life could be useful to her? What could his own heavy arms and befuddled brain accomplish that would earn him his own respect, that would in turn allow him to accept her love?   (Morrison 1990: 127)

She looks up at him and sees the vacuum where curiosity ought to lodge. And something more. The total absence of human recognition – the glazed separateness.   (Morrison 1990: 36)

This book has presented an account of the lives of working class people drawn from personal testimony. Throughout, the work has dealt with the cultural condition of the working class. I have tried to express what I feel to be the conditions that consign many to inarticulacy and silence. This has been based upon an analysis of the conditions of their articulacy, and the testimony has required a deep contextualization in order for it to express the sense that coheres at the heart of working class life. Yet, in the last chapter, we did see the forms of expressivity and the forms of relation they mediate which have emerged from this context. The testimony of older people suggests a pretty clear experience of social decay, but the present conditions have deep continuities with those former conditions. The cultural conditions of the working class have obviously changed little. What it *means*, the sense the flesh has of itself, emerges from processes of domination and symbolic violence that have remained unchanged, broadly, throughout this century.

What has clearly changed is the institutional superstructure, the state bureaucracy, that must now manage the 'fit' between the labouring population and the economic positions open to them. The most visible cleavage within this society is that between the securely employed and those who left school to Youth Training and the 'new' economic conditions and whose lives are ones of insecurity and marginality. There can be little wonder that the most dispossessed fractions of the working class share few of the dispositions of the traditional habitus, and that they thus excite discussions about an urban underclass. But such change has not, in itself, been the focus of this work. Indeed, much of what has been written here would have been true throughout the era of industrial capitalism. However, it does seem that the social decay, that many working class people live with, does seem to have become an issue for the middle classes.

None of this has really concerned me in this work. What I have tried to reveal is the powerful sense of alienation from human expressivity that seems to mark these lives. This is why I have used, throughout, phenomenological ideas that focus upon the phenomenal-body as the pre-discursive communicative medium that frames our lived sense of the realms through which we move. The damage done to individuals through the processes of subjection and demoralization that we looked at in the last chapter, leads to the construction of subjectivities around a fatal shrine of silence, around a sense of the body as unable. An imbuing of a practical sense that afflicts the gesturing body in its seamless interweaving of the moment's movement, comportment, heaves from the world. Instead of the gesturing gaiety so evident in the thrill-filled comportment of privileged students a sense of the body that proclaims its own pleasure in its signification, a pleasure born of objective value and of being encouraged into possibilities and a variety of experience, we have the comportment of beings shorn of the pleasure of those privileged individuals whose position allows them to remain what they perceive themselves to be, the paradigm examples of virtuous humanity, able to move through the world with the gentle mocking seriousness which is a prerequisite for playing the games of culture (that are, after all, their games) and reap the symbolic profits of seeming and being that are denied to those who are excluded from:

the ranks of those who have been able, not necessarily to make their whole existence a sort of children's game, as artists do, but at least to maintain for a long time, sometimes a whole lifetime, a child's relation to the world. (All children start life as a baby bourgeois, in a relation of magical power over others and, through them.)

(Bourdieu 1984: 54)

For many working class kids, the baby's magical power over others is soon lost, as class's inscriptions overlay the flesh too young, and a series of early beginning, ever-recurring, never-ending negative injunctions ensure that their most personal sense of being is constituted amidst a fundamental sense of inadequacy; which renders the generative capacities of the body-subject inhibited in the processes of incorporation of the very techniques of comportment and performative competence that frame the life of the successful adult. Their experience of themselves is not that characterized by Merleau-Ponty when he suggests that as a sentient subject he experiences himself as a 'repository stocked with natural powers at which I am the first to be filled with wonder' (Merleau-Ponty 1962: 215).

For those condemned to a life lived under a socially constituted gaze that makes of them an inability to be other than what they must do, life originates in a comportment that cannot secure its own conditions of value and thus must secure them through life among their own kind. This relation to self is revealed in the comportment that constitutes this form of being. It is clear in the restricted expressivity, in the impoverished gestural and postural ranges of many working class people. And this impoverishment is manifest in the manner with which they participate in the culture that is left them as their own. It is at the heart of working class life and their most personal relationships. It is why, in their personal space, there is so much silence and so much television, 'Wiyaht [without] telly on in ahr 'ouse thi's nowt to talk abaht.' As one woman put it:

X: At mi sister's thi 'ave t' have telly [television] on all time cos thi' just dun't 'ave 'owt t' talk abaht [about]. We find it 'ard gu'in' rahnd [round]. At 'ouse yer can gu rahnd an' thi'll leave telly on while yer the'er an' yer feel uncomfortable an' if ever yer see 'em elsewhe'er, all thi can talk abaht is video's or shoppin' an' after 'alf an 'our it's pauses an' thi's nowt t' talk abaht. It's like thi' 'ave t' be watchin' sumaht [something] or du'in' sumaht t''ave 'owt [anything] t' talk abaht.

S: Ahr general is that du yer think?

X: Ah think it's pretty general, Ah mean, when people gu aht, it's lads an' lasses gu'in' from boozer to boozer an' clubbin', an' thi talk abaht that (S: Yeh, abaht that activity, yer mean?) yeh, but yer gu [go] in boozer's, well rahnd us it's not right nice anyway, but yer dun't see much conversation du yer?

I think the reasons for this are fundamental and of profound consequence for the lives of working people. What may seem like disparate elements of working class life are connected by their relation to culture, and by the consequences that this has for their relation to being and hence to each other. It is part of why they like the films and music that they do, and why they spend their leisure time as they do. But more significant than the details of their life-style, is their relation to those practices which issue from their relation to the world, from their being-in-the-world and it is this that I have tried so hard to illuminate.

Phenomenological writings draw attention to a level of pre-epistemic responses to others that root us, through our inter-corporeal expressivity, in a shared world that our individuated existences presuppose. The emphasis in such writings is often upon the pleasure involved in communication and in corporeality as an expressive medium. However, there is an important issue that arises from such considerations that the previous piece of transcription makes explicit. What if the social conditions of a people's being-in-the-world curtail their capacity to extend their expressive capacities or otherwise corrupt their experience of their capacity to make meaning through the fluid flow of the constancy of their being in space? And this has surely been the central message of this book. It is a set of links that are bound to be tenuous: how can one connect, uncontestably, the effects of place and position with its transmutation into the life of being? It is a set of questions not helped by common-sense ideas about space, objects and our relation to both as involving the relation of two discrete types of substance, matter and mind and two discrete realms; one of the object and the other of the subject; about which we can make a categorical distinction between the objective and the subjective. Hence, throughout, any consideration of the significance of the personal testimony has called on abstract ideas in order to trace the effects upon being of place and position. Only in this way can we understand their significance and see clearly that class is a fundamental modality of being-in-the-world and that it is fundamental because it is world-constituting for the body-subjects it constitutes.

Yet what we have seen in this work is a frustration involved in the very grounds of these people's coming-to-be, of the generative potentialities that are part of normal human being. And alongside this we have even seen a self-willed turning away from processes of self-generation and development that have begun, but which the individual finds painful in these conditions. Social deprivation is a line that runs throughout working class life and finds its most complete manifestation in the displaced men and women who rot alone in council flats and bed-sits and suffer a depth of privation from the human sociality which phenomenological writings reveal as the conditions of well-being that is almost as profound as the punishment of solitary confinement used in prisons as one of the sternest mediums of discipline and control. There can be little wonder that people in this category suffer huge amounts of mental illness and parasuicide, and are one of the main categories of drug users. We would do well to understand their condition existentially and phenomenologically; instead they are turned over to public health professionals and social workers because no human response is economically feasible.

I have tried to offer a glimpse into how this position, predicament, and its actualization in the place that is the site of daily life, is one of deprivation. It is as though their position and the environmental conditions that issue from it, have destroyed in these people the possibility of finding value or worth in their generative human capacities and their spontaneous development through inter-relations with others. Their experience of class is embedded in a world that demands to be dealt with. A realm that demands an alert comportment absorbing individuals in a reality that in its injunctions, frustrations and dangers instils forms of silent strain that sap the will. It is a mode of engagement in a realm whose possibilities are, at best, frustrating, at worst, negating, and which thus demands the forms of comportment engaged in coping. As the testimony shows, many are involved in a world that too many know nothing other than; hence what is linguistically constituted takes form within the parameters of what they expect; it follows the delineated contours of the plausible, and is held within the world as it has been imbued – a world that emerges from structures of power never seen, only felt. So they do not know the circumspection involved in their thought, and hence justice never arises as a hope beyond the living critique of 'whingeing' or 'moaning'; that gut response to sickening injustice we all feel, confronted with the petty exercises that confirm our own powerlessness.

Frustration, boredom and a certain dull resentment are the product of living a life constantly confirming the limits of one's world. Frustration is embedded in the long duration of personal time as each negotiates the dispropriation which leaves each the simple pleasures of the resigned hedonism celebrated in the comic-irony of a culture that must confront the paucity of the range and quality of its pleasure: a choice of the necessary made an elective affinity, and celebrated in Blues music, the pure sensual kinaesthetic pleasures of eating, drinking, dancing, sex, going out, the search for pleasures in the rudiments of those given in the body;

some nice snap t' 'ave a good trough at; plenty'r beer, a shag, some decent kip an' a good shit, the'r in't much mo'ore t' life.

It is not only that the basics of life are constituted as *pleasures* but that the articulation also denotes a *way* of eating, a modality of pleasure, an involved, un-stylized eating in which the mouth is filled and messes made: 'a good trough', has its own aesthetic sensuousness which is neither aesthetic in a formal sense nor sensuous in the usual sense of the word. This is a philosophy of finding pleasure in what one has, for those who can have nothing beyond the universal. It is a practical realization of life that, only for the fortunate among the working class, allows them *any* allowance of quality and then, only when they are lucky. For they know the fallacy involved in believing that there is a *human* world that is not bought with the capital one embodies or has. And it is a philosophy, practically realized, spontaneously, without consideration, which covers all things, even sexual partners. It makes many working people, when they articulate these principles, robust and offensive to the middle classes whose privileged manners and position allow them access to the very possibility of dignity, respect and sophistication, and allow them the added symbolic profit of a humanist good-faith that can never know the grounds of its vacuous inauthenticity. From the margins, or with them at least in sight, human existence becomes radically clear, and leaves these people, from too young an age, seeking to realize the life-style of the adult working class because that life-style is a response to conditions that begin too young and then never end. In a world in which one is taught that one is nothing, that one has no status-signifiers to constitute identity around, one can only be absorbed in the project of work as a routine of the adult (as opposed to the school of the child) and the life-style it inaugurates.

The education system is the chief institutional site through which they come to learn the dominant criteria of evaluation and realize their own competence as negatively valued. In such conditions of degradation, their relation to language follows the contours of their relation to the world. Coming to comport themselves; to realize a relation to themselves through the medium of their flesh; a living pride amidst their stigma; they unknowingly establish the form of life that gives life to the system of reference their language-use co-ordinates, realizes, and affirms and embed the patterns of experience, relation, response and perceptions that their language use constitutes in their way of living as a mediated way of being that emerges from particular conditions of possibility that they have no say in the conditions of. The rootedness of their language-games in the usages of the world that they live has consequences for their most personal experience of life. Embedded in an essentially practical realm of being, being excluded from the conditions of acquisition of language-games that would shape apperception in a way that might transform their relation to culture, they remain trapped and subject to a world that they can salvage little from. Lacking the instruments of perception, they lack the personal resources to establish modes of personal relation that allow for the constitution of a realm of value beyond the instrumentality of a realm of personal space that is increasingly being colonized by the commodity form and by an endless need to consume. Their position, and the relation to self and language that it implies, limits strongly their preferences in social life and inhibits the development of capacities through which they might forge a different way of inhabiting the world. It prevents the possibility of their using the space that is left them in different ways, because they lack the means to appropriate culture in other possible ways. Hence, their lives march on, through the endless realization of the same limited round of practices. This is why there is so much discontent and so much inertia because both make perfect sense as a response to the sensory impoverishment of their lives. What is latent in both senses is that, political conditions aside, the remedy of their discontent and frustration, the virtual impossibility of their founding experiences of value in their lives, demands more than an act of will to change the fundamental conditions of their experience of life. They need different ways of being: different ways of relating to the practices through which they live, a different relation to culture and thus the ability to found a culture that is their own but based upon conditions that allow for mutual self-realization. However, this is foreclosed upon by the very conditions of their culture. Avoiding the transmutation into the life of being of the bleak instrumentality of a brutal world in which each has only the worth of their manifest wealth, demands a distancing of that world and a long and slow acculturation into conditions of perception that allowed apperception to become signified in dimensions of humanity through forms of inter-relation absorbed in the pleasure of the refined word. But these conditions are inseparable from the cultural conditions that ensure these people's worthless marginality. To found a world on the kind of relation the Greeks called *philia* (Bourdieu and Eagleton 1992: 116), a refusal of instrumentality and a valuing of personal relationships for the joys of association and the pleasures of involvement in the mutual projects of talk as an end in itself, would require the adoption of a relation to language that was akin to the bourgeois relation, one of distance and ease that allowed them to develop the dispositions of contemplation amidst realized practices, and it would demand the forms of acculturation acquired in formal education. As Bourdieu concludes:

The principle of the most important differences in the order of life-style and, even more, of the 'stylization of life' lies in the variations in objective and subjective distance from the world, with its material constraints and temporal urgencies. Like the aesthetic disposition which is one dimension of it, the distant, detached or casual disposition towards the world or other people, a disposition which can scarcely be called subjective since it is objectively internalized, can only be constituted in conditions of existence that are relatively freed from urgency. The submission to necessity which inclines working-class people to a pragmatic, functionalist 'aesthetic', refusing the gratuity and futility of formal exercises and every form of art for art's sake, is also the principle of all the choices of daily existence and of an art of living which rejects specifically aesthetic intentions as aberrations. (Bourdieu 1984: 376)

It is the possibility of any other experience and any other relation to that experience that is foreclosed upon through the relation to culture that their position consigns them to. This is at the heart of the sense of alienation manifest in their frustration at what amounts to a denial of possibilities, 'The best we can 'ope fo' is a video an' a shag, if wi lucky! [*Laughs*]' as one man expressed the limits of his life's pleasures. But it is not just frustration at the extent of possibilities, it is alienation born of dispropriation of the instruments, techniques and modalities through which they might find rest from their aimless, restless, boredom that is broken only by work. An experience they loathe but which is their only access to public life, and all they are prepared for. As one man put it:

X: Ah'm boored rigid when Ah'm on 'oliday. After two days Ah want t' gu back. Ah du honest! [*laughs*] Thi's *nowt* t' du. All Ah du is sit in front 'r telly an' get fat. An' tha' gets fed up wi' telly. (S: Yet works shit?) Ah know it is, Ah 'ate it but if Ah'm not the'er, Ah'm fuckin' lost!

Such utterances are heavily mimetic in nature; they denote a relation to the world that is heavily ingested by the body's sense of its position and relation; the realm of the deepest sense of the phenomenal body's acquisition of its fundamental orientation to a world; and they use prosody to a remarkable degree, a prosody that is carried in the sonority generated through a style of articulation that involves a whole way of holding and moving, of patterning the continuingly gesturing body. Utterances like, 'Fuckin' w'k Ah do fo' undred an' ten spunkin' quid; Ah feel like wipin' mi fuckin' arse on it', rely upon a primary and deep familiarity with the degradation of hard, ill-remunerated, physical work such that one can share the humiliation and indignity but at a linguistic level, it works through a prosody that relies upon a practical sense of the immediacy of meaning, of rendering harsh realities done upon the body, like discipline, through a huge stock of ready-to-hand expressions that illustrate that these people can assimilate the nuances of words; that new forms of linguistic behaviour are assimilated to pre-linguistic reactions. Clearly, they are *as* capable of spontaneously producing new forms of linguistic reactions that link intimately with insights into the world, of 'seeing' perceptual phenomena. However, it is their position and its consequences for the mediation of their being that create for them their conditions of frustration. It is as though something has got in the way, fractured their human powers to achieve self-fruition. It is as though these people are perceptually damaged, and what looks like a natural absence of capacity in fact emerges from a taught inability and the damage that comes from being made to be intimidated by the expressive medium itself, such that they remain throughout life afraid of special categories of linguistic use, and thus alienated from a range of perceptual and expressive tools that enable one access to the possibility of founding worthwhile relations and a life in which one can be actively engaged in a realm of non-alienated human value based in a companionship based upon something more engaged than the kind of sterile consumption that so marks the dispossessed.

This, I have tried to show, is embedded in their relation to culture, which emerges from their economic position within England, and from their experience of school, the labour market and the state agencies that mediate their relation to it, adding to the damage inflicted by the school. By debasing their sense of their own linguistic productions and inculcating a sense of the legitimate usage, its value and superiority, the school imbues working people with a sense of themselves as stigmatized in relation to dominant markets and ensures a fractured experience of the social; an experience of degradation and not grace.

This experience of formal education has consequences for their relation to the disposition of learning, one that makes it an experience of anxiety that can be confronted only through a heightened, even extreme, tension. Moreover, their exclusion from the linguistic competence taught in school has repercussions for them. Without the linguistic and dispositional competences that would begin to make an enlarged realm of schemata of perception and appreciation open to them, there remain dimensions of experience and inter-relation that are foreclosed upon prematurely for these people. Their socially mediated relation to language, as the medium through which we acquire, gradually, a deepening relationship to meaning and significance, means that there are ranges of competence, expressivity and perception, or kinds of experience, they remain on the outside of. Without access to the means to appropriate significances beyond the realm of the reality their practices oblige them to know, they can take little from the realm of existence beyond what is given in their condition. And so their consciousness remains tied to the world of their practices; remains absorbed in their dispositional being, purely phenomenal, never getting beyond the primacy of experience contained in a realm of existence governed by their function. This operates in the manner of their practices and accounts for the perceived baseness and vulgarity that strikes more cultivated eyes looking at the leisure practices of working people. Exclusion from the conditions of possibility of something akin to aesthetic experience, ensures that perception must conform to the schemata through which they experience their everyday environment. This is perhaps why Bourdieu suggests that 'aesthetics can only be . . . a dimension of the ethics (or, better, the ethos) of class' (Bourdieu 1990e: 47).

I am not suggesting that working people should be able to appreciate fine art, or that they would be better off partaking of other cultural practices, but it seems to me that much of their culture can be understood to issue from this condition. To return to the quotation at the beginning of the chapter about silence among families and in pubs and the focus of interaction being the activity; this seems to me to emerge from conditions which ensure that individuals are able to constitute so little linguistically beyond what shows up in the particular domain and our involvement in it.

The education system and their experience of the state agencies which mediate the labour market create the general conditions for the world's disclosure, given in the comportment their position encourages them to imbue, being limited. In this way, tied to this form of being, they are held within the bounds of a particularly limited form of engagement with the world, one that is sensorily impoverished, perceptually deprived and which does not facilitate many forms of self-realization. This impoverishment of their way of being has cognitive effects because being locked out of the means to appropriate the secondary and special forms of language-use that education provides access to, means that there are dimensions of experience, dependent upon a developing acquisition of linguistic techniques, that they remain effectively shielded from. In important respects, their abilities to perceive different aspects in perception are reduced to that given in the assignment-relations given in the implicitness of the everyday world which we perceive as simply to-hand, there and given. Bourdieu illuminates this phenomenon through the study of artistic perception, but it has wider repercussions in working class life, and is part of a more general human relationship to the sensible and perceptible. Human beings have a capacity to acquire new techniques of perception embedded in the linguistic practices of human cultures. We have an extraordinary capacity to absorb, spontaneously, the meaning of words such that words we understand seem always to exhibit or manifest their meaning, always, already, for us, without conscious effort. So deeply do we assimilate the network of the linguistic field in which words take their place that we do not normally have to interpret their meaning. Language ties into and issues from the way the world is disclosed through comportment; it is part of the totality of involvement-relations that mediate being-in-the-world. However, the very transparency of these processes allows us to overlook, or to mis-categorize as natural, processes that are of profound consequence in the lives of working people because the deep internalization of meaning, such that we come to inhabit the world as though it were immanently constitutive of sense in itself, means that the complete process whereby we imbibe a totality of involve-ment-relations, a referential-whole that is the background of practices of our form of life, is like the acquisition of a second nature. Here, Wittgenstein's insights are of the highest importance. Discussing the phe-nomena of secondary sense, or our capacity to understand such devices as metaphor whose sense relies upon a deviation from the primary, everyday sense, Mulhall makes a series of observations that seem relevant:

What the phenomenon of secondary sense is therefore designed to highlight is one further and important consequence of our capacity to continuously perceive the meanings of words. Here, our feeling that words have a physiognomy – our sense that they have absorbed their meanings to the point at which they appear to mani-fest them, to make a unique gesture even in isolated or alien contexts – is manifest in their availability for us as elements of a new gesture language, as a means by which to articulate a further set of spontaneous reactions, upon which a further range of language use can then be erected. In this respect, for Wittgenstein, our attachment to words – our tendency to assimilate them – is like the acquisition of a second nature: just as pre-linguistic reactions that are a part of human nature form the precondition for acquiring language in the first place, so the acquisition of those forms of linguistic behaviour shapes that nature and leads in its turn to a new realm of spontaneous *linguistic* reactions. It is as if humans inherit language twice, and the second inheritance is made possible by – and so is expressive of – the depth of the first: for only when our first inheritance of language has come to inform our lives to such a degree and in such a way that each and every word of it is available to us as a unique gesture do we find ourselves possessed of the reactive substratum that is essential for our inheritance of a further range of language and experience. And this second inheritance is portrayed as a fundamental medium of human indi-viduation and intimacy: terrain upon which the specificity of one person's inner life might find more and more finely-grained articulation.   (Mulhall 1995: 77–8)

We have seen throughout that these processes of individuation allow both for forms of intimacy and for exclusion; that within social structures they form the basis of social evaluations that are the social conditions constitu-tive of personal experiences of grace and abjection, but this is not the impli-cation that I want to consider here. Whilst clearly we all become possessed of an initial, primary gesture language, those who are privileged with access to the legitimate culture and the spaces through which it is acquired, the complete private and public world constituted by the modal trajectory through select schools (or the essentially aristocratic experiences of the top pupils in state schools) on through elite universities, share an experience that inaugurates a relation to culture and language that is one of endless refinement, of never-still development. It is the inauguration of a teleological process of the self which is embedded in a relation to the world that is distinguished even without pursuing difference. As Mulhall acknowledges, this acquisition of a 'second nature' amounts to a process of speciation as though through our acquisition of our 'second inheritance' or acquisition of culture we become part of specific races, particular categories of being recognizable through the reactions, responses and characteristic kinds of look and sound that are typical of our form of life. We have already seen the deeper effects of this process. However, I want to consider the conclusion Mulhall reaches concerning the status of language and our form of life; the practical, background, patterns of response and use, which are fundamental to individuation and the realization of forms of intimacy. The centrality of a vocabulary of self-expression through which a domain of feeling is constituted is eloquently described by Taylor:

> We could think of the feeling vocabulary as simply describing pre-existing feelings, as marking distinctions which would be there without them. But this is not adequate because we often experience in ourselves or others how achieving, say, a more sophisticated vocabulary of the emotions makes our emotional life, not just our description of it, more sophisticated. Reading a good, powerful novel may give me the picture of an emotion which I had not previously been aware of. But we cannot draw a neat line between an increased ability to identify and an altered ability to feel emotions which this enables. (Taylor 1985: 26)

The argument here is that our feelings involve a certain articulation of our context, and that this characterization can be made in more refined ways which can transform the feelings. The conclusion is clear:

> What we can feel thus depends on what we *can* articulate – and I do not say what we *do* articulate but what is intelligible and, therefore, articulable for us in the language we possess. What we can see, what sense we can make of things, what kind of person we are: these are connected and depend on what we can articulate. (Dilman 1993: 33)

In principle, such reasoning is correct; however, as an argument it seems to me to be an idealization of particular sets of linguistic practices which have certain social conditions of existence which are not universal. The problem arises if certain kinds of linguistic technique are not universally and uniformly accessible. Yet, as we have seen, 'Language is the most active and elusive part of the cultural heritage which each individual owes to his background' (Bourdieu 1994: 8) and it is too easy to assume too great a similarity in what its use establishes and it is too easy to take for granted that the language of ideas and 'the second-order language of allusions and cultural complicities are second nature to intelligent and gifted individuals' (Bourdieu 1994: 8). Yet, contrary to the 'illusion of linguistic communism' (Bourdieu and Wacquant 1992: 43) and apart from the primary inheritance of language that we acquire in our primary milieu, for some, their relationship to language and the perceptual possibilities it brings into existence cannot be taken for granted. Clearly, language-use is mediated by the forms of practical life that are the grounds of its development; and, in labouring communities, or communities of people whose relation to a public world is even more tenuous because of unemployment, the conditions, both personal and social, of forms of linguistic use aimed at the generation of self, other and genealogical descriptions may be absent. Moreover, the kinds of vocabularies that foster the generation of coherent and cogent narratives of self must bear some relation to the language of the education system which, Bourdieu reminds us, 'is very unequally distant from the language actually spoken by the different social classes' (Bourdieu 1994: 8). If there is a sense in which all normal human beings have a transparent relationship to the linguistic skills of our primary cultures, it is also true that we do not all have a transparent relationship to language. There are social conditions for acquiring the ability to lucidly linguistically constitute a consciousness that thinks the world as a flawless narrative. And we cannot forget that the sites designed to formally inculcate such techniques have left such an indelible mark of inability that these people, often, never fully acquire more sophisticated linguistic skills, particularly written ones. Indeed, for many the socially mediated nature of their relationship to language has been so traumatic as to mean that in certain conditions they are effectively dispossessed of their own instruments of expression.[1] So, if the acquisition of forms of linguistic behaviour shapes our nature, leading to new forms of linguistic reactions which alter and deepen our relationship to our nature and being, and if this process is continued and extended so that we are possessed of a new reactive substratum that allows for a further range of language and experience, then if a group's relation to language was, because of social organization and institutional structures, damaged, such that its conditions of existence constrained their capacity to realize capacities that are effectively part of its generative possession of being, then wouldn't this be a critical lever with which to criticize the society? Because, if Mulhall, Taylor et al., are correct, in the light of Bourdieu's work it seems clear that conditions which impede the capacities of individuals to develop in these ways curtail the conditions of being human that we all, in principle, ought to have a right to.

If a 'second inheritance', a gradually deepening relation to forms of linguistic use is, indeed, the 'terrain upon which the specificity of one person's inner life might find more and more finely-grained articulation' (Mulhall 1995: 78); such that 'What we can feel thus depends on what we *can* articulate' (Dilman 1993: 33), then if individuals are inhibited from access to the means of possessing the instruments and confidence through which to constitute a realm experienced as a unique domain of subjective self-realization, or 'inner life', isn't one of the consequences of this the condition that Mulhall describes as 'aspect blindness':

In this respect, aspect-blindness locks the sufferer out of language as an expressive medium: he is incapable of manifesting the reactions and related behaviour which alone would confer sense upon the attribution of such feelings to him. In his alienation from (rather than assimilation of) language, he is condemned to an impoverished inner life; he lacks the second nature which language confers upon human beings.   (Mulhall 1990:51)

Wittgenstein's model is that we have a tendency to assimilate words within the patterns of linguistic behaviour that shape our second nature, leading to the progressive acquisition of newer forms of spontaneous linguistic reactions. Gradually, a whole range of expressive behaviours and ranges of experience are overlaid through this deepening relation to language and the social that it mediates. However, social position and the exclusion that it can involve for certain groups can lock people out of these processes of self-actualization. If this is so, then another question arises from this analysis and it might be posed in the following way: 'what consequences does it have for those individuals locked out of language as an expressive medium? Does it not mean that they have an impoverished relationship to their humanity and the humanity of others? And if we accept Heidegger's insight that comportment reveals, in practical responses, an attitude to existence, and to being, then if social conditions create an instrumental attitude towards one's being and the being of others, forms of being dominated by the awareness of calculations of value, of the use of other human beings who do not show up, naturally, unreflexively, as beings-in-themselves with a subjectivity like one's own, then we can begin to see, around us in the social world, forms of life that are damaged, fractured shadows refracted by the light of the forms of being framed in the light of the legitimate culture. Forms of being that relate internally to the possibility of each; one public and proud, unconsciously enjoying the fruits of life in the light, the other shameful and dismal, living in caves of ill-formed pleasure. In these conditions, they are consigned to an impoverished relation to a medium that is fundamental to human individuation and intimacy. They lack access to the means to develop gradually, securely, through social fields that would bring value through possession of dispositions towards sensitivity. Moreover, in these conditions the acquisition of these potentials would introduce them to a medium of further misery. Given the grounds for the constitution of an inner life, with this landscape of the heart, framed by necessity, with ever more conviction, one might begin to see why, for a large section of the working class, 'Their homes, however, remained some of the worst in Britain' (Campbell 1984). We might see that class is not simply a socio-economic cum political–cultural category, but a space of being whose contours are forged in processes that demand a psycho-analytic treatment, an understanding of class as a psychic space resonating with terror and anxiety, a realm of the body socially constituted through position to know the world primarily through pain and degradation, love and lovelessness, grace and agony, beauty and ugliness; the fundamental co-ordinates that shape the body's experience of a primal world that undergirds the social experience of a primal body there before all judgements begin, and living long after the fundamental ones have settled its form of life.

In the light of these insights we might begin to recognize an aspect of working class experience that is manifest within their speech and yet which it is easy to overlook or ignore in a focus upon the content of the speech.[2] If it is natural for us to acquire such mediums of expressive self-actualization, and not merely to imbue the second nature of alienated beings which effectively thwarts self-development, then we might expect those who have managed to found some sensitivity, to experience the absence of something that is of profound importance in human existence. It is a result of their exclusion from a developed relation to the expressive medium through the social conditions that their being issues from and which their language-use thus circles around, that explains the sense of absence that is at the heart of their experience of life. It is because this condition becomes part of the phenomenal body, part of the very grounds of the relation to the self that their comportment constitutes, a process of socially grounded speciation so deep that it seems to belong to the realm of nature and the gene, that they *feel the presence* of an absence, a dissatisfaction in all that they do, that belongs to the manner of their cultural appropriation and not merely to their practices. They accept what they do as part of the available to be done, but their alienation emerges as much from the way that practices are participated in, the way that space is seized and rendered meaningful. It is the paucity of the ability of working people to render their world that leaves many feeling that there is something missing from their lives that ought to be there. This sense is clear in the speech of one woman in conversation with a male friend:

X: If Ah'd known yer wo gu'in' aht [out], A'd a come along. Ah wo sat in 'ouse on mi own wi' nowt [nothing] to du an' Ah wo thinkin' abaht [about] gu'in' in *Masons* [*pub*] an' Ah'd a gone if Ah'd known ye'd bi in.

Y: It's shit in the'er, it's all just on parade, what clothes yer wear, wot car yer drive . . .

Z: Ah know, that's why Ah'r dun't like it . . .

X: It is, it's shit rahnd 'ere. If ye'v got '*alfe* a brain it's awful. If yer talk abaht music or 'owt [anything] to people rahnd 'ere thi just look at yer like yer sumat [something] strange. Ah se' to W [*husband*], Ah just can't stand it anymo'ore an' Ah'll get upset abaht it an' hi'll draw up a list o'r places an' things wi could do but wi never du, du 'owt, wi stuck 'ere. Ah mean, A'm bo'ored [bored] wi' 'im an' he's prob'ly bo'ored wi me. It's soul-destroyin'. Yer know, Ah sit an' Ah can't remember the last interestin', witty conversation Ah'ad: Ah just can't remember the last conversation Ah really enjoyed: in't that sad? Ah mean, Ah'm not clever, far from it, never 'ave been, but A'm so sick o'r it, sick o'r life. It's just so borin' an' people are so dead.

This expresses the alienation of the people she meets from the capacity to see and participate in life through a developing realm of spontaneous linguistic reactions which produces that alchemy capable of transforming what a certain philosophy of existence might see as sense-data into that living value-given world that is culture; that transformation of the ordinary into space that is immanent with the presence of the human meaning that association and a civic, public culture make possible yet which these people's conditions render implausible. This woman is expressing the inadequacy of these people's ability to found a world of meaning and association beyond the stale practices and forms of commodity-driven pleasure and association that are involved in public space reduced to the mode of estranged association that a realm reduced to the gaze, to being seen and desired in, is. Yet it is important to note the form of her expression. In making the observations that she does, she clearly is not seeking a profit of distinction. This is clear in her insistence that 'Ah'm not clever' which declares her shared objective position and identity with the people she describes, acknowledging that she is a product of the same cultural conditions. Rather, her words have the character of a lament for the complete paucity of basic forms of human association in this culture. She is lamenting the absence of a realm of simple conversation she feels life ought to have. It is striking the desperation that she feels trapped in a world in which there is so little fulfilment and in which people lack the resources to make meaningful, and less bleak, a world of such circumscribed pleasures. It is a sense of despair that comes through in the words of one man:

S: What did yer gu t' doctors fo'?

D: Just a problem am 'avin' wi' mi 'ealth. Ah keep gettin' these right bad 'eadaches an' Ah'm feelin' knackered, an' then when Ah gu t' bed Ah dun't sleep? A'm fed up . . .

S: S' many o'r us feel like that, it's part o'r us life-style . . .

D: Naow, Ah know, I mean, in ahr lives watchin' a film is all the'r 'is t' look forrard tu, that else a football match an' then ne'et aht [night out] at weekend 'cos that's we'er the's opposite sex. But 's [our] lives are just so borin', it's the same all the time, every fuckin' day's the same. Ye' need to bi part o'r a group an' 'ave some conversation but the's nowhe'er to gu. An', Ah mean, this 'll fuckin' bi it fo' rest o'r ma life.

This man clearly articulates the grounds of this alienation in the sense of entrapment in such a limited horizon of possibility, within a cultural life that offers such a limited number of alternatives. Yet the absence these people allude to is not just one of opportunity; it concerns their inability to find a meaning to their lives founded in something of human value. That is, in something that en-values *them* in giving value to *it*: that peculiar phenomenon that genuine association brings through engaging and thus fulfilling our being-in-the-world, without which we are sick. I have spoken here of 'meaning' because, in a sense, our own tradition uses this idea in this way; people speak of 'life lacking meaning' and it is this more practical application, as opposed to the more cognitive and linguistic connotations that the word has, that I want to use because perhaps what these people are really describing is the lack of sense to their lives. What both these people articulate, in different ways, is that the background of sense, the referential whole that embeds human existence in a practically realized sense that nourishes being, is insufficient to fill their life with a vibrancy and quality of relation to one another; with the result that being is experienced as transparently meaningless, a set of routines simply to be gone through, a routine of small talk circumscribed by the possibilities of a world into which they can no longer be absorbed.

In such conditions, in which things of such radical importance to human existence become so difficult to realize within the realm of public and communal life, there can be little wonder that individual pathology, sickness, social decay and various kinds of abuse and victimization ensue. Both of these people refer to distress and physical discomfort, the second overtly to sickness. This is the thin line between physiology and psychology, what I alluded to earlier as 'socio-somatic', where our moral condition transmutes into physical ill-health. The absence these people feel acutely is part of the human inheritance of sense and meaning that Mulhall illuminates through insights drawn from aspect-perception. Part of these people's need is to be able to realize spontaneously new aspects, new realms of being, something apart from the deadness and alienation. Yet such a shift requires a complete reconfiguration of the grounds of their being and far-reaching economic and social change. What is clearly expressed in the testimony is that the conditions of that development, and its fulfilment if developed, are absent. Yet these very expressions exhibit a desire for something beyond a life of being consumed by sign-driven desires for people reduced to agglomerations of signs to be consumed with alcohol and drugs; something that might allow them to find some peace in their generative human capacities and in a mutuality founded in respect and a degree of dignity.

They need something that operates as an aesthetics for them but in the practical mode of their being-in-the-world, not something that makes them want to go to the theatre or opera. 'Ah think everybody needs a bit o'r beauty in their life an' I've got mi daughter, but people rahnd 'ere an't got none' is how one man perceptively put it. But the communication, like the community, has gone, and, with the talk of the shared life of work gone, there has emerged an absence of association; not merely a lack of the conversation that was once the community's founding, spoken-of experience of life, but the emergence in its place of a distrust and misanthropy that makes life a difficult daily chore of few moments of meeting or pleasure. What has gone is anything approximating to what, in orthodox political theory, was called 'civil society'. Habermas renders this sphere with a definition of particular relevance to the lives of these people:

civil society is composed of those voluntary associations and coalitions separate from the state and the economy that secure the communicative dimension of the life-world. Civil society is composed of those more or less spontaneous coalitions, organizations and movements which respond to the resonance that societal problems have found in the private sphere, and which condense them and amplify them in the direction of a public sphere.   (Habermas 1992)

It is this sphere of association once founded upon the communal dispositions of work, the union movement and the Labour Party that, with those sites changed irrevocably, has disappeared for working people, especially the young, and its absence is manifest in the emptiness and anxiety felt by so many. A woman in her mid eighties expressed, poignantly, this loss:

At least we 'ad some community, when we wo growin' up in t' depression, wi 'ad the community arahnd [around] us. But all that's gone nahr [now], but wi'r in same state and cos the'r in't the community anymore an' it's w'se. A'm glad A've 'ad ma time . . .

In this sense, at the level of social description, understanding working class life is simple. The happiest are those, in a sense the most dominated, who are happy to live within the range of possibilities that are available. However, many more live, daily, reconciled in silent misery to their position and its lot, rarely articulating the deep yearning the oppressed know for a life that is better, without the pain of the endless daily injunctions that confirm their position and their confinement. However, to understand the extent to which the opportunities immanent in a place become internalized as a sense of limits and of reality demands something that goes beyond a description of place and the routines of life that go on there. Recognizing this phenomenon of habituation to the world as it is given to us in our flesh as realized categories of being and, for the dominated, as involving, throughout life, a deep, unremitting form of repressed suffering, is critical if we are to understand one of the central effects of the structures of inequality that our society exists through. It seems that the advanced societies, the forms of statehood that they demand, produce racialized categories of people. In some societies this symbolic violence is visited upon first-generation migrant labour, and in some it is carried out upon indigenous peoples. A process of internal imperialism which characterizes social space within the nation-state and which involves the deep alienation that is at the heart of working people's sense of the social and of themselves and their relations. This is a condition necessary for the reproduction of these societies which shapes the contours of the environments in which individuals must shape their destiny, and it is a condition that affects the very grounds of personal existence, in which every personal aspect of life is touched and shaped to such a degree that the world in which people live becomes taken for granted as the absolute world. For the dominated, with the range of possibilities closed, with so little opportunity, part of the very definition of their condition, lack the means even to realize, fully, the extent of their dispossession. Impoverished conditions and social domination, exclusion from the totality of resources that humans require in order to satisfy the conditions of their existence, lead to the multiple forms of social decay and personal pathology that characterize the lives of the urban poor today. Their position seems to foreclose upon the possibility of developing the relations with others, and with one's own embodied being, that would offer the possibility of a life of worth possessed of sense; instead their existence seems to take place on the brink of nonsense. And part of that condition of the absurd is that we lack even the belief in a hope of there ever being another way to be. From conditions of absence people do not know the feel of a brighter culture; like people from a cold clime, their flesh knows only the brief spots of localized heat. That warmth might consume the flesh in an iridescence possessed of the ambience that covers the world, remains beyond the range of projective possibilities. As one man captured the circumscription involved in the lives of local people:

X: What tha's gorra remember is these people rahnd [around]'ere dun't know 'owt else, thi' dun't know ahr [how the] other 'alfe live, thi' *dun't* know ahr other'alfe'r Rother'am live, thi' *dun't know* ahr thi' live on Moorgate, the'r like dogs barkin' in' back yard. Thi can bi nicest dogs in world but in the'r backyard that's their patch an' the'll bark an' bark.

Or as Bourdieu puts it:

Perhaps the most ruthless call to order, which in itself no doubt explains the extraordinary *realism* of the working classes, stems from the closure effect of the homogeneity of the directly experienced social world. There is no other possible language, no other life-style, no other form of kinship relation; the universe of possibles is closed. Other people's expectations are so many reinforcements of dispositions imposed by the objective conditions.   (Bourdieu 1984: 381)

It is a point expressed movingly by a man in his early twenties:

I cun't [could not] think owt [anything] else. Wot else wo the'r? . . . I 'ad to do it t' get' money in? Fuckin 'ell it wo disgusting wern'it? Yer w'k fo fucking next to nowt! But yer see, then, I din't know nowt . . . ohnny [only], I'd just left school, I wo straight on't building site w'king mi bollocks off an like . . . that's all, Ah mean, a lot o'r' people dun't know any different, so thi just carry on wi the life-style, fucking goin aht [out] wi lads, getting pissed up, gonna gym, gonna work, getting in money, seein wife, havin' a kid 'an that, fuckin gettin an 'ouse, [*Voice goes up for stress*] that's it, *that's their life,* that's *our life that.* So thi don't know any fucking better really do thi? . . . [*pause*] . . . it's fuckin rubbish.

Notes

1 Introduction: Dead Man's Town

1 One can add, here, that one has to be concerned by the gap that has opened up between producers of discourse on the social and those condemned to live beyond a civil or public realm.

2 I was fascinated by parallels in Paul Gilroy's *The Black Atlantic* (Verso, 1993).

3 In *The Myth of Sisyphus*, Camus writes of, 'that odd state of the soul in which the void becomes eloquent, in which the chain of daily gestures is broken, in which the heart vainly seeks the link that will connect it again' (Camus 1975: 19).

4 Clearly, this does not constitute a denial that there may be important areas of difference in people's experience. Obviously the world of the man is not the world of the woman. It is simply to claim that there is some level of shared experience that makes these people recognizable as the beings they are and in terms of which they share a perceptual realm that is significant in their association.

5 The concept is taken from Pierre Bourdieu. It is a term he has developed in order to suggest a way of enacting being, where the enactment constitutes ways of feeling the presence of the world. The habitus involves what is involved in more ordinary senses of 'ways of perceiving' the social world but its stress is on the place of habituation and embodied techniques rather than upon cognition. I develop this notion later.

6 Which is not a profound thing to say, except that it does raise the important question of why only some *appear* parochial, and pay the appropriate price for this, which usually involves remaining in their original conditions.

7 See the second transcribed quote on page 207: the woman speaking about her feelings of violation.

2 Introducing some concepts: practice, habitus, ethos, doxa, reflexivity

1 I am indebted to the books by A. P. Munford (Munford 1995) and M. Jones (Jones 1995) for the historical information that is used here.

2 For the information in this chapter I am deeply indebted to Rotherham Borough Council, to its *Social Policy Bulletin,* to its publication *Rotherham: A Poverty Profile* by Steve Griffiths (Griffiths 1995) and to the Factsheets of the 1991 Census that are produced under the title *Rotherham in Profile* (Rotherham Borough Council, 1994). I also found useful the publications *The Rotherham Economic Strategy* by A. G. Carruthers (Carruthers 1992) and Rotherham Training and Enterprise Council's *Labour Market Assessment 1992–1993* (Rotherham Training and Enterprise Council, 1993).

3 The series of studies by Champion and Green, *In Search of Britain's Booming Towns* (1985), *Local Prosperity and the North–South Divide* (1988) and *The spread of Prosperity and the North–South Divide* quoted in *Rotherham: Economic Strategy: A Technical Report* by A. G. Carruthers and published by Rotherham Borough Council.

4 These losses break down as follows:

Doncaster: Hickleton 896; Brodsworth 2069; Askern.
South Yorkshire: Kilnhurst 505; Cadeby 954; Manvers 1169; Cortonwood 839; Brookhouse 706; Dinnington 933.
Barnsley: Bullcliffe 309; Kinsley Drift 444; Parkmill 365; Barrow 1263; Darfield 709; Woolley 1747; Emley Moor 247; Dodworth 1261; South Kirby 1471; North Gauber 737.
North Yorkshire: Glass Houghton 602; Ackon Hall 1326; Savile 521; Nostell 613; Ledstone Luck 446.
Others: Mansfield, Sutton, Whitwick, Askern, Yorkshire Main, Prince of Wales; Wath, Barnburgh, Shire Oaks, Treeton, Fryston, Wheldale, Redbrook, Royston, Dearne Valley, Barnsley Main, Denby Grange.

5 No author's name was given with this short piece.

6 Given the objectivity of the structures of meaning, the work itself will be read through the canons of the dominant aesthetic and it is thus hard to escape the realm of parody and cliché.

7 Roger Dataller *From a Pitman's Notebook,* p. 183 quoted in Hearne 1995, p. 307.

8 These last two contributions suggest the importance of something that I discuss later, the place of this type of talk in working class life.

9 I've transcribed this as 'fAther' because of the South Yorkshire pronunciation which pronounces the 'a' in 'father', 'hard' and short, unlike the Southern soft, longer 'a' that renders it 'farther'.

10 The oral historian concerned with earlier phases of working class culture has it easier. As I have experienced myself, the older ones who grew up with the co-ordinates of work are full of important stories whereas, for the young of today, one fears that their lives are simply a void. They will likely never have the kind of rich narratives of life to tell that their parents and grandparents have as a rationalized economy unifies the relation of working people, the world over, to the economy.

3 Class and the objectifying subject: a reflexive sociology of class experience

1 See p. 297, note 3, chapter 4, for a discussion of the meaning of 'occurrent'.
2 And this insight is one that emerges from the dialectic of embodiment, for if the world is disclosed through the uncovering, or bringing to light, involved in public forms of comportment, then this process is also a covering over of other ways of the world being disclosed. Clearly, from this Heideggerian perspective, in which all cognition is perspectival, there can be no free-floated, unlocated comprehension of entities or the world. It is thus better to be aware, in a developed way, of the grounds of sense.
3 That is, statistically probable.
4 Kafka quoted in Steiner 1985: 87.
5 Obviously, in person, one has pre-verbal, gestural cues in manner, bearing, intonation, eye-contact as well as a knowledge of the person across time.
6 There is a wide literature in social science concerning this. Of particular interest is feminist philosophy concerned with acts of knowing. For example, Pearsall 1989.
7 Something that a Labour government has recently made even more aggressive to help wean people from their dependency culture.

4 A landscape with figures?

1 Lawrence had an intuitive appreciation of the insights of phenomenological writings, perhaps because of the nature of the phenomena that concerned him which make clear why it is erroneous to regard Lawrence as a romantic, irrational writer.
2 John McLeish, *Universities and Left Review* 1(2), Summer 1957, p. 29. Quoted in Mulhern 1996.
3 The concept is taken from Dreyfus (1994) and is one I use throughout the book, to refer to 'the way of being of isolated, determinate substances' (Dreyfus 1994: 71). For Heidegger, 'the ways of being of equipment *and* substances, and of actors *and* contemplators, presuppose a background understanding of being – originary transcendence or being-in-the-world' (Dreyfus 1994: 61). In this way, Heidegger wants to illuminate a more fundamental involvement of people with their environment than that of self-referential mental content and external world of objects. As Dreyfus puts it: 'According to Heidegger three modes of disturbance – conspicuousness, obstinacy, and obtrusiveness – progressively bring out both Dasein as a thoughtful subject and occurrentness as the way of being of isolated, determinate substances . . . we can see these three modes of breakdown as increasingly serious disturbances in which a conscious subject with self-referential mental states directed towards determinate objects with properties gradually emerges' (Dreyfus 1994: 71). The problem with the metaphysics of the present-at-hand and the spectatorial premise is that it is based upon the theoretical attitude, upon disengagement and disinterested contemplation, which fails to understand the fundamental stance of engagement: 'By

looking at the world theoretically we have already dimmed it down to the uniformity of what is purely present-at-hand' (Heidegger 1962: 177). In the situation of the scholar, retiring from the world in order to think about its essential nature, this metaphysics comes readily to hand and it is easy to become implicitly perceptually involved in the Cartesian vision of the world as an assortment of substances with extension and 'thinking things' whose basic relation to the world 'has for the most part been represented exclusively by a single exemplar – knowing the world' (Heidegger 1962: 86). Our being-in our environment is not a spatial relationship but one of involvement and we encounter the phenomena of world not through a pure form of 'perceptual cognition', as collections of sense-data or such reductionist categories, but as part of a field of intelligibility that concerns us because it is the grounds of our practical engagement with the world. Cooper expresses the point with some panache: 'For unless things are first "lit up" in virtue of the roles they play within our practical concerns, nothing would stand out for us to then "stare" at and submit to "perceptual cognition". The lacuna in the Cartesian tradition is its failure to ask how the extended thing we represent to ourselves should ever have emerged as discriminable items for perceptual attention. The traditional question, "How do we know things?" is insufficiently basic, for it presupposes a prior mode of access to them, the practical dealings which enable things to "show up". Experiencing things as present-at-hand is necessarily derivative from, "later than", this "proximal" encounter with them. In fact, we only switch to observing things present-at-hand when something goes wrong in our everyday dealings with equipment. Only when the hammer malfunctions does it become "conspicuous" as a mere physical object, a fusion of wood and metal which we now need to inspect in abstraction from its usual functional role. Descartes' mistake was to take this parasitic spectatorial stance towards the object as the primary one, and then to identify the "real" object with this "dimmed down" lump of extended matter. One may as well insist that a symphony is "really" just some vibrations in the air' (Cooper 1996: 26–7).

4 See the studies cited in Gross (1992) of human cataract patients given sight after being blind since birth by operations to remove the cataracts over their eyes. They could not identify, without touch, familiar objects. Gross also cites the case of S.B. who was given his sight back at 52 years of age, who had great difficulty identifying objects visually which he did not already know by touch.

5 In the sense that the patterns of comportment adopted to deal with this space disclose the a version of English society that then has consequences for the individual's life-chances and future experience.

6 Advanced level for access to higher education.

7 We will look in detail at this in chapter 7.

8 Given that, usually, individuals like their own dispositions, and only under specific conditions learn the possibility of disliking them.

9 Toni Morrison's brilliant *The Bluest Eye* (1990) is superb in its rendering of these aspects of the significance of the world that haunt the being-in-the-world

of individuals from dominated groups. Critics of this work suggest it is my task to make this background explicit. Morrison does so, but one has to wonder whether such a burden of proof, and of talent, can be justifiably thrust on any single individual.

10 I am indebted to Stephen Mulhall's exposition here. See Mulhall 1996: 90–104.

11 The kinds of answer that questions like 'What do you think of Rotherham?' or 'Describe this?' might evoke. We will look at the reasons why these kinds of questions do not make much sense in the next chapter, even though perceptually, we have already begun to see why such questions do not evoke a response, or, if they do, not a revealing one. Although, as we will see, even though such questions did not usually gain a response that was revealing, I did occasionally, especially early on in my interviewing, ask such naive questions! And I do consider one woman's answer to this question later.

12 For instance, people might say that the flowers of the town centre look nice or that the centre is kept clean and looks nice whilst still, in general conversation, producing accounts of life in which the town shows up, and is encountered, negatively.

13 This is clearly why middle class students who do not share this trajectory through the place and who are able to look forward to mobility do not share this experience of place. One might say that it is a class experience masquerading as an experience of place.

14 It is interesting also that this man is expressing the point that the decline he is so aware of is not, in itself, to do with the nature of the space that historically this area has been left: the terraced housing, the high level of council owned accommodation, the poor quality of the buildings.

15 This accounts for the problems involved when two people come together who are divided by a relation of power. Each depiction of the world must be an aggression upon the other.

16 Obviously, it is the general condition of all human beings' accession to being but it is particularly true of labouring people's being-in-the-world because their being is maintained at this level by the routines of work, because they rely for their income on motor-skills and because of their dispossession of the instruments that would allow them a different, mediated relation to being.

17 Hence Dewey used the term 'body-mind' for 'mind'. Clearly, the intent is similar to Merleau-Ponty's in using the term 'Body-Subject'.

18 This is a fascinating statement by which the person meant that university-educated people do not have to live among an objectively stigmatized group whose marks they share regardless of personal quality and among whom they are trapped, whilst experiencing the realm in which they live as threatening.

19 Here he euphemizes because he is uncomfortable with recognizing in words this judgement, uncomfortable with taking up a position of superiority from which to make this judgement, because he doesn't feel socially instituted to adopt such a distance.

20 By 'funded', Ostrow is trying to capture the sense of ourselves as deeply invested; something we are at stake in.

5 Understanding the barriers to articulation

1 Were my bodily hexis different, then I would disturb the sphere of interaction through which access is made available.
2 And this is as true of left-wing critics. This was clearly manifest in publishers' initial responses to the work. One insisting that the 'work is insufficiently attuned to the cross-currents in popular culture in late capitalism' and another insisting that my account descended into cliché.
3 It is difficult to communicate the kind of hyper-tense vigilance this demanded and I often felt great strain throughout interviews.
4 We will see later that a feature of working class space is that working people establish tacitly an agreement not to instate these forms of competence.
5 Although the whole story of their social experience and of their objective being, as with any of us, is not wholly expressed in, and not therefore wholly captured by, their speech. And this is why, throughout, I have employed instruments of objectification that facilitate the articulation of the lived experience of their social being; what their speech emerges from but often leaves under-described. In this sense, reconstructing their lives unavoidably means using resources that, on first acquaintance, seem remote from the world that they describe.

6 Necessity and being working class

1 Mention must be made here of the dockers whose own terrible struggle was met with a stunning conspiracy of silence by the Labour Party.
2 The culture of the university has been transformed by feminist ideas and the demand for the highly euphemized, hyper-coherent discourse of political correctness, falls unduly harshly on working class men. Whilst much feminist analyses is highly sophisticated, there is often a huge difference between that and the attitudes it fosters which are often thinly veiled justifications of class racism of the worst kind. It allows a lot of privileged women to adopt a whole battery of insult and negation in the service of their own personal life-strategies. It is a point Curthoys makes with some integrity: 'The women I'm speaking of were, then, in terms of the society they lived in, highly privileged people. They had been born at the right time, had had access to education, and now had a relatively high degree of job security and material comfort. Yet how did this group, these friends of mine in the women's movement, see themselves? They saw themselves as oppressed, as victims, as underdogs . . . They recognized their material advantages in some ways, but at bottom identified themselves as part of an oppressed group – women . . . And I began to wonder how this was possible. For the people I'm talking about regarded themselves as socialists of some kind, as opposed to capitalism . . . How could socialists so easily identify themselves, the relatively privileged, as oppressed? How could socialists have become so blind to the exploitation and struggles of working class and/or colonised men? How had they come to identify the relative privilege and power of the middle-class men they combated in their working lives with the position of all men? . . . We

are now confronted with the anomaly that many socialist feminists talk constantly about "men" and "women" in no-class-differentiated ways, refuse to cope with the fact that upper- and middle-class women are privileged in this society and in world terms, and evince – in my experience – remarkably little empathy or political allegiance with working class men . . . My point is: what about working class men? As long as middle class women identify themselves as the oppressed, they have a theoretical basis for continuing to exert class privilege, for asserting their own interests over those of working class men. And for Socialists, Marxists, this just won't do . . . to focus on sexism out of context, to remain wilfully blind to the realities of class privilege and exploitation in this way, must locate a class-blind feminism as politically reactionary' (Curthoys 1988).

3   So, he is no socialist and yet that someone who was always on the right of the Labour Party can make this point means the point is not particularly controversial.

4   Which is why a fundamental burden involved in this project was the strain of being aware that the text itself, and not merely the transcribed testimony, must create what Steiner characterises as an 'iconic presence' (Steiner 1984: 87).

5   A sense that social theory and the academy would do well to understand the conditions of, in the same way that Bourdieu has done. They might then grasp the distastefulness of discussions of agency and empowerment in the context of the very ubiquity of these kinds of conditions. We learn more from paying attentive treatment of the lives of people than we do from futile discussions of grand questions posed for the pleasure of grandeur they allow us to satisfy. Such exercises of conscience can only benefit those positioned in fields that allow for the symbolic profits of good-conscience, they do nothing for those enmired in a malaise of ill-being born of a misery that begins in poverty and ends in the complete wastage of personal life that each must endure, alone.

6   I am aware here that this is a second, slightly different sense of 'necessity' that exists as a consequence of economic necessity but I am happy to cover both senses with the one term because they seem to me, as I hope this makes clear, so intimately linked.

7   This is an argument I feel great sympathy for and would use in the face of those who say this book is repetitive.

8   Except, of course, for those who are lucky enough to have the right breaks in life or who win the lottery.

9   This is why posture and this sense of the flesh can betray dominated individuals within fields of social power, because the relations of power embodied at the heart of comportment function mimetically and, as a form of practical sense, the grounds of comportment mean that individuals are possessed of the sense of their flesh inscribed in their flesh through the constitutive inter-relation of the structurally disparate fields.

10   I am using the notion of 'aspect perception' here.

11   Elvis Costello, "Spike" Plangent Visions Music Inc., 1988.

7 The culture of necessity and working class speach

1 This does not contradict what we have seen emerge in the previous chapters, that these people have a strong sense of where and what they are. However, I think that an accurate rendering of their social condition and the sense of their lives, necessarily involves an objectification that relies upon schemes that are not those *of* working class people, since, on the whole, it is part of the political conditions of their dispossession that they do not have 'schemes' through which to objectify their existence. This makes the paradox of writing about working class people's lives clear. This is a point confirmed by the analysis that I have offered which shows that the sense of their experience is not presented wholly and simply in their speech.

2 See note 7 on page 295.

3 I believe this is also true of working women's speech. It does seem part of a working class tradition that celebrates the base and vulgar. We will consider this later. However, since most of the transcription comes from men, I'll focus upon working class male speech.

4 And, from what I can tell, this is true of female workers who work shifts and work in manual, labour-intensive jobs.

5 Which is why middle class people find it so vulgar because it is a context in which the forms of capital of dominated individuals can be emblematized as a celebration.

6 This is obvious in the conversations that students often have about the 'locals'.

7 One must remember that for some workers, particularly construction workers who work around portable toilets, their experience of using toilets during their daily life can be an abject one, especially when they have the job of removing the portable toilet from the site. Furthermore, one finds the same 'trench humour' among nurses.

8 This ethos can often contradict statements, concerning ethnic groups and gender (just as the hyper-coherence which intellectuals strive for is often contradicted by their non-verbal cues, with which they often betray a practical intolerance for different and marginal individuals).

9 Hobnail working boots.

10 Raining.

11 Hence the often remarked difference of how we sound when recorded and our sense of how we sound.

12 A set of dispositions that is true of women from the most dominated and economically marginal sectors of the working class.

13 One thinks, for example, of the nurse's walk which is that of someone who must adopt a comfortable walk that can be managed for the full shift, as opposed to the more stylized manners of women whose social position demands an 'appropriate' stylization of deportment.

14 Imagine it being decreed that those whose degrees were awarded before the current vogue for modularization, had to go back to university and do another degree to guarantee their competence?

15 Especially working class men since as a group they fail in the English education

system in alarming numbers. As Adonis puts it: 'the mass of "white working-class males" – to take the group defined by Chris Woodhead, the chief Inspector of Schools – continue to languish in an almost anti-education culture in under-performing comprehensive schools. The comprehensive revolution has not removed the link between education and class but strengthened it . . . So bad is the situation that the Chief Inspector of Schools feels compelled to write that:

> the failure of boys, and in particular white working-class boys, is one of the most disturbing problems we face within the whole education system. Research shows that white working-class boys are the least likely to participate in full-time education after the age of sixteen, and that white boys are the most likely to be completely unqualified on leaving compulsory education . . . The fact is that our most disadvantaged children, especially boys, remain disadvantaged at the end of their schooling.

The very children most dependent upon state education are thus the children most failed by the system' (Adonis 1998: 51–4).

16 As we saw in chapter 4.

17 The effort this man went to for this money tells us something about the value of money in the condition of its absence but having looked at the issue of necessity, we can leave this, here.

18 One wonders whether this has something to do with why young, single working class women have children.

19 This raises the important question of the fashionableness, among the intelligentsia, for all kinds of minority politics and why there is a pervasive resistance to recognizing the oppression of what might, in these terms, be seen to be an ethnic group who constitute the majority of this society.

20 And also those working class women who do menial work.

21 There is also an issue here of the extent to which this is a 'reading' of the bodies of vulnerable people and an allocation to them of values that are attributed to them to stigmatize still further those already stigmatized by powerful interests within the dominated fractions of the dominant class. By which I mean, it is not at all a straightforward question that the groups characterized by middle class people as 'hard' do actually possess the insensitivities the term is commonly held to denote. It seems to me a description that emerges from the relationship between the classes and a 'reading' based on the two forms of being. However, putting this issue aside and accepting the dominant stereotypes of working *men*, there is still an issue that many marginalized and stigmatized groups have to imbue such traits as a response to their stigmatization. In such conditions, one does have to be hard in order to live up to the pain exclusion involves.

22 The point is an astute one, if working class people invest themselves in elite skills, they then need access to the spaces through which to practise those skills and be remunerated, which aren't available, or accessible, in their own communities. Hence, it makes most sense to invest oneself in ubiquitous skills which are ill-remunerated and poorly valued but which one can practise within the immediate sphere of one's community if one is unemployed.

8 Conclusion

1 This is clearly why this work has struggled to deploy a model of the relation of identity, self-hood and being that is less logocentric.
2 This is why conceptual analysis is so important as a means to lay clear the grounds of phenomena and allow us to recognize deeper aspects that are emergent within phenomena but which too close a focus upon the literal content of speech may obscure.

References

Adonis, A. and Pollard, S. 1998. *A Class Act*. London: Penguin.

Adorno, T. 1974. *Minima Moralia*. London: Verso.

Agee, J. and Evans, Walker. 1969. *Let Us Now Praise Famous Men*. London: Panther.

Barney Dews, C. L, and Leste Law, C. 1995. *This Fine Place So Far From Home*. Philadelphia: Temple University Press.

Barrett, C. 1988. Wittgenstein, Leavis and Literature. *New Literary History* 19: 2.

Barthes, R. 1986. *The Rustle of Language*. New York: Hill and Wang.

Berger, J. 1972. *Ways of Seeing*. London: Penguin.

Black, M. 1992. *D. H. Lawrence Sons and Lovers*. Cambridge University Press.

Bourdieu, P. 1974. The School as a Conservative Force: Scholastic and Cultural Inequalities. In *Contemporary Research in the Sociology of Education*, ed. J. Eggleston, London: Methuen.

  1977. *Outline of a Theory of Practice*. Cambridge University Press.

  1979. *Algeria 1960*. Cambridge University Press.

  1981. Men and Machines. In *Advances in Social Theory and Methodology: Toward an Integration of Micro- and Macro Sociologies*, ed. K. Knorr-Cetina and A. Cicourel, London: Routledge and Kegan Paul.

  1983. The Philosophical Institution. In *Philosophy in France Today*, ed. A. Montefiore, Cambridge University Press.

  1984. *Distinction*. London: Routledge.

  1988. *Homo Academicus*. Cambridge: Polity Press.

  1990a. *The Logic of Practice*. Cambridge: Polity Press.

  1990b. *Photography*. Stanford University Press.

  1990c. *In Other Words*. Cambridge: Polity Press.

  1990d. The Scholastic Point of View. *Cultural Anthropology* 5 (4): 380–91.

  1990e. *The Love of Art*. Stanford University Press.

  1991. *Language and Symbolic Power*. Cambridge: Polity Press.

  1993a. *Sociology in Question*. London: Sage.

  1993b. *The Field of Cultural Production*. Cambridge: Polity Press.

1994. *Academic Discourse*. Stanford University Press.

1996a. Understanding. *Theory, Culture and Society* 13 (2): 17–37.

1996b. *The State Nobility*. Cambridge: Polity.

1998. A Reasoned Utopia and Economic Fatalism. *New Left Review* 227: 125–30.

Bourdieu, P. and Eagleton, T. 1992. Doxa and Common Life. *New Left Review* 191: 111–21.

Bourdieu, P, and Passeron, J-C. 1979. *The Inheritors*. London: University of Chicago Press.

Bourdieu, P. and Wacquant, L. J. D. 1992. *An Invitation to Reflexive Sociology*. Cambridge: Polity Press.

Brierley, W. 1983. *Means-Test Man*. Nottingham: Spokesman.

Campbell, B. 1984. *Wigan Pier Revisited*. London: Virago.

Camus, A. 1975. *The Myth of Sisyphus*. London: Penguin.

Carruthers, A. G. 1992. *The Rotherham Economic Strategy*. Rotherham Borough Council.

Code, L. 1991. *What Can She Know? Feminist Theory and the Construction of Knowledge*. New York: Cornell.

Collier, A. 1994. *Critical Realism*. London: Verso.

Compton, J. J. 1989. Merleau-Ponty's Thesis of the Primacy of Perception and the Meaning of Scientific Objectivity. In *Merleau-Ponty: Critical Essays*, ed. H. Pietersma. Washington, DC: Center for Advanced Research in Phenomenology.

Cooper, D. E. 1990. *Existentialism*. Oxford: Basil Blackwell.

1991. Ineffability. *The Aristotelian Society*. Supplementary volume 65.

1992. Inverting the Image: Dreyfus's Commentary on Heidegger. *Inquiry* 35: 233–48.

1996. *Thinkers of Our Time: Heidegger*. London: The Claridge Press.

Cosgrove, D. 1984. *Social Formation and Symbolic Landscape*. London: Croom Helm.

Coward, R. 1994. Whipping Boys. *The Guardian Weekend*, 3 September.

Curthoys, A. 1988. *For and Against Feminism*. London: Allen and Unwin.

de Beauvoir, S. 1952. *The Second Sex*. New York: Knopf.

Dewey, J. 1934. *Art as Experience*. New York: Perigee Books.

Dilman, I. 1993. *Existentialist Critiques of Cartesianism*. London: Barnes and Noble Books, Macmillan.

Dreyfus, H. 1994. *Being in the World*. New Baskerville: Massachusetts Institute of Technology.

Dwyer, P. *Sense and Subjectivity*. New York: E. J. Brill.

Fogelin, R.J. 1995. *Wittgenstein*. London: Routledge.

Foucault, M. 1977. *Discipline and Punish*. London: Penguin.

Frank, A. W. 1991. For a Sociology of the Body: An Analytical Review. In *The Body: Social Process and Cultural Theory*, ed. M. Featherstone, M. Hepworth and B. S. Turner, London: Sage, 36–102.

Friere, P. 1970. *The Pedagogy of the Oppressed*. New York: Herder and Herder, 1970.

Galbraith, J. K. 1992. *The Culture of Contentment*. London: Penguin.

Garner, L. 1995. Hard Times on Easy Street. *The Sunday Times Magazine* 12 November.

Gash, N. 1979. *Aristocracy and People*. London: Edward Arnold Ltd.

Gerth, H. and Wright Mills, C. 1946. *From Max Weber: Essays in Sociology*. New York: Oxford University Press.

Gilroy, P. 1996. *The Black Atlantic*. Verso: London.

Goffman, E. 1971. *The Presentation of Self in Everyday Life*. London: Penguin.

1990. *Stigma*. London: Penguin.

Gregg, P. 1996. We Work, It Hurts: Why Job Fears are Rising. *The Observer* 16 June.

Griffiths, S. 1995. *Rotherham: A Poverty Profile*. Rotherham Borough Council.

Gross, R. D. 1992. *Psychology*. London: Hodder and Stoughton.

Habermas, J. 1992. *Faktizität und Geltung*. Frankfurt: Suhrkamp.

1993. *Moral Consciousness and Communicative Action*. Cambridge, MA: The MIT Press.

Hall, H. 1993. Intentionality and World: Division I of *Being and Time*. In *The Cambridge Companion to Heidegger*, ed. C. Guignon. Cambridge University Press.

Harré, R. 1979. *Social Being*. Oxford: Basil Blackwell.

Hart, J. 1991. *Damage*. London: Arrow Books.

Hearne, R. 1995. Roger Dattaller of Rawmarsh. In *Aspects of Rotherham*, ed. M. Jones, Barnsley: Wharncliffe Publishing Limited.

Heidegger, M. 1962. *Being and Time*. New York: Harper and Row.

1977. *Basic Writings*. London: Routledge and Kegan Paul.

Hillmore, P. 1996. Excuse Me, is this Seat taken? *The Observer* 14 April.

Hoggart, R. 1957. *The Uses of Literacy*. London: Penguin.

Hutton, W. 1996a. Fool's Gold in a Fool's Paradise. *The Observer* 2 June.

1996b. *The State We're In*. London: Vintage.

Jay, M. 1984. *Adorno*. Cambridge: Harvard University Press.

Jones, M. 1995. *Aspects of Rotherham*. Barnsley: Wharncliffe Publishing Limited.

Kalnins, M. 1992. *D. H. Lawrence: Selected Poems*. London: J. M. Dent & Sons Ltd.

Kellner, D. 1989. *Jean Baudrillard: From Marxism to Postmodernism and Beyond*. Cambridge: Polity.

Koch, M. 1996. Class and Taste: Bourdieu's Contribution to the Analysis of Social Structure and Social Space. *International Journal of Contemporary Sociology* 33 (2):187–202.

Kozol, J. 1992. *Savage Inequalities*. New York: HarperPerennial.

Langer, M. M. 1989. *Merleau-Ponty's Phenomenology of Perception*. London: Macmillan.

Lawrence, D. H. 1992. *Selected Poems*. London: Everyman's Library.

1994a. *Lady Chatterly's Lover*. London: Penguin.

1994b. *Sons and Lovers*. London: Penguin.

Levi, P. 1988. *The Drowned and the Saved*. London: Abacus.

Levin, D. M. 1990. Justice in the Flesh. In *Ontology and Alterity in Merleau-Ponty*, ed. G. A. Johnson. Evanston: Northwestern University Press.

Macann, C. 1993. *Four Phenomenological Philosophers*. London: Routledge.

Marx, K. 1975. *Economic and Philosophical Manuscripts of 1844*. In K. Marx and F. Engels, *Collected Works*, 3. London: Lawrence and Wishart.

1976. *Capital*. London: Penguin.

Mazis, A. 1989. Merleau-Ponty, Inhabitation and the Emotions. In *Merleau-Ponty: Critical Essays*, ed. H. Pietersma. Washington, DC: Center for Advanced Research in Phenomenology.

McCann, G. 1988. *Marilyn Monroe*. Cambridge: Polity Press.

McCarthy, T. 1993. *Ideals and Illusions*. Cambridge, MA: MIT Press.

McGinn, M. 1997. *Wittgenstein*. London: Routledge.

Merleau-Ponty, M. 1962. *Phenomenology of Perception*. London: Routledge.

1963. *The Structure of Behaviour*. Pittsburgh: Beacon Press.

1964. *The Primacy of Perception*. Evanston: Northwestern University Press.

1968. *The Visible and the Invisible*. Evanston: Northwestern University Press.

1969. *Humanism and Terror*. Boston: Beacon Press.

1973. *The Prose of the World*. Evanston: Northwestern University Press.

1995. *Signs*. Evanston: Northwestern University Press.

Morrison, T. 1990. *The Bluest Eye*. London: Picador.

Mulhall, S. 1990. *On Being In The World*. London: Routledge.

1995. Re-Monstrations: Heidegger, Derrida and Wittgenstein's Hand. *Journal of the British Society for Phenomenology* 26 (1): 65–85.

1996. *Heidegger and Being and Time*. London: Routledge.

Mulhern, F. 1996. A Welfare Culture? *Radical Philosophy* 77: 26–37.

Munford, A. P. 1994. *Rotherham: A Pictorial History*. Chichester: Phillimore.

1995. *Around Rotherham*. London: Alan Sutton Publishing Ltd.

Nagel, T. 1979. *Mortal Questions*. Cambridge University Press.

Nbalia, D. 1991. *Toni Morrison's Developing Class Consciousness*. London: Associated University Press.

Nietzsche, F. 1974. *The Gay Science*. New York: Random House.

Ortner, S. B. 1974. Is Female to Male as Nature Is to Culture? In *Woman, Culture, and Society*, ed. M. Z. Rosaldo and L. Lamphere. Stanford University Press.

Ostrow, J. M. 1981. Culture as a Fundamental Dimension of Experience: A Discussion of Pierre Bourdieu's Theory of Human Habitus. *Human Studies* 4 (3): 279–97.

1990. *Social Sensitivity*. New York: State University of New York Press.

Parsons, T. 1992. Thick on the Ground Thick in the Head. *The Times* 3 October.

Pearsall, M. 1989. *Women, Knowledge and Reality*. London: Unwin Hyman, Inc.

Rilke, R. M. 1993. *Letters to a Young Poet*. New York: W. W. Norton & Company, Inc.

Rotherham Borough Council. 1994. *Rotherham in Profile*. Planning Department of Rotherham Borough Council.

1995. *Social Policy Bulletin*. Social Policy Department of Rotherham Borough Council.

Rotherham Training and Enterprise Council. 1993. *Labour Market Assessment 1992–1993*. Rotherham Training and Enterprise Council.

Searle, J. 1983. *Intentionality: An Essay in the Philosophy of Mind*. Cambridge University Press.

Sennett, R. and Cobb, J. 1973. *The Hidden Injuries of Class*. New York: Vintage Books.

Steiner, G. 1984. *George Steiner: A Reader*. Harmondsworth: Penguin Books.

1985. *Language and Silence*. London: Faber & Faber.

1989. *Martin Heidegger*. University of Chicago Press.

Strawson, P.F. 1959. *Individuals*. London: Methuen.

Taylor, C. 1985. *Philosophy and the Human Sciences*. Cambridge University Press.

1989a. *Sources of the Self*. Cambridge University Press.

1989b. Embodied Agency. In *Merleau-Ponty: Critical Essays*, ed. H. Pietersma. Washington, DC: Center for Advanced Research in Phenomenology.

1993a. Engaged Agency and Background in Heidegger. In *The Cambridge Companion to Heidegger*, ed. C. Guignon, 317–36. Cambridge University Press.

1993b. To Follow a Rule. In *Bourdieu: Critical Perspectives*, ed. C. Calhoun, E. LiPuma, and M. Postone, 45–60. Cambridge: Polity Press.

Willis, P. 1977. *Learning to Labour*. Westmead: Saxon House.

Wittgenstein, L. 1958. *Philosophical Investigations*. Oxford: Basil Blackwell.

1970. *Zettel*. Berkeley: University of California Press.

1972. *On Certainty*. New York: Harper Torchbooks.

1980. *Culture and Value*. Oxford: Basil Blackwell.

Wolfe, A. 1989. *Whose Keeper? Social Science and Moral Obligation*. Berkeley: University of California Press.

X, Malcolm. 1992. *The Autobiography of Malcolm X*. New York: Ballantine Books.

Zukin, S. 1991. *Landscapes of Power*. Berkeley: University of California Press.

Index